Consumption and Spirituality

Routledge Interpretive Marketing Research

EDITED BY STEPHEN BROWN, *University of Ulster, Northern Ireland*

Recent years have witnessed an 'interpretive turn' in marketing and consumer research. Methodologies from the humanities are taking their place alongside those drawn from the traditional social sciences.

Qualitative and literary modes of marketing discourse are growing in popularity. Art and aesthetics are increasingly firing the marketing imagination.

This series brings together the most innovative work in the burgeoning interpretive marketing research tradition. It ranges across the methodological spectrum from grounded theory to personal introspection, covers all aspects of the postmodern marketing 'mix', from advertising to product development, and embraces marketing's principal sub-disciplines.

16 Consumption and Spirituality
*Edited by Diego Rinallo, Linda
Scott, and Pauline Maclaran*

*Also available in Routledge Interpretive
Marketing Research series:*

Representing Consumers
Voices, views and visions
Edited by Barbara B. Stern

Romancing the Market
*Edited by Stephen Brown, Anne
Marie Doherty and Bill Clarke*

**Consumer Value: A framework
for Analysis and Research**
Edited by Morris B. Holbrook

Marketing and Feminism
Current Issues and Research
*Edited by Miriam Catterall,
Pauline Maclaran and Lorna Stevens*

Consumption and Spirituality

Edited by Diego Rinallo, Linda Scott,
and Pauline Maclaran

Routledge
Taylor & Francis Group
NEW YORK   LONDON

First published 2013
by Routledge
711 Third Avenue, New York, NY 10017

Simultaneously published in the UK
by Routledge
2 Park Square, Milton Park, Abingdon, Oxon OX14 4RN

Routledge is an imprint of the Taylor & Francis Group,
an informa business

Library of Congress Cataloging-in-Publication Data
   Consumption and spirituality / edited by Diego Rinallo, Linda Scott,
and Pauline MacIaran.
      p. cm.
   Includes bibliographical references and index.
   1. Consumption (Economics)—Religious aspects.   I. Rinallo, Diego,
1973– II. Scott, Linda M.   III. Maclaran, Pauline.
   HC79.C6C6728 2012
   201'.73—dc23
   2012003023

ISBN13: 978-0-415-88911-7 (hbk)
ISBN13: 978-0-203-10623-5 (ebk)

Typeset in Sabon
by IBT Global.

Contents

PART III
The Commodification of the Spiritual

PART IV
The Consumption of Spiritual Goods

PART V
Issues of Method and Representation

Figures

Foreword
For What We Are About to Receive . . .

For as long as I can remember, I've been a consumer of spirituality. As a blue-collar kid, brought up in a very religious household—fundamentalist, in fact—I spent most of my slumdog childhood consuming old-time religion. Dragged along by my holy-roller mother, who was catholic in her taste if not Catholic in her theology, I traipsed from mission hall to meeting house, from Sunday school to Sally Army, from Genesis to Revelation (and back again), in an unrelenting cycle of spiritual overconsumption. Whether it was listening to firebrand preachers, watching people speaking in tongues, witnessing miracle cures of the halt and lame, attending to personal testimonials of the I-was-lost-but-now-I'm-found variety, or singing along with stirring songs of praise like "Deep and Wide," "Fishers of Men," "Way, Far Beyond Jordan," and "Jesus Wants Me for a Sunbeam," I had religion rammed down my throat on a daily basis, plus several times on Sundays. It was a deathless diet of fiery furnaces, lions' dens, burning bushes, graven images, Our Fathers, imminent Ends, days of judgment, tablets of stone, sloughs of despond, lakes of fire and backsliding down slippery slopes to Sodom and Gomorrah, or someplace equally purgatorial.

Ah, happy days . . .

Anyway, after fifteen years or so of sitting on hard wooden benches, doing time in draughty tents and tabernacles, taking part in putative revivals and short-lived great awakenings—while praying that the power of prayer would help me make the miraculous transition from sinner to saved—I'd pretty much had my fill of signs and wonders, trials and tribulations, and ever-nourishing hellfire and brimstone. And, unlike Lot's petrified wife, I never looked back.

Nor am I especially unusual. As James Twitchell shows in *Adcult USA*, consumption and spirituality have long been closely intertwined. If not quite the Cain and Abel of Western capitalism, they are definitely its Samson and Delilah. Many pioneers of the advertising/marketing profession—F. W. Ayer, Bruce Barton, Marion Harper, Claude C. Hopkins, Helen Lansdowne, Theodore MacManus, Rosser Reeves, Dorothy L. Sayers, to name but a few—were children of the manse or raised in evangelical circumstances. Numerous scholarly commentators, not least those associated with the iconic Consumer Odyssey, have noted strong parallels between selling soap and saving souls. The apocalyptic linguistic construction "you're doomed, unless" is a constant refrain in marketing and advertising, where the "unless" is usually followed by "you buy our cure for . . . halitosis . . . heartburn . . . baldness . . . bloating . . . trapped wind . . . bingo wings . . . or whatever the latest marketer-invented, socially-incapacitating condition happens to be.

Lest you think that I'm making marketing mock—oh ye of little faith!—I should acknowledge that I myself have employed "spiritual" selling tactics throughout my academic career, such as it is. I've co-edited a book called *Marketing Apocalypse*; I've organised conferences on devotional themes; I've written several scholarly essays that employ religious motifs or use the Bible as their point of departure; I've spent much of the past fifteen years yelling "ye must be born again" to unimpressed audiences of my academic peers. I guess I'm the marketing equivalent of that sad old man with a sandwich board and megaphone, who wanders round the town centre on Saturday afternoons shouting "Repent. Repent. Repent." I know exactly what crying in the wilderness feels like.

I also know what crying "Hallelujah" feels like. And I can't deny that the H-word was repeatedly uttered on reading this volume. Not only does it feature many of the academic luminaries who have previously graced the Interpretive Marketing Research series—thus providing a wonderful tribute to the late, lamented Barbara B. Stern, whose *Representing Consumers* inaugurated this series back in 1998—but *Consumption and Spirituality* is a testament to the wonder-working power of great writing. All of the contributors are esteemed literary stylists and, at a time when students are increasingly reluctant to read the dreary academic articles that clog our journals, Diego, Linda, and Pauline remind us that all is not lost, that scholarly salvation is still possible, and that in the beginning was the Word. Praise the Lord and pass the iPad.

Stephen Brown
Series Editor, Interpretive Marketing Research

Acknowledgments

We would like to thank the following people for their advice and support throughout the development of this project: Stephen Brown for his help to get the project off the ground and for his ongoing encouragement; Stacy Noto, Editorial Assistant at Routledge, who has guided us tirelessly through the production processes; three reviewers for their many constructive and insightful comments; and Russ Belk, Rob Kozinets, John Sherry, Darach Turley, Steve Gould, Eric Arnould, and Lorna Stevens, who all participated in various conference sessions with us and whose insights have been invaluable for this project. Diego Rinallo would like to thank Simone Messina for the ongoing conversation on spirituality, branding and consumption started during the supervision of his M.Sc. thesis, which helped shape some of the ideas expressed in the introductory chapter of this book.

Diego Rinallo
Linda Scott
Pauline Maclaran

1 Introduction

Unravelling Complexities at the Commercial/Spiritual Interface

Diego Rinallo, Linda Scott, and Pauline Maclaran

Spirituality *and* consumption? Really? This book brings together two topics that in the eyes of many go uneasily together. Spirituality is sublime. It smells of incense and everything that is good in humans. Consumption is instead mundane, materialistic, and ultimately soulless. The idea of spiritual consumption may thus be considered an oxymoron, a contradiction in terms. For sure, it triggered negative reactions from some of our informants (not to mention colleagues). Why would business school professors be interested in studying spirituality? Shouldn't this topic be left to more respected disciplines? Do we really need to frame humanity's spiritual search as consumption? Is there something to gain from calling spiritual seekers consumers? These were some of the questions we were asked. We believe that these reactions arise from a cultural tension that is at the centre of both age-old speculation in philosophy, theology, and social science, and the life of countless individuals in postmodern societies: the difficult relationship between matter and spirit, sacred and profane. And yes, we also believe that, as marketing and consumer researchers, we may add something to the debate that would be missed by sociological, cultural, or anthropological analyses of spirituality. Before defending this assertion, which might be easily dismissed as disciplinary colonialism, let us introduce briefly what we mean by spirituality and the way the concept is treated in the disciplines that have it as a subject of study.

SPIRITUALITY VS. RELIGION

Spirituality is not the same as religion. This affirmation would have sounded odd a few decades ago. Experiences that would now be considered spiritual were labelled as religious in influential work such as William James' (1902/1982) *The Varieties of Religious Experiences* and Rudolf Otto's (1917) *The Idea of The Holy*. With the counterculture of the 1960s, this began to change. Already in 1964, Abraham Maslow suggested that spirituality can be found outside of institutionalised churches. According to the founder of humanistic psychology, experiences such as "the holy; . . .

humility; gratitude and oblation; thanksgiving; awe before the mysterium tremendum; the sense of the divine, the ineffable; the sense of littleness before mystery; the quality of exaltedness and sublimity; the awareness of limits and even of powerlessness; the impulse to surrender and to kneel; a sense of the external and of fusion with the whole of the universe; even the experience of heaven and hell" (Maslow, 1964, p. 54) can be felt by the religious and the non-religious alike. In the decades that followed, many observed that "religion is giving way to spirituality" (Heelas and Woodhead, 2005). The divorce of spirituality from religion can be ascribed to two distinct but related phenomena: the secularisation of society and the postmodern behaviour of spiritual seekers, who mix and match from different sources to customise their spiritual beliefs and practices.

According to theories of secularisation (Hammond, 1985; Wilson, 1969), modernisation of society would inexorably lead to the demise of religion. One can easily trace an antecedent of this body of work in Max Weber's (1922/1978) disenchantment thesis, according to which the scientific revolution and the Protestant Reformation in the fifteenth and sixteenth centuries resulted in a rationalisation and intellectualisation of individual and social life and in a corresponding decline in religious beliefs and practices. After enjoying decades of unchallenged supremacy, the more extreme versions of the secularisation thesis were empirically disconfirmed. Studies show that some European countries are indeed becoming more secular, whereas in the United States religion is on the rise (Berger, Davie, and Fokas, 2008). The American religious market is a competitive arena where different institutions and groups invest to maintain and develop their membership, resulting in greater overall demand for religious services. Europe is instead still characterised by quasi-monopolistic religious markets as in many countries the once state religions still enjoy a dominant position. As a consequence, institutionalised religions have reduced incentives to market themselves, resulting in reduced participation rates (Finke, 1997; Finke and Stark, 1988; Iannaccone, 1991; Stark, 1997; Stark and Bainbridge 1985; Stark and Finke, 2000; Warner, 1993). Studies from other regions of the world suggest that religion is as alive today as it ever was (Berger, 1999). This is true also for countries where state atheism was enforced and organised religions had to go underground, including former Eastern Bloc countries and China.

Clearly, the secularisation of Europe is the exception rather than the rule. A much more defensible aspect of secularisation theory highlights the loss of authority of religious institutions on various spheres of public and private life. Social functions that used to be ascribed to religion are now dealt with by specialised institutions (Luckmann 1967; Wilson 1982), which are governed according to their own specific logic. Over the centuries, with its institutional separation from the state, science, medicine, education, art, economy, etc., religion has thus lost its ability to morally overarch all of society in a sort of "sacred canopy" (Berger, 1967).

Starting from the 1960s, the reduced authority of institutionalised religions has led to an increased individual freedom to create beliefs based on a variety of competing (but from an individual point of view complementary, at least to a certain extent) spiritual resources (Roof, 1999). Such degree of freedom is unprecedented, as in most periods of human history spiritual innovators, unless successful in creating new religions, have been marginalised and sometimes physically suppressed. Globalisation has been a trigger of this spiritual mix and match at least from the early nineteenth century, where the British Empire was instrumental to the first contacts between Westerners and 'exotic' spiritualities (Owen, 2004). Today these trends continue, as multicultural societies are increasingly tolerant of alternative, emerging, and foreign religions and spiritualities. Creativity in the spiritual domain is however often seen as intrinsically incoherent (e.g., do-it-yourself religion, Baerveldt, 1996; pick-and-mix religion, Hamilton, 2000) and often denigrated as it is largely based on the exchange of goods (books, DVDs, crystals, divinatory tools) and services (courses, workshops, retreats, therapy and counselling sessions) for money (e.g., spiritual supermarket/marketplace, Lyon, 2000; Roof, 1999; religious consumption à la carte, Possamai 2003; religious consumerism, York, 1995).

Secularisation and the spiritual bricolage of consumers (we do not of course share the negative connotations that critics ascribe to the phenomenon) have thus contributed to disconnecting spirituality from institutionalised churches. Not only has religion a much-decreased impact on the various social and cultural domains it once dominated; it has also lost its monopoly on religious beliefs and practices as consumers create their own spirituality and new religious movements, which often lack a priestly caste and avoid institutionalisation. Moreover, as consumer researchers have occasionally noted, even mundane brands such as Harley Davidson or Star Trek may assume sacred qualities and stimulate spiritual breakthrough (more on this below).

Based on these theoretical developments, social scientists have attempted to obtain operational definitions of religion vs. spirituality (Emmons and Paloutzian, 2003; Gorsuch, 1984; Hill, 2005; Hill et al., 2000; Moberg, 2002; Pargament, 1999; Turner et al., 1995; Zinnbauer and Pargament, 2005; Zinnbauer et al., 1997, 1999). Despite extensive theoretical and empirical work, there is not widely accepted operationalisation of the two terms (Moore, Kloos, and Rasmussen, 2001). Religion is often seen as community-oriented, formalised, organised, and consisting of an organised system of beliefs, practices, and rituals designed to facilitate closeness to God. Spirituality is instead more individualistic, less formal, and institutionalised to a reduced degree, and it is considered a subjective, personal quest to understand the ultimate questions about life, meaning, and the sacred. Interestingly, religion (e.g., Zinnbauer et al., 1999) is often associated with "negative" qualities (e.g., it is dogmatic and may lead to fundamentalist behaviours), whereas spirituality is more positively connoted (e.g., it may lead to expanded self-awareness).

SPIRITUALITY IN SOCIAL SCIENCE

As hinted above, over the last few decades spirituality emerged as a topic of study in a variety of disciplines (see Holmes, 2007, for a brief review). *Psychology* has recently moved beyond its initial negative views on religion and spirituality. According to Freud (1927/1961), religion was an expression of individual neuroses. The father of psychology dismissed mystical experiences as regression to primary narcissism (Freud, 1930/1989). Following his lead, spiritual experiences were usually considered pathological, even psychotic (Group for the Advancement of Psychiatry, 1976; Horton, 1974), forcing the discipline to find criteria to distinguish spiritual experiences from psychopathology (Caird, 1987; Hood, 1976; Jackson and Fulford, 1997). Many schools of psychology, including humanistic, Jungian, and transpersonal, now recognize that spirituality is an important aspect of psychological development and wellbeing. Beyond psychology, in the *health sciences*, interest in spirituality has skyrocketed (Gorsuch, 2002; Prasinos, 1992; Young-Eisendrath and Miller, 2000). Moreover, there is growing empirical research on the impact of spirituality and religiosity on various measures of mental and physical health (Koenig, 2001; Koenig et al., 2001; Mueller et al., 2001). Other studies also focus on the effect of specific practices, such as prayer (e.g., Masters and Spielmans, 2007) or meditation (e.g., Ospina et al., 2007).

Anthropology has a long tradition of studying and providing thick descriptions of "other" spiritualities (for a general introduction, see Morris, 2006). However, the insider-outsider boundary and fear of "going native" often led to situations where "extraordinary" experiences observed or even personally experienced by the fieldworker would be explained away or even subjected to self-censorship (Turner, 1994; Young and Goulet, 1994; see also Favret-Saada, 1980; Stoller, 1987, for significant exceptions). Critiques of the imperialistic past of the discipline together with ethical considerations have led to the acceptance of methods and representation styles more respectful of the legitimacy of other cultures' spiritual practices and belief systems (Arweck and Stringer, 2002).

In *Sociology* debates on spirituality are usually situated within broader analyses of religions, with key subjects being secularisation and related themes (fundamentalism, religious revivalism), globalisation, and the de-institutionalised (or post-institutionalised) nature of new religious movements, like the New Age or Neo-Paganism. Spirituality per se, given its 'subjective' nature, has received more limited attention (see, however, Flanagan and Jupp, 2007), even though several key thinkers in sociology are arguably relevant to make sense of spirituality under the conditions of postmodernity (think of Giddens [1991] on the substitution of traditional authority with self-authority, or Foucault's [1988] technologies of the self as a framework for interpreting spiritual practices).

Getting closer to the topic of this book, *management* and *organisation studies* are also devoting some attention to organisational spirituality (Benefiel,

2003; Biberman and Tischler, 2008) and spirituality in the workplace (Biberman and Whitty, 2000; Giacalone and Jurkiewiez, 2002; Mitroff and Denton, 1999), and to the related issue of including spirituality into management education (Barnett et al., 2000; Bento, 2000; Delbecq, 2000, 2005; Epstein, 2002; Harlos, 2000; Neal, 1997). Similarly to research in psychology and health sciences, this stream of research has attempted to measure the impact of various measures of spirituality on organisational performance. The question typically asked is: "Would organisations be more productive and innovative, and individuals be able to live more satisfying lives, if they felt inwardly connected to their work, fellow workers, and workplace?" (Sheep, 2006, p. 357). Also, business leadership is said to benefit from spiritual values and practices (Benefiel, 2005; Miller, 2000; Reave, 2005; Vaill, 2000). Despite criticism based on instrumentality and negative consequences of workplace spirituality (Boje, 2008; Lips-Wiersma et al., 2009), enthusiasts propose that organisation studies are experiencing a "spiritual turn," which is saluted as a response to the crisis of meaning in organisations (Drive, 2007).

To sum up, in social science, there is growing interest on the subject of spirituality and its impact on culture, society, and individuals. Let us now turn to examine relevant debates in consumer research, which have been influenced by these developments in social science and have, in turn, influenced marketing theory and practice.

SPIRITUALITY AND CONSUMER RESEARCH

In consumer research, spirituality per se has attracted limited explicit attention. Notable exceptions are Hirschman (1985), on the spiritual significance of consumption objects; Holbrook (1999), on spirituality as a typology of consumer value; Gould (1991), on spiritual self-awareness as a goal for the management of energy through product use; and Moisio and Beruchashvili, 2010, on the model of wellbeing proposed by contemporary support groups, which is spiritual and therapeutic at the same time. Spirituality is, however, an element of the liberatory postmodernist quest to re-enchant human life (Firat and Venkatesh, 1995). Moreover, it is inherent, albeit in an implicit manner, in two influential and debated streams of research: (1) materialism, and (2) the sacred (as opposed to profane) aspects of consumer behaviour. Other relevant streams of research (not reviewed here) regard superstition (which is, however, negatively connoted as excess of belief, gullibility; see Kramer and Block, 2008; Mowen and Carlson, 2003) and magical thinking (Arnould et al., 1999; Fernandez and Lastovicka, 2011; St. James et al., 2011) in consumer behaviour.

Materialism

Materialism is the idea that everything is made of matter. Such a view is in direct contraposition with the religious or philosophical belief that the material universe has a spiritual fundament (Vitzhum, 1995). Most religions see the Divine as transcendent, that is, dwelling outside of creation rather than immanent in it. Put differently, the creator is separated from the physical creation, which is often considered a distraction to the soul's spiritual journey, when not intrinsically evil. Accordingly, excessive pursuit of material goods is criticized as a hindrance to spiritual pursuits (see Belk, 1983).

In consumer research, materialism is conceived as the search for happiness through consumption (Belk, 1984, 1985; see also Burroughs and Rindfleisch, 2002; Richins, 1991; Richins and Dawson, 1992). If the physical world is all that there is, the implication is that happiness can only be experienced during one's lifetime. Whether one can actually find happiness in material possessions is open to debate. Happiness through consumption is, at most, transient (Belk et al., 2003). Growing evidence suggests that higher levels of materialism lead to reduced happiness and life satisfaction (Richins and Dawson, 1992; Burroughs and Rindfleisch, 2002; Emmons, 1999; La Barbera and Gürhan, 1997). Conversely, individuals with more spiritual strivings are more satisfied with their life (Emmons, 1999) and are less materialistic (Burroughs and Rindfleisch, 2002; Pace, 2012; Stillman et al., 2012).

However, it would be naive to conclude that materialism and spirituality oppose each other. Religious and spiritual beliefs are reified in material culture (McDannell, 1995; Morgan, 1999; Moore, 1995) in the form of sacred images, devotional and liturgical objects, buildings and other places of worship, works of art, mass-produced consumption goods and entertainment products, and the practices surrounding these material objects (rituals, ceremonies, prayer, mediation, display, pilgrimage, worship, magic, study, etc.). Such consumption is not, however, exempt from critiques, ranging from bad taste (e.g. in the case of Catholic kitsch) to the more extreme accusation of spiritual materialism, particularly frequent in the case of the New Age movement (Rindfleish, 2005; Trungpa, 1973).

Gould (2006) warns against conflating spirituality with spiritual materialism. He defines the latter as "the coopting of spiritual meanings and practices in the service of the material life of the self and then conflating them by rationalising that one is engaging in spirituality. For instance, one may use spiritual practices to reduce tension so one can get along better in the world as opposed to using them to seek some sort of spiritual fulfilment or enlightenment" (Gould, 2006, p. 65). Based on a Buddhist perspective, Gould (1992, 2006) suggests that spirituality can fruitfully engage with matter in ways different from asceticism. For example, alcohol, whose abuse is condemned by ascetic religious paths, may be employed under the right circumstances for spiritual transformation, like experiencing altered states of consciousness that might accelerate one's spiritual pursuits. From this perspective, consumption of goods, services, and experiences can indeed provide the material means to achieve spiritual goals.

Sacred and Profane in Consumer Behaviour

In 1989, Belk, Wallendorf, and Sherry argued that consumption may be a vehicle for experiencing the sacred. Drawing from Émile Durkheim (1915) and Mircea Eliade (1959), in their groundbreaking article, Belk et al. (1989) proposed that two processes are evolving in contemporary societies. One is the increased secularisation of society and institutional religions (at the time they were writing, the secularisation thesis had already been the subject of ample debate in the sociology of religion). The other is the sacralisation of the secular in the spheres of politics, science, art, and consumption. Belk et al. (1989) further described the consumer behaviour processes inherent in sacralisation (e.g., ritual, pilgrimage, gift-giving, collecting, inheritance), the perpetuation of sacredness (e.g., separation of the sacred from the profane, ritual, bequests, tangibilised contamination), and desacralisation (lack of separation of the sacred from the profane, rationalisation and routinisation of ritual, intentional divestment rituals, loss of sacred object or of people taking care of them). These themes are also reflected in related research by Belk and his colleagues (Belk et al., 1988, on divestment rituals that enable the sale of once-sacred possessions at a swap meet; O'Guinn and Belk, 1989, on the sacralisation of the secular in a religious theme park; Belk and Wallendorf, 1990, on the sacred meanings of money; see also Hirschman, 1988).

Interestingly, the work of Belk et al. was influenced by sociological theory at a time when the interest on spirituality was yet to come. In their discussion of the sacred, spirituality is hardly mentioned. Since the Belk et al. (1989) publication, the sacred has become a frequently invoked conceptual category to refer to those aspects of consumer behaviour that go beyond the satisfaction of functional needs, including those that do not necessarily involve transcendent or ecstatic experiences. As sharply observed by Iacobucci (2001), consumer research can fruitfully distinguish the sacred (in the lower case) inherent in exceptional experiences from the Sacred (upper case) "involving an individual's experience with religion, spirituality, worship, and God" (p. 110). However, the work of Belk and his colleagues suggested that the sacred aspects of consumer behaviour "can be clinically described and interpreted, thereby enhancing our understanding of consumer behavior" (Belk et al., 1989, p. 2), helping the legitimisation of metaphors and constructs based on religion, spirituality, and magic in subsequent consumer research.

For example, Fournier (1998) draws on theories of animism to develop brand-consumer relationship theory; others have conceived certain types of brand-consumer relationship as based on devotion (Pichler and Hemetsberger, 2007; Pimentel and Reynolds, 2004). Reference to the sacred, re-enchantment, and transcendence is also frequent in studies of extraordinary consumer experiences as different as river rafting (Arnould and Price, 1993; Arnould et al., 1999), consumer gatherings such as the mountain men rendezvous (Belk and Costa, 1998) and the Burning Man event (Kozinets, 2002; Kozinets and Sherry, 2003; Sherry and Kozinets, 2003, 2007), skydiving (Celsi et al., 1993), and mountain climbing (Tumbat and Belk, 2011). Spiritual elements are also present in experiences that immerse consumers in artificial, marketer-made consumptionscapes, such as disco clubs (Goulding et al., 2002, 2009), art exhibitions (Chen, 2009), and retail spaces (Borghini et al., 2009; Dion and Arnould, 2011; Kozinets et al., 2002, 2004; Sherry, 1998; Sherry et al., 2009).

Brands (and the communities forming around them) are also sometimes described by scholars (and experienced by consumers) in spiritual or even religious ways. In their ethnography of Harley Davidson bikers, Schouten and McAlexander (1995) observe that the "Harley consumption experience has a spirituality derived in part from a sense of riding as a transcendental departure from the mundane", linked to several aspects including "the increased closeness to nature, the heightened sensory awareness, the mantric throbbing of the engine, the constant awareness of risk and the concomitant mental focus, and, in group riding, the consciousness of oneself as an integral part of a larger group or purpose" (p. 50). Muñiz and Schau (2005), in their analysis of the brand community centred on the Apple Newton, identify several supernatural, religious, and magic motifs in their informants' narratives. Belk and Tumbat (2005) develop the notion of brand cult and identify the sustaining myths that underlie the religious aspect of Macintosh consumption. Also popular management books are now available with suggestions on how to create brand cults and turn customers into "true believers" (Atkin, 2004; Ragas and Bueno, 2002).

Spiritual elements are perhaps even more prominent in entertainment brands based on science fiction, fantasy, and horror genres (e.g., X-Files, Kozinets, 1997; Star Trek, Kozinets, 2001; Star Wars, Brown et al., 2003), which are often based on the commercial exploitation of stories set in the same narrative universe through a variety of media and products (books, movies or television shows, comic books, role playing games, videogames, action figures, merchandising, etc.; see Jenkins, 2003, 2006, on transmedia storytelling). By introducing "fantastic" elements, these brands familiarize their audiences with supernatural beings (e.g., angels, vampires, fairies, aliens) and phenomena (e.g., magic, miracles) that are not supposed to exist from a secular, atheist standpoint. Although criticized as further steps in the secularisation of religion, these mass-produced entertainment products can reinvigorate faith and make religious messages nearer to younger generations, as suggested by theological work on popular culture (Ostwalt, 2003). Entertainment brands, however, can introduce their audiences to alternative histories, mythologies, cosmologies, and theologies in ways that traditional religions might find threatening. This is evident in religious organisations' opposition to the Da Vinci Code for its representation of Mary Magdalene as Jesus' wife, to Harry Potter for popularizing sinful magic, and even to Hello Kitty for being a current-day incarnation of pre-Christian cat goddesses, believed to be devils in disguise. Rather than being worshipped per se, these entertainment products can, however, shape sacred consumption practices and, more importantly, transcendent experiences (Rinallo, 2009a).

Going Beyond Current Debates

As a whole, consumer research has mostly been concerned with the sacralisation of the secular (Iacobucci, 2001). The objective of this book is not only to revisit and expand such scholarship, but also to look at the commodification of the spiritual in the context of both organized religion and "do it yourself" spirituality. The numerous contributions in the book look at how a variety of agents—religious institutions, spiritual leaders, marketers, and consumers—interact and co-create spiritual meanings in a post-disenchanted society. From a marketing perspective, the book examines not only religious organizations, but also brands and market systems and the way they infuse, whether intentionally or not, their products, services, and experiences with spiritual meanings that flow freely in the circuit of culture and can be appropriated by consumers even without purchase acts. In this respect, our approach is to a certain extent similar to work that has examined religious themes and fakery in popular culture and the way it may inspire authentic spiritual experiences (Chidester, 2005; Forbes & Mahan, 2000). However, as a whole, the chapters in the present collection, which are mostly authored by marketing scholars, show a finer-grained understanding of the mechanisms of cultural production in a globalized, capitalistic marketplace.

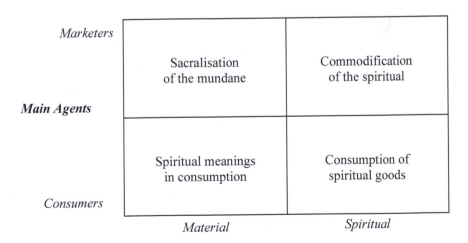

Figure 1.1 The consumption and marketing of spirituality: An overview.

THE CONSUMPTION AND MARKETING OF
SPIRITUALITY: MAPPING THE FIELD

As anticipated above, our two inter-related themes are the "commodification of the spiritual" and the "sacralisation of the mundane." When deciding how to organize the many contributions we received, we resorted to a traditional "business school" 2 x 2 matrix (see Figure 1.1). Although many studies in this volume look at both marketers and consumers, in most cases they privilege either the supply or demand side. As a result, our categorisation of each contribution in one of the figure's four cells is not as arbitrary as it could appear. In addition, a final section will look at issues of method and representation when studying consumers' spiritual experiences.

Part I, titled "Marketers' Sacralisation of the Mundane," explores how marketers and brands call on spiritual meanings to enhance the value of their products, services, and experiences. This theme has received scant attention in marketing and consumer research (see, however, Thompson, 2004; Thompson and Coskuner-Balli, 2007, on the socio-historical patterning of spiritual and magical aspects of the natural health's and community-supported agriculture's marketplace mythologies). Chapter 2 by Diego Rinallo, Stefania Borghini, Gary Bamossy, and Robert V. Kozinets looks at a highly provocative example of marketplace appropriation of religious symbols: Dolce & Gabbana's launch of a collection of rosaries as fashion accessories. These high-priced religious emblems are typically worn around the neck to direct onlookers' gaze to the wearer's body as an object of beauty, a trend started initially by the pop star Madonna. Exploring the contested meaning of this practice, Rinallo et al. show that although many consumers stigmatise fashion designers for being vain, ignorant of the "real" meaning of the rosary, or even blasphemous, other consumers see instead branded rosaries as objects devoid of religious significance, "just decorative objects" whose provocative nature enables wearers to stand out in a crowd. Perhaps the most interesting group, however, are those consumers for whom branded rosaries have a dual nature, sacred and profane at the same time: they partake of the transformative power of fashion but at the same time they draw consumers near to God.

A different type of marketplace appropriation is discussed by Elif Izberk-Bilgin in Chapter 3 on the ways in which the halal movement in Turkey forges a faith-based market. There has been a recent surge of interest in Islamic marketing with notable scholars (Izberk-Bilgin, 2012; Jafari, 2012; Sandıkçı and Ger, 2010; Sandıkçı and Rice, 2011) highlighting how marketers have ignored the complexity of economic, political, and socio-cultural forces shaping the Islamic marketplace. In a similar vein, Izberk-Bilgin's study counters previous claims that Islam is anti-modern and anti-market, and it shows how Islamic ideology is negotiated and made compatible with the modern capitalist marketplace.

In contrast to this example of institutionalised religious marketplace appropriation, the final chapter in Part I, Chapter 4 by Mary Johnstone-

Louis, examines the commercialisation of New Atheism, a 21st-century anti-religious movement that positions atheism as a brand and constructs unbelief as a commodity. This fascinating study, somewhat ironically creating belief around non-belief, illustrates how New Atheism popularises its message using a range of marketing tools and techniques to establish its authority and develop a devote community of followers. Emphasizing one of the key underpinning themes of our book, this chapter powerfully illustrates the diversity of religious practices that exists today and how new types of marketplace mediators arise—mediators that are different to traditional religious institutions.

Part II, "Consumers' Search for Spiritual Meanings in Consumption of the Mundane," discusses how consumers infuse their everyday consumption patterns with spiritual meanings and how they transform the profane into the sacred. In this respect, we are honored to have a contribution (Chapter 5) from the leading pioneer of the sacred and profane in consumer research, Russell V. Belk. His early work on the sacralisation of the secular (e.g., Belk et al., 1989) did a tremendous job of illustrating how the human need for spirituality and transcendence can be found in popular culture and consumption activities. Just over twenty years ago, he and his colleagues showed how consumers can sacralise not only objects and people, but also places, experiences, and times. In his current chapter, Belk turns attention on a mythic figure associated with Christmas, namely, Santa Claus, a figure that was, of course, popularised by Coca-Cola as fat and jolly with a red suit and white beard. Belk argues that this quasi-commercial Santa myth has become as sacralised as the original Christian story on the birth of Christ and, indeed, that Santa provides an alternative 'religious' myth that in many cases is more powerful and pervasive for contemporary consumers than the story of Jesus.

Another mythic figure in Western culture is the vampire, most recently revived for contemporary popular culture through the TV series *Buffy the Vampire Slayer* and the *Twilight* novels. Focusing on *Twilight*, Margo Buchanan-Oliver and Hope Jensen Schau (Chapter 6) provide a topical and timely analysis of spirituality in popular culture by exploring how the consumption of this media narrative provides spiritual and moral instruction. They show how the vampire myth questions normative social and sexual roles, thereby enabling consumers to act as 'mythic bricoleurs' in their identity projects while enacting what Buchanan-Oliver and Schau refer to as the commodification of mass worship.

Switching to another contemporary media narrative, Stephen Brown (Chapter 7) engages us with his usual indomitable style by bringing to life the dynamics of spiritual consumption through his tale of a family visit to the *Wizarding World of Harry Potter* in Orlando, Florida. Using his widely recognised literary mode of representation, he vividly conveys the heightened emotions and antagonisms that can occur during this commercialised pilgrimage and act of brand worship. Reflecting Ritzer's (2005) thesis on how the enchantment found in theme parks and shopping malls ultimately succumbs to increased rationalisation and ultimately annihilates itself, Brown's tale humorously illustrates how the quasi-spiritual nature of brands can equally enable them to fall from grace. Taking Dante's *Inferno* as his departure point, he recounts a less than spiritual encounter with this iconic cultural brand.

The final chapter in Part II (Chapter 8) is by Alan Bradshaw, who offers us an overlooked theoretical lens with which to better understand the sacred in consumer culture, Colin Campbell's (2008) *Easternization of the West* thesis. Better known for his *Romantic Ethic*, this later work by Campbell has been little acknowledged to date by consumer researchers. In it Campbell argues that a shift in worldview has taken place and that we are now in an era of Easternization, a cultural change that has permeated all facets of our lives and especially religion. As part of his thesis, Campbell undertakes a systematic analysis of the contingencies of the sacred and the devotional, locating manifestations of the sacred in consumption as part of this worldview. Thus, Bradshaw argues, he provides consumer culture theory (CCT) with the missing explanatory link for the sacralisation of the mundane.

Part III, "The Commodification of the Spiritual," looks at how religious institutions and spiritual leaders market their products and services. Religious pluralism has stimulated the rise of the so-called economics of religion approach (Finke, 1997; Finke and Stark, 1988; Iannaccone, 1991; Stark, 1997; Stark and Bainbridge 1985; Stark and Finke, 2000; Warner, 1993), which applies economic concepts such as supply and demand to model the religious behaviours of individuals and groups. According to such an approach, competition among religious institutions stimulates greater "marketing" efforts to attract and/or keep their members, resulting in increased rates of religious participation. The work of these scholars finds a parallel in those contributions that have examined the promotional practices currently adopted by religious institutions, which are increasingly similar to those of market-oriented multinational corporations (Shawchuck et al., 1992). These texts, which often have evocative titles (e.g., *Shopping for Faith*, Cimino and Lattin, 1999; *Shopping for God*, Twitchell, 2007; *Brands of Faith*, Einstein, 2008; *Jesus in Disneyland*, Lyon, 2000; *Consuming Religion*, Miller, 2005; *Selling God*, Moore, 1995; see also Sargeant, 2000; Twitchell, 2004) often provide vivid case studies of the increasingly sophisticated marketing practices currently adopted by religious institutions. The theme of religious marketing has also surfaced in marketing journals (Belk, 2000; Bonsu and Belk, 2010; a recent special issue of the *International Journal of Nonprofit and Voluntary Sector Marketing* [2010, Vol. 15, n. 4]; and numerous articles in the *Journal of Islamic Marketing*). Interestingly, the use of overtly commercial marketing strategies by religious organisations may be negatively perceived by consumers (Attaway, Boles, and Singley, 1997; Kenneson and Street, 1997; McDaniel, 1986; McGraw, Schwartz, and Tetlock, 2012).

The first chapter in Part III by Robin Croft (Chapter 9) suggests that the commodification of the spiritual is not necessarily a modern phenomenon. Croft tracks how relics of saints and other holy people have formed a significant role for many centuries in religious rites of many cultures, elevating profane possessions to sacred status. Using a case study of Glastonbury Abbey in the medieval period, he shows how monks at the abbey centred the spiritual and commercial bases of the community on what was England's largest relic collection and created a thriving pilgrimage business that relied on various marketing techniques (and manipulations!) to sustain it.

Moving to contemporary times, Mara Einstein (Chapter 10) discusses how major religious institutions are using branding to re-confirm or, in some cases, re-establish an identity. As she highlights, the use of branding and other marketing techniques is an increasing imperative if these institutions wish to remain part of the cultural conversation or be chosen as cultural resources for identity projects. Using two recent advertising campaigns as case studies—"I'm a Mormon" for The Church of Jesus Christ of Latter-Day Saints and "Inspired by Muhammad" for Islam—Einstein demonstrates how religious branding is being used not only to gain more followers, but also to enhance the religion's image and create a stronger sense of "corporate" identity.

The final chapter in Part III by Catherine Dolan (Chapter 11) explores how single women represent a promising market segment for Pentecostal-charismatic Christianity in Kenya. Her richly detailed study of 'Single Women Ministries' that commodify the private sphere and present marriage as spectacle, illustrates the blurring of boundaries among religion, commerce, and entertainment. Dolan argues that these charismatic spectacles counter Christianity's concept of marriage as a sacred sphere outside the marketplace and reframe marriage as a means for material success and happiness. Taking a more critical stance, this study also shows that as this 'gospel of prosperity' extends into ever more domains, it is not only blurring the distinction between the sacred and secular, but also calling into question the nature of intimacy and marriage itself.

Part IV, "The Consumption of Spiritual Goods," looks at the proliferation of spiritual goods and the rich ways in which they are consumed. The sacred is often mediated through material objects, goods, and places. All three chapters in Part IV focus on specific places that are conducive to spiritual experiences. Much CCT research has dealt with sacred places (Belk, Wallendorf, and Sherry, 1989) that might play multiple roles for consumers: cultural epicenters (Holt, 2002), pilgrimage sites (O'Guinn and Belk, 1989), liminal contexts where self-experimentation and personal transformation are possible and where meaningful relationships are built (Arnould and Price, 1993; Belk and Costa, 1998; Kozinets, 2002), and temporary retreats where a mythical past is reconstructed and the disenchantment and commercialisation of everyday life is resisted (Belk and Costa, 1998; Kozinets, 2002; Maclaran and Brown, 2005).

Part IV contributes to this literature in showing how the processes of place meaning creation are more complex than previously thought. First, some places are interpreted, imagined, exploited, transformed, and narrated by different communities with conflicting agendas, thus providing contradictory sources of identity value for consumers (as we see in Chapter 14 by Scott and Maclaran). Second, we suggest that processes of meaning generation interact with the physicality of their material form and the uniqueness of their geographical location—all aspects that have been downplayed so far. Whether a well whose healing waters are associated with divine compassion or a hill whose top draws men near to the Gods, the natural environment may structure memory and myth making and facilitate the manifestation of the sacred in ways similar to the marketplace-created environment. Darach Turley's Chapter 12, which investigates pilgrimages to a Holy Well dedicated to St. Brigid in the West of Ireland, aptly illustrates both of these points The bizarre array of quasi-religious artefacts and personal belongings left at the site by the travelling community creates tensions and contested meanings with the settled local community. At the same time, his study also shows the syncretic blending of Pagan and Christian myth and its grounding in the Irish landscape.

The remaining two chapters in this section by Richard Kedzior (Chapter 13) and Linda Scott and Pauline Maclaran (Chapter 14) also look at pilgrimages, but this time of the New Age variety. In each case, the focus is on commercialisation and the role of the marketplace in mediating the meanings created by spiritual seekers and spiritual providers. Kedzior explores the visitor experience of vortex energy in Sedona, Arizona, arguing that the marketplace simultaneously creates tensions and offers their resolution. As such, consumption mediates access to the sacred and spiritual. In a similar vein, Scott and Maclaran show local vendors producing pilgrimage experience, acting independently of any single religious institution, yet using history and landscape, along with an eclectic selection of stories and practices from established faiths, to produce a distinctly 21st-century spiritual experience for a new generation of independent pilgrims.

Studying spiritual experiences, particularly in interpretive consumer research, poses special challenges to researchers who have to question the impact of their religious worldview (or lack thereof) on their relationship with informants and interpretation of research findings. Part V, "Issues of Method and Representation," explores research issues that emerge when studying spirituality and consumption. John F. Sherry, Jr. (Chapter 15) focuses on the "spatial turn" in scholarly research, claiming that it will reshape marketing and consumer research, just as the interpretive turn has already done. Social scientific and humanistic traditions offer many insights into enquiry on the spirit of place, and the previous part has just illustrated the importance of understanding the elusive nature of place in relation to the intersection of consumption and spirituality. Sherry draws on such traditions to take us on an auto-ethnographic wander through his university office and to comprehend the blending of mystical and material elements that are its genius loci.

Chapter 16 by Stephen Gould introduces personal introspection as a further method to apprehend spiritual phenomena. Introspecting on his own consciousness and subconscious, he introduces us to the hermeneutics of spirituality, materialism, and introspection, a hermeneutics that problematises well-known dualities such as the sacred/profane, material/non-material, and phenomenal/epiphenomenal. Presenting spirituality as a spiritual practice, Gould incorporates many thought exercises for the reader to develop his or her own meditative-introspective practices.

Robert V. Kozinets and John F. Sherry, Jr. (Chapter 17) bring Part V and, indeed, the volume to a triumphant conclusion with their idea of auto-themataludicization, a concept that develops new insights into the nature of contemporary spiritual consumption as well as its representation. They suggest that autothematalucization, defined as "a contemporary process in which consumers collectively create of their own initiative, customized, meaningful, and playful spiritual experiences in a particular location, following some particular, and likely proscribed theme," encapsulates the search for meaning in a consumer society that is disenchanted with conventional religions. Make your own world and play with your reality—in fact, make your own reality is their ultimate message and an appropriately upbeat note on which to finish our journey into spirituality and consumption.

CONCLUSION

Let us conclude with some autobiographical notes on how the idea for this book emerged. In the summer of 2007, we spent a week together at the Avalon Witch Camp, a retreat organized by members of the Reclaiming tradition, which is part of the Neo-Pagan movement. The Witch Camp was set in Glastonbury, which as Scott and Maclaran explain in this volume is a place of spiritual significance for its associations to Arthurian legends and England's pre-Christian heritage. We like to think of the week we spent together as our own Spiritual Consumer Odyssey. We took part in several consciousness-altering practices, including ritual, divination, ecstatic dance, and meditation. Like many of the other participants at this event, we shopped for spiritual merchandise, we visited sacred places such as the Chalice Well, and we climbed the hill known as the Tor. More importantly, we talked to the other participants and compared their views on spirituality with our own.

During the Witch Camp, there were ongoing comparisons of field observations among the three of us, which yielded considerable variation in interpretation based on, among other factors, our gender, age, and degree of involvement with the Neo-Pagan community and alternative spiritualities more in general. We had extensive conversations about feminist theology and the impact of feminine representations of the Divine on the lives of both women and men; witchcraft as a metaphor for women's power; the role played by works of fictions like Marion Zimmer Bradley's *Mists of Avalon* on the experience that we and other participants were living at Glastonbury (according to some, the Tor is the site of legendary Avalon); what it meant to practice magic today, in supposedly rational and disenchanted societies; and the mechanisms through which the marketplace shapes spiritual experiences. We extended our conversations, in spirit, to the colleagues whose work would come spontaneously to our mind during our observations. Could spiritual seekers escape the market? Were the consecration rituals in which we were taking part a way to sacralise the mundane and enchant commodities? Was the event we were attending best described as a community, a subculture, a tribe, a hypercommunity? Were participants' motivations escapist or emancipatory? What were the differences with mountain men rendezvous, Star Trek fan gatherings, or the Burning Man event?

The idea for this book was born after extensive debate with many colleagues, often (but not always) in the context of special sessions at consumer research conferences (Scott and Maclaran, 2009; Rinallo, 2009b, 2010). The unexpected, but profound interest for the topic convinced us that spirituality is a highly relevant phenomenon for marketing and consumer research. Sometimes the influence of spirituality may simply help us to better understand how and why consumers behave as they do in particular contexts; at other times, spirituality may inspire us to seek entirely new contexts and ways of understanding. Whatever the extent of spirituality's influence on our research, there can be no doubt regarding its significance to contemporary consumer culture. In this volume, we have brought together some of the many complexities at the intersection of commerce and spirituality. With the help of our insightful contributors, we hope we have unravelled some of these complexities for other researchers in the field while also opening up new mysteries for researchers to pursue in the future.

REFERENCES

Arnould, Eric J., and Linda L. Price. 1993. "River Magic: Extraordinary Experience and the Extended Service Encounter." *Journal of Consumer Research* 20 (June): 24–45.

Arnould, Eric J., Linda L. Price, and Cele Otnes. 1999. "Making Consumption Magic: A Study of White-Water River Rafting." *Journal of Contemporary Ethnography* 28 (February): 33–68.

Arweck, Elizabeth, and Martin D. Stringer, eds. 2002. *Theorising Faith: The Insider-Outsider Problem in the Study of Ritual.* Birmingham: University of Birmingham Press.

Atkin, Douglas. 2004. *The Culting of Brands: When Customers Become True Believers.* New York: Portfolio.

Attaway, Jill S., James S. Boles, and Rodger B. Singley. 1997. "Exploring Consumers' Attitudes toward Advertising by Religious Organizations." *Journal of Marketing Management* 13 (Fall/Winter): 71–83.

Baerveldt, Cor. 1996. "New Age-Religiositeit als Individueel Constructieproces" [New Age-Religiosity as a Process of Individual Construction]. In *De Kool en de Geit in de Nieuwe Tijd: Wetenschappelijke Reflecties op New Age* [The Fence, the Hare, and the Hounds in the New Age: Scientific Reflections on New Age], edited by Miranda Moerland, 19–31. Utrecht: Jan van Arkel.

Barnett, Carole K., Terence C. Krell, and Jeanette Sendry. 2000. "Learning to Learn about Spirituality: A Categorical Approach to Introducing the Topic into Management Courses." *Journal of Management Education* 24 (5): 562–580.

Belk, Russell W. 1983. "Worldly Possessions: Issues and Criticisms." In *Advances in Consumer Research*, Vol. 10, edited by Richard P. Bagozzi and Alice M. Tybout, 514–519. Ann Arbor: Association for Consumer Research.

Belk, Russell W. 1984. "Three Scales to Measure Constructs Related to Materialism: Reliability, Validity, and Relationships to Measures of Happiness." In *Advances in Consumer Research*, Vol. 11, edited by Thomas Kinnear, 291–297. Provo, UT: Association for Consumer Research.

Belk, Russell W. 1985. "Materialism: Trait Aspects of Living in the Material World." *Journal of Consumer Research* 12 (December): 265–280.

Belk, Russell W. 2000. "Pimps for Paradise: Paradisal Versions Proffered by Missionaries, Monetary Funds, and Marketers." *Marketing Intelligence and Planning* 18 (6/7): 337–334.

Belk, Russell W., and Janeen A. Costa. 1998. "The Mountain Man Myth: A Contemporary Consuming Fantasy." *Journal of Consumer Research* 25 (December): 218–240.

Belk, Russell W., Guliz Ger, and Søren Askegaard. 2003. "The Fire of Desire: A Multisited Inquiry into Consumer Passion." *Journal of Consumer Research* 30 (3): 326–351.

Belk, Russell W., John F. Sherry, Jr., and Melanie Wallendorf. 1988. "A Naturalistic Inquiry into Buyer and Seller Behavior at a Swap Meet." *Journal of Consumer Research* 14 (March): 449–470.

Belk, Russell W., and Gülnur Tumbat. 2005. "The Cult of MacIntosh." *Consumption, Markets & Culture* 8 (3): 205–217

Belk, Russell W., and Melanie Wallendorf. 1990. "The Sacred Meanings of Money." *Journal of Economic Psychology* 11 (March): 35–67.

Belk, Russell W., Melanie Wallendorf, and John F. Sherry. 1989. "The Sacred and Profane in Consumer Behavior: Theodicy on the Odyssey." *Journal of Consumer Research* 16 (June): 1–38.

Benefiel, Margaret. 2003. "Irreconcilable Foes? The Discourse of Spirituality and the Discourse of Organizational Science." *Organization* 10: 383–391.

Benefiel, Margaret. 2005. *Soul at Work: Spiritual Leadership in Organizations*. New York: Seabury Books.

Bento, Regina F. 2000. "The Little Inn at the Crossroads: A Spiritual Approach to the Design of a Leadership Course." *Journal of Management Education* 24 (5): 650–661.

Berger, Peter L. 1967. *The Sacred Canopy: Elements of a Sociological Theory of Religion*. New York: Doubleday.

Berger, Peter L. 1999. *The Desecularization of the World: Resurgent Religion and World Politics*. Grand March: Eerdmans.

Berger, Peter, Grace Davie, and Effie Fokas. 2008. *Religious America, Secular Europe? A Theme and Variations*. Aldershot: Ashgate.

Biberman, Jerry, and Len Tischler, eds. 2008. *Spirituality in Business: Theory, Practice, and Future Direction*. New York: Palgrave Macmillan.

Biberman, Jerry, and Michael Whitty, eds. 2000. *Work & Spirit: A Reader of New Spiritual Paradigms for Organizations*. Scranton, PA: University of Scranton.

Boje, David. 2008. "Critical Theory Approaches to Spirituality in Business." In *Spirituality in Business: Theory, Practice and Future Directions*, edited by Jerry Biberman and Len Tischler, 160–187. New York: Palgrave Macmillan.

Bonsu, Samuel K., and Russell W. Belk. 2010. "Marketing a New African God: Pentecostalism and Material Salvation in Ghana." *International Journal of Nonprofit and Voluntary Sector Marketing* 15: 305–323.

Borghini, Stefania, Nina Diamond, Robert V. Kozinets, Mary Ann McGrath, Albert Muñiz, and John F. Sherry, Jr. 2009. "Why Are Themed Brandstores So Powerful? Retail Brand Idelogoy at American Girl Place." *Journal of Retailing* 85 (3): 363–375.

Brown, Steven, Robert V. Kozinets, and John F. Sherry. 2003. "Teaching Old Brands New Tricks: Retro Branding and the Revival of Brand Meaning." *Journal of Marketing* 67 (July): 19–33.

Burroughs, James E., and Aric Rindfleisch. 2002. "Materialism and WellÔøD° > Being: A Conflicting Values Perspective." *Journal of Consumer Research* 29 (3): 348–370.

Caird, Dale. 1987. "Religion and Personality: Are Mystics Introverted, Neurotic or Psychotic?" *British Journal of Social Psychology* (26): 345–346.

Campbell, Colin, 2008. *The Easternization of the West: A Thematic Account of Cultural Change in the West*. London: Paradigm Publishers.

Celsi, Richard L., Randall L. Rose, and Thomas W. Leigh. 1993. "An Exploration of High-Risk Leisure Consumption Through Skydiving." *Journal of Consumer Research* 20 (1): 1–23.

Chen, Yu. 2009. "Possession and Access: Consumer Desires and Value Perceptions Regarding Contemporary Art Collection and Exhibit Visits." *Journal of Consumer Research* 35 (6): 925–940.

Chidester, David. 2005. *Authentic Fakes: Religion and American Popular Culture*. Berkley: University of California Press.

Cimino, Richard, and Don Lattin. 1998. *Shopping for Faith: American Religion in the New Millennium*. San Francisco, CA: Jossey-Bass.

Delbecq, André. 2000. "Spirituality for Business Leadership: Reporting on a Pilot Course for MBAs and CEOs." *Journal of Management Inquiry* 9: 117–129.

Delbecq, André. 2005. "Spiritually Informed Management Theory: Overlaying the Experience of Teaching Managers." *Journal of Management Inquiry* 14: 242–246.

Dion, Delphine, and Eric Arnould. 2011. "Retail Luxury Strategy: Assembling Charisma through Art and Magic." *Journal of Retailing* 87 (4): 502–520.

Drive, Michaela. 2007. "A 'Spiritual Turn' in Organization Studies: Meaning Making or Meaningless?" *Journal of Management, Spirituality, & Religion* 4: 56–86.

Durkheim, Émile. 1915. *The Elementary Forms of the Religious Life*. London: Allen & Unwin.

Einstein, Mara. 2008. *Brands of Faith: Marketing Religion in a Commercial Age*. New York: Routledge.

Eliade, Mircea. 1959. *The Sacred and the Profane: The Nature of Religion*. Translated by Willard R. Trask. New York: Harper & Row.

Emmons, Robert A. 1999. *The Psychology of Ultimate Concerns: Motivation and Spirituality in Personality*. New York: Guilford.

Emmons, Robert A., and Raymond F. Paloutzian. 2003. "The Psychology of Religion." *Annual Review of Psychology* 54: 377–402.

Epstein, Edwin M. 2002. "Religion and Business: The Critical Role of Religious Traditions in Management Education." *Journal of Business Ethics* 38: 91–96.

Favret-Saada, Jeanne. 1980. *Deadly Words: Witchcraft in the Bocage*. Cambridge: Cambridge University Press.

Fernandez, Karen V., and John L. Lastovicka. 2011. "Making Magic: Fetishes in Contemporary Consumption." *Journal of Consumer Research* 38 (2): 278–299.

Finke, Roger. 1997. "The Consequences of Religious Competition: Supply-Side Explanations for Religious Change." In *Rational Choice and Religion, Summary and Assessment*, edited by Lawrence A. Young, 45–64. New York: Routledge.

Finke, Roger, and Rodney Stark. 1988. "Religious Economies and Sacred Canopies: Religious Mobilization in American Cities." *American Sociological Review* 53 (1): 41–49.

Firat, A. Fuat, and Alladi Venkatesh. 1995. "Liberatory Postmodernism and the Reenchantment of Consumption." *Journal of Consumer Research* 22 (December): 239–267.

Flanagan, Kieran, and Peter C. Jupp, eds. 2007. *A Sociology of Spirituality*. Aldershot (UK): Ashgate.

Forbes, Bruce D., and Jeffrey Mahan, eds. 2000. *Religion and Popular Culture in America*. San Francisco: University of California Press.

Foucault, Michel. 1988. "Technologies of the Self." In *Technologies of the Self: A Seminar with Michel Foucault*, edited by Luther H. Martin et al., 16–49. Amherst: University of Massachusetts Press.

Fournier, Susan. 1998. "Consumers and their Brands: Developing Relationship Theory in Consumer Research." *Journal of Consumer Research* 24 (March): 343–353.

Freud, Sigmund. 1961. *The Future of an Illusion*. Original edition 1927. Garden City, NY: Doubleday.

Freud, Sigmund. 1989. *Civilization and its Discontents*. Original edition 1930. Edited by James Strachey. New York: Norton.

Giacalone, Robert A., and Carole L. Jurkiewiez, eds. 2002. *The Handbook of Workplace Spirituality and Organisational Performance*. New York: M. E. Sharpe Inc.

Giddens, Anthony. 1991. *Modernity and Self Identity. Self and Society in the Late Modern Age*. Cambridge: Polity Press.

Gorsuch, Richard L. 1984. "The Boon and Bane of Investigating Religion." *American Psychologist* 39: 228–236.

Gorsuch, Richard L. 2002. *Integrating Psychology and Spirituality*. Westport, CT: Greenwood.

Gould, Stephen J. 1991. "The Self-Manipulation of my Pervasive, Perceived Vital Energy Through Product Use: An Introspective-Praxis Perspective." *Journal of Consumer Research* 18 (2): 194–207.

Gould, Stephen J. 1992. "Consumer Materialism as a Multilevel and Individual Difference Phenomenon: An Asian-Based Perspective." In *Meaning, Measure, and Morality of Materialism*, edited by Floyd Rudmin and Marsha Richins, 57–62. Provo, UT: Association for Consumer Research.

Gould, Stephen J. 2006. "Cooptation Through Conflation: Spiritual Materialism Is Not the Same as Spirituality." *Consumption, Markets and Culture* 9 (1): 63–78.

Goulding, Christina, Avi Shankar, and Richard Elliott. 2002. "Working Weeks, Rave Weekends: Identity Fragmentation and the Emergence of New Communities." *Consumption, Markets and Culture* 5 (4): 261–284.

Goulding, Christina, Avi Shankar, Richard Elliott, and Robin Canniford. 2009. "The Marketplace Management of Illicit Pleasure." *Journal of Consumer Research* 35 (February): 759–771.

Group for the Advancement of Psychiatry. 1976. *Mysticism: Spiritual Quest or Mental Disorder?* New York: Group for the Advancement of Psychiatry.

Hamilton, Malcom. 2000. "An Analysis of the Festival for Mind-Body-Spirit, London." In *Beyond New Age: Exploring Alternative Spirituality*, edited by Steven Sutcliffe and Marion Bowman, 188–200. Edinburgh: Edinburgh University Press.

Hammond, Philip E. 1985. *The Sacred in a Secular Age: Toward Revision in the Scientific Study of Religion*. San Francisco: University of California Press.

Harlos, Karen P. 2000. "Toward a Spiritual Pedagogy: Meaning, Practice, and Applications in Management Education." *Journal of Management Education* 24 (5): 612–627.

Heelas, Paul, and Linda Woodhead. 2005. *The Spiritual Revolution: Why Religion Is Giving Way to Spirituality*. Oxford: Blackwell.

Hill, Peter C. 2005. "Measurement in the Psychology of Religion and Spirituality: Current Status and Evaluation." In *Handbook of the Psychology of Religion and Spirituality*, edited by Raymond F. Paloutzian and Crystal L. Park, 43–61. New York: Guilford Press.

Hill, Peter C., Kenneth I. Pargament, Ralph W. Hood, Jr., Michael E. McCullough, James P. Swyers, David B. Larson, and Brian J. Zinnbauer. 2000. "Conceptualizing Religion and Spirituality: Points of Commonality, Points of Departure." *Journal for the Theory of Social Behaviour* 30: 51–77.

Hirschman, Elizabeth. 1985. "Primitive Aspects of Consumption in Modern American Society." *Journal of Consumer Research* 12 (September): 142–154.

Hirschman, Elizabeth. 1988. "The Ideology of Consumption: A Structural-Syntactical Analysis of 'Dallas' and 'Dynasty.' " *Journal of Consumer Research* 15 (3): 344–359.

Holbrook, Morris B., ed. 1999. *Consumer Value: A Framework for Analysis and Research*. New York: Routledge.

Holmes, Peter R. 2007. "Spirituality: Some Disciplinary Perspectives." In *A Sociology of Spirituality*, edited by Kieran Flanagan and Peter C. Jupp, 23–42. Ashgate: Aldershot (UK).

Holt, Douglas B. 2002. "Why Do Brands Cause Trouble? A Dialectical Theory of Consumer Culture and Branding." *Journal of Consumer Research* 29 (June): 70–90.

Hood, Ralph W. 1976. "Conceptual Criticism of Regressive Explanations of Mysticism." *Review of Religious Research* 17: 179–188.

Horton, Paul C. 1974. "The Mystical Experience: Substance of an Illusion." *Journal of the American Psychoanalytic Association* 22: 364–380.

Iacobucci, Dawn. 2001. "Commonalities between Research Methods for Consumer Science and Biblical Scholarship." *Marketing Theory* 1 (1): 109–133.

Iannaccone, Laurence R. 1990. "Religious Practice: A Human Capital Approach." *Journal for the Scientific Study of Religion* 29: 297–314.

Iannaccone, Laurence R. 1991. "The Consequences of Religious Market Structure: Adam Smith and the Economics of Religion." *Rationality and Society* 3 (2): 156–177.

Izberk-Bilgin, Elif. 2012. "Infidil Brands: Unveiling Alternative Meanings of Global Brands at the Nexus of Globalization, Consumer Culture, and Islamism." *Journal of Consumer Research* (December), in press.

Jackson, Mike, and K. W. M. Fulford. 1997. "Spiritual Experience and Psychopathology." *Philosophy, Psychiatry, & Psychology* 4 (1): 41–65.

Jafari, Aliakbar. 2012. "Islamic Marketing: Insights from a Critical Perspective." *Journal of Islamic Marketing* 3 (1): 22–34.

James, William. 1982. *The Varieties of Religious Experience: A Study in Human Nature*. Original edition 1902. New York: Penguin.

Jenkins, Henry. 2003. "Transmedia Storytelling." *MIT Technology Review*, January 15. Accessed December 11, 2011. http://www.technologyreview.com/Biotech/13052/

Jenkins, Henry. 2006. *Convergence Culture*. New York: New York University Press.

Kenneson, Philip, and James L. Street. 1997. *Selling Out the Church: The Dangers of Church Marketing*. Nashville: Abingdon.

Koenig, Harold G. 2001. "Religion, Spirituality, and Medicine: How Are They Related and What Does It Mean?" *Mayo Clinic Proceedings* 76: 1189–1191.

Koenig, Harold G., Michael E. McCullough, and David B. Larson, eds. 2001. *Handbook of Religion and Health*. Oxford: Oxford University Press.

Kozinets, Robert V. 1997. " 'I Want to Believe': A Netnography of the X-Philes' Subculture of Consumption." In *Advances in Consumer Research*, Vol. 24, edited by Merrie Brucks and Deborah J. MacInnis, 470–475. Provo, UT: Association for Consumer Research.

Kozinets, Robert V. 2001. "Utopian Enterprise: Articulating the Meanings of Star Trek's Culture of Consumption." *Journal of Consumer Research* 28 (June): 67–87.

Kozinets, Robert V. 2002. "Can Consumers Escape the Market? Emancipatory Illuminations from Burning Man." *Journal of Consumer Research* 28 (1): 67–88.

Kozinets, Robert V., and John F. Sherry, Jr. 2003. "Dancing on Common Ground: Exploring the Sacred at Burning Man." In *Rave and Religion*, edited by Graham St. John, 287–303. New York: Routledge.

Kozinets, Robert V., John F. Sherry, Jr., Benét DeBerry-Spence, Adam Duhachek, Krittinee Nuttavuthisit, and Diana Storm. 2002. "Themed Flagship Brand Stores in the New Millennium: Theory, Practice, Prospects." *Journal of Retailing* 78: 17–29.

Kozinets, Robert V., John F. Sherry, Jr., Diana Storm, Adam Duhachek, Krittinee Nuttavuthisit, and Benét DeBerry®ÔøD° > Spence. 2004. "Ludic Agency and Retail Spectacle." *Journal of Consumer Research* 31 (3): 658–672.

Kramer, Thomas, and Lauren Block. 2008. "Conscious and Nonconscious Components of Superstitious Beliefs in Judgment and Decision Making." *Journal of Consumer Research* 34 (6): 783–793.

La Barbera, Priscilla A., and Zeynep Gürhan. 1997. "The Role of Materialism, Religiosity, and Demographics in Subjective Well-Being." *Psychology & Marketing* 14 (1): 71–97.

Lips-Wiersma, Marjolein, Kathy Lund Dean, and Charles J. Fornaciari. 2009. "Theorizing the Dark Side of the Workplace Spirituality Movement." *Journal of Management Inquiry* 18 (4): 288–300.

Luckmann, Thomas. 1967. *The Invisible Religion*. New York: Macmillan.

Lyon, David. 2000. *Jesus in Disneyland: Religion in Postmodern Times*. Cambridge: Polity Press.

Maclaran, Pauline, and Stephen Brown. 2005. "The Center Cannot Hold: Consuming the Utopian Marketplace." *Journal of Consumer Research* 32 (September): 311–323.

Maslow, Abraham H. 1964. *Religions, Values, and Peak-Experiences*. Columbus, OH: Ohio State University Press.

Masters, Kevin S, and Glenn I. Spielmans. 2007. "Prayer and Health: Review, Meta-Analysis, and Research Agenda." *Journal of Behavioral Medicine* 30 (4): 329–338.

McDaniel, Stephen W. 1986. "Church Advertising: Views of the Clergy and General Public." *Journal of Advertising* 15 (March): 24–29.

McDannell, Colleen. 1995. *Material Christianity: Religion and Popular Culture in America*. New Haven, CT: Yale University Press.

McGraw, Peter, Janet A. Schwartz, and Philip E. Tetlock. 2012. "From the Commercial to the Communal: Reframing Taboo Trade-offs in Religious and Pharmaceutical Marketing." *Journal of Consumer Research* 39 (June): 157-173.

Miller, Bob. 2000. "Spirituality for Business Leadership." *Journal of Management Inquiry* 9 (2): 132–134.

Miller, Vincent J. 2005. *Consuming Religion: Christian Faith and Practice in a Consumer Culture*. New York: Continuum International.

Mitroff, Ian, and Elizabeth Denton. 1999. *A Spiritual Audit of Corporate America*. San Francisco: Jossey-Bass.

Moberg, David O. 2002. "Assessing and Measuring Spirituality: Confronting Dilemmas of Universal and Particular Evaluative Criteria." *Journal of Adult Development* 9 (1): 47–60.

Moisio, Risto, and Beruchashvili, Mariam. 2010. "Questing for Well-Being at Weight Watchers: The Role of the Spiritual-Therapeutic Model in a Support Group." *Journal of Consumer Research* 36 (February): 857–875.

Moore, Robert L. 1995. *Selling God: American Religion in the Marketplace of Culture*. New York: Oxford University Press.

Moore, Thom, Brett Kloos, and Rachel Rasmussen. 2001. "A Reunion of Ideas: Complementary Inquiry and Collaborative Interventions of Spirituality, Religion, and Psychology." *Journal of Community Psychology* 29 (5): 487–495.

Morgan, David. 1999. *Visual Piety: A History and Theory of Popular Religious Images*. Berkeley, CA: University of California Press.

Morris, Brian. 2006. *Religion and Anthropology: A Critical Introduction*. Cambridge: Cambridge University Press.

Mowen, John C., and Brad Carlson. 2003. "Exploring the Antecedents and Consumer Behavior Consequences of the Trait of Superstition." *Psychology & Marketing* 20 (12): 1045–1065.

Mueller Paul S., David J. Plevak, and Teresa A. Rummans. 2001. "Religious Involvement, Spirituality, and Medicine: Implications for Clinical Practice." *Mayo Clinic Proceedings* 76: 1225–1235.

Muñiz, Albert M., and Hope J. Schau. 2005. "Religiosity in the Abandoned Apple Newton Brand Community." *Journal of Consumer Research* 31 (March): 737–747.

Neal, Judith A. 1997. "Spirituality in Management Education: A Guide to Resources." *Journal of Management Education* 21 (1): 121–139.

O'Guinn, Thomas C., and Russell W. Belk. 1989. "Heaven on Earth: Consumption at Heritage Village, USA." *Journal of Consumer Research* 16 (September): 227–238.

Ospina, Maria B., Kenneth Bond, Mohammad Karkhaneh, Lisa Tjosvold, Ben Vandermeer, Yuanyuan Liang, Liza Bialy, Nicola Hooto, Nina Buscemi, Donna M. Dryden, and Terry P. Klassen. 2007. "Meditation Practices for Health: State of the Research." *Evidence Report/Technology Assessment* 155: 1–263. Ostwalt, Conrad E. 2003. *Secular Steeples: Popular Culture and the Religious Imagination*. Harrisburg, PA: Trinity Press International.

Otto, Rudolf. 1950. *The Idea of the Holy*. Translated by J. W. Harvey. London: Oxford University Press. Original work published in German in 1917.

Owen, Alex. 2004. *The Place of Enchantment. British Occultism and the Culture of the Modern*. Chicago: University of Chicago Press.

Pace, Stefano. 2012. "Does Religion Affect the Materialism of Consumers? An Empirical Investigation of Buddhist Ethics and the Resistance of the Self." *Journal of Business Ethics*, in press.

Pargament, Kenneth I. 1999. "The Psychology of Religion and Spirituality? Yes and No." *International Journal for the Psychology of Religion* 9: 3–16.

Pichler, Elisabeth A., and Andrea Hemetsberger. 2007. " 'Hopelessly Devoted to You'—Towards an Extended Conceptualization of Consumer Devotion." In *Advances in Consumer Research*, Vol. 34, edited by Gavan Fitzsimons and Vicki Morwitz, 194–199. Duluth, MN: Association for Consumer Research.

Pimentel, Ronald W., and Kristy E. Reynolds. 2004. "A Model for Consumer Devotion: Affective Commitment with Proactive Sustaining Behaviors." *Academy of Marketing Science Review* 5: 1–45.

Possamai, Adam. 2003. "Alternative Spiritualities and the Cultural Logic of Late Capitalism." *Culture and Religion* 4 (1): 31–45.

Prasinos, Steven. 1992. "Spiritual Aspects of Psychotherapy." *Journal of Religion and Health* 31 (1): 41–52.

Ragas, Matthew W., and Bolivar J. Bueno. 2002. *The Power of Cult Branding: How 9 Magnetic Brands Turned Customers into Loyal Followers (and Yours Can, Too)*. New York: Crown Business.

Reave, Laura. 2005. "Spiritual Values and Practices Related to Leadership Effectiveness." *The Leadership Quarterly* 16 (5): 655–687.

Richins, Marsha L. 1991. "Social Comparison and the Idealized Images of Advertising." *Journal of Consumer Research* 18 (1): 71–83.

Richins, Marsha L., and Scott Dawson. 1992. "A Consumer Values Orientation for Materialism and Its Measurement: Scale Development and Validation." *Journal of Consumer Research* 19 (December): 303–316.

Rinallo, Diego. 2009a. " 'Living a Magical Life': Sacred Consumption and Spiritual Experience in the Italian Neo-Pagan Community." In *Advances in Consumer Research*, Vol. 36, edited by Ann L. McGill and Sharon Shavitt, 60–63. Duluth, MN: Association for Consumer Research.

Rinallo, Diego. 2009b. "Mythical Places of Origin, Pilgrimage Destinations, Promised Lands: Perspectives on the Consumption of Sacred Places." Special Session, *Consumer Culture Theory Conference*, Ann Arbor, June.

Rinallo, Diego. 2010. "Marketplace Shaping of Spiritual Experiences: Current Theory and Prospects." Roundtable, *Association for Consumer Research European Conference*, London, June.

Rindfleish, Jennifer. 2005. "Consuming the Self: New Age Spirituality as 'Social Product' in Consumer Society." *Consumption, Markets and Culture* 8 (4): 343–360.

Ritzer, George. 2005. *Enchanting a Disenchanted World*. Thousand Oaks, CA: Pine Forge Press.

Roof, Wade C. 1999. *Spiritual Marketplace: Baby Boomers and the Remaking of American Religion*. Princeton, NJ: Princeton University Press.

Sandıkçı, Özlem, and Guliz Ger. 2010. "Veiling in Style: How Does a Stigmatized Practice Become Fashionable?" *Journal of Consumer Research* 37 (1): 15–36.

Sandıkçı, Özlem, and Gillian Rice. 2011. *The Handbook of Islamic Marketing*. Northampton: Edward Elgar.

Sargeant, Kimon H. 2000. *Seeker Churches: Promoting Traditional Religion in a Nontraditional Way*. New Brunswick, NJ: Rutgers University Press.

Schouten, John W., and James H. McAlexander. 1995. "Subcultures of Consumption: an Ethnography of the New Bikers." *Journal of Consumer Research* 22 (June): 43–61.

Scott, Linda, and Pauline Maclaran. 2009. " 'Roll Your Own' Religion: Consumer Culture and the Spiritual Vernacular." In *Advances in Consumer Research*, Vol. 36, edited by Ann L. McGill and Sharon Shavitt, 60–63. Duluth, MN: Association for Consumer Research.

Shawchuck, Norman, Philip Kotler, Bruce Wrenn, and Gustav Rath. 1992. *Marketing for Congregations: Choosing to Serve People More Effectively*. Nashville: Abingdon.

Sheep, Mathew L. 2006. "Nurturing the Whole Person: The Ethics of Workplace Spirituality in a Society of Organizations." *Journal of Business Ethics* 66 (4): 357–375.

Sherry, John F., Jr., 1998. "The Soul of the Company Store: Nike Town Chicago and the Emplaced Brandscape." In *Servicescapes: The Concept of Place in Contemporary Markets*, edited by John F. Sherry, Jr., 109–150. Chicago: NTC Business Books.

Sherry, John F., Jr., Stefania Borghini, Mary Ann McGrath, Albert Muñiz, Nina Diamond, and Robert V. Kozinets. 2009. "Allmother as Image and Essence: Animating the American Girl Brand." In *Explorations in Consumer Culture Theory*, edited by John F. Sherry, Jr., and Eileen Fischer, 137–149. London: Routledge.

Sherry, John F., Jr., and Robert V. Kozinets. 2003. "Sacred Iconography in Secular Space: Altars, Alters and Alterity at the Burning Man Project." In *Contemporary Consumption Rituals: A Research Anthropology*, edited by Cele Otnes and Tina Lowrey, 291–311. Mahwah, NJ: Lawrence Erlbaum.

Sherry, John F., Jr., and Robert V. Kozinets. 2007. "Comedy of the Commons: Nomadic Spirituality at Burning Man." In *Consumer Culture Theory*, edited by Russell W. Belk and John F. Sherry, Jr., Vol. 11 of *Research in Consumer Behavior*, 119–147. Oxford: Elsevier.

St. James, Yannik, Jay M. Handelman, and Shirley F. Taylor. 2011. "Magical Thinking and Consumer Coping." *Journal of Consumer Research* 38 (4): 632–649.

Stark, Rodney. 1997. "Bringing Theory Back in" In *Rational Choice Theory and Religion, Summary and Assessment*, edited by Lawrence A. Young, 3–24. New York: Routledge.

Stark, Rodney, and William S. Bainbridge. 1985. *The Future of Religion: Secularization, Revival and Cult Formation*. Berkley, CA: University of California Press.

Stark, Rodney, and Roger Finke. 2000. *Acts of Faith: Explaining the Human Side of Religion*. Berkeley, CA: University of California Press.

Stillman, Tyler F., Frank D. Fincham, Kathleen D. Vohs, Nathaniel M. Lambert, and Christa A. Phillips. 2012. "The Material and Immaterial in Conflict: Spirituality Reduces Conspicuous Consumption." *Journal of Economic Psychology* 33: 1–7.

Stoller, Paul. 1987. *In Sorcery's Shadow: A Memoir of Apprenticeship among the Songhay of Niger*. Chicago: Chicago University Press.

Thompson, Craig J. 2004. "Marketplace Mythology and Discourses of Power." *Journal of Consumer Research* 31 (1): 162–180.

Thompson, Craig J., and Gokcen Coskuner-Balli. 2007. "Enchanting Ethical Consumerism: The Case of Community Supported Agriculture." *Journal of Consumer Culture* 7: 275–304.

Trungpa, Chögyam. 1973. *Cutting Through Spiritual Materialism*. Berkeley: Shambala.

Tumbat, Gülnur, and Russell W. Belk. 2011. "Marketplace Tensions in Extraordinary Experiences." *Journal of Consumer Research* 38 (June): 42–61.

Turner, Edith. 1994. "A Visible Spirit Form in Zambia." In *Being Changed by Cross-Cultural Encounters. The Anthropology of Extraordinary Experience*, edited by David E. Young and Jean-Guy Goulet, 71–95. Peterborough, Ontario: Broadview Press.

Turner, Robert P., David Lukoff, Ruth T. Barnhouse, and Francis G. Lu. 1995. "Religious or Spiritual Problem: A Culturally Sensitive Diagnostic Category in the DSM-IV." *Journal of Nervous and Mental Disease* 183 (7):435–444.

Twitchell, James B. 2004. *Branded Nation: The Marketing of Megachurch, College Inc., and Museumworld*. New York: Simon & Schuster.

Twitchell, James B. 2007. *Shopping for God: How Christianity Went from in Your Heart to in Your Face*. New York: Simon & Schuster.

Vaill, Peter. 2000. "Introduction to Spirituality for Business Leadership." *Journal of Management Inquiry* 9 (2): 115–117.

Vitzthum, Robert. 1995. Materialism: *An* Affirmative History and Definition. Amherst, NY: Prometheus.

Warner, R. Stephen. 1993. "Work in Progress Toward a New Paradigm for the Social Study of Religion in the United States." *American Journal of Sociology* 98 (5): 1044–1093.

Weber, Max. 1978. *Economy and Society.* Original edition 1922. Berkeley: University of California Press.

Wilson, Bryan R. 1969. *Religion in a Secular Society.* London: Penguin.

Wilson, Bryan R. 1982. *Religion in Sociological Perspective.* Oxford: Oxford University Press.

York, Michael. 1995. *The Emerging Network: A Sociology of the New Age and Neo-Pagan Movements.* Lanham, MD: Rowman and Littlefield.

Young, David, and Jean-Guy Goulet, eds. 1994, *Being Changed by Cross-Cultural Encounters. The Anthropology of Extraordinary Experience.* Peterborough, Ontario: Broadview Press.

Young-Eisendrath, Polly, and Melvin E. Miller, eds. 2000. *The Psychology of Mature Spirituality: Integrity, Wisdom, Transcendence.* London: Routledge.

Zinnbauer, Brian J., and Kenneth I. Pargament. 2005. "Religiousness and Spirituality." In *Handbook of the Psychology of Religion and Spirituality,* edited by Raymond F. Paloutzian and Crystal L. Park, 121–142. New York: Guilford.

Zinnbauer, Brian J., Kenneth I. Pargament, Brenda Cole, Mark S. Rye, Eric M. Butter, Timothy G. Belavich, Kathleen M. Hipp, Allie B. Scott, and Jill L. Kadar. 1997. "Religion and Spirituality: Unfuzzying the Fuzzy." *Journal for the Scientific Study of Religion* 36 (4): 549–564.

Zinnbauer, Brian J., Kenneth I. Pargament, and Allie B. Scott. 1999. "The Emerging Meanings of Religiousness and Spirituality: Problems and Prospects." *Journal of Personality* 67 (6): 889–919.

Part I

Marketers' Sacralisation of the Mundane

2 When Sacred Objects Go B®a(n)d

Fashion Rosaries and the Contemporary Linkage of Religion and Commerciality

Diego Rinallo, Stefania Borghini, Gary Bamossy, and Robert V. Kozinets

"Not only has religion become a consumption object, consumption has become a religion in which wealth and opulence are venerated." (O'Guinn and Belk, 1989, p. 237)

Is nothing sacred? Is everything sacred? Is there no in-between?

Ever since the Odyssey returned its divine verdict on the sacred state of the American economy, consumer researchers have been seeking and finding holiness throughout a range of ostensibly drab, everyday objects and activities. Exploring "the admixture of the religious and the commercial" in the Heritage Village context of "televangelism, neo-fundamentalism, and the religious right," O'Guinn and Belk (1989, p. 227) asked if "commodities" could be "sacralized within the religious sphere, where opposing values presumably would be strongest." Their positive answer to this question, they asserted, was "evidence of refashioned contemporary linkages between an economic system and religion" (O'Guinn and Belk, 1989, p. 237).

Emphasizing the literally iconic nature of the consumption object, Schouten and McAlexander (1995, p. 50) find that "so strong is the Harley-Davidson motorcycle as an organizing symbol for the biker ethos that it has become, in effect, a religious icon around which an entire ideology of consumption is articulated." Setting a now-standard formula, they then proceed to articulate numerous "religious aspects of the subculture," including the "transcendental departure" of the ride, reverence of objects such as the motorcycle, creation of shrines, principles of brotherhood, religious and Satanic naming conventions, rituals, proselytism and missionary work, and a "gospel" or ideology (Schouten and McAlexander, 1995, pp. 50–51).

Belk and Tumbat (2005) return to the company's genesis in order to argue the religious equivalence of the Apple brand and its supportive community. They state this equivalence in no uncertain terms: "The Mac and its fans constitute the equivalent of a religion. This religion is based on an origin myth for Apple Computer, heroic and savior legends surrounding its co-founder ... CEO Steve Jobs, the devout faith of its follower congregation, their belief in the righteousness of the Macintosh, the existence of one or more Satanic opponents, Mac believers proselytizing and converting non-believers, and the hope among cult members that salvation can be achieved by transcending corporate capitalism" (Belk and Tumbat, 2005, pp. 207–208). Such analysis appears even more valid today, with the religious overtones accompanying worldwide consumer commotion after Job's passing in 2011.

Muniz and Schau (2005) also locate the seeds not only of the sacred, but also of religion, within Apple's seeming supernatural successes. Studying the amazing life-after-death phenomenon of the Apple Newton brand community, they find that "supernatural, religious, and magical motifs are common in the narratives of the Newton community. There are strong elements of survival, the miraculous, and the return of the creator" (Muniz and Schau, 2005, p. 739).

Related to this, popular culture has been increasingly viewed as another source of the sacred, with people investing more and more of their psychic energies into the acts of fandom.[1] Attempting to explain the pervasiveness of religious comparisons and metaphors within the ostensibly mundane Star Trek fan community, Kozinets (2001, p. 78) theorized that "Perhaps most important of all, the fact that parallels to religion and the sacred are found so prevalently in Star Trek discourse and debate demonstrates the remarkable level of affective investment that some (perhaps many) contemporary consumers can collectively make in a commercial product such as Star Trek." A vast variety of popular media can easily be read as sources of alternative religious narratives, including but certainly not limited to The Matrix, Avatar, Lost, The Lord of the Rings, 2001: A Space Odyssey, Buffy the Vampire Slayer, Battlestar Galactica, and others.

These past investigations explore the religious-commercial interface in the context of popular culture and media, religious media and theme parks, objects such as transportation and technological products, and their associated narratives and communities. This chapter continues these intriguing investigations in the bridging of the religious and the commercial in the unique cultural context of fashion. What happens when we start to examine the interface between believe-or-baste-in-eternity religious objects and the gone-in-a-minute fashion economy where people actually invest a lot of their psychic energy and moment-to-moment yearning? What then?

Our investigation focuses on the complex case of the rosary, a Christian prayer instrument that entered the realm of profane consumption in the 1980s. At that time, the iconoclastic pop icon Madonna Ciccone wore rosaries and cross necklaces in her videos and in a popular—but banned—Pepsi commercial notable for its mix of sexuality and Catholic symbolism, thereby popularizing its status as a fashion accessory. More recently, Italian fashion designers Dolce & Gabbana launched a collection of high-priced rosaries. The purpose of our chapter is to explore, using a variety of analytic means, the contested meaning of this practice. The chapter begins with a historical overview that develops our brief introduction. We develop our method, present findings, and then discuss some of our provisional conclusions.

CONSUMING THE ROSARY: A BRIEF HISTORY

The rosary is one of the most popular prayers of the Catholic Church. In the most common of its current forms, this parentally-minded devotional consists of fifty repetitions, also known as five "decades" of repetition, of "Hail Mary," each preceded by the "Our Father" prayer and followed by a "Glory Be to the Father." The Latin term *rosarium* originally referred to a garden, an anthology of texts, or a rose wreath. By reciting a sequence of Hail Mary's, the faithful follower was believed to also be creating a symbolic wreath of roses for the Blessed Virgin. Each decade of repetition is associated with a meditation on specific moments in the life of Mary and Jesus, moving from the Annunciation to their ascension in Heaven. The term rosary also refers to the closed strings of beads that are used as a counting device. The custom of using beads on a string to help the memory in the recitation of prayers is very ancient and not distinctly Catholic, as it is also found in Hinduism, Buddhism, Islam, and the Eastern Churches. However, in those contexts, strung prayer beads are not referred to as "rosaries."

According to a later legend, the rosary was revealed to St. Dominic (ca. 1170–1221), the founder of the Dominican Order, by Mary herself. In this vision, Mary exhorted Dominic to use the rosary as a spiritual weapon against the Albigensian heresy. Historically speaking, the rosary developed between the 12th and 15th centuries through a coalescence of various forms of previously existing devotions to Christ and the Virgin (Winston, 1993; Winston-Allen, 1997). During the 16th century, such devotion to the Virgin Mary was banned and vilified by the Protestant Reformation as a despised emblem of papist superstition. As a consequence, the Catholic Church strongly supported the rosary in an attempt to defuse and counter Reformation doctrine and practices (Lysaght, 1998). The rosary was thus aggressively promoted through predications, "instruction" books, and, especially, the establishment of rosary confraternities (associations whose members tried to recite the entire rosary at least once a week; see Dillon, 2003; McClain, 2003).

The Dominican monk Jacob Springer established the first rosary confraternity in Cologne in 1475. Such confraternities soon diffused through Germany and other countries under the supervision of the Dominicans. Unlike other associations, they welcomed a variety of members, including women, which was quite uncommon at the time (especially for a "fraternity"). They were populist, requiring no formal vows or membership fees, and they quickly grew in membership and influence. In 1573, the Catholic Church institutionalized the Feast of the Holy Rosary, in commemoration of the Christian victory over the Turks in the naval battle of Lepanto (1571). Over the centuries, new formal associations were formed to diffuse the rosary and to build its influence. These associations were supported by many popes, among whom Leo XIII (who declared October the month of the rosary), Pious XI, Pious XII, John XXXIII, John Paul II (who added five more mysteries to the existing ones), and, currently, Benedict XVI are probably the most noteworthy. In the 19th and 20th centuries, the rosary also gained prominence because of its relation to apparitions of the Virgin Mary seen with a rosary in her hands in Lourdes (1858) and Fatima (1917).

The history of the rosary points to its status in miracles and divine apparitions, to flowers and gardens, to weapons, to ideological campaigns and Catholic counter-offenses, and to community and influence building. Today, however, the rosary—which was originally never meant to be an adornment—is also employed as a fashion accessory.

In 1985, pop star Madonna Ciccone was the first to start a craze for rosaries when she wore them on her "Like a Virgin" tour and video.[2] More recently, the use of rosaries as necklaces was promoted by Italian fashion designers Dolce & Gabbana (D&G). Beginning with their 2003 spring/summer fashion show, D&G proudly displayed new D&G-branded rosaries displayed on half-naked male models with sculpted, smooth physiques as well as on sensual female models wearing provocative black embroidery lingerie. Branded rosaries were offered for sale at D&G shops for prices up to several hundred dollars. Other marketers were quick to imitate this new trend in the months that followed, and consumers could easily find cheaper fashionable rosaries from retailers such as H&M and street vendors. Celebrities such as David Beckham and Britney Spears were among the first to adopt this new craze, quickly followed by fashion-conscious consumers.

The reaction of religious spokesperson towards the appropriation of religious symbols by celebrities and fashion designers was firm and resolute. The use of rosary beads was condemned as an illegitimate use of rosary beads that denoted a lack of respect, desecration, bad taste, and even overt blasphemy. Catholic Church leaders affirmed, "it is a great pity if they [rosaries] are only being used as a decoration and not for devotional purposes. . . . People are wearing them as fashion accessories and are not mindful of their religious significance" (BBC, 2004). How are we to understand this conflict between the religious history of the rosary and its much more recent utilization as a sexy, perhaps sassily superficial, symbol of fashion-ability and dissent? Before proceeding to our consumer-oriented findings, our next section describes the method we used for the investigation.

METHODOLOGY

Our approach is based on personal interviews and observation, extended through historical analysis. We have conducted interviews with about twenty-five Italian informants of various ages (i.e., from 9 to 78 years old), genders (both women and men), sexual orientation (both gay and straight), levels of religiosity (practicing Catholics, believers but not practicing Catholics, non-believers), and uses of the rosary (as a prayer instrument, as an adornment, and those not using it). Many of these interviews have been long and phenomenological in nature (McCracken, 1988; Thompson et al., 1989), whereas a few of them have been developed as informal and thus insightful conversations on the issue investigated.

Informants were invited to discuss their consumption of rosaries, level of religiosity, relation with fashion and media, and any personal experience that could be related to the role played by the rosaries in their life. Pictures of fashion models, celebrities, and advertisements were also employed to elicit interpretations. Most informants were interviewed in their homes in order to help create a reassuring sense of personal comfort. This situation allowed a more naturalistic enquiry and gave our informants the opportunity to show us their favorite rosaries and the places where they keep or display them.[3]

Data were analyzed and codified following methodological recommendations of qualitative methods (e.g., McCracken, 1988; Spiggle, 1994; Thompson, Locander, and Pollio, 1989). In addition, an ongoing inquiry has been developed on media press releases and archives to reconstruct and monitor the use of rosaries by fashion designers and celebrities and the social debate that has arisen around these uses. This contributed to a deep and throughout understanding of the phenomenon from a broad cultural point of view.

RESEARCH FINDINGS

The Religious Rosary

Our research findings illuminate the different meanings attributed to rosaries by consumers. For many of our research participants, the rosary only has traditional and religious significance. Our older informants were all raised in a less secularized era: for them, ritual praying is institutionalized as an important part of their daily routine. These primarily older female respondents pray the rosary on their own, among small groups of friends, or in community circles; silently or aloud; in their homes, in neighbors' homes, or in church. These prayers are often routine, in specific moments of the day, such as in the morning before getting up or the night before going to sleep—or as the "need" arises. The rosary prayer is offered more in certain periods of the liturgical calendar, such as Advent, Lent, and the month of May, when the Marian celebrations take place.

In this context, for these people, the rosary is employed to '*draw near to God*,' to ask God or the Madonna to grant a special request; to commemorate loved ones who have passed away. Rosaries are bought in a Church or a local shop, but more often they are purchased in souvenir shops during pilgrimages in places of religious significance. Most often of all, rosaries are given as a gift from family, friends, neighbors, or educators. Many informants have small collections of rosaries, each of which elicits memories, emotions, stories: '*This used to be my mom's,*' '*I bought this during a journey to the Holy Land,*' '*this is the one I want to be buried with.*' A rosary may thus become a cherished possession (e.g., Belk, 1988; Wallendorf and Arnould, 1988) whose sacredness has several sources: it materializes religious symbols (i.e., the Cross or Crucifix, the image of the Virgin Mary), it is used to pray, and it is often blessed by priests.

For most of our younger informants, who are "*believers, but not practicing Catholics,*" the rosary is still a sacred object, but it only plays a minor role in their daily life. Many of them have one or more rosaries. These rosaries were often received in moments of religious significance (e.g., the First Communion, Confirmation) by family or educators. However, they do not know how to use them to pray in the 'official' way. That is, they do not know the "correct" or "official" sequence of prayer offerings and only have a rough idea of the different Mysteries that the rosary prayer represents. For these informants, rosaries are most typically stored away, together with other cherished objects that are owned but not actively used.

Our more religious informants tended to express negative reactions to the "profane" use of the rosary as a fashion accessory. Although the intensity of the reaction varied, their comments resonated with the official positions of Church officials. Fashion designers and celebrities alike were accused of exploiting religious symbols to obtain media coverage: "*It's a provocation,*" "*they just want to create a scandal.*"

According to these faithful consumers, the "real" motivation underlying the fashionable promotion of rosaries is that of making money: the ultimate profane goal. Consumers who wear rosaries as necklaces also are stigmatized. They are seen, as activists tend to see wrongdoing consumers in Kozinets and Handelman (2004), as ignorant: '*they don't even know its religious meaning,*' they '*have no personality of their own as they are subjugated by advertising,*' they '*show doubtful taste,*' they '*lack respect for those who believe,*' and they are even '*blasphemous*' and '*shouldn't be allowed to do that.*'

The Fashionable Rosary

Our more fashion-conscious informants offered a different perspective. The following verbatim exemplifies many of the themes that emerged from our analysis.

> There's nothing wrong in these D&G rosaries. It's not like they [D&G] are desecrating or profaning something. These [branded] rosaries are not sacred or blessed objects. They are two separate things . . . I mean, that one [the religious rosary] is not to be worn, not to be shown, you put it in your pocket or inside, under the t-shirt. The Dolce & Gabbana rosary was fashionable, it was to be looked at, to be shown. With an open shirt, for example. It was conspicuous, it was like "come on, look

at me", it attracted attention to my pectorals, to my nice sun-tanned, muscular chest. . . . I liked to wear it as everybody used to notice it. In a disco, it's cool, it attracts the attention. . . . Yes, I liked it, because everybody paid me a lot of compliments, not because of the rosary. The rosary was like the cherry on the cake . . . and I was the cake!" (Simone, gay male, 27 years old)

Similarly to many other fashion-conscious informants, Simone sees branded rosaries as objects devoid of religious significance. Perhaps his ideas resonate with Durkheim's (1912) and Belk, Wallendorf, and Sherry's (1989) view that sacred and profane correspond to opposing and distinct realms of social life. Branded rosaries are unproblematic. They are simply stylish accessories whose provocative nature and 'out-of-context' quality enable wearers to stand out in a crowd and direct attention to their '*nice*' physique. The rosary thus partakes of the transformative power of fashion: it makes you look beautiful, and it makes others look at you and see how beautiful you are. This idea resonated in the narratives of both male and female consumers, both straight and gay: our informants show considerable agency in the manner they use fashion as part of their desire to transform themselves for the gaze of desiring others.

When D&G rosaries were initially introduced, many of our informants were immediately aware of them, but assumed the role of risk avoiders. Good early majority citizens, they waited before making a purchase, as the fashion rosary was perceived to be too '*risky*' from both a financial ('*It cost a lot!*') and a social ('*I was unsure of my friends' reaction*') point of view. However, the quick adoption of branded rosaries by celebrities and fashionistas reassured these consumers about social risks, while the appearance of more affordable fashion rosaries by H&M and other street vendors reduced the financial barriers to purchase. Some informants who ended up wearing fashion rosaries initially interpreted D&G rosaries as a '*lack of respect*.' However, interestingly, eventually, seeing the rosaries in popular circulation, they were seduced by the notion that this was a case of decommodification, not desecration, aestheticism over atheism.

> I liked these rosaries. Wearing them made me beautiful. At beginning I felt a little guilty. I felt embarrassed with myself. I used to say: "perhaps it's not the case". But I ended up wearing them. I convinced myself, everybody was wearing one. I saw nothing wrong in that. Surely I wasn't desecrating anything. Those crosses weren't like the religious ones. . . . I was employing them over clothes. Over low-necked dresses that were provocative. (Chiara, female, 22 years old)

After a couple of years of being '*cool*,' branded rosaries have shown the typical short life cycle of fashion, and by 2011 they became far less fashionable (however, there are rumors of an impending comeback). Within this relatively short fashion cycle, some of the initial concerns about the social risks of its use have re-appeared: "*It's out of fashion now. I wouldn't like myself. I wouldn't have the nerve to be seen with a rosary now. It is nonsense now, you know? It was one of those fashions that don't last long. . . . Should I wear one now, I'd hide it, I wouldn't wear it with an unbuttoned shirt*" (Marco, male, 21 years old). Even in 2011, a rosary proudly worn on the chest would attract the gaze. However, the wearer now risks a panoptical gaze (Foucault, 1977; Rinallo, 2007), a gaze that sanctions an illegitimate aspect, now totally out of context at discos or on the beach.

The Polysemic Rosary

Rosaries are among the most sanctified objects of popular religion. Rosaries can also be fashionable branded goods. Can they, for some, in some ways, be both things? According to some of our fashion-conscious informants, branded rosaries are not purely profane possessions, but something liminal and in-between, something simultaneously sacred, sexy, swanky, and secular.

> I'm a very religious person. I've always worn a Cross around my neck. In the past, I used to wear a wooden cross, but more recently it was a Swarovski Crucifix that I received as a gift from my sister. . . . I received a D&G rosary by a friend of mine, it was one of her usual moves to make me wear something peculiar. However, I have to admit that I appreciated a lot this gift. At the end, I like wearing peculiar things. I see this [the rosary] as something that could let me combine the two things. I was wearing a Cross, and at the same time, it was branded. It was nice to wear it under an unbuttoned shirt; other times, I used to wear it on a turtle-neck sweater. It was nice. (Clara, female, 21 years old)

For these consumers, branded rosaries and crosses may have a dual nature, both sacred and profane at the same time. As religious objects, they draw consumers nearer to a sense of the divine, to God. However, they also make consumers feel more beautiful, more desirable, and more desired. Clara, with her traditional upbringing and religious consciousness, would not pray with a branded rosary and would also not bring it to a priest to be blessed, whereas other informants used a rosary to pray to God for "profane" (rather than unselfish) favors such as sex.

Perhaps it is unsurprising at this point that the sacred and the profane commingle in our commercial culture. Clearly, we have moved a long way beyond Durkheim's (1912) idea of a fundamental dichotomy between sacred and profane, to the extent that they can be conceived as separate worlds. The commingling of sacred and profane is perhaps a frozen step between the sacralization and desacralization processes of Belk et al. (1989), and it is akin to the simultaneously commercial-and-religious status of objects such as Harley bike, Star Trek collectibles, Heritage Village (may it rest in peace) visits, Apple Newtons, and iPads.

A brand like D&G, with its rich mix of gay and straight meanings, high-class luxury, and streety sexuality, may enable consumers to express their own conflict-ridden and juxtaposed life projects, goals, and meanings through an admixture of interstitial projections, objectives, and symbols. Anthropologies of the marketplace continue to teach us that the black-and-white, either-or partitions of economic rationality are far from what they have been assumed to be. Our next section offers some initial and necessarily succinct analysis of these findings and points to some directions for future theory and additional investigation.

THE PASSION OF THE FASHION

Religion appears to be quite adaptable in a consumer-centered world; it responds to social, cultural, and market forces. It adapts, but it leaves its explanatory mythologies in all sorts of places, including the marketplace and brands. (Muniz and Schau, 2005, p. 746)

For centuries, the rosary proved to be a malleable instrument to promote the Catholic faith, one that could be adapted to different local conditions and political agendas. We find that the history of the rosary is an interesting example of the interplay between the "great tradition," which comprises the major continuing component of a religion, and the "little tradition," which consists of the way such components are appropriated, modified, and reimagined over time by local communities and individuals (Redfield 1956; see also Marriott, 1955; Spiro, 1982; Stewart, 1991). The rosary, a local practice, was appropriated and "universalized" by the Catholic Church and heavily promoted. At the same time, local communities adapted the rosary to their needs in a process of parochialization. The marketplace appropriation of the rosary may be interpreted as consumer culture's attempt to also, simultaneously, and likely temporarily "universalize" the rosary and promote it as a decorative object. Through phenomenological interviews with informants of various ages, levels of religiosity, gender, and sexual orientation, we find a unique spin on this combined universalizing-parochializing function.

By investigating the complex web of meanings surrounding the use of the rosary in its commercial and religious dimensions, we seek to broaden the understanding of the interrelations of consumption object, brand, religion, community, and history in contemporary postmodern consumer culture. We find that the religious and historically established attribute of *sacredness* contributes a powerfully marketable quality to rosaries, which holds both in terms of their attraction and rebellious possibilities. The appropriation, manipulation, and monetization of sacred meanings by fashion brands such as D&G open our eyes to emergent new forms of material culture that embody the sometimes turbulent, sometimes-peaceful, and sometimes ecstatic coexistence of the religious and the commercial.

Our findings suggest that we might further involve the brand, its meanings and histories, as others (e.g., Belk and Tumbat, 2005; Kozinets, 2001; Kozinets et al., 2004; Muniz and Schau, 2005; Sherry, 1998; Shouten and McAlexander, 1995) have, as we examine the religiosity of brands and consider the flows of meanings among commercial (e.g., corporate), non-commercial (e.g., religions and churches), and communal cultural players. In our study, we found celebrity icon Madonna and fashion icons D&G to be powerfully transformative and transgressive cultural actors acting with much of the religious, meaning-making force of cultural creators unto themselves. As such, our study draws into focus the contingency of terms such as religion and legitimacy, suggesting the temporary and liquidly shifting nature of style, stigma, and the sacred.

As Paul Ricoeur (1975) suggested, thoughts cannot exist outside of ideology. The individual human being, as a socialized social being, can only hop from one shared ideological position to another. Similarly, consumers' rosary adoption processes reveal that no positions are found beyond the faithful consumption position. As with Kozinets' (2001, p. 85) media devoted consumers, "although the consumers in this study exhibited a range of consumption meanings and practices, these were structured by social and institutional forces such as their own social situation, the articulations of subculture members, institutional practices, and cultural producers."

As we see in this study, consumers sensitive to the influence of strong cultural forces represented by brands adhere to a new system of values and take part in performances where conventional meanings are juxtaposed and transformed through transgression, be it mild or extreme. Rosary consumers have choices, but they are structured. They can consume the transgressive religious ideology of the branded rosary in a way that sees it as legitimate, illegitimate, or irrelevant. But in each case, they are operating from "within the interpretive confines of an ideological structure" in a manner that is both individually driven, but also, perhaps even largely, "superintended" by cultural forces largely beyond their control (Kozinets 2001, p. 85). For when the fashion rosary stopped being featured in magazines and discos, when it stopped being fashionable, it also stopped being transgressive and returned to being the religious prayer object that it had long been held to be, dormant, perhaps, until the next rosary fashion revival. The marketplace and its powerful brands set consumers free. But simultaneously, it keeps them contained within a new, temporary, evanescent web of meanings, now embedding them and their beliefs in the quick-burning fashion cycle and an associated system of power. We believe that further investigation of these commercial interrelations may prove fruitful for enhanced understanding of the complex and dynamic contemporary world of spirituality and consumption.

NOTES

1. "Fandom" is an emic term meaning a fan community. It is noteworthy that the term fan is derived from the Latin "fanaticus," meaning a devotee of the temple, and thus has definite religious connotations.
2. Over the years, Madonna has frequently used Catholic symbols. In 1987, in her "La Isla Bonita" video, she is shown using a rosary to pray, bowing to an altar full of sacred images but, at the same time, abandoning herself to carnal fantasies. Nineteen eighty-nine was the year of the highly controversial "Like a Prayer," with its mix of sacredness and sensuality, which caused Catholic Church protests and the ban of the Pepsi commercial, which was to accompany the launch of the video. In 2005, the album "Confession on a Dancefloor" hinted in its title at one of the Catholic Church's sacraments. In the following "Confessions" tour, Madonna appeared crucified from a giant Swarovski crystal cross and wearing a crown of thorns, triggering a threat of excommunication by the Vatican.
3. To view a 16-minute video ethnography of our informants' discussions of these tensions and uses (Borghini, Rinallo, and Bamossy, 2007), go to: http://vimeo.com/23546426

REFERENCES

BBC. 2004. "Church Fears Rosary Fashion Craze." *BBC News*, October 29. Accessed February 15, 2006. http://news.bbc.co.uk/1/hi/business/3964667.stm

Belk, Russell W. 1988. "Possessions and the Extended Self." *Journal of Consumer Research* 15 (September): 139–168.

Belk, Russell W., and Gülnur Tumbat. 2005. "The Cult of Macintosh." *Consumption, Markets and Culture* 8 (September): 205–218.

Belk, Russel, Melanie Wallendorf, and John F. Sherry. 1989. "The Sacred and the Profane in Consumer Behavior: Theodicy on the Odyssey." *Journal of Consumer Research* 16 (1): 1–38.

Borghini, Stefania, Diego Rinallo, and Gary J. Bamossy. 2007. "Fashion Iconography," Film presented at the Association for Consumer Research European Conference Film Festival, Milan. Video available at http://vimeo.com/23546426

Dillon, Anne. 2003. "Praying by Number: The Confraternity of the Rosary and the English Catholic community, c. 1580–1700." *History* 88 (291): 451–471.

Durkheim, Emile. 1912. *The Elementary Forms of Religious Life. Translated by Karen E. Fields.* New York: The Free Press.

Foucault, M. 1977. *Discipline and Punish: The Birth of the Prison.* New York: Vintage Books.

Kozinets, Robert V. 2001. "Utopian Enterprise: Articulating the Meanings of *Star Trek*'s Culture of Consumption." *Journal of Consumer Research* 28 (June): 67–88.

Kozinets, Robert V., and Jay M. Handelman. 2004. "Adversaries of Consumption: Consumer Movements, Activism, and Ideology." *Journal of Consumer Research* 31 (December): 691–704.

Kozinets, Robert V., John F. Sherry, Jr., Diana Storm, Adam Duhachek, Krittinee Nuttavuthisit, and Benét DeBerry-Spence.(2004. "Ludic Agency and Retail Spectacle." *Journal of Consumer Research* 31 (December): 658–672.

Lysaght, Patricia. 1998 "Attitudes Towards the Rosary and Its Performance in Donegal in the Nineteenth and Twentieth Century." *Béaloideas* 66: 9–58.

Marriott, M. 1955. "Little Communities in an Indigenous Civilization." In *Village India: Studies in the Little Community*, edited by M. Marriott, pp. 171–222. Chicago: University of Chicago Press.

McClain, Lisa. 2003. "Using What's at Hand: English Catholic Reinterpretations of the Rosary, 1559–1642." *Journal of Religious History* 27 (2): 161–176.

McCracken, Grant. 1988. *The Long Interview*. Newbury Park, CA: Sage. Muniz, Albert, and Hope Jensen Schau. 2005. "Religiosity in the Abandoned Apple Newton Brand Community." *Journal of Consumer Research* 31 (March): 737–747.

O'Guinn, T. C., and R. W. Belk. 1989. "Heaven on Earth: Consumption at Heritage Village, USA." *Journal of Consumer Research* 16 (September): 227–238.

Redfield, Robert. 1960. *The Little Community and Peasant Society and Culture*. Chicago: University of Chicago Press.

Ricoeur, Paul. 1975. *Lectures on Ideology and Utopia*. Chicago: University of Chicago Press.

Rinallo, Diego. 2007. "Metro/Fashion/Tribes of Men: Negotiating the Boundaries of Men's Legitimate Consumption" In *Consumer Tribes: Theory, Practice, and Prospects*, edited by Bernard Cova, Robert V. Kozinets, and Avi Shankar, pp. 76–92. New York: Elsevier/Butterworth-Heinemann.

Schouten, John W., and James H. McAlexander. 1995., "Subcultures of Consumption: An Ethnography of the New Bikers." *Journal of Consumer Research* 22 (June): 43–61.

Sherry, John F., Jr. 1998 "The Soul of the Company Store: Nike Town Chicago and the Emplaced Brandscape." In *Servicescapes: The Concept of Place in Contemporary Markets*, edited by John F. Sherry, Jr., pp. 109–146. Lincolnwood, IL: NTC Business Books.

Spiggle, Susan 1994. "Analysis and Interpretation of Qualitative Data in Consumer Research." *Journal of Consumer Research* 21(December): 491–503.

Spiro, Melford E. 1982. *A Great Tradition and its Burmese Vicissitudes*. Berkeley: University of California Press.

Stewart, C. 1991. *Demons and the Devil: Moral Imagination in Modern Greek Culture*. Princeton, NJ: Princeton University Press.

Thompson, Craig, W. Locander, and H. Pollio. 1989. "Putting Consumer Experience Back into Consumer Research: The Philosophy and Method of Existential-Phenomenology." *Journal of Consumer Research* 16: 133–146.

Wallendorf, Melanie, and Eric Arnould. 1988. " 'My Favorite Things': A Cross-Cultural Inquiry into Object Attachment, Possessiveness, and Social Linkage." *Journal of Consumer Research* 14 (March): 531–547.

Winston, Anne 1993. "Tracing the Origins of the Rosary: German Vernacular Texts." *Speculum* 68 (3): 619–636.

Winston-Allen, Anne. 1997. *Stories of the Rose: The Making of the Rosary in the Middle Ages*. University Park, PA: Pennsylvania State University Press.

3 Theology Meets the Marketplace

The Discursive Formation of the Halal Market in Turkey

Elif Izberk-Bilgin

The intriguing link between modernity and religion has inspired an ongoing debate among scholars. Classical sociologists have maintained that modernity, with its emphasis on individualism and scientific thinking, posed a threat to the mystical and communal nature of religion. It has been suggested that modernity 'disenchants' the world, rendering the role of the divine and the sacred trivial in everyday life (Weber, 1922/1978). Others in postmodern milieu have argued that modernity paradoxically fosters the quest for religious affiliation as the disenchanted and alienated modern individual desperately seeks for meaning in life (Firat and Venkatesh, 1995).

Consistent with this latter view, consumer researchers have reaffirmed the prominent role of religion in contemporary life (O'Guinn and Belk, 1989). Recent studies have illustrated how the postindustrial world leaves consumers looking for communal affection and religious affiliation in the least expected venues. For instance, Kozinets (2001) demonstrates how Star Trek fans seek to legitimize a commercial articulation of popular culture as religion; Muniz and Schau (2005, p. 745) find that members of brand communities seek to mimic the communal nature of religion by applying "religious language, narrative, and philosophy to what is clearly a secular situation." Other studies have found undertones of religiosity among consumer activist groups and in anticonsumerist events (Kozinets and Handelman, 2004; Sherry and Kozinets, 2007). Collectively, these studies have highlighted the fascinating dialectical relationships among religion, consumption, and the market.

This study seeks to advance our existing theoretical understanding of the symbiotic relationship between religion and the market by examining how marketplace institutions synthesize the ideals of modernity with religious teachings to negotiate faith and modernity. Of particular interest to this research is the discursive formation of the halal[1] market. The recent emergence of the halal industry on a global scale represents an excellent example of the religion-market interface, where we can examine how modern discourses (e.g., scientific thinking, industrialism, capitalism) are appropriated by Islamic actors to legitimize the consumer demand for Islamically suitable marketplace offerings.

This study draws from a discourse analysis of quarterly journals, reports, and books published over a span of six years by GIMDES (Food and Perishable Commodities Auditors and Certification Association), a non-governmental organization spearheading the institutionalization of the halal movement in Turkey. Founded in 2005, GIMDES has come to play a crucial role in the market as the single issuer of halal certificate. As such, it provides an excellent means to historically trace the institutionalization of a faith-based market.

ISLAM, MODERNITY, AND MARKET

Islam has frequently been interpreted as a critique of modernization, capitalism, and consumerism (Barber, 1996; Huntington, 1993; Ray, 1993). Writing in the shadow of the Iranian revolution and subsequent rise of Islamic political movements, scholars have casted Islam as an authoritative religion that is against social change and modernist ideas such as democracy and capitalism (Turner, 1994). Ahmed (2004, p. 264), for example, likens the relationship between Islam and modern societies to "a fight between two opposed philosophies. . . . One is based on secular materialism, the other on faith; one has rejected belief altogether, the other placed it at the center of its world-view." Likewise, Lewis (2002) characterizes modernity as an alien force that has caused Muslims great suffering and brought about the demise of the Islamic civilization. According to Lewis (2002, p. 19), the "invasion of foreign ways of life" has led the Muslim subject to witness "an undermining of his authority in his own country" and even challenged "his mastery in his own house," thanks to "emancipated women and rebellious children." Arguing that the ideological conflict between Islam and modernity has fueled Islamist movements, Lewis reinforces the view echoed by many prominent scholars of political Islam (Ayoob, 2008; Tibi, 1983) that dogmatic interpretations of Islam have been appropriated as a political and militant rhetoric, contesting rapid modernization and Westernization.

Often implied in these accounts is that Islam is also anti-market. For example, Webb (2005) argues that Islamic values such as collectivism and moderation are not compatible with the ideals of individualism and material accumulation that bolster a modern market economy. Turner (1974, p. 237) notes that Weberian theories attribute the absence of "a capitalist spirit" in Islamic societies to the "patrimonial economic and political structure." It has also been noted that Islamic teachings embody Marxist undertones and Islamist fundamentalism has replaced Marxism in the Third World (Ray, 1993). Kozinets and Handelman (2004, p. 702) agree with the view that Islamic fundamentalism constitutes "one of the most powerful threats to global consumerist ideology today." As a result, in both public and academic discourse, Islam has been generally understood as a religion with anti-modern and anti-consumerist ethos.

However, until recently, scholars exploring Islam's relationship with modernity and markets have not taken into account the varying class-based interpretations of Islam. The latest research shows that different class positions within the Muslim community generate different readings of Islam, leading to various consumption ideologies and practices. For example, low-income and low-cultural capital Turkish Muslims are highly critical of secularization and capitalism, which they perceive as Western inventions. And this criticism often translates into an aversion to global brands in the marketplace (Izberk-Bilgin, 2010). In contrast, upper-middle income, young, and urban Muslims, thanks to higher economic means, not only embrace many Western values, albeit with an Islamic twist, but also seek to connect with their global peers through their consumption of global brands to feel more like "global citizens" (Pink, 2009).

Other research shows that governments and private businesses in Muslim countries are increasingly blending Islamic teachings with modern management principles and capitalist ethics to stimulate economic development and enhance global competitiveness of local industries. More specifically, Rudnyckyj (2009) finds that businesses utilize 'spiritual training' that combines Islamic history and practices with Western management principles in an effort to enhance transnational competitiveness of Indonesian enterprises. In a similar fashion, Wong (2007) finds that Malaysia's ruling party has been employing Islam as a discursive engine of national development and urging masses that the Islamic values of "abstemiousness, frugality, family and diligence could be marshaled and distilled into a force for modernization and moderation, enabling economic growth and productivity." Perhaps as a result of this marriage of Islam with capitalist principles in the Muslim world, we witness the formation of a halal industry with global ambitions.

THE MUSLIM CONSUMER AND THE ISLAMIC CONSUMPTIONSCAPE

A recent Pew study, *Mapping the Global Muslim Population*, finds that Muslims, at 1.8 billion strong, make up approximately a quarter of the world's population (Miller, 2009). Even more noteworthy is the growth rate of the Muslim population in North America and Europe. In the next two decades, the Muslim population is projected to increase 180% in Canada and 140% in United States, whereas the growth is expected to be more than 100% in Italy, Norway, Finland, and Sweden (Miller, 2009). In contrast to the widespread perceptions of a uniform Muslim profile, this impressive consumer segment represents a mosaic of believers from 200 countries with greatly varying income and education levels, religious practices, and political ideologies.

Paralleling the growth of this heterogeneous demographic, various Muslim-friendly products have been emerging in European and American markets over the last two decades. Currently, the global Islamic market is estimated to be worth 2.1 trillion dollars (ogilvynoor.com) and caters to Muslims from different socio-economic backgrounds with a broad spectrum of offerings from Sharia compliant credit cards to halal champagne. The emergence of Islamic dolls, alcohol-free perfumes, gender-segregated resorts, and Muslim colas also imply a new Muslim consumer who is conservative in values but apt to engage with the global consumer culture (Pink, 2009). The tech-savvy, globally traveled, and ambitious Muslim consumers are not unlike their Western counterparts in using consumption as a means to construct an Islamic identity and lifestyle. Dubbed as YUMMIES (Al-Azmeh, 1993), these young, upwardly mobile Muslims are the engines of a global halal industry.

While halal is synchronous with the birth of Islam, the global halal market has experienced dramatic growth in recent years. The renewed interest in halal can be attributed to a combination of several socio-economic factors. First of all, today's Muslims are more affluent and better educated compared with their parents and preceding generations. Secondly, young and educated Muslims are, in a postmodern milieu, keenly cognizant of the ill-effects of industrialization and globalization on the environment and human health. Lastly, halal sensitivity is accentuated by the revival of Islamist movements, which propagated a Muslim identity divorced from national consciousness or any other form of loyalties. Particularly for the middle-class Muslims, the most convenient and prominent way of enacting that identity position is through the consumption of halal and other Muslim-friendly products.

Perhaps as a result of this identity-enhancing value and Muslim actors' increasing adoption of modern consumption patterns, the notion of halal has expanded beyond Islam's regulatory realm of usury and dietary norms. Halal offerings now include everyday consumer goods like toothpaste, cosmetics, and over-the-counter drugs, in addition to more conventional Shariat-compliant services such as restaurants, butchers, and mortgages. Halal is also applied in business-to-business domains with the advent of halal supply chains, manufacturing processes, and storage practices.

THE HALAL MARKET IN TURKEY

The prominently secular façade of the Turkish marketplace significantly changed with the proliferation of faith-based offerings such as Islamic media, movies, music, novels, toys, swim suits, resorts, beauty shops, and cafes in the 1990s. The scope of offerings is telling: the debut of Islamized versions of existing products reflects the heated culture war between the pro-secular Muslims and the Islamists.[2] As Navaro-Yashin (2002, p. 223) notes, "As Islamists came to forge identities in distinction from secularists, they radically changed the sorts of things they bought and sold. They wore different clothes, ate only certain kinds of food, frequented particular shops, started special businesses of their own. The rise of the Islamist movement in popularity and power is indissoluble from the development of specialized businesses for 'Islamic goods' and the formation of market networks for believers."

Indeed, the rise of the halal market is inseparable from the surge of pro-Islamist parties to power and the integration of Islamic capital—that is, the accumulations of the conservative businessmen—into the post-1980s economy. Following the military coup in 1983, Turkey has witnessed a major shift from a state-controlled to a liberal market economy during the Özal administration. The market augmenting policies of the Özal years changed the etatist trajectory of the state not only by considerably limiting the role of government in the economy, but, most importantly, incorporating the previously excluded groups of conservative businessmen and religious sects into the national economic landscape. For example, the interest-free banking law of 1983 was instrumental in enticing the Islamic bourgeoisie to turn significant amounts of under-the-pillow savings into investments. These investments, in turn, promoted the growth of Islamic businesses, particularly newspapers and TV stations, which allowed Islamic groups to annunciate a visible identity and strengthen their solidarity (Demir et al., 2004). Paralleling the economic visibility of Islamic bourgeoisie was its rising political influence. As pro-Islamic parties successively came to power, they awarded Islamic businesses with contracts. Backed by such governmental support and remittances of Turkish guest workers living abroad, this new breed of conservative entrepreneurs, also known as Anatolian Tigers, established many Islamic enterprises, noticeably expanding their economic and political influence in Turkish society.

Many of these Anatolian tigers are the backbones of the halal movement in Turkey. They play a fundamental role in the formation of the halal industry by both championing the demand for halal products and supplying the market with Islamic goods. The public face of the halal movement is GIMDES, which states its mission as "verifying that the halal qualifications, hygiene standards, and the nutrition value of foodstuff, cleaning agents, cosmetic products and pharmaceuticals are according to Islamic norms, issuing halal certification to the same, and exposing those that hinder the society's need and demand for 'halal food', 'righteous wealth', and 'healthy living' to the public" (gimdes.org)." With this mission in mind, the organization has joined the halal network of key international institutions such as World Halal Council and World Halal Forum, receiving accreditation from fellow member organizations (e.g., JAKIM of Malaysia). Currently, GIMDES oversees the halal certification process, performs audits of manufacturing facilities, and trains halal certifiers. GIMDES also seeks to increase public awareness by organizing annual conferences and halal expos, publishing a bi-monthly magazine, maintaining an informative website, and offering resources to help consumers lead a halal lifestyle.

GIMDES is a noteworthy example to the Islamist activists' space-making for and discursive formation of a new market within a prominently secular marketplace with little halal consciousness. Similar to the other grassroots organizations leading contemporary movements (e.g., organic, fair-trade), GIMDES is primarily interested in creating halal awareness, distinguishing halal from other market offerings, and positioning it vis-à-vis the global and local socio-historical contexts. A narrative analysis of GIMDES literature reveals that modernity, industrialization, and capitalism are the key ideological resources that the halal movement appropriates in framing its agenda. On the one hand, the movement defines itself as a counterforce to Western modernization, and, on the other hand, it strongly relies on scientific studies and modern marketing techniques to legitimize and commercialize the halal concept. The following offers an analysis of how halal advocates selectively adopt the key tenets of modernism to forge the halal movement in Turkey.

CONTESTING MODERNITY: HISTORICIZING HALAL AS A CURE TO MODERNIST ILLS

GIMDES accounts construe the halal movement as a countervailing force to social and economic problems posed by Western modernity. Underlying this countermodernist stance is the perception that Western individualism and the capitalist motives of modern markets have undermined the solidarity of umma, the Muslim community. According to GIMDES narratives, thanks to the strict observance of halal, Muslims have ruled over the world and have led a pristine life marked by benevolence and solidarity for centuries. This romanticized order is believed to have come to an end, however, when Western culture started infiltrating the Turkish society. In halal proponents' narratives, the West is constructed as a "bandit" who forcefully enters the immaculate realm of Islam and cunningly introduces habit-forming non-halal products with deceiving marketing techniques in order to transmute Islamic lifestyles. The following excerpt from GIMDES's Food Report[3] demonstrates this view:

> Western bandits raided our house, going into every corner and scattering everything we owned. What we've left is an umma scattered like loose prayer beads. . . . In return for the lifestyle we've lost, what we've been left with is an alien, intoxicating, supposedly modern lifestyle that's imposed upon us . . . until recently Muslims could easily know what is halal and haram but now we're faced with products that are new to us like Coca-Cola, chips, marshmallow, and mayonnaise. . . . We have to question these products. It's become evident that they're harmful to both our health and our soul.

The characterization of Western countries as "bandits" finds an equally interesting match in halal narratives' portrayal of industrialization and capitalism. In historicizing halal and justifying its revitalization, halal advocates frequently construe the Western modes of production as evil, jeopardizing human health and overrating capitalist motives at the expense of moral principles. This demonization is evident in elaborate, scary-tale descriptions of factories as alienating places with "giant boilers, extractors, and gears" that have replaced "our homespun" methods with soulless processes and "dubious" ingredients. This repelling image is further reinforced by claims that large corporations driven by capitalist motives use inconceivable ingredients such as "lice, blood, human hair, hog bristle" (Büyüközer, 2007, pp. 10–18) in their products, which are then marketed in appealing packages for Muslims' consumption.

The concern over the growing use of genetically modified organisms (GMOs) in the agro-business, in particular, has fueled the halal debate, allowing GIMDES to dramatize the consequences of making non-halal choices. Progressive approaches in food biotechnology such as GM crops are perceived as the reflections of the greedy and imperialist agendas of multinationals who are seeking to play God. In appealing to the 'conscious Muslim,' GIMDES narratives criticize the public for remaining blissfully ignorant against the threat posed by Western producers, who are said to "transmute our foods."

> The industrial movement, which has been rapidly growing under the control of the infidels, laid its hands on our food. It has significantly transmuted the contents of our food. . . . What should a Muslim do? Should he wake up and break free from this system or should he continue to sleep?[4]

The monstrous consequences of "continu(ing) to sleep" are illustrated in elaborate conspiracy theories, which suggest that Western powers use GMOs to change Muslim consumers' DNA structure and, thereby, manipulate them. The following quote from an article discussing the dangers of GMOs illustrates an interesting take on these conspiracy theories:

> How do they [the capitalist powers] control our DNA in order to shape our society as they wish? . . . thanks to a game that is played on our genes. . . . They analyze the blood samples taken from our people and then develop viruses that would mislead our DNA. And then, they sell these viruses to us. How? Through the British chips, French-Jew's patented yoghurt, and the German gummy bears that have sneaked into the farthest corners of our streets.[5]

Halal proponents' decided skepticism toward Western modernity tempts them to create sci-fi scenarios that would suggest that non-halal goods are intended to overtake Muslims' body and soul, rendering them submissive to imperial motives. The pervasive suspicion that is embodied in GIMDES narratives regarding Western modernization naturally spills over to pro-secular elites and the Westernization project in Turkey. Halal proponents argue that the modernization efforts, which most noticeably began in 1923 with Kemalist reforms and the abolishment of the Islamic Empire, not only introduced foreign ways and ideologies, but also aimed to expunge the Muslim identity and their halal sensitivity.

For many orthodox Muslims, the secularizing reforms like the abolishment of the caliphate, the closing down of religious shrines, and the replacement of the Islamic canon law with the Swiss code marked a significant shift from an Islamic state and signaled the end of Islamic civilization. Changes like replacing the Arabic alphabet—the holy language of Islam—with Latin in instruction, when coupled with the annihilation of polygamy and enforcement of civil marriages, deeply touched the daily life of the population. Seen through this socio-historical lens, the republican era secularization efforts represent a break from Islamic traditions and practices, significantly diminishing the prevalent halal consciousness during the Ottoman times.

Today, this lost halal consciousness is associated with a wide range of contemporary problems, from the dissolution of communal ties to the increasing cancer rates that seemingly represent Muslims' fall from grace. Consider the following quote:

> As a society we witnessed a period in which we were suddenly thrown out of power. Western culture was rammed down our throat. Sadly, today we're faced with an alien lifestyle . . . our people have problems, particularly, with the foodstuff that represents the fabric of our life. The essence of these problems is the frustrations with the foreign substances that don't belong to our culture and don't fit with our norms. . . . We're also confronted by a series of health problems. In the past, coronary problems or hypertension weren't at a concerning level, but today millions of people are diagnosed with these problems and even more with cancer. When we evaluate these problems, we have to consider the issues of halal-haram. The halal certification matter didn't come out of the blue; there is a reason why it became an issue worldwide.[6]

As the above excerpt demonstrates, an eroding halal consciousness is blamed for the rise in modern-age problems, and, by the same token, halal consumption is positioned as the cure for these modern ills. In situating halal choices as the solution to modern ailments, GIMDES narratives construct the secular mindset and the social structures as the most important impediments against the movement. The secular mindset, like its Western counterpart, is said to be motivated by capitalist anxieties rather than moral responsibilities, thereby tempting manufacturers to cut corners and use Islamically unacceptable ingredients. The secular regime is also criticized for leaving the halal movement short-handed of the necessary talent and expertise to rule over on halal matters. It is argued that the regime has not only eradicated Islamic jurisdiction by replacing the independent fatwa (religious decree) institution with a state-controlled one, but also jeopardized the future of the movement by failing to produce Islamic scholars via its secular education system.

> Since issues of halal and haram relate to Islamic jurisdiction, these decisions are to be made by Islamic scholars. However, our religious scholars lack knowledge of technology. On the other hand, the people who have pursued scientific studies lack the basic knowledge of Islamic norms and canon law because the utterly secular education system deprives individuals of the basic religious teachings. . . . Following the collapse of Ottoman empire, the powers that sought to extinguish religion tried to annihilate the fatwa institution, the heart of Muslim life. During that period, the Islamic scholars were massacred and executed. They were to be replaced by a new generation of scholars programmed to suit their [secular] regime.[7]

As these narratives demonstrate, halal proponents justify the emergence of the halal movement and discursively construct the need for halal certification vis-à-vis two ideological rivals: Western modernity and the Westernization project in Turkey. Accordingly, adopting modern practices and secularism have swayed Turkish people away from their "true path," the ordained halal lifestyle. Having lost their halal consciousness, Muslims have fallen from grace as evident in the declining communal affection and increasing rates of diseases in Turkish society. As such, GIMDES discursively forges its quest for halal as a cure to modern ills.

EMBRACING MODERNITY: LEGITIMIZING AND COMMERCIALIZING HALAL VIA SCIENTIFIC STUDIES AND MODERN MARKETING TECHNIQUES

Although halal proponents are critical of modernity, they selectively embrace modern ideas and practices. One such idea is the indisputable authority of scientific methods over other ways of knowing. Because modernism has privileged science and technology over other forms of knowledge (Firat and Venkatesh, 1995), scientific methods like clinical studies and experiments have assumed tremendous authority, becoming the predominant means through which opinions and beliefs can be legitimized. Because Islamist actors leading the halal movement are themselves a product of modernity, they realize that rejecting science altogether would call on social stigmatization, which would not only further marginalize their social position in the eyes of the mainstream, but also jeopardize the movement. While this is not to suggest that the halal narratives solely rely on scientific evidence to convince consumers to make halal choices, it is noteworthy how meticulously GIMDES strives to support Quranic verses on halal with scientific studies published in European and American journals.

For example, an article advocating the halalness of vinegar, which is widely believed to be haram due to the alcohol content resulting from fermentation, provides detailed accounts of Prophet Mohammad's praise for vinegar and introduces various fatwas, reflecting distinguished Islamic scholars' views on vinegar. This canonical evidence is then complemented with information from Western medical sources regarding the health benefits of vinegar.[8] Another article opens with verses from the Quran on haram and offers an elaborate medical account of the role that hormones found in forbidden foods play on human metabolism.[9] Through a series of articles, GIMDES magazines also explore the adverse consequences of potentially haram consumption goods from cosmetics to cancer-inducing chemical compounds (e.g., BPA) and emulsifiers.

What is noteworthy in GIMDES's use of scientific evidence is the excessive use of scientific terms and statements in English, both of which can be interpreted as an explicit attempt to assert the reliability and validity of its claims. Seeking to establish rapport with the public, GIMDES has also assembled a board of *scientists* in addition to the initial team of Islamic scholars. These 'technical' experts regularly publish informative articles on a variety of topics in GIMDES's magazine and on its website. While it may seem counterintuitive that the movement would position itself as a counterforce to modernity and then rely on scientific knowledge to legitimize its pleas for halal consumption, this is not surprising granted that Islamic actors are embedded in a modern market society. Employing scientific claims also allows the movement to broaden its appeal to unlikely audiences such as natural health aficionados and organic fans among the pro-secular segments.

Embracing modern marketing strategies and trends to reach these skeptical, pro-secular audiences represents another way in which halal proponents co-opt modernism. GIMDES narratives notably draw from the natural health marketplace discourses (Thompson, 2004) to position halal as the wholesome choice claiming that halal, by nature, is free of pesticides, GMOs, and other harmful chemicals. Halal is even argued to be superior to organic agriculture in the global fight against biotechnology and GMOs:

> It's not possible for the humanity to survive the GMO catastrophe without the help of Islam. Official sources indicate that even the organic agriculture projects undertaken in Europe are not 100% pure. The only way to safeguard a healthy lifestyle for humanity is through halal certification of everything, starting from embryo and seed.[10]

The movement also caters to the ethical consumers by positioning halal as fair trade. Contending that social justice is the essence of Islam, GIMDES narratives underscore that halal is an overarching notion, encompassing the investing, sourcing, and manufacturing aspects of production. As such, GIMDES claims to inspect the labor conditions to ensure that halal-certified manufacturers employ good manufacturing practices. Drawing from contemporary marketplace discourses such as organic, natural, and fair trade not only allows the movement to expand its audience to include pro-secular consumers in Turkey as well as health-conscious, ethical consumers overseas, but also lobby state officials and local manufacturers for a mandatory halal certification on the basis that would boost Turkish exports.

CONCLUSION

Through a discourse analysis of GIMDES archives, this study outlines the ways in which the halal movement in Turkey co-opts the tenets of modernity in its quest to institutionalize halal certification and forge a faith-based market. In contrast to previous claims that Islam is anti-modern and anti-market, this study shows how Islamists appropriate modernism and capitalism with religious teachings to form a consumptionscape that is compatible with their ideology. From this standpoint, Islamists closely resemble Thompson's (2004) cultural creatives who gave considerable impetus to the natural health market. Like their postmodern counterparts, Islamists selectively use modern cultural and ideological mores to make space for a halal market within a predominantly secular consumptionscape. Turkey's halal movement becomes more meaningful when read as an Islamist endeavor, both contesting and accommodating the prevalent social structures and ideologies.

NOTES

1. The concept of halal is similar to Kosher and denotes a range of goods that are produced according to Islamic principles.
2. Islamist refers to those individuals who are not just "much more pious than other Muslims, but also search for an alternative Islamic life politics and a new social order" (Saktanber 2002, p. 257).
3. Food Report, March 28, 2008, http://www.gidaraporu.com/yasam-tarzimiz_p.htm, last accessed on March 7, 2012.
4. Food Report, July 3, 2006, http://www.gidaraporu.com/yeni-dunya-dergisi-helal-haram_p.htm, last accessed on March 7, 2012.
5. "Turkey Is Still an Open Market for GMOs," *GIMDES magazine*, August 2009, p. 22.
6. Food Report, August 15, 2009, http://www.gidaraporu.com/adapazari-helal-gida_p.htm, last accessed March 7, 2012.
7. "The Quest for Halal Food and Halal Certification in the World," *GIMDES magazine*, October 2009, p. 21.
8. "Vinegar from Wine?," *GIMDES magazine*, April 2010, pp. 16–19.

9. "The Effects of Forbidden Foods on Human Hormones and Behaviors," *GIMDES magazine*, June 2010, pp. 4–8.
10. "New World Order and Halal Food," *GIMDES magazine*, April 2010, p. 4.

REFERENCES

Ahmed, Akbar S. 2004. *Postmodernism and Islam: Predicament and Promise.* New York: Routledge.
Al-Azmeh, Aziz. 1993. *Islams and Modernities.* London: Verso.
Ayoob, Mohammed. 2008. *The Many Faces of Political Islam: Religion and Politics in the Muslim World.* Ann Arbor: University of Michigan Press.
Barber, Benjamin R. 1996. *Jihad Vs. Mcworld.* New York: Ballantine Books.
Büyüközer, Hüseyin K. 2007. *Food Report Once More.* Istanbul: Çevik.
Demir, Ömer, Mustafa Acar, and Metin Toprak. 2004.), "Anatolian Tigers or Islamic Capital: Prospects and Challenges." *Middle Eastern Studies* 40 (6): 166–188.
Firat, Fuat A., and Alladi Venkatesh. 1995. "Liberatory Postmodernism and the Reenchantment of Consumption." *Journal of Consumer Research* 22 (4): 239–267.
Huntington, Samuel P. 1993. "The Clash of Civilizations?" *Foreign Affairs* 72 (3): 22–50.
Izberk-Bilgin, Elif. 2010 "Lifting the Veil on Infidel Brands: Islamist Discourses of Anticonsumerism." In *Advances in Consumer Research*, edited by Margaret C. Campbell, Jeff Inman, and Rik Pieters, 686–687. Duluth, MN: Association for Consumer Research.
Kozinets, Robert V. 2001. "Utopian Enterprise: Articulating the Meanings of Star Trek's Culture of Consumption." *Journal of Consumer Research* 28 (1): 67–88.
Kozinets, Robert V., and Jay M. Handelman. 2004. "Adversaries of Consumption: Consumer Movements, Activism, and Ideology." *Journal of Consumer Research* 31 (3): 691–704.
Lewis, Bernard. 2002. "The Roots of Muslim Rage." *Policy* 17 (4): 17–26.
Miller, Tracy. 2009. "Mapping the Global Muslim Population," Pew Research Center.
Muñiz Jr., Albert M., and Hope Jensen Schau. 2005. "Religiosity in the Abandoned Apple Newton Brand Community." *Journal of Consumer Research* 31 (4): 737–747.
Navaro-Yashin, Yael. 2002. "The Market for Identities." In *Fragments of Culture: The Everyday of Modern Turkey*, edited by Deniz Kandiyoti and Ayşe Saktanber, 221–254.
London: I. B. Tauris. O'Guinn, Thomas C., and Russell W. Belk. 1989. "Heaven on Earth: Consumption at Heritage Village, USA." *Journal of Consumer Research* 16 (2): 227.
Pink, Johanna, ed. 2009. *Muslim Societies in the Age of Mass Consumption.* Newcastle upon Tyne: Cambridge Scholars Publishing.
Ray, Larry. 1993. *Rethinking Critical Theory: Emancipation in the Age of Global Social Movements.* Thousand Oaks, CA: Sage.
Rudnyckyj, Daromir. 2009. "Market Islam in Indonesia." *Journal of the Royal Anthropological Institute* 15: S183–S201.
Saktanber, Ayşe. 2002. *Living Islam: Women, Religion and the Politicization of Culture in Turkey.* London: I. B. Tauris.
Sherry, John F., and Robert V. Kozinets. 2007. "Commedy of the Commons: Nomadic Spirituality and the Burning Man Festival" In *Consumer Culture*

Theory, edited by Russell W. Belk and John F. Sherry, 119–151. San Diego: JAI Press. Thompson, Craig J. 2004. "Marketplace Mythology and Discourses of Power." *Journal of Consumer Research* 31 (1): 162–180.

Tibi, Bassam. 1983. "The Renewed Role of Islam in the Political and Social Development of the Middle East." *Middle East Journal* 37 (1): 3–13.

Turner, Bryan S. 1974. "Islam, Capitalism, and the Weber Theses." *The British Journal of Sociology* 25 (2): 230–243.

Turner, Bryan S. 1994. *Orientalism, Postmodernism, and Globalism*. New York: Routledge.

Webb, Dan. 2005. "On Mosques and Malls: Understanding Khomeinism as a Source of Counter-Hegemonic Resistance to the Spread of Global Consumer Culture." *Journal of Political Ideologies* 10 (1): 95–119.

Weber, Max. 1922/1978. *Economy and Society*. Berkeley: University of California Press.

Wong, Loong. 2007. "Market Cultures, the Middle Classes and Islam: Consuming the Market?" *Consumption Markets & Culture* 10 (4): 451–480.

4 No Gods. No Masters?
The "New Atheist" Movement and the Commercialization of Unbelief

Mary Johnstone-Louis

University of Oxford biologists are improbable online purveyors of jewelry. But celebrity scientist Professor Richard Dawkins has recently entered the accessories trade, peddling "atheist jewelry" through his namesake organization, the Richard Dawkins Foundation for Reason and Science (RDFRS). Through the RDFRS virtual store, one can purchase earrings, necklaces, and brooches bearing a stylized scarlet letter "A" for "atheist," along with a wide range of apparel, videos, paraphernalia, and promotional items under the brand banner "I Believe Science". These items signal not simply an affirmation of science, but also a commitment to atheistic dogmata, a disavowal of belief in the theistic, the spiritual, and the supernatural.

The RDFRS is a flagship portal for the "New Atheism," a 21st-century anti-religious movement. Through their employ of a mix of market maneuvers, Richard Dawkins, Daniel Dennett, Sam Harris, and the late Christopher Hitchens emerged as the paterfamilias of the New Atheism. In late 2007, these men gathered in front of a fireplace and, flanked by bookcases, filmed two hours of un-moderated conversation about the future of atheism. The resulting footage, available in DVD and online, conjures the image of four urbane intellectuals and was promoted as a dialogue between "The Four Horsemen of the Anti-Apocalypse." Building on bestselling books by each of the Four at the time, this video aimed to brand the nascent New Atheist movement and consolidate its message. The Four have remained the most recognizable faces of the New Atheism, an all-male irreligious priesthood (Shores, 2010) marketed as figureheads ushering in a clarion call for a godless era (McGrath, 2011, p. 3).

Disbelief has a long and public history, and neither the content of their communication nor the scale of their ambitions makes this voluble present-day variant of atheism "new." Rather, it is the skilled and persistent use of the market that seems to set Dawkins et al. apart from their Enlightenment predecessors. Primarily through consumer offerings including music, best-sellers, branded accessories, and ticketed gatherings, the movement engages in what Benford and Snow (2000, p. 615) have described as three core provocations of collective action: "diagnostic framing" (i.e., problem identification and attribution of who/what is to blame), "prognostic framing" (i.e., the articulation of a solution), and "motivational framing" (i.e., a call to action). New Atheist framing presents all faith as downscale, deceptive, and ultimately dangerous; emphasizes science as the means to truth; and appeals to an altruistic urgency to "save" or "improve" oneself and others through the embrace of "reason" as manifest through atheism/"anti-theism."

This trend emerges at a time when secularization theory tends to posit that, rather than fading away, contemporary belief is simply becoming more varied. A related phenomenon, noted by a large body of scholarship such as that which this volume contains, is the extensive use of marketing techniques by spiritual and religious groups. These twin developments have shaped the context in which the New Atheism competes. Through examination of electronically gathered material produced by and about the "Four Horsemen," his chapter investigates how, following Thompson, the New Atheist framing presents consumers with "selfmythologizing narratives," offering "resistance to one discourse of power" (i.e., religion) and "subordination to another" (i.e., the movement's troika brand message; Thompson, 2004, pp. 172–173).

LITERATURE REVIEW

By the 1960s, many scholars, building on work by Marx, Durkheim, and Weber, converged on the "secularization thesis," arguing that as societies industrialized, interest in religious and spiritual matters would decline. Nevertheless, by the 1990s, sociologist Peter Berger famously argued that rather than secularizing, industrialized countries appeared to be undergoing "a shift in the institutional location of religion" (1999, p. 10). Building on this conclusion, Einstein suggested that secularization theory might explain the decline of "organized religion," but posited that faith often appeared to have moved from "pew to pixel" (2007, p. 5). Scholars including Arnould and Price (1993), Kozinets (2001, 2002), Thompson (2004), Holt (2004), and Lofton (2011) concur, exploring how the purportedly secular market has become the prime contender for a new institutional location of religious activity, a master maker of myth and meaning.

Indeed, from the early days of the United States, the separation of church and state meant religious leaders competed for adherents and financial support. This historical situation led to a early fusion of religion and marketing in the U.S. context, which had a profound effect on both the development of the advertising industry (Belk, et al., 1989; O'Guinn and Belk, 1989; Twitchell, 2007, pp. 78–83, 271) and the religious landscape of the United States (see Hatch, 1989; Noll, 1995; Finke and Stark, 2005; Moore, 1995). Einstein points to the effects of a mediatized, commercialized environment on many Western consumers' approaches to belief and spirituality, observing that, "[P]eople get their faith from something other than a religious institution . . . [they] attend movies, read books, participate in religious chat rooms . . . wear t-shirts with logos . . . buy religious rock albums . . . [and] religious/self help books" (2007, pp. 5–8). In an overview of the relationship between marketing and Christianity in 20th-century America, Twitchell (2007) describes the proliferation of Christian camps, concerts, clothing, and accessories; logos and bumper stickers, children's toys, and books; testimonials and online communities; as well as celebrity spokespeople. Einstein documents similar market activity by Kabbalah, a tradition originally open only to adult male Orthodox Jews but endorsed in the 2000s by celebrities including Madonna, the Material Girl herself (2007, pp. 147–149). Religious advertising is visible throughout the world, confounding the secularization theory that predicted religion would disappear from public life. But rather than disappearing, it would appear that much religious activity has simply migrated into the marketplace.

The result, however, is not only the sacralization of consumption, but also a proliferation of market offerings for those interested in metaphysical matters. Three outcomes of this phenomenon are important to note. First, the loudest religious voices often appear to dominate public attention (Noll, 1995). Second, shared consumption practices may appear to become, in some cases, as powerful a cohesive as creedal content, creating something akin to religious "brand communities" (Muniz and O'Guinn, 2001; Twitchell, 2007, p. 15). A third outcome is consumer choice. The market for spiritual and religious entertainment, products, and services has tracked with the "explosive growth" of the American economy and media industry (Einstein, 2007, p. 27). Roof (2001) has documented the increase of religious "shopping" in the United States as "baby boomers" ease from one faith practice to another; not through affiliation with traditional institutions, but through the purchase of a mutable mélange of spiritual goods and services. This is the context within which the New Atheism competes.

NO GODS. NO MASTERS?

Although the New Atheists do not position themselves as a religious group, New Atheist brand leaders have self-consciously employed the market in order to codify and popularize their agenda, establish authority, define community, and inspire devotion and action; that is, to support Benford and Snow's three tasks necessary for the construction of collective action frames. These entrepreneurial skeptics use the market to construct unbelief as a "collectively produced commodity" (Twitchell, 2004, p. 53). Like Christian "pastorpreneurs" (Twitchell, 2007), New Atheist "skeptopreneurs" belong to a "new class of cultural meditators [that] resemble classical religious leaders . . . [as] religion inhabits new spaces, is mediated by new classes of people, and is practiced in new ways" (Miller, 2003, pp. 76–77). As some televangelists and celebrity author-pastors have shifted from more traditional pastoral roles, skeptopreneurs have moved—often from the role of scientist or public intellectual—to usher in the New Atheism's début on the public stage.

The aim of this section is to introduce readers to the "Four Horsemen"—the master skeptopreneurs. Whereas a proliferation of writers, celebrities, and spokespeople (e.g., scientists Stephen Hawking and P. Z. Myers, comedians Ricky Gervais and Bill Maher, Rebecca "Skepchick" Watson, the producer of an annual pin-up calendar of scientists and skeptics, and authors Ian McEwan and Salman Rushdie) have affiliated themselves in various degrees to the New Atheism, Harris, Dawkins, Dennett, and Hitchens remain emblematic, serving as arbiters of doctrine and brand managers. This is particularly true of Dawkins. Reflecting on his symbolic importance, one journalist described his visit to an annual meeting of the Council for Secular Humanism in the United States: "Mingling with conference participants . . . the anticipation of Dawkins' appearance was palpable. . . . Some said they came to conference . . . from quite far away . . . because Dawkins was going to speak. It was something akin to the excitement that I once noted among participants at an evangelical conclave before a sermon by Billy Graham" (Larson, 2010).

How did the Four rise to their present prominence? McGrath argues that in breaking the American cultural taboo of the need to be polite about religion in the wake of the September 11, 2001 ("9–11"), attacks on the United States, Sam Harris uncovered a market for books that did the same (2011, p. 5). Indeed, books have long been the bedrock of religious advertising in the United States, with a few runaway bestsellers tending to open up a genre and establish the credibility of leaders (Einstein, 2007, p. 41; Moore, 1995, p. 16). Sam Harris's *The End of Faith: Religion, Terror, and the Future of Reason* (2004) spent more than thirty-five weeks on the *New York Times* bestseller list, popularizing the assertion that all religion is dangerous and that its antidote is something called "reason." Indeed, 9–11 is often cited as the inauguration of the New Atheist movement, a moment of "diagnostic framing" about which Richard Dawkins wrote just days after the event: "The [terrorists'] insane courage . . . came from religion. To fill a world with religion . . . is like littering the streets with loaded guns. Do not be surprised if they are used" (2001).

Harris's subsequent bestseller titles, *Letter to a Christian Nation* (2006) and *The Moral Landscape: How Science Can Determine Human Values* (2010), can be easily read as prognostic and motivational frames. He is introduced on the elite TED Talks website as a man who is "[a]dored by secularists, feared by the pious . . . [for] argu[ing] that religion is ruinous and, worse, stupid—and that questioning religious faith *might just save civilization*" [author's italics]. He has made numerous television appearances on major networks and contributes regularly to some of the world's most-read newspapers and websites. In 2005, he appeared in the documentary film *The God Who Wasn't There* by self-described atheist filmmaker Brian

Flemming, and he is the founder of "Project Reason," a charity intended to combat the influence of "dogmatism, superstition, and bigotry" through media and events. Harris is an author and popularizer before he is an academic, obtaining his PhD in neuroscience the year before publishing *The Moral Landscape*.

Richard Dawkins's 2006 book *The God Delusion* drove the growth of the New Atheist market category (Smith, 2007) and cemented Dawkins's position as chief of the "demigods of modern atheism" (Larson, 2010). *The God Delusion* popularized the evidentialist argument that belief in God is tantamount to belief in "fairies at the bottom of the garden." The book has been widely translated, and Dawkins's website catalogues dozens of "fleas," his nomenclature for books written in response to his iconic bestseller. By 2006, Dawkins was already well established as an author of popular science books, including *The Selfish Gene* (1976), *The Blind Watchmaker* (1986), and *The Ancestor's Tale* (2004). An evolutionary biologist who left his research career in favor of science popularization, Dawkins was the University of Oxford's first Charles Simonyi Professor for the Public Understanding of Science (1995–2008). He is recognized for TV programs including *The Root of All Evil?*, *The Enemies of Reason*, and *Faith School Menace?* Online, he founded the aforementioned RDFRS, which is branded "A Clear Thinking Oasis" and is the best-known of many web portals for New Atheist activities (but with the inimitable feature that events are searchable by the criteria "Richard speaking: Yes/No").

Tufts University philosophy professor Daniel C. Dennett's book *Breaking the Spell: Religion as a Natural Phenomenon* joined the New Atheist canon in 2006. Dennett remains more involved than either Dawkins or Harris in the current academic debate about theism. He promulgates New Atheist motivational frames, saying, e.g., "If we don't understand religion, we're going to miss our chance to improve the world in the 21st century." Also, although he is a tenured academic, he positions himself as "an autodidact," a thinker who "defies easy categorization, and refuses to affiliate himself with accepted schools of thought." This posture reinforces the popular New Atheist icon and prognostic frame of the "freethinker." Dennett's work casts "science" and "nature" as self-evident conduits of truth, and faith, in contrast, as backwards and obsolete, firmly in the "diagnostic frame." Famously, when told that friends had prayed for him as he faced a health crisis, Dennett reported that he "resisted the urge to ask them: 'Did you sacrifice a goat?' " (2006).

The late Christopher Hitchens earned his place among the New Atheist leadership with his bestseller *God Is Not Great: How Religion Poisons Everything* (2007). Long a bestselling author and public intellectual, Hitchens cited 9–11 as his inspiration to become more outspoken about his "antitheism," promoting the diagnostic frame that faith is dangerous and leads to suffering. The cancellation, due to ill health, of a 2011 appearance at the American Atheists Conference prompted Hitchens to draft a letter to "fellow-

unbelievers," encouraging them that "[o]ur theocratic enemy is in plain view
. . . and we must learn new ways of combating [faith] in the public sphere,
just as we have learned to free ourselves of it in private" (Myers, 2011). Commentators have noted that the text contains notable literary parallels with
letters purportedly written by St. Paul at the end of his life to the nascent
Christian church. The message has been widely circulated and has become
something of an emblem among online New Atheist communities.

It is not so surprising that an aggressively secular movement—declaring
to be neither religious nor especially commercial—would claim a brand
proposition of "reason" while also appearing to invoke ritual and symbol
to endure. What is novel is the New Atheists' strategic embrace of the
market to disseminate diagnostic, prognostic, and motivational frames,
offering consumers the apparent ability to "buy in" to atheist identity and
activism. Although the movement is less than a decade old, its market
offerings range from techno music to children's camps, lettered bracelets
(sold with shipping by Christmas and reminiscent in style of the erst-
while popular 'WWJD—What Would Jesus Do?' design), and youth choir
performances, to holidays (with associated greeting cards), de-baptism
certificates, and a plethora of other rituals and assemblies. The following
section details several trends in the commercialization of unbelief, touching on Richard Dawkins's activities as the de facto New Atheist brand
manager, emphasizing the movement's emphasis on children, and not-
ing its use of conversion and symbolic figures to propagate its three-part
brand meaning.

COMMERCIALIZING UNBELIEF

Richard Dawkins's own website is an apt place to begin. Under the scarlet
"A" logo, Dawkins promotes humanist choirs and family festivals, including "multi-cultural, multi-generational and multi-disciplinary celebrations
of science," complete with inspirational speeches and "amazing science
songs performed by . . . children and adults." One may donate money to a
scarlet-letter humanitarian charity branded "Non-Believers Giving Aid" or
to the student society version, "Non-Prophet Week." In a manner not dis-
similar to the calling of Christian Bible translators, one can also respond
to the appeal for volunteers to translate the "Four Horsemen" series into
world languages.

Dawkins's logo choice of a red letter "A" is not accidental in its affiliation with Nathaniel Hawthorne's *The Scarlet Letter*. The narrative of
persecution for holding socially unacceptable beliefs is a consistent feature of New Atheist discourse, and it forms an important aspect of identity formation and market messaging for the group. In fact, this symbol
captures the narrative of the New Atheists' 'OUT Campaign,' a prognostic and motivational device that, through events, apparel, and web

communities, encourages nonbelievers to "Come out, reach out, speak out": "Atheists have always been at the forefront of rational thinking and beacons of enlightenment . . . we are not going to allow those that would condemn us to push us into the shadows. . . . COME OUT of the closet! You'll feel liberated, and your example will encourage others to COME OUT too" (OUT Campaign).

On other websites, Dawkins endorses events such as the British Humanist Association's "Ancestor's Trail," a nature walk "shared experience for non-religious people" inspired by his book, *The Ancestor's Tale*, which the BHA recommends reading to "hugely amplify your pilgrimage experience" (Ancestor's Trail). He supports music and film festivals such as "Rock Beyond Belief" and the International Freethought Film Festival, and he has supported public campaigns on busses and billboards internationally (the original "Atheist Bus Campaign," which Dawkins fronted with "atheist babe" Ariane Sherine, ran in London in 2008 under the tagline "There's Probably No God. Now Stop Worrying and Enjoy Your Life"). He promotes many other authors, such as A. C. Grayling, the self-described "velvet version" of the New Atheists, who wrote *The Good Book: A Secular Bible* (2011).

Dawkins website also hosts "Converts' Corner," a space signified by the logo of a Catholic prayer rosary transmuting into a strand of DNA, to publically share a "de-conversion" testimony of how you "lost your religion (or have been encouraged to come out of the closet) as a result of reading *The God Delusion* or other Dawkins books" (Converts' Corner). "De-conversion" is a key ritual of the New Atheism. Opening *The God Delusion*, Dawkins writes, "If this book works as I intend, religious readers who open it will be atheists when they put it down." Sam Harris's TED speaker profile encourages readers to "Read Sam Harris and wake up." The theme of individual awakening and liberation, of one being "lost" in religion and coming to see, is reflected in aforementioned testimonies of atheist catharsis shared online, as well as through globally active movements of "apostasy" or "debaptism," typically marked by events and certificates. In a characteristic move by the National Secular Society in the United Kingdom, more than 100,000 certificates of debaptism ("in the name of human reason") have been purchased online (Debaptize Yourself!). Filmmaker Brian Flemming popularized events such as the Rational Response Squad's Blasphemy Challenge, which gave DVDs of *The God Who Wasn't There* to the first 1,001 people to submit videos of themselves denying the existence of the Christian Holy Spirit (a ritual interpreted to signify a point of spiritual "no return"). Celebrity New Atheists as well as members of the Four participated in the highly publicized event.

Religious marketing is often aimed at both current believers and potential converts, and New Atheist marketing appears to be no different. As Einstein has observed when examining cryptic symbols often employed in Christian t-shirts and accessories, Dawkins's "A" and logos on offer from other New Atheist groups are devised to be conversation starters. "The Brights," an "international constituency for individuals whose worldview is free of supernatural and mystical elements," suggest that a lapel pin bearing their logo will provide "many opportunities to respond to curious persons," allowing the wearer to "divulge/discuss your *naturalistic worldview* in amiable and informative ways" (The Brights' Bulletin).

For New Atheist branding, the propositions of "reason" and "self-improvement" are central prognostic frames: American Atheists claim that in embracing atheism, one becomes a "freethinker," a member of a group that is "intelligent, well-educated, positive, and upbeat" (American Atheists). For US$2.50 for a pack of 10, the organization sells tracts containing "An Invitation to the Intellectual Elite," encouraging their members to purchase pamphlets to keep on hand so that "next time you encounter a fundamentalist (or a Gideon Bible), you can quickly leave a rational view behind you" (Atheists Store). (Whether such a tactic would appear engaging to a member of the "intellectual elite" of course remains unclear.)

Notably, the New Atheism has inspired a medley of market innovations aimed at children and teenagers. Popular musical homages include Baba Brinkman's 'Rap Guide to Evolution,' They Might Be Giants,' 'Here Comes Science' album (at time of writing, the number 1 seller in Amazon's children's music category), and techno music series "Symphony of Science" produced by electronic musician John Boswell. Dawkins has authored an illustrated children's book, *What Is a Rainbow, Really?* (2011). On other websites, baby blankets bearing the statements "I gave up superstitious mumbo jumbo for Lent" are available, as is a children's line of "freethinkers" baseball jerseys. The "Religion Kills" line of apparel offers not only the aforementioned children's sportswear and baby blankets, but items ranging from kitchen aprons to teddy bears. (In the adult market, "Free Thinker" classic thong underwear is for sale, as are lingerie designs declaring "Guilty of Independent Thought").

Also in the children's market, Camp Quest, a "Summer Camp Beyond Belief!" offering "fun, friends, and freethought for kids ages 8–17" is marketed with the tagline "I evolved!", capturing the spirit of religion as backwards or out of date. The camp is currently held in five countries and endorses an array of toys, books, and apparel for "little freethinkers". A recent Camp Quest blog observes that parents may find: "It's easy to give Valentine's Day short shrift with it coming right on the heels of Darwin Day," while providing ideas of how to celebrate the latter (Camp Quest). In New Atheist marketing to both children and adults, Charles Darwin serves as not only a scientific but also a metaphysical prophet, a bearded figure whose name and writings are invoked with authority, used to adjudicate conflict, and celebrated through products such as *The Genius of Charles Darwin* video and a jewelry range modeled on his "tree of life" drawing; both are available on Dawkins's website.

DISCUSSION AND CONCLUSION

The advocates, events, and accouterments that characterize the commercialization of unbelief are remarkably similar in both form and function to those of religious marketing. Song, camps, and iconic imagery instill clear perceptions of good and evil, of "in" and "out," and emphasize personal and global improvement through embrace of atheistic beliefs. The definition of religion, of course, has been debated by great thinkers from Douglas to Mauss to Weber and is unlikely to be resolved here. However, in evaluating the New Atheism through the lens of religious marketing, it is useful to consider a description such as that offered by Geertz, who suggests that religion may be:

1. a system of symbols which acts to (2) establish powerful, pervasive, and long-lasting moods and motivations in men by (3) formulating conceptions of a general order of existence and (4) clothing these conceptions with such an aura of factuality that (5) the moods and motivations seem uniquely realistic. (1966, p. 4)

The New Atheism, at least in its marketing, appeals to a system of symbols (Scarlet "A," Charles Darwin), establishes motivations in men (fighting a common enemy in theists for the personal and common good) and combines a general order of existence with an aura of factuality (science as the primary means to truth, atheist elites as gatekeepers of "reason") to present a message that appears uniquely realistic, distinctively linked to independent thought and cleverness. The use of diagnostic, prognostic, and motivational frames to inspire consumer devotion is evident in even an exploratory review of New Atheist material for this study.

"Mythic archetypes" of consumption are often "grounded in the most fundamental concerns of human experience . . . struggles between the weak and the strong . . . humanity's relationship to the natural world" (Thompson, 2004, pp. 162, 172), creating powerful tropes. The New Atheist market positioning as elite and intellectual builds on post-Enlightenment cultural tropes such as individual freedom from superstition, supremacy of reason, and science as passport to Truth, each of which facilitates diagnostic framing through the New Atheist brand. The archetype of a scientist in a white lab coat uncovering universal realities resonates with the New Atheists' use of "reason" to position religion, by contrast, as an obsolete throwback and its adherents, when not dangerous, as obtuse and hoodwinked. Much as Kozinets observed in his study of anticorporate Burning Man participants' use of Disney and the archetype of "the consumer," "religion" writ large "provides an important foil against which to discursively distinguish" (2002, p. 25) the New Atheism and engage in prognostic and motivational framing. Consumption is as much a means to express what one *is* as what one is *not* (Bourdieu, 1984, pp. 56–57), and the New

Atheist brand proposition is, in many ways, a class proposition, employing the foil of "unenlightened" religious people to bolster atheism's ostensibly elite brand identity.

Lacking a traditional church or set of religious practices and not-withstanding its diagnostic frame to join the "intellectual elite," the New Atheism has been birthed via consumer culture. In their marketing approach, the New Atheism behaves less like an organic assembly of elite, autonomous "free thinkers" than a group marked by arbiters of doctrine, symbolic figures, emphasis on conversion, and clear group identity. As Thompson has observed:

> Broadly defined social institutions . . . family, religion, professional work, education, and medicine—all produce discourses through which social hierarchies and status distinctions are constructed and legiti-mated, and through which normative identity positions . . . are institu-tionalized. These institutions and concomitant social roles have been thoroughly interpenetrated by marketing discourses (via advertising, fashion, and mass media) and the capitalist lifestyle ideals that infuse all facets of consumer culture. (2004, pp. 172–173)

Originally attributed to 20th-century American activist Margaret Sanger, the phrase in the title of this chapter has been adopted by atheist groups, and at the time of this publication, it is readily visible on various New Athe-ist websites. But can it be said of the New Atheists that they have "No gods and no masters?" While avidly secular and purporting to provide mean-ing outside institutions, the movement uses framing devices to aggressively advocate one way to Truth, eschewing the pastiche religion typical of many Westerners since the Baby Boomers (Roof, 2001). Through their market-ing, this group thus appears to be bringing the secular closer in line to the sacred. As contemporary secularization theory has argued, the religious becomes more secular and, vice versa, the New Atheism appears to make the secular more religious. In this way, the New Atheism can be understood as one among many modern voices that call on metaphysical matters but compete largely through market means.

REFERENCES

American Atheists. Accessed April 20, 2011. http://www.atheists.org/Support/Uhl_Challenge

Ancestor's Trail. Accessed April 20, 2011. http://www.ancestorstrail.net/thinking.htm.

Arnould, E.J. and L.L. Price. June 1993 "River Magic: Extraordinary Experi-ence and the Extended Service Encounter." *Journal of Consumer Research*, 20: 24–45.

Atheists Store. Accessed April 20, 2011 https://atheists.org/store/

Belk, R. W., M. Wallendorf, and J. Sherry, Jr. June 1989. "The Sacred and the Profane in Consumer Behavior: Theodicy on the Odyssey." *Journal of Consumer Research* 16: 1–38.

Benford, R. D., and D. A. Snow. 2000. "Framing Processes and Social Movements: An Overview and Assessment. *Annual Review of Sociology* 26: 611–639.

Berger, P., ed. 1999. *The Desecularization of the World: Resurgent Religion and World Politics*. Grand Rapids, MI: W. B. Eerdmans.

Bourdieu, P. 1984. *Distinction: A Social Critique of the Judgment of Taste*. Cambridge, MA: Harvard University Press.

The Brights' Bulletin. Accessed April 20, 2011. http://www.the-brights.net/movement/bulletin/bulletin.html?b=36.

Camp Quest. Accessed April 20, 2011. http://www.campquest.org/.

Converts' Corner. Accessed February 20, 2011. http://richarddawkins.net/letters/converts.

Dawkins, R. 1976. *The Selfish Gene*. Oxford: Oxford University Press.

Dawkins, R. 1986. *The Blind Watchmaker*. New York: W. W. Norton.

Dawkins, R. September 15, 2001. "Religion's Misguided Missiles." *The Guardian*. Accessed April 20, 2011. http://www.guardian.co.uk.

Dawkins, R. 2004. *The Ancestor's Tale*. Boston: Houghton Mifflin.

Dawkins, R. 2006. *The God Delusion*. New York: Bantam Books.

Debaptize Yourself! Accessed April 20, 2011. http://www.secularism.org.uk/debaptise-yourself.html

Dennett, D. November 3, 2006. "Thank Goodness!" *The Edge*. Accessed April 20, 2011. http://www.edge.org.

Einstein, M. 2007. *Brands of Faith*. New York: Routledge.

Finke, R. and R. Stark. 2005. *The Churching of America 1776–2005*. *Rutgers*: Rutgers University Press.

Geertz, C. 1966. "Religion as a Cultural System." In *Anthropological Approaches to the Study of Religion*, edited by M. Banton, 1–46. London: Tavistock.

Grayling, A.C. 2011. *The Good Book*. London: Bloomsbury.

Hatch, N. 1989. *The Democratization of American Christianity*. New Haven: Yale University Press.

Harris, S. 2004. *The End of Faith: Religion, Terror, and the Future of Reason*. New York: W.W. Norton.

Harris, S. 2006. *Letter to a Christian Nation*. New York: Knopf.

Harris, S. 2010. *The Moral Lanscape: How Science Can Determine Human Values*. New York: Free Press.

Hitchens, C. 2007. *God Is Not Great: How Religion Poisons Everything*. New York: Twelve.

Holt, D.B. 2004. *How Brands Become Icons: The Principles of Cultural Branding*. Boston: Harvard University Press.

Kozinets, R. June 2001. "Utopian Enterprise: Articulating the Meanings of Star Trek's Culture of Consumption." *Journal of Consumer Research* 28:67–88.

Kozinets, R. June 2002. "Can Consumers Escape the Market? Emancipatory Illuminations from Burning Man." *Journal of Consumer Research* 29: 20–38.

Larson, E. J. October 19, 2010. "Dining with Dawkins in the Humanist Bosom." *Religion Dispatches*. Accessed April 20, 2011. http://www.religiondispatches. org.

Lofton, K. 2011. *Oprah: The Gospel of an Icon*. Berkeley. University of California Press.

McGrath, A. 2011. *Why God Won't Go Away: Engaging with the New Atheism*. London: Society for Promoting Christian Knowledge.

Miller, V. 2003., *Consuming Religion*. New York: Continuum International.

Moore, R. L. 1995. *Selling God: American Religion in the Marketplace of Culture.* New York: Oxford University Press.

Muniz, A., and T. O'Guinn. 2001. "Brand Community." *Journal of Consumer Research* 27: 412–432.

Myers, P. Z. April 22, 2011. "Hitchens' Address to American Atheists." *Pharyngula.* Accessed April 24, 2011. http://scienceblogs.com/pharyngula/2011/04/hitchens_address_to_american_a.php.

Noll, M. 1995. *The Scandal of the Evangelical Mind.* Grand Rapids, MI: W. B. Eerdmans.

O'Guinn, T. C., and R. W. Belk. September 1989. "Heaven on Earth: Consumption at Heritage Village, USA."*Journal of Consumer Research* 16: 227–238.

OUT Campaign. Accessed April 20, 2011. http://outcampaign.org/.

Roof, W. C. 2001. *Spiritual Marketplace: Baby Boomers and the Remaking of American Religion.* Princeton, NJ: Princeton   University Press.

Shores, M. November 1, 2010. "Will 'New Atheism' Make Room for Women?" *Ms. Magazine Blog.* Accessed April 20, 2011. http://msmagazine.com/blog.

Smith, D. August 12, 2007. "Believe It or Not: The Sceptics Beat God in Bestseller Battle." *The Guardian.* Accessed April 20, 2011 http://www.guardian.co.uk/.

Thompson, C. June 2004. "Marketplace Mythology and Discourses of Power." *Journal of Consumer Research* 31 (1): 162–180.

Twitchell, J. 2004. *Branded Nation* New York: Simon & Schuster.

Twitchell, J. 2007. *Shopping for God.* New York: Simon & Schuster.

Part II

Consumers' Search for Spiritual Meanings in Consumption of the Mundane

5 The Sacred in Consumer Culture

Russell V. Belk

It has become commonplace in the sociology of religion, consumer research, and discussions of consumer culture to maintain that religion and consumption are opposing forces in contemporary life (e.g., Burroughs and Rindfleisch, 2002). These views are reflections of the broader secularization thesis that maintains religion is losing its power as other institutions such as consumption, science, and entertainment become dominant. From this perspective, it appears that consumer culture is ascendant, the sacred is being replaced by the secular, and religion is being forced to adapt in order to compete in a marketplace with multiple sources of meaning (e.g., Hoover, 2000; Miller, 2004; Roof, 1999; Twitchell, 2007). The resulting marketing and consumption of religion and religious objects and icons are found by some to be shocking, ironic, and tacky, with these practices seen as profaning the sacred religions that they objectify (e.g., Einstein, 2008; McDannell, 1995; Moore, 1994). These arguments can be broadly classified as being about the secularization of the sacred.

An opposite perspective concerns the sacralisation of the secular (e.g., Belk, Wallendorf, and Sherry, 1989). It suggests that we have a deep-seated need for the spiritual and transcendent and that we increasingly find it in popular culture and consumption institutions (e.g., Chidester, 2005; Detweiler and Taylor, 2003; Hulsether, 2000; Lyon, 2000). Many of us seem to have made a religion of technology (e.g., Cobb, 1998; Davis, 1998; Ellul, 1964; Kozinets, 2008; Noble, 1997). Groups of us worship certain consumption objects like Macintosh computers (e.g., Belk and Tumbat, 2005; Kahney, 2004), iPods (e.g., Kahney, 2005; Levy, 2006; Sheffield, 2006), or even discontinued offerings like the Apple Newton (Muñiz and Schau, 2005). Some seek a utopian paradise in such secular but sacralized earthly locales as Hawaii (Costa, 1998), mountain man rendezvous (Belk and Costa, 1998), or Burning Man festivals (Kozinets, 2002). For others the sacred is found in virtual reality (e.g., Castronova, 2007; Heim, 1993; Wertheim, 1999), science fiction worlds (e.g., Cowan, 2010; Kozinets, 2001), or certain retailing, branding, and advertising environments (e.g., Ritzer, 1999; Shachar, Erdem, Cutright, and Fitzsimons, forthcoming; Sheffield, 2006; Sherry, Kozinets, and Borghini, 2007). All of these contexts have one thing in common: they are secular contexts that have acquired at least some characteristics and functions of the sacred.

In this chapter, I would like to further interrogate the changing distinctions between the sacred and the secular by examining a particular contested battleground between the two: the increasingly global celebration of Christmas. Christmas celebrations involve a particularly interesting contestation because religious, commercial, and folk cultures have all contributed to these celebrations in various ways. Regardless of whether these systems of meaning are antagonistic or synergistic, by examining their confluence, we should learn something about the nature of the sacred in contemporary culture.

WHAT IS THE SACRED?

Before considering Christmas and sacredness, we should be clear about what we mean by the sacred. For Durkheim (1915), all societies divide things into the sacred and the profane, and this distinction as well as the beliefs, rituals, and myths surrounding it, constitute religion. Drawing primarily on Durkheim (1915, 1953), and Eliade (1958, 1959), Belk, Wallendorf, and Sherry (1989) derive a set of twelve properties of the sacred:

1. *Hierophany*, something sacred reveals itself to us.
2. *Kratophany*, the sacred encompasses both desired goodness and feared evil power.
3. *Opposition to the Profane*, the extraordinary sacred counters the ordinary profane.
4. *Contamination*, the contagious ability of the sacred transmits its power to that with which it comes into contact.
5. *Sacrifice*, worshippers approach the sacred through offerings, self-abnegation, and submission.
6. *Commitment*, the participant's identity is linked to the sacred via focused emotional attachment.
7. *Objectification*, we condense the sacred into key symbols.
8. *Ritual*, in order to approach the sacred, we must enact certain scripted behaviors.
9. *Myth*, narrative accounts tell of our place in the world vis-à-vis the sacred.
10. *Mystery*, we cannot understand the sacred through rational thought.
11. *Communitas*, those who participate in sacred rituals enjoy a shared egalitarian antistructure.
12. *Ecstasy and Flow*, these are ecstatic states of the group and individual communing in the sacred.

Thus, in its most universal form, the sacred does not necessitate a god, transcendence, or the supernatural. For example, nature or the clan could be the focus of the sacred, as with animism and totemism. In fact, for Durkheim (1915), totemism is the most basic form of religion.

As Belk, Wallendorf, and Sherry (1989) demonstrate, it is possible for consumers, individually or collectively, to sacralize a wide variety of secular consumer goods. They offer examples of sacred places, times, experiences, things (both tangible and non-tangible), and beings (both human and non-human). This allows a broad catalogue of things that are sacred or that may become so through meeting certain sacralization criteria and undergoing specific sacralization processes. These include the processes of ritual, pilgrimage, gift-giving, collecting, or inheritance, as well as criteria of quintessence or external sanction through a thing's incorporation into a sacralizing institution like a museum. But they also note that just as these processes and criteria can sacralize objects that come from the profane world, their neglect can mean that these objects can lose their sacred power and slip back into the realm of the profane.

CHRISTMAS AND SACRALIZING THE SECULAR

As Miller (1993) notes, before there was Christmas, the ancient Romans celebrated Kalends (January 1), Saturnalia (December 17–21), and Dies Natalis Solis Invicti or the Birth Day of the Sun God Sol Invictus (December 25), complete with feasting, drinking, gift-giving, and masquerades, as well as attendant criticisms of excess and crass materialism in such practices. Sol Invictus was the one of several Roman gods competing against Christianity in Rome and had come from the Vedic sun cult of Mithra by way of India, China, Turkey, and Persia (Count and Count, 1997; Restad, 1995). It is no coincidence that somewhere between the years of 354 and 360 C.E., the Christian church chose December 25 as the date on which to establish the Christmas festival. It was intended to replace, and has clearly succeeded, in replacing these earlier non-Christian holidays as the grand feast day of the Western world. But whereas Christmas began as a Christian holy day in the West, it has become something much larger than this as we shall see.

Although the Christian church established Christmas as the day to celebrate the birth of Christ, the holiday celebration did not catch on immediately and has gradually evolved over the years since it was established. Although Christmas spread with Christianity and became fused with many local seasonal celebrations like the Norse Yule throughout the Middle Ages and through to Puritan England and Colonial America, its celebration was officially opposed, suppressed, and sometimes outlawed (Barnet, 1954; Gillis, 1996; Golby and Purdue, 1986; Marling, 2000; Nissenbaum, 1996; Restad, 1997; Schmidt, 1995; Waits, 1993). This resistance was only partially based on religious opposition. The holiday was also associated in many places with raucous, rebellious, and licentious behaviour, which was also opposed on moral grounds. As department stores began to promote

Christmas merchandise in the mid- to late 19th century, Christmas was also critiqued as becoming excessively materialistic and commercial. In some estimations, Christmas celebrations were about to die out in the 19th century until works like the Christmas stories of Charles Dickens, the poem now known as "T'was the Night Before Christmas" by Clement Moore, and the Santa Claus illustrations by Thomas Nast in *Harper's Bazaar* began to revitalize the holiday in the popular imagination (Belk, 1993). Since the 1940s, a number of Christmas movies and television specials have added to the nostalgic rendering of Christmas as a family holiday, at least in the West (Connelly, 2000; Kuper, 1993; Svehla and Svehla, 1998; Thompson, 2000).

But contemporary Christmas celebrations have also become increasingly non-religious and commercial, especially as Christmas has spread to non-Western countries (Belk and Kimura, 2005; Moeran and Skov, 1993; Plath, 1963; Santino, 1996; Zhao and Belk, 2005). Christmas is now widely celebrated in China and Japan and has a growing commercial presence in a number of Buddhist, Hindu, and Muslim countries throughout the world. Miller (1993) suggests that Christmas has become the first global consumer holiday, if largely in a secular and non-religious sense. Likewise, adapting to the Western Christmas was seen as a necessary mark of immigrant acculturation, even if the immigrants were Jewish, Muslim, or Buddhist (Heinze, 1990; Newall, 1989; Pleck, 2000). As Christmas has grown in global popularity, a number of sustained criticisms of Christmas have re-emerged (e.g., Flynn, 1993; Horsley and Tracy, 2001; Waldfogel, 1993, 2009). Some of these criticisms see the commercialization of Christmas and the consumer materialism it fosters as profaning and diluting the sacred Christian holy day and subverting its meaning (e.g., Coleman, 1957; Flynn, 1993; Horsley, 2001). Waldfogel's (1993, 2009) arguments are instead economic: as gift-givers, we do not know recipients' desires as well as they do, so we would be better off avoiding gifts and spending the money on ourselves. Although he entirely misses the non-economic principles that lie behind gift-giving (e.g., Belk, 1996; Sherry, 1983), the primary spur to the "wasteful" Christmas gift-giving that Waldfogel indicts is Santa Claus, to whom I now turn.

SANTA AS SACRED

In one widely accepted account, the Christmas icon we know in much of the world as Santa Claus began as a Christian saint, Saint Nicholas (Bowler, 2005; Jones, 1978). Saint Nicholas, the 4th-century bishop of Myra in what is now Turkey, is said to have performed acts of kindness, including tossing three bags of gold through the window of a home in which a man's three daughters would have been sold into slavery and prostitution were it not for the dowries that the gold provided. Not only do these gifts provide parallels to the contemporary gift-giving of Santa Claus, the miracle-per-forming Nicholas also provides a sacred predecessor. By the Middle Ages in Europe, gift-giving in the name of the saint occurred on Saint Nicholas Day, December 5. Only gradually with the Protestant Reformation did the celebration of the birth of Christ on December 25th begin to take hold as the Protestants tried to move away from the Catholic veneration of Saints (Bowler, 2005). In Germany, the church offered Christkindlein, the Christ Child, as the gift-bringer in competition with Saint Nicholas. But the trans-formation was not that simple, as different parts of Europe had different gift-bringers, including females like the Italian Befana. Furthermore, there are alternative predecessor mythologies in which the European seasonal gift-giver was a goddess (Curtis, 1995), a shaman (van Renterghem, 1995), or a wild man (Siefker, 1997).

Belk (1987) argues that the primary unification of the various European Christmas gift-bringer figures took place in the immigrant culture of the United States. The same can be said of the overall Christmas celebration as immigrants brought such traditions as the Christmas tree, stockings hung on the fireplace mantle, Christmas cookies and candies, Christmas carols, various Christmas decorations, Christmas cards, and Christmas shopping as well as handmade gifts (Belk, 1989). Just as elements such as the Ger-man Christmas tree, the Dutch Christmas cookie, and the British Christmas card became a part of the American Christmas celebration, so were the vari-ous European predecessor figures combined in the popular image of Santa Claus and then re-exported to Europe and other parts of the world. Coca-Cola also played a role in the popular image of Santa Claus, with advertis-ing featuring a series of depictions of Santa and Coke by the Swedish artist Haddon Sundblom painted for the company between 1931 and 1963. It is such non-religious Christmas motifs and icons that allow Christmas to be celebrated by non-Christians around the world. As Belk and Kimura (2005) show, although Christmas is widely celebrated in Japan and involves familiar Christmas decorations, many Santa Clauses, gift-giving, and customs such as Christmas cakes, the celebration is almost entirely non-religious.

Although the contemporary image of Santa Claus comes more from folk culture and commercial culture than from the ancient religious traditions of Saint Nicholas, there are a number of parallels between Santa and Christ that support Belk's (1987) conclusion that Santa is the god of materialism. The parallels include miracles (traveling around the world in a single night, a bottomless bag of toys, flying reindeer), omniscience ("he knows if you've been bad or good"), immortality, living in the heavenly snow-white purity of the North Pole, and reigning from his shopping mall throne with elves as apostles and reindeer as manger animals. Furthermore, Belk (1987) notes that we can see children's

> letters to Santa as secular prayers pledging "good" behavior if they are
> granted, and offerings of cookies and milk as sacrifices placed upon

the fireplace mantle altar. It is also possible to see Santa's travels as parallel to Christ's journeys and secular Christmas carols about Santa as hymns. Just as Christ brought his gifts of love and salvation to earth and then ascended to heaven, Santa brings his gifts of toys and treats to houses and then ascends up the chimney. (p. 90)

Hagstrom (1966) uses Durkheim's specification that sacredness involves something that can be profaned and something celebrated in social rituals to declare that Santa is sacred.

Dell deChant (2002) takes this argument further and presents a detailed argument that rather than Santa and the commercial Christmas forming a secular alternative to the Christian sacred Christmas celebration, they should be seen as an alternate and increasingly dominant religion. In this view, the economy of consumer culture is seen as a cosmological religion like the religions that Christianity once conquered in installing its transcendent religion (deChant, 2002). Within this new religion, Santa is God and the Santa stories are his supporting mythology. Consumer Christmas shopping is the chief ritual that sustains this new religion, and advertisements act as secondary myths about the transformative power of buying. Department stores and shopping malls have become our sacred sites of pilgrimage, and the expenditure of money buying Christmas gifts marks our key sacrifice.

Although deChant (2002) is not alone is positing materialism and consumption as our new religion, he suggests an elaborate cycle of consumption holidays/holy days throughout the year, culminating in the United States in the High Holy season from Thanksgiving and Black Friday to Christmas Day, Gift Return Day, and New Year's Day. After the excess and indulgence of this season comes a ritual fasting period from Christmas until Super Bowl Sunday. The sacred calendar of the new consumer religion put forward by deChant (2002) is replete with holidays that may have once served other Christian or civic religions, including Easter, the Fourth of July, and Memorial Day, but that have now been taken over by the new religion of consumerism. The triumph of this new religion is evident in part of deChant's (2002) conclusion:

> Far more profoundly than Jesus, the annual rebirth of Santa is seen, felt, and celebrated in the season of their overlapping advents. Santa, not Jesus, signals the beginning of the Christmas holy-day cycle, arriving with the season and announcing the formal commencement of its mythico-ritual cycle. After Harbinger Weekend [pre-Thanksgiving] his presence becomes increasingly prominent. By Pilgrimage Friday [Black Friday or the day after Thanksgiving that starts the Christmas shopping cycle], he is ubiquitous. He shows up on television specials and in holiday films, at football games and holiday basketball tournaments. He is seen with the president. We find him wherever we turn: in songs on the radio and songs our children sing, on greeting cards, at churches

and hospitals, riding in parades, ringing bells for the poor and ringing up sales for Wal-Mart and Sears. Above all, we find him sitting in palatial splendour at the sacred center of every shopping mall in the postmodern world. Like the great seasonal gods of antiquity, he has made his annual return; with this theophany, the High Holy Days begin. Every year, we are there to greet him, even as he is there to greet us. (pp. 196–197)

Although this is an America-centric version of the Sacred Santa meta-myth, as deChant (2002) calls it, it could be argued that the United States is the birthplace of contemporary consumer culture, and that just as Christianity has many denominations and variants, so too can the religion of consumer culture. But whether we fully accept deChant's formulation, it should jolt us out of the complacent assumption that monotheistic world religions have a monopoly on the sacred. While Belk, Wallendorf, and Sherry (1989) emphasize the role that consumers play in sacralising and resacralizing consumption objects, places, persons, experiences, times, and beings, deChant (2002) begins to show the role of advertising in creating the sacred.

This is a topic taken up by Sheffield (2006). Although she stops short of calling advertising a religious ritual and instead refers to it as having religious dimensions, Sheffield argues that advertising is a sacrament that sacralises commodity-totems, which thereby allow those who consume them to feel part of a totemic clan that shares the mystical power of the totem. She suggests the iPod as an example of a commodity whose meaning is mediated by advertising for the totemic clan that reveres it. Drawing on Taylor (1999), she suggests that money has become God because it is the key to purchase that allows us membership in the affluent clan whose totems we worship. Sheffield (2006) does not single out Santa Claus as the key sacred figure in all of this, but notes that shopping and consuming are most like religious rituals during the Christmas holiday season thanks to the mediating sacrament of advertising. She also compares the mediating and sacralising role of advertising to the mediating and sacralising role of Siddhartha in Buddhism, Moses in Judaism, and Muhammad in Islam. Although none of these figures is taken to be divine like Jesus Christ in Christianity, they mediate between humans and God and thereby act to transmit the sacred, mysterious, and God-like to humankind. If money (Taylor, 1999) or the consumer economy (deChant, 2002) is sacred, Santa should be seen as no less of an intermediary. That is, if advertising sacralises branded commodity-totems, Santa sacralises our participation in the consumer economy.

CONCLUSION

It is interesting to contemplate the implications of deChant's (2002) inversion of the alignment of the sacred with traditional world religions in favour of an alignment of the sacred with the purported new world religion of consumer capitalism. Seen as the chief God of an alternative religion, Santa's failure to capture the popular imagination in a book and a series of crèches showing him praying at the manger cradle of the baby Jesus (Bakewell, 1984) is understandable. This scene would be like showing Krishna in a Christmas crèche; these are alternative ideologies that may compete with one another but cannot be accommodated and combined. Some evidence exists that Santa and the commercial Christmas are now dominant. It is hard to imagine children lining up to see "Jesus" the way they queue up to see "Santa." Although children do sometimes address their letters to Santa to "heaven," it is clearly Santa whom they are addressing (Clark, 1995). Children's letters to Santa are far less apt to ask for peace and good will toward men than they are to ask for consumer goods specified by brand name (e.g., O'Cass and Clarke, 2002; Otnes, Kim, and Kim, 1994a, 1994b). Likewise in the world of fiction, we have depictions of families ostracized not for their lack of Christian piety at Christmas, but for their lack of commercial spirit that ties their community together (Grisham, 2001). The sin or taboo behaviour here is failing to worship Santa Claus, Frosty the Snowman, Rudolf the Red-Nosed Reindeer, and the rest of the Christmas pantheon exhorting us to participate in the shopping, feasting, decorating, and other rites of excess of the high holy season. But even within the commercial Christmas, there is a pre-industrial lament that should the sacred Santa emphasize quantity over quantity or production-line efficiency over caring and craftsmanship, something vital, humane, and sacred will have been lost from the postmodern commercial Christmas celebration (e.g., Belk and Bryce, 1993; Vinge, 1985). The Victorian virtues of home, family, and magical childhood are also alive and well in the Santa Claus myth (Gillis, 1996). Moreover, this set of cover values helps disguise the deeper consumerist core values of the season. In this sense, the emphasis on love, giving, family, and enchanted childhood help to camouflage the more crass, indulgent, and commercial basis of the contemporary Christmas holiday, just as Santa himself does.

If looking backwards helps put the shift from secularization of the sacred to sacralisation of the secular into perspective, looking forwards helps put our continuing need for the sacred into perspective. This is not only true in science fiction (e.g., Cowan, 2010; Kozinets, 2001), but in the sciences as well. In February 2011, the NASA Kepler Observatory announced the discovery of more than 1,200 potentially habitable planets in our universe, vastly increasing the chance of intelligent life beyond our solar system. If a being from one of these planets had the means to visit Earth (some 2,000 light years away), it would likely find us as insignificant as the ants whose ant hills we pass on a country road. If this were to happen, what would it do to our notions of gods and religions? It would no doubt shake our sacred ontologies to their core and at the same time prompt new ones. But it would not diminish our need for the sacred.

REFERENCES

Bakewell, Nicholas. 1984. *Santa and the Christ Child*. Los Angeles, CA: Kneeling Santa.

Barnet, James H. 1954. *The American Christmas*. New York: Macmillan.

Belk, Russell. 1987. "A Child's Christmas in America: Santa Claus as Deity, Consumption as Religion." *Journal of American Culture* 10 (Spring): 87–100.

Belk, Russell 1989. "Materialism and the Modern U.S. Christmas." In *Interpretive Consumer Research*, edited by Elizabeth Hirschman, 115–135. Provo, UT: Association for Consumer Research.Belk, Russell. 1993. "Materialism and the Making of the Modern American Christmas." In *Unwrapping Christmas*, edited by Daniel Miller, 75–104. Oxford: Oxford University Press.

Belk, Russell. 1996. "The Perfect Gift." In *Gift Giving: A Research Anthology*, edited by Cele Otnes and Richard F. Beltramini, 59–84. Bowling Green, OH: Bowling Green University Popular Press.

Belk, Russell, and Wendy Bryce. 1993. "Christmas Shopping Scenes: From Modern Miracle to Postmodern Mall." *International Journal of Research in Marketing* 10 (August): 277–296.

Belk, Russell, and Janeen Costa. 1998. "The Mountain Man Myth: A Contemporary Consuming Fantasy." *Journal of Consumer Research* 25 (December): 218–240.

Belk, Russell, and Junko Kimura. 2005. "Christmas in Japan: Globalization versus Localization." *Consumption, Markets and Culture* 8 (September): 325–338.

Belk, Russell, and Gülnur Tumbat. 2005. "The Cult of Macintosh." *Consumption Markets and Culture* 8 (September): 205–218.

Belk, Russell, Melanie Wallendorf, and John F. Sherry, Jr. 1989. "The Sacred and the Profane in Consumer Behavior: Theodicy on the Odyssey." *Journal of Consumer Research* 16 (June): 1–38.

Bowler, Gerry. 2005. *Santa Claus: A Biography*. Toronto: McClelland and Stewart.

Burroughs, James, and Aric Rindfleisch. 2002. "Materialism and Well-Being: A Conflicting Values Perspective." *Journal of Consumer Research* 29 (December): 348–370.

Castronova, Edward. 2007. *Exodus to the Virtual World: How Online Fun Is Changing Reality*. New York: Palgrave Macmillan.

Chidester, David. 2005. *Authentic Fakes: Religion and American Popular Culture*. Berkeley, CA: University of California Press.

Clark, Cindy D. 1995. *Flights of Fancy, Leaps of Faith: Children's Myths in Contemporary America*. Chicago: University of Chicago Press.

Cobb, Jennifer. 1998. *CyberGrace: The Search for God in the Digital World*. New York: Crown.

Coleman, Arthur D. 1957. *Keeping Christmas Christian*. New York: Greenwich.

Connelly, Mark, ed. 2000. *Christmas at the Movies: Images of Christmas in American, British, and European Cinema* London: Tauris.

Costa, Janeen Arnold. 1998. "Paradisal Discourse: A Critical Analysis of Marketing and Consuming Hawaii." *Consumption, Markets and Culture* 1 (4): 303–346.

Count, Earl W., and Alice L. Count. 1997. *4000 Years of Christmas: A Gift from the Ages*. Berkeley, CA: Ulysses Press.

Cowan, Douglas E. 2010. *Scared Space: The Quest for Transcendence in Science Fiction Film and Television*. Waco, TX: Baylor University Press.

Curtis, Bruce. 1995. "The Strange Birth of Santa Claus: From Artemis the Goddess and Nicholas the Saint." *Journal of American Culture* 18 (4): 17–32.

Davis, Erik. 1998. *Techgnosis: Myth, Magic and Mysticism in the Age of Information*. New York: Three Rivers Press.

deChant, Dell. 2002. *Sacred Santa: Religious Dimensions of Consumer Culture*. Cleveland, OH: Pilgrim Press.

Detweiler, Craig, and Barry Taylor. 2003. *A Matrix of Meanings: Finding God in Pop Culture*. Grand Rapids, MI: Baker.

Durkheim, Emile. 1915. *The Elementary Forms of Religious Life*. London: Allen and Unwin.

Durkheim, Emile. 1953. *Sociology and Philosophy*. Translated by D. F. Pockock. London: Cohen and West.

Einstein, Mara. 2008. *Brands of Faith: Marketing Religion in a Commercial Age*. London: Routledge.

Eliade, Mircea. 1958. *Patterns in Comparative Religion*. London: Sheed and Ward.

Eliade, Mircea. 1959. *The Sacred and the Profane: The Nature of Religion*. Translated by Willard R. Trask. New York: Harper and Row.

Ellul, Jacques. 1964. *The Technological Society*. Translated by John Wilkinson. New York: Vintage Books.

Flynn, Tom. 1993. *The Trouble with Christmas*. Buffalo, NY: Prometheus Books.

Gillis, John R. 1996. *A World of Their Own Making: Myth, Ritual, and the Quest for Family Values*. New York: Basic Books.

Golby, John M., and A. W. Purdue. 1986. *The Making of the Modern Christmas*. Athens, GA: University of Georgia Press.

Grisham, John. 2001. *Skipping Christmas*. New York: Doubleday.

Hagstrom, Warren O. 1966. "What Is the Meaning of Santa Claus?" *American Sociologist* 1 (November): 248–252.

Heim, Michael. 1993. *The Metaphysics of Virtual Reality*. Oxford: Oxford University Press.

Heinze, Andrew R. 1990. *Adapting to Abundance: Jewish Immigrants, Mass Consumption, and the Search for American Identity*. New York: Columbia University Press.

Hoover, Stewart M. 2000. "The Cross at Willow Creek: Seeker Religion and the Contemporary Marketplace." In *Religion and Popular Culture in America*, edited by Bruce David Forbes and Jeffrey H. Mahan, 145–159. Berkeley, CA: University of California Press.

Horsley, Richard. 2001. "The Gospel of the Savior's Birth." In *Christmas Unwrapped: Consumerism, Christ, and Culture*, edited by Richard Horsley and James Tracy, 113–138. Harrisburg, PA: Trinity Press.

Horsley, Richard, and James Tracy, ed. 2001. *Christmas Unwrapped: Consumerism, Christ, and Culture*. Harrisburg, PA: Trinity Press.

Hulsether, Mark D. 2000. "Like a Sermon: Popular Religion in Madonna Videos." In *Religion and Popular Culture in America*, edited by Bruce David Forbes and Jeffrey H. Mahan, 77–100. Berkeley, CA: University of California Press.

Jones, Charles W. 1978. *Saint Nichols or Myra, Bari, and Manhattan*. Chicago: University of Chicago Press.

Kahney, Leander. 2004. *The Cult of Mac*. San Francisco, CA: No Starch Press.

Kahney, Leander. 2005. *The Cult of iPod*. San Francisco, CA: No Starch Press.

Kozinets, Robert V. 2001. "Utopian Enterprise: Articulating the Meanings of *Star Trek*'s Culture of Consumption." *Journal of Consumer Research* 28 (June): 67–88.

Kozinets, Robert V. 2002. "Can Consumers Escape the Market? Emancipatory Illuminations from Burning Man." *Journal of Consumer Research* 29 (June): 20–39.

Kozinets, Rovert V. 2008. "Technology/Ideology: How Ideological Fields Influence Consumers' Technology Narratives." *Journal of Consumer Research* 35 (April): 865–881.

Kuper, Adam. 1993. "The English Christmas and the Family: Time Out and Alternative Realities." In *Unwrapping Christmas*, edited by Daniel Miller, 157–175. Oxford: Oxford University Press.

Levy, Steven. 2006. *The Perfect Thing: How the iPod Shuffles Commerce, Culture, and Coolness*. New York: Simon and Schuster.

Lyon, David 2000. *Jesus in Disneyland: Religion in Postmodern Times*. Cambridge: Polity.

Marling, Karal Ann. 2000. *Merry Christmas! Celebrating America's Greatest Holiday*. Cambridge, MA: Harvard University Press.

McDannell, Colleen 1995. *Material Christianity: Religion and Popular Culture in America*. New Haven, CT: Yale University Press.

Miller, Daniel. 1993. "A Theory of Christmas," in *Unwrapping Christmas*, edited by Daniel Miller, 3–37. Oxford: Oxford.

Miller, Vincent J. 2004. *Consuming Religion: Christian Faith and Practice in a Consumer Culture* New York: Continuum.

Moeran, Brian, and Lise Skov. 1993. "Cinderella Christmas: Kitsch, Consumerism, and Youth in Japan." In *Unwrapping Christmas* , edited by Daniel Miller, 101–133. Oxford: Oxford: Oxford University Press.

Moore, R. Laurence. 1994. *Selling God: American Religion in the Marketplace of Culture*. Oxford: Oxford University Press.

Muñiz, Albert M., Jr., and Hope Jensen Schau. 2005. "Religiosity in the Abandoned Apple Newton Brand Community." *Journal of Consumer Research* 31 (March): 737–747.

Newall, Venetia. 1989. "A Moslem Christmas Celebration in London." *Journal of American Folklore* 102 (April–June): 186–189.

Nissenbaum, Stephen. 1996. *The Battle for Christmas*. New York: Alfred A. Knopf.

Noble, David F. 1997. *The Religion of Technology: The Divinity of Man and the Spirit of Invention*. New York: Alfred A. Knopf.

O'Cass, Aron, and Peter Clarke. 2002. "Dear Santa, Do You Have My Brand? A Study of the Brand Requests, Awareness and Request Styles at Christmas Time." *Journal of Consumer Behaviour* 2 (1): 37–53.

Otnes, Cele, Kyungseung Kim, and Young Chan Kim. 1994a. "Yes, Virginia, There Is a Gender Difference: Analyzing Children's Requests to Santa Claus." *Journal of Popular Culture* 28 (Summer): 17–30.

Otnes, Cele, Young Chan Kim, and Kyungseung Kim. 1994b. All I Want for Christmas: An Analysis of Children's Brand Requests to Santa Claus." *Journal of Popular Culture* 27 (Spring): 183–195.

Plath, David W. 1963. "The Japanese Popular Christmas: Coping with Modernity." *Journal of American Folklore* 76 (October–December): 309–317.

Pleck, Elizabeth H. 2000. *Celebrating the Family: Ethnicity, Consumer Culture, and Family Rituals*. Cambridge, MA: Harvard University Press.

Restad, Penne L. 1995 *Christmas in America: A History*. Oxford: Oxford University Press.

Ritzer, George. 1999. *Enchanting a Disenchanted World: Revolutionizing the Means of Consumption*. Thousand Oaks, CA: Pine Forge Press.

Roof, Wade. 1999. *Spiritual Marketplace: Baby Boomers and the Remaking of American Religion*. Princeton, NJ: Princeton University Press.

Santino, Jack. 1996. *New Old-Fashioned Ways: Holidays and Popular Culture*. Knoxville, TN: University of Tennessee Press.

Schmidt, Leigh Eric. 1995. *Consumer Rites: The Buying and Selling of American Holidays*. Princeton, NJ: Princeton University Press.

Shachar, Ron, Tülin Erdem, Keisha Cutright, and Gavan Fitzsimons. forthcoming. "Brands: The Opiate of the Nonreligious Masses?" *Marketing Science*, 30 (1): 92–110.

Sheffield, Tricia. 2006. *The Religious Dimensions of Advertising*. New York: Palgrave Macmillan.

Sherry, John F., Jr. 1983. "Gift Giving in Anthropological Perspective." *Journal of Consumer Research* 10 (September): 157–168.

Sherry, John F., Jr., Robert Kozinets, and Stefania Borghini. 2007. "Agents in Paradise: Experiential Co-Creation through Emplacement, Ritualization, and Community." In *Consuming Experience*, edited by Antonella Carú, 34–47. Oxon, UK: Routledge.

Siefker, Phyllis. 1997. *Santa Claus, Last of the Wild Men: The Origins and Evolution of Saint Nicholas Spanning 50,000 Years*. Jefferson, NC: McFarland and Company.

Svehla, Gary J., and Susan Svehla. 1998. *It's Christmas Time at the Movies*. Baltimore, MD: Midnight Marquee Press.

Taylor, Mark C. 1999. *About Religion: Economies of Frith in Virtual Culture*. Chicago: University of Chicago Press.

Thompson, Robert J. 2000. "Consecrating Consumer Culture." In *Religion and Popular Culture in America*, edited by Bruce David Forbes and Jeffrey H. Mahan, 44–55. Berkeley, CA: University of California Press.

Twitchell, James. 2007. *Shopping for God: How Christianity Went from in Your Heart to in Your Face*. New York: Simon and Schuster.

van Renterghem, Tony. 1995. *When Satan Was a Shaman: The Ancient Origins of Santa Claus and the Christmas Tree*. St. Paul, MN: Llewellyn Publications.

Vinge, Joan. 1985. *Santa Claus: The Movie*. New York: Berkley.

Waits, William B. 1993. *The Modern Christmas in America*. New York: New York University Press.

Waldfogel, Joel. 1993. "The Deadweight Loss of Christmas." *American Economic Review* 83 (December): 1328–1336.

Waldfogel, Joel. 2009. *Scroogenomics: Why You Shouldn't Buy Presents for the Holidays*. Princeton, NJ: Princeton University Press.

Wertheim, Margaret. 1999. *The Pearly Gates of Cyberspace*. New York: W. W. Norton.

Zhao, Xin, and Russell Belk. 2005. "Sinolization of a Western Holiday: The Sweethearts' Christmas." *Advances in Consumer Research* 32: 8.

6 Consuming Spirituality and the Spirituality of Consuming Media Narratives
Why Vampirism, Why *Twilight*, Why Now?

Margo Buchanan-Oliver and Hope Jensen Schau

"Myth created by literature has now become the very space of definition of human behavior" (Edwards 1989, p. 102), and "myths determine our . . . culture," representing "constants which transcend history and time" and "reassert basic human needs and desires in the face of adverse social conditions" (p. 104). In Edwards's discussion of *Le Vol du Vampire*, she notes Tournier's assertion that a literary work acts like a vampire, sucking the blood from the reader's imagination in order for a process of identification to be enabled between the text and the reader. The identification is a recognition of the "primordial longing" (p. 105) in readers for the myths of the past. White (1971) extends the reach of Tournier's text to illuminate current mores and times: "Writers . . . are inviting their readers to interpret new experiences in the light of traditional sources of archetypal patterns" (p. 23).

It is just such an approach, drawn from such a mythical repository, that Stephanie Meyer, the author of *The Twilight Saga*, employs. Her media narratives (four novels, three feature films, with another in production and one in planning) play on consumers' primordial fears and desires, deploying mythical characters (vampires, werewolves, gods/goddesses) who are represented from cultural memory and redrawn in the contemporary world(s) of the reader.

THE CULTURAL AND SPIRITUAL TRAJECTORY OF THE VAMPIRE

In this chapter, we will focus on the mythical figure of the vampire and its long cultural and spiritual trajectory in European and American popular consciousness as evidenced in consumption narrative in general and *The Twilight Saga* in particular. However, as Dresser (1989) notes, not only is the *myth* of the vampire subscribed to, but perhaps vampires are themselves real. Her study of 574 persons asked whether they believed that "vampires exist as real entities," to which 27% replied in the affirmative (p. 69), but we constrain discussion to the socio-cultural artifact and discuss the ebb and flow of the cultural reverence for vampirism.

The vampire is an ancient being, globally diffused and folkloric in origin that erupted into the European imagination in the vampire manias of the 1730s. He was considered an enurgumen—the devil's avatar, and his dead body held the "entrapped soul [which] lived eternally under the devil's control" (Twitchell, 1981, p. 8). In early accounts, the vampire was not believed to be a victim of attack but was commonly held to be a sinner, especially a suicide. Such sins against the church carried "sufficient promise of damnation to incite the devil" (p. 9), and "the church, the state, and the community recognized . . . the terrible potency of the vampire myth and capitalized on it to enforce their own standards of conformity" (p. 10).

The crime against God and nature embodied by the vampire was first enacted in his inability to die. Dresser (1981) cites Becker, an anthropologist, who asserts that the truth of the vampire is that "our bodies are our doom . . . regulated by 'earthly laws of blood and animality' and that only the spiritual aspects of man can transcend his lower materialistic self" (p. 154). Whereas humans are condemned to suffer death for our rebellion against God in the Garden of Eden, the vampire is 'free' to experience eternity, the province of the divine and the saved. Consequently, the myth of the vampire "is a perennial horror-passion play reflecting the entire truth of the human condition and the hope [of eternity] beyond it" (Becker, 1975, in Dresser, 1981, p. 154).

The criminality of the vampire is exacerbated further in his drinking of human blood. At a primitive level, this is an act appropriating the vanquished's life force and powers by the victor and, latterly, condemned by the Church (Deuteronomy 12:16; Genesis 9:4; Leviticus 17:11). However, as Twitchell (1981) notes, the paradox inherent in the Christian mythos of the rite of communion, as the path to resurrection and eternal life (John 6:53–57), is predicated on the drinking of blood (sacramental wine) and the eating of flesh (the communion wafer), actions that the vampire mirrors and bodily incorporates. In such trangressive acts are spirituality, religion, and myth intertwined in the figure of the vampire.

ROMANTIC HORROR AND SPIRITUAL RAPTURE

Vampire scholars (Auerbach, 1995; Dresser, 1989; Twitchell, 1981) trace the rise of the vampire from early folkloric sources through to its popular cultural efflorescence in the Romantic novel. Romanticism involved the remembrance of the remote, the dead, and the unknown and carried with it connotations of magic, the suggestive, and the nostalgic (Praz, 1970). These Romantic ideas were embodied in the characters named the Fatal Men, frequently personified as monks: men of "mysterious . . . origin, [exhibiting] burnt-out passions, suspicion of a ghastly guilt, melancholy habits, pale face, [and] unforgettable eyes" (p. 61). They were also exemplified in the figure of the Byronic Hero who exists in a state of moral torture and lives a life saturated with painful/pleasurable sensation: "the great object of life is sensation, to feel that we exist, even though in pain" (pp. 74 and 91, footnote 53). Praz (1970) notes that Byron was not only the progenitor of Romantic heroism but also for the vampiric fashion to follow, as exemplified in Mérimée's story, *Vampire* (in *La Guzla*, 1827), whose accursed hero drags to destruction the woman he loves. Such tales spread quickly throughout Europe and then to the American tales of Poe, in which the desire for "complete fusion with the beloved being . . . ends in vampirism [and] . . . nervous ecstasy" (p. 147). These are the literary tales of terror that Meyer memorializes for her audience and the qualities she ascribes to Edward Cullen, the vampire hero of *The Twilight Saga*.

The Romantic horror inherent in these tales of vampire terror includes both ecstatic dread and exhultation. Horror is dreamlike, uncanny, and the realm of the marvelous, and the monsters we imagine are always " 'out there' . . rising from the ooze of the sub-conscious" (Twitchell, 1985, p. 22) as sublimated projections of fear and desire.

Such sublimation in vampire mythology is enacted in the surrogate sex act and remembered in the relationship between sexual ecstasy and religious ecstasy most vividly represented in St. Teresa of Avila's rapture, which culminates in the piercing of her heart by an angel's flaming dart. Her ecstasy has been understood to be an expression of her spiritual desire to be one with God and of the spiritual reception of the saint by God: "serving Him as lover, even as she becomes Him" (Laguardia, 1980, p. 528). It has also been read as an eroticized transference for her "suppressed sexuality . . . [which is] the representation of an orgasm . . . and rapture metaphors of the same" (Laguardia, 1980, p. 530, footnote 11).

Meyers' descriptions of Bella and Edward's spiritual recognition of each other as soulmates (especially in her references to Edward's eyes, which remember the Fatal Man, the vampire, and the Byronic hero), and their pain and pleasure experienced in the delay of and then the rapturous enactment of their sexual consummation, and the metaphysical transformations that act occasions in Bella are evidence of the "chain of memory" (Hervieu-Léger, 2000) that myth and religion enable. Meyer, in her constant traversing between religious, Romantic, and vampire metaphor, enables an imaginative identification by her readers of the primordial longings that these myths incorporate and encourages her readers to interpret their lives and experiences "in the light of traditional sources of archetypal patterns" (White, 1971). Such a "chain of memory" creates a shared understanding and links individuals to communities of believers in the articulated myths and rites. This acute identification and communality is a feature of *Twilight* fan narratives:

> *Twilight* is about love. True, abiding, affirming, unconditional love. It is about love that is ordained, fated. It is this sort of love that I want someday. . . . I think this love story is what makes fans read the books,

watch the movies and participate in the [fan] community. So many stories these days are about hooking up and inconsequential relationships.
This is a story about commitment that exceeds human desires. The
body is merely an artifact. Edward intends to love Bella into her human
old age. Their love is eternal. . . . When they finally release their carnal
desires the union is blessed—more than just physically satisfying . . . I
want that. (Robin interview, October 22, 2009)

Robin echoes many fans' mythic yearning for a love that surpasses human
frailty and understanding. The *Twilight* community identifies with and
endorses the concept of an eternal love that is built on spiritual commitment to another and can be only partially expressed in physical intimacy.

The Twilight Saga explicitly grapples with spiritual concerns such as the
existence of deities, souls, and afterlives. This is evidenced in fans' discussion:

Edward's eyes are central to the story and often betray him. Bella relies
on Edward's eyes, not his words, to determine the truth from mundane
issues like whether he is 'thirsty', to serious issues regarding his love for
her and his belief in the existence of God. The meaning is very thinly
veiled; eyes are the window to the soul. Bella insists that Edward's eyes
reveal his good intentions and prove he has a soul. (Devone interview,
February 16, 2009)

Here, Devone asserts that the vampire, Edward Cullen, can and does serve
God's will and not the Devil's imperative. Edward's eyes are proof of his
virtue and his soul. Moreover, his suppression of carnal desire and bloodlust are unnatural in the vampire clan and make him unique.

Traditionally, the vampire has acted as a subversive agent enabling the
erotic imagination in the vampiric surrogacy of the sex act to be played out
with deadly physical, moral, and spiritual consequences. For even while
the vampire is conceptualized as wanton, insatiable, and sexually ambivalent, vampiric consummation privileges blood lust over explicit sexual contact. The bodily act of the vampire primarily concerns appropriation of
life force and spiritual domination. Edward and the rest of the Cullens
work tirelessly, at great self-sacrifice, to maintain human life and preserve
spirituality. Even when Bella chides him for his beliefs and begs for sexual
release, Edward holds fast to his convictions in the hopes that Bella's soul
can still be saved. The *Twilight* community reveres this sacrifice and service
to humanity:

Carlisle [Cullen—Edward's father] devotes his existence to helping
humans as a doctor. . . . Edward places Bella's soul above his own
desire and incurs great discomfort. In fact, the Cullens are role models
for loyalty and service. If those aren't righteous objectives, what is?
(Genna interview, October 16, 2009)

This spiritual dimension of the Cullens' vampirism is a chronic tension as most other vampires that inhabit the story are not virtuous, following the traditional vampire bloodlust lore.

THE SIN OF LUST AND VAMPIRIC ASCETICISM?

Previous vampire literature proscribes the immediate gratification of the vampire's blood lust and the pyscho-sexual gratification of the human victim. Such consummation results in the death of the human victim as a result of the vampire act and her consequent damned, eternal search for further gratifications. Consuming the vampire is a subversive act. It is an act against the dominant culture, an act against decency, an act against nature. Rather than physical penetration resulting in new life, the vampiric act results in perversion, in death, and, more importantly, in the creation of the undead—a species unable to be regulated by human governments. The sin of lust that is suppressed in polite society or deferred to the realm of the imagination is unleashed to dominate behavior as a single imperative.

In *Twilight*, the erotic expression of sublimated desire is described in attenuated, excoriating detail, what MacKendrick (1999) calls pleasure-in-tension. The delaying of the act of vampiric penetration, physical penetration, and spiritual union between Edward and Bella (not until the beginning of the fourth novel) may remember transgressive Romantic and religious representations of the voluptuousness of pain and the sado-masochist cannibalism of religious ecstacy, but it presages a change in the status of the figure of the vampire.

An oft quoted passage from the *Twilight* text, where Edward says, "And so the lion fell in love with the lamb," exemplifies this change in status. Bella responds, "What a stupid lamb," to which Edward replies, "What a sick, masochistic lion." This exchange so strongly resonates with the members of the *Twilight* community that they discuss the segment frequently, use it in their signature files in the online forum, create fan art around it, and even tattoo it on their person (see Figure 6.1).

In *The Twilight Saga*, for Bella and Edward (prey and hunter/lamb and lion), these moments of physical penetration and spiritual connection are delayed until marriage. Lust is held in control not by the female human protagonist but by the male vampire; abstinence is endured by Edward despite Bella's persistent desire for consummation.

This is not only an inversion of the vampire myth, the Romantic myth of the Fatal Man, and the Byronic Hero but also inverts cultural expectations of the female figure, *La Belle Dame Sans Merci* (Praz, 1970, p. 199, citing Keats' poem of the same name), who cruelly refuses her lover's advances and condemns her lover to an unsatisfied death. In the *Twilight* media narrative,

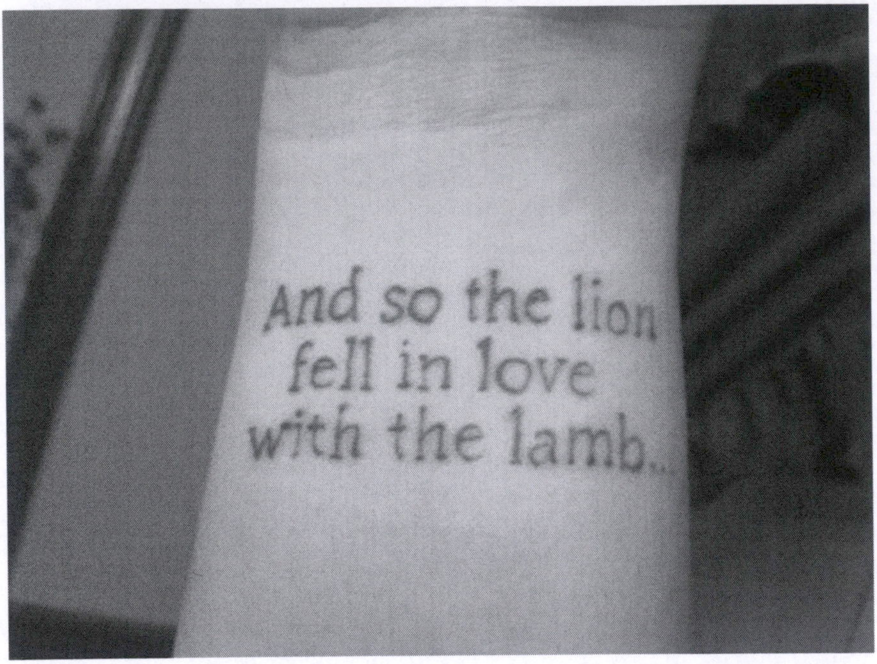

Figure 6.1   Lion quote tattoo.

it is the male who memorializes physical control in order to sanctify marriage and enacts a new spiritual asceticism. Ironically, the female 'victim' reifies the demon of desire, and the vampire is re-written as a sainted monk.

Once again we remember the religious contexts of myth. The religious ascetic—commonly a monk—who lives a life of abstinence and denial of the flesh is also, as Bataille (1957) perversely reminds us, "prompted by desire and desire alone and in this resembles an erotic man." However, his desire is a quest for the grace of God, just as St. Teresa desired. But Edward's monkish restraint—let us dwell here on the paradox of the vampire enacting the central, ascetic, monastic rite of sexual continence—may not only preserve the life of his beloved (if he couples with her as a human, she will die), it is also tempered by his desire to sanctify his love in marriage, keep Bella's soul unblemished (his own is beyond hope), and live a conventional life. The irony of this position for a vampire should not go unnoticed. Indeed, the details of the marriage arrangements, the wedding gown and the ceremony, are lingered over to express the conventional wish fulfillments of Meyer's contemporary audience. *Twilight* fans respond to this traditional approach to marriage and monogamy:

> Bella doesn't want to get married. Her own parents didn't stay married and she doesn't have faith in the institution. . . . Edward tells her that the

divorce rate in the vampire community is much lower. In fact, it seems that vampires mate for their entire existence. . . . Edward insists that while his soul is already lost, he will preserve Bella's at all costs. He wants Bella to have the traditional experience of prom in the first book and in the fourth book he requires that the traditions of marriage and of the wedding ceremony are strictly adhered to. Edward is old-fashioned. He asks Charlie [Bella's father] for his blessing. Bella's dress is white. The relationship is consummated after the wedding. I love that. I want to meet a man who puts my soul about his own desire. I want a mate who loves me above himself. We all want that. (Sara interview, October 11, 2009)

Edward's disciplining of his body and the imposition of his will against lust and desire not only re-enacts a historical religious metanarrative but also symbolically conveys social desire and realities. The metatheme of the *Twilight* narratives concerns questions of choice for the central protagonists: the choice to be good or evil, the choice to be human (mortal) or vampire (eternal), the choice to have sex before marriage or not ("the wages of sin are death"). The religious binaries of choice—good/evil, mortal/eternal, saved/sinner—offered in the text are nowhere more evident than in the use of the religious image of choice/temptation—the apple—in promotional imagery and its prominence in fans' narratives:

The apple is iconic Twi-imagery. It is the forbidden fruit. Bella falls for the vampire, the forbidden love and risks her soul to love him. It is precious. I want to find a love worth risking it all on. (Bailey interview, November 2, 2008)

I know Stephenie is a Mormon but it plays out like any other Catholic or Christian tale. Don't be tempted. Don't go astray. Be a good girl. The twist is that Edward the 'demonic' vampire is the moralizing force. He saves Bella from her own desire and keeps her chaste even though it causes him pain to deny her desire. . . . He may inadvertently offer the apple to Bella, but he won't let her sin. (Miranda interview, May 25, 2010)

See Figures 6.2, 6.3, and 6.4 for pictures depicting *Twilight* apple tattoos that exemplify this temptation in the consumption narrative (and are physically inscribed in fans' lives) and Edward's strict policing of desire to save Bella's soul.

As Auerbach (1995) has charted, the vampire may present as a revolutionary figure, but he is always a reactionary. The vampire tale is always a morality play in which order is restored and social norms are affirmed (Dresser, 1989). The vampire is a mutating phenomenon who embodies the cultural and political mores inherent in the desires and manifestations of fear of the times. For Auerbach, vampires are chameleons who "shape themselves to personal and national moods" (p. 5) and who "go where power is" (p. 6). In

Figure 6.2   Apple and lion quote.

Figure 6.3   Apple tattoo with heart quote.

the American 1920s, 1930s, 1940s, and 1950s, they exemplified the sexual decadence and formality of Europe and in their overthrow asserted American imperial authority; and in their portrayal of social isolation and exclusion, they

Figure 6.4 Apple tattoo.

affirmed the value of the patriarchal familial and communal unit; in the 1960s and 1970s, they explored alternative sexualities via lesbian and homosexual vampirism; in the 1980s, they became mortal in the face of the AIDS epidemic and became agents of oppression for "the restored patriarchal family" (p. 181); in the 1990s, they become 'good'—good women, good citizens, good family members; their blood feeding became "the exchange" (p. 185)—an empathetic act. They retreat to the margins of society segregated from the mass and are, therefore, as exemplars of the "Other" complicit in a restorative paternalistic morality (p. 187). It is this latter manifestation that the *Twilight* narratives vivify, reflecting the socio-cultural mores of early 21st-century times. The characters and the results of their actions can be seen as mapping to a neo-conservative desire in the socio-cultural and religious framings of America, which manifests itself in binaries of good and evil, patriarchal dominance, and the triumph of right (Lyon, 2000). As Lind (2004), asserts:

For the neoconservatives, religion is an instrument of promoting moral-ity . . . in order to ensure social order." (Curtis, *The Power of Night-mares: The Rise of the Politics of Fear*, BBC Documentary 2004)

The Vampire and Neoconservatism

Neoconservativism is described by Schneider (1999) as religiosity, family values, authoritativeness, and materialism, and in North America he notes the high appreciation of religious identities by contemporary males and females. Mishra (1989) further notes neoconservatism's populist approach, its authoritarian social doctrine with its emphasis on the traditional family and traditional gender roles and its need to maintain law and order (pp. 173–174), whereas Evans (1989) comments on the role of the family as a "universal, traditional . . . homogenous social form because biologically natural and God-given," which perceives that any threat to the family is a "social demoralization [which] threatens the natural order" (p. 83). These are contemporary socio-cultural and political themes that fans explore in their reflections on the texts:

> Edward is chivalrous. He denies his own pleasure to keep Bella virtu-ous even though he has given up on his own virtue. . . . Bella, although resistant, finds herself a mother whose only ambition is keeping her baby safe and her man pleased. So despite her initial faux assertions of feminism, she falls into the traditional mode. I'm not sure I like that les-son, but it is surprising how Twi-moms is the biggest [*Twilight*] forum online. (Claudia interview, February 10, 2009)

Claudia is disconcerted that the narrative centers on this 'faux' or inauthen-tic feminism but notes that the largest *Twilight* community is composed of mothers who, when you read the forums, appear to uphold traditional gender roles.

> I don't know what the harm is in having a story that favors sex within marriage. Sure monogamy isn't modern and definitely not postmodern, but at the end of the day, what's wrong with sex being more than a momentary distraction? Girls should reconsider their own worth and not sell themselves short. After all, biology dictates that we live with the material consequences of sex. We have the babies. We get more of the diseases. (Daniela interview, January 6, 2010)

Here, Daniela indicates that controlling sex is a biological imperative. Women are more vulnerable than men, in that they are by nature left with the consequences of their desires and have increased responsibilities.

Through these themes, Meyer may be seen to be mirroring a neocon-servative lens. As *Brittanica Online Encyclopedia* notes (Neoconservatism

[Political Philosophy], p. 3), neoconservatives pay attention to cultural matters and the mass media because they believe that "a society defines itself and expresses its values through these means." Because society has become "amoral, adrift and degenerate" due to the " 'adversarial' counterculture of the 1960's, which dismissed traditional values and religion as old-fashioned, irrelevant, or even reactionary" they advocate religion as "a kind of social cement." There is certainly a moral worldview in *The Twilight Saga* that is recognized in this review:

> This intense movie [*Eclipse*] has plenty of thrilling moments and moral worldview elements that almost overcome its occult origins as a vampire story and its use of pagan American Indian mythology to fashion a moral tale about good versus evil. As such, it also supports marriage before sexual activity, protection of the weak, and setting aside one's differences with others to fight great evil. (*Christian Movie Review*)

Lyon (2000) recognizes religion's transformative power and notes that religion "has to do with faith, identity, and non-cognitive aspects of life, such as emotion" (p. 23). Fans of *The Twilight Saga* speak with high emotion about its transformative impact on their lives and their views of family, motherhood, and traditional gender roles:

> I want it all like Bella. I want to be a wife, a mother, a gorgeous immortal woman who can kick ass. . . . I might even stay home and walk barefoot through the kitchen if I could have it all. (Sasha interview, February 18, 2009)

Yet, there is an inherent tension in these narratives that may reflect more complexity in American social realities. Certainly, there is the male invocation to 'just say no' to sex before marriage; male control of the courtship and the insistence on marriage; the transformation experienced by the female through marriage; the fulfillment of motherhood; and the privileging of the family unit. These are all neoconservative concepts. But there is also the transformation of the female protagonist, Bella, into the most powerful being of the vampire clan; her unique ability to reconcile warring factions; her declarations of sexual desire; and her gendered ability to bring forth a daughter borne of hybrid beings—humans and vampires—who will be the most powerful being of them all. What are we to make of these liminalities? Where are the moral absolutes of good (human, religious) versus evil (vampires, occult)? Where is the overarching patriarchy in the supernatural power accreted to Bella and her daughter, Renesmee? Where is the dominant male voice in these narratives that invokes right and dispenses justice amongst warring clans? As one fan explains:

Some people try to tell me that Bella is weak and that Edward is controlling. Well, Edward may want to be in control but when Bella gets pregnant, she insists on having the baby. When Bella is a newborn vampire, she is stronger. When the final conflict comes, Bella is the most gifted immortal . . . In fact, many of the female characters are strong: Jane, Alice, Victoria. . . . Renesmee is gifted and brilliant. Carlisle [Cullen, Edward's father] leads by consensus. Mates are equal partners. In the *Twilight* world women can definitely hold their own. Can't these Twi-haters read? (Caitlin interview, March 12, 2010)

Perhaps these are instances of the uncertainties of our postmodern world in which differing socio-cultural, religious, and political agendas and competing individual and communal identities collapse together to create multiple realities about ourselves and the myths that reflect us, creating a "bricolage of beliefs" (Lyon, 2000, p. 18). In this way, perhaps we are more like the vampire than we know: a liminal, mutable creature reshaped by each generation to serve their needs and desires. In this "bricolage of belief," *Twilight* can be read as both a celebration of and a riposte to the stereotype of neoconservative religious practice.

Twilight is a media brand that is inherently spiritual and spiritually consumed. It is at once about spirituality, spiritual meanings of consumption, and the commodification of mass worship. It is about spirituality in that it raises sexuality above the momentary hedonic experience. It also problematizes questions about souls and morality. It collapses the erotic imaginary of the vampire with the rapture of the sex act and religious rapture, and it vivifies the sublimation of the body in the life of the ascetic.

But perhaps most interestingly, it deploys a historical figure of sin and transgression—the vampire—to instruct in traditional morality and reflect the neoconservative and spiritual tenor of the times. We should not be surprised. Auerbach (1995) reminds us of the perennial attraction the figure has always offered as a cultural consumption site and of its mutability:

Posing as revolutionaries, they [vampires] are consummate turncoats, more formidable in their flexibility than their love, their occult powers, or their lust for blood. It is impossible either to exorcise or to trust a species whose immortality has given them supreme adaptability. (p. 8)

REFERENCES

Auerbach, Nina. 1995. *Our Vampires, Ourselves*. Chicago and London: University of Chicago Press.

Bataille, Georges. 1957. *Erotism: Death and Sensuality*. Translated by Mary Dalwood. San Francisco: City Light Books.

Becker, Ernest. 1975. *Escape from Evil*. New York: Free Press.

Dresser, Norinne. 1989. *American Vampires: Fans, Victims and Practitioners.* New York: W. W. Norton and Company.

Edwards, Rachel. 1989. "Myth, Allegory and Michel Tournier." *Journal of European Studies* 19: 99–121.

Evans, David T. 1989. "Section 28: Law, Myth and Paradox." *Critical Social Policy* 9: 73–95.

Hervieu-Léger, Danièle. 2000. *Religion as a Chain of Memory.* Great Britain: Polity Press.

Laguardia, Gari. 1980. "Santa Teresa and the Problem of Desire." *Hispania* 63 (3): 523–531.

Lind, Michael 2004. In *The Power of Nightmares: The Rise of the Politics of Fear,* produced by Adam Curtis, BBC Two Documentary, shown October 20–November 3. Accessed April 20, 2011. http://en.wikipedia.org/wiki/Neoconservatism

Lyon, David. 2000. *Jesus in Disneyland: Religion in Postmodern Times.* Cambridge, MA: Polity Press.

MacKendrick, Karmen. 1999. *Counterpleasures.* Albany: State University of New York Press.

Mérimée, Prosper. 1827. "*Vampire*", in *La Guzla, ou choix de poésies illyriques recueillies dans la Dalmatie, la Bosnie, la Croatie et l'Herzégowine.* Paris: F.-G. Levrault.

Mishra, Ramesh. 1989. "Riding the New Wave: Social Work and the Neo-Conservative Challenge." *International Social Work* 32 (17): 171–182. "Neoconservatism (Political Philosophy)," *Britannica Online Encyclopedia.* Accessed April 20, 2011. http://www.britannica.com/EBchceked/topic/1075556/neoconservatism.

Praz, Mario. 1970. *The Romantic Agony.* London and New York: Oxford University Press.

Schneider, Andreas. 1999. "US Neo-Conservatism: Cohort and Cross-Cultural Perspective." *International Journal of Sociology and Social Policy* 19 (12): 56–86.

"Twilight Saga: Eclipse: It All Begins with a Choice." *Christian Movie Review.* Accessed April 20, 2011. http://www.movieguide.org/reviews/movie/the-twilight-saga-eclipse.html.

Twitchell, James. 1981. *The Living Dead: A Study of the Vampire in Romantic Literature.* Durham, NC: Duke University Press.

———. 1985. *Dreadful Pleasures: An Anatomy of Modern Horror.* London and New York:Oxford University Press.

White, John, J. 1971. *Mythology in the Modern Novel: A Study of Prefigurative Techniques* Princeton, NJ: Princeton University Press.

7 The Devil Has All the Best Brands
Raising Hell in a House of Horrors

Stephen Brown

Through me is the way to the city of woe.
Through me is the way to eternal pain.
Through me is the way of the damned.
Abandon all hope, ye who enter here.

—Dante, *Divina Commedia: Inferno*, Canto 3

The road to hell, as each and every one of you knows, is paved with good intentions. Well, I'm here to tell you folks that it's also strewn with off-ramps and on-ramps and confusing cloverleaf junctions, to say nothing of signposts and stop lights and toll booths and traffic jams and contraflows and cone zones and spiralling slip roads to subterranean parking garages, the nine circles of hell of our time.

Dante didn't know the half of it, amigos. Harken to a tale of horror.[1]

My intentions, let me state openly at the outset, were good. Everything started swimmingly, what's more. Our tickets were booked beforehand, Express Plus tickets no less. Our Bates brand theme motel was within easy driving distance of Universal Studios, the second-largest tourist trap in the Sunshine State. The immigration officers at Orlando International Airport let me through relatively unmolested (hey, what's a full-body cavity search between friends?), and the counter staff at Alamo car rental went the extra mile, as you'd expect. True, our flight from London was delayed—Dante had his Virgil, I made do with Virgin—and we got in pretty late. I had very little sleep before our big day and was denied my necessary flagon of extra-strong coffee before setting off. "What's the hurry?" I naively asked my darling daughters. "Sure, there's plenty of time before it opens. Time for a waffle or several or even a stack of delicious American-style pancakes, swimming in maple syrup. Just like the good old days in Wisconsin Dells, when you were little."

The girls looked at me askance. Their memories of Wisconsin Dells evidently differed from my own.[2] Indifferent to my entreaties, they took their seats in the Chevy. Seatbelts fastened, arms folded, lips pursed, they waited until I caved in to their implacable demands, which wasn't long once my wife sided with the rebels. Whimpering, in vain, for a Starbucks or something, I settled myself behind the wheel, slipped the Chevy into gear, and, thanks to a combination of clutchlessness, cluelessness, and coffeeless-ness, kangaroo-hopped through the parking lot past the picture-windowed restaurant. "Beatrice," our brittle-voiced sat-nav, was still speaking to me at this stage, although it was hard to hear her over the tutting, spluttering, and all too audible eyeball rolling. The passengers had a point, in fairness, because my record with rentals is less than distinguished. Car hire clerks still talk about me, I'm reliably informed, in the environs of Salt Lake City, where my importunate demands at the Hertz desk were surpassed only by my untimely encounter with a tow truck. But let's not go there, brothers and sisters. Once was more than enough for anybody.[3]

Such unhappy memories, of course, were far from my mind as we cruise-controlled our way toward International Drive, while Beatrice kept us on track with occasional omnipotent interjections. Arabica deprivation aside, I was in as good a mood as I get (i.e., somewhere between wrong-side-of-the-bed and bear-with-a-sore-head). Yes, the traffic was heavy. Yes, congestion was rife. Yes, I was struggling with the left-hand/right-hand drive switcheroo, as eighteen-wheelers whizzed past, air-horns parping like the Last Trump. Yes, the interstate experience was hellish, purgatorial, the automotive equivalent of eternal damnation. However, we were wending our way to the one and only Wizarding World of Harry Potter, the biggest thing to hit the theme park industry since Six Flags Over Guantánamo. What's not to like?

I should perhaps explain at this early stage in the proceedings that I belong to a family of Potterphiles. My daughters are in the demographic sweet-spot for the boy wizard brand, and both my wife and I are big fans of the books. If truth be told, I started to lose interest around volume five of the seven-novel saga because I felt that the books were becoming a bit bloated and, if not exactly boring, much less brilliant than before. My better half and her daughters would have none of this, though. Harry Potter just got better and better and better as far as they were concerned. Arguments to the contrary were neither brooked nor entertained. Accordingly, every new book was bought on the day of release. Every new movie was attended over the opening weekend. Every extras-stuffed DVD was pre-ordered on Amazon and then viewed on repeat, on repeat, on repeat. As if that weren't enough, every audio-book was acquired—initially on cassette, CD thereafter—and listened to *ad nauseam* during boring car journeys. Unlike many besotted aficionados, admittedly, we never actually queued at midnight for the latest brick-sized bulletin about The Boy Who Lived. But, all things considered, our commitment to the series was absolute. As a family, we adored Harry Potter. As a family, we worshipped the brand. As a family, we deified J. K. Rowling. As a family, we venerated Hogwarts, glorified Hagrid, revered Hermione, idolised Hippogriffs, and prayed that Harry and Co. would survive their apocalyptic encounters with Lord Voldemort, which they invariably did, praise be to God. As a family, in short, we were duty bound to make the pilgrimage to Harry's shrine in Universal Studios, where the Wizarding World was packing them in.

The last three words are all-important, compadres, because "packing them in" was my undoing. That and the unfortunate Starbucks shortfall, previously described. Things started to go awry at the main entrance, just off Universal Boulevard, when Beatrice was unaccountably struck dumb and the parking garage alternatives on offer were much too much for the driver's befuddled brain. Hence, I may have missed a turn or two or three or more. However, instead of supportive words of encouragement for their endearingly hapless, characteristically scatter-brained father, whose bottomless pocketbook had been plumbed full fathom five for this worshipful trip, my passengers were unsparing in their censure, unspoken though it was.

"What's the rush?" I joshed once more. "There's plenty of time, ladies. It doesn't open until 9.00 a.m. It's only 8.30. A leisurely breakfast, a cup of coffee, a . . . whoops, missed the turn again."

The communal screech spoke volumes; seven hefty volumes of Harry Potter adulation, all told. Clearly I was missing something. The girls were as pumped as I'd ever seen them. They were ready to rumble and then some. How was I to know that The Wizarding World of Harry Potter was unable to cope with the crowds? How was I to know that they were turning people away at the entrance and telling them to come back another day? How was I to know that the lines for the rides were so long that they stretched all the way to Walt Disney's rival resort down the road, much to Mickey and Minnie's annoyance? How the hell was I to know that my own "torment the customer" imperative had been taken so literally by Harry Potter's Mephistophelean marketing department? Surely nobody pays any attention to academics. Surely nobody bothered to read my flatulent article in *HBR*.[4] Surely nobody believed me when I claimed that denial marketing turns diffident customers into slavering lustomers. Surely I wasn't going to suffer under a marketing lash of my own making.

Lashing was the least of my problems.

After much moan-inducing manoeuvring and more than a few imaginary daggers plunged into my unprotected back by appreciative family members, we descended to the "Spiderman" level of Universal's gigantic parking garage. I felt like something of a superhero myself, having gotten there in one piece and without the benefit of Beatrice's robotic commands. But my daughters didn't see it that way. With nary a word of thanks, the car doors were flung open before the Chevy had stopped. Unfettered, the girls were up and away, power-walking towards the staircase, my wife in hot pursuit. Mustering what little dignity I possessed—as a sagacious scholar at an illustrious, ivy-clad academic institution, I naturally endeavour to remain dignified at all times—I locked up, looked around, and lumbered after them with a mega-grande latte in mind. A monster muffin, maybe. A calorie-engorged cinnabon, even. Heck, I'm on holiday. Relax. Rejoice. Refuel. Recovery position. . . .

I mounted the stairs. I boarded an escalator at "The Simpsons" level. I ascended past "E.T." and the "Hulk" and then found myself in the middle of a vast glass-vaulted walkway, which stretched into the far distance. I could just see my darling daughters one hundred yards ahead, picking their way through the surprisingly enormous crowds at this ungodly hour.

Before going any further, I feel obliged to inform you that, desk-shackled sluggard though I am, I haven't completely gone to seed. I work out once in a while. I keep within spitting distance of fit. I jog six times per week, except when the weather's bad (as it often is in Ireland). I own a rowing machine, which I'll get round to using one of these days (it's right beside the dusty multi-gym in my garage). I am, if not exactly a finely-tuned athlete (let alone a buff habitué of Muscle Beach), in fairly good shape for my age. Granted, that shape is ever-more malformed as my body gradually disintegrates on its bone yard-bound journey. But compared to some of the morbidly obese Americans waddling along the moving walkway, with a wallow and a wheeze, I was a veritable spring chicken. Had I been smeared in KFC's secret blend of herbs and spices, I might have been in trouble with the famished among them. As it was, I sailed past the slow-moving multitudes and caught up with Linda and the girls where the walkway spilled onto Universal Citywalk, a hyperreal urban assortment of stores and bars and cinemas and restaurants and—bliss was it in that dawn to be alive—a friendly neighbourhood Starbucks.

There is no time to tarry, I was told. Try to keep up, I was instructed. Breakfast can wait, I was informed. Muffins are fattening, I was reminded. A teeny-weenie take-out espresso is so not on the agenda right now, I was notified with asperity. A tiny tantrum was thrown. A desolate tear was shed. A comforting thumb may have been sucked at some point, although I can't be certain. All I recall is that my pleas were ignored as we sped through Citywalk's ersatz streets. We flew past Fossil, zoomed by Katie's Candy Company, hot-footed it around Pat O'Brien's authentic Irish pub, leapt down the steps outside Jimmy Buffet's Margaritaville, with its seaplane becalmed in Lone Palm concrete, and hurtled across a lagoon-spanning bridge to Islands of Adventure's so-called Port of Entry. The box office, basically.

The crowds were big, in every sense of the word. The sun was up, as it usually is in the Sunshine State. The temperature was rising steadily, the humidity ditto. Things were going to get real ugly, real soon. But not for us. Thirty seconds later, we were in, high-fiving *en famille*. The bovine herd looked on in fury, but they only had themselves to blame. They should have bought Express Plus tickets beforehand, like we did. Better luck next time, mother-suckers!

Ordinarily, I'm sure you agree, a tiny moment of theme park triumph would be celebrated with a delicious Danish pastry at Ali Baba's coffee bar, right next to the Port of Entry. Not on this occasion. Dismissing my whinging and wheedling and weeping and wailing, the girls galloped off, God knows where. We darted down a street that looked like a plastic homage to the Prince of Persia, complete with phoney minarets, pseudo souks, and pre-recorded calls of multi-cultural-minded muezzins. We crossed another bridge over troubled water, which was tightly wrapped in the bright green coils of an Incredible Hulk roller-coaster, only to find ourselves in a New York lookalike, where the buildings were bedecked with gigantic cut-outs of Spiderman, Thor, the Silver Surfer, and several additional Marvel marvels. Stan Lee, it seems, is alive and well and art-directing in Orlando, although I wasn't given time to pay my respects.

We hurried past Dr. Doom's Free Fall, a ride that rises 150feet into the air and then drops its passengers faster than gravity—eat your heart out, Isaac Newton—then made our way through the Toon Lagoon, which boasts Popeye and Bluto's Bilge Barges, as well as a wet 'n' wild log flume that'd put hairs on the chest of a lumberjack or a dampener on his libido at least. We rounded a corner, panting. The gates of Jurassic Park—yes, *those* gates, the iconic gates from the movie—lay directly ahead. I turned to the girls and said, "We're not in Kansas anymore." They looked back at me, less out of love than pity, wondering whether it was wise to be seen in public with this man. I think we already know the answer to that, Toto.

There was only one problem. The gates of Jurassic Park were locked. Or, rather, a metal barrier had been placed across the access road, and security staff stood sentinel on either side, unsmiling. Stopped in our tracks by this unanticipated turn of events, the girls soon brought me up to speed. The Harry Potter part of the park opened at 9.15 a.m., and, for some reason known only to Universal Studios, they held the crowds back a little while longer. It was for safety purposes, apparently. No it wasn't, I replied mirthlessly, it was for consumer psychology purposes because it ramped up the excitement, the enthusiasm, the expectation, and, on this particular occasion, the rage of an ageing marketing academic who recognised tormenting the customer when he saw it but never actually expected to get hoist by his own petard. This wasn't so much torment as torture. This was satanic. This was demonic. This was iniquitous. This was living proof of my late mother's words of Biblical wisdom: "Be sure your sins will find you out."

It was good to get a breather, though. We were nearly there. We could see our destination, Hogwarts Castle, looming over the Jurassic Park treetops. Conspiratorially, the girls quickly outlined their strategy, which they'd assembled from stray comments on various social networking websites. Our objective was to get to Hogwarts pronto because that's where the signature ride, Harry Potter and the Forbidden Journey, was situated. A moment's delay could mean hours in line. Seriously. There was no time to hang about. As soon as the barrier came down, it was hell for leather, all systems go-go-go, devil take the hindmost. "Don't dilly-dally, daddy. No dithering. No dawdling. No dandering.⁵ No way."

And there was me thinking that we were on holiday, a nice relaxing break from the belting rain back in Belfast. Damn you and all your devilish work, Rowling! May your name go down in infamy alongside Judas, Caligula, Savonarola, and Simon Cowell. Several years ago, when God-fearing religious fundamentalists burnt Harry Potter books as sacrilegious testaments to witchcraft, wizardry, and wickedness, I poked fun at their neo-medieval attitudes.[6] A decade later, I ruefully realise they were right all along.

Right or wrong, it was time to get medieval on the asses of the surrounding throng, which simmered in the early-morning sunshine. The crowd had built up considerably on account of Universal's fan frenzy-fanning tactic. Everyone was anxious. Everyone was twitchy. Everyone was waiting for the off. It was like the start of the London Marathon. Except in Jurassic Park. In Orlando. In the hot, hot heat of the Sunshine State.

A uniformed guard made an officious announcement. "Running is not permitted in the park." However, her protective clothing belied the stentorian statement. She'd clearly been trampled in the past. Either that or she'd had a close encounter with a voracious velociraptor. Or possibly her cosmetic surgery had gone tits-up, so to speak. But who am I to talk?

The barrier was removed in three shakes of a pterodactyl's tail, and, surging forward as one, phalanxes of Potterphiles plunged into the sainted Steven Spielberg's theme park within a theme park. The collective pace was slow to start, but once the security personnel were behind us, all pretence was abandoned, along with the halt, the lame, and the physically incapacitated. Perambulation be damned. Accelerate or else. Ain't no saunter, sister. Faster pussycat, kill, kill. . . .

Now, I'm not exactly proud of what happened next. I'm only 'fessing up because I cannot tell a lie. In my honorary capacity as the George Washington of postmodern consumer research, where nothing less than absolute Truth will do, I'm duty bound to furnish an unflinching account of the horrors that I witnessed and, yes, participated in to my everlasting shame. Look, it wasn't my fault that the buck-toothed ten-year-old behind me ran straight into my bony elbow. And, anyway, American orthodontists can do wonders for youngsters nowadays. Nor, for that matter, was I to blame when the sprightly senior citizen in front tripped over his own feet (after his trailing leg inadvertently clipped mine). I stopped to help him up but stomped on his twisted ankle by accident and, well, I couldn't really stick around after that. There is no truth, by the way, in the scurrilous rumour that I fibbed to speeding soccer mom about a ravenous T-Rex right behind her. Granted, she glanced around whilst sprinting, forgot to look where she was going, and collided with a rock-hard tree trunk, regrettably. But it had nothing to do with me. You know what women are like when it comes to way-finding. The female brain wasn't wired with a sense of direction. It's scientifically proven. Just ask Beatrice.

The real problem, you must appreciate, is competition. It does funny things to people. It renders them bestial, brutish, sub-human. It awakens the devil within. Not me, obviously, because I am a paragon of virtue who wouldn't dream of toppling trashcans on a steep incline so that they bounce and bound and barrel into the unsuspecting crowds below, bowling over entire extended families like ninepins, and bulldozing through large parties of boy scouts, who are supposed to be prepared for untoward occurrences. I gather there's a badge for surviving trashcan cascades, although I might have been misinformed.

Be that as it may, there's a lesson here for ivory tower academics who sit in their plush offices penning "critical" articles about the horrors of capitalism, the cheating, the lying, the malfeasance, and more. Meanwhile, the poor bloody marketing infantry on the front line—the guys who are trying to make the sale, move the merchandise, close the deal or deliver on time—are caught up in a life or death struggle that's not of their own making but can't be avoided, otherwise they'll also fall victim. The killing fields of capitalism are full of bleeding-heart managers who do good all the way to the gallows. Even the most Jekyll of organisations can end up as a Hyde of themselves. Google, for example.[7]

Indeed, much the same could be said about many big name brands, from Nestlé to Nike, from Facebook to Ford, from Sony to Starbucks, although I'd forgive the latter anything for a Frappuccino right now. My point is that there's an angel and a demon within everyone, corporations included. The devil might not have all the best brands, but, given sufficient time, he has his wicked way with most of them.

Anyway, to return to my trail of woe, we managed to wend our way through dinosaur central—up hill, down dale, selflessly stopping to help those less fortunate than ourselves—and into the one, the only, The Wizarding World of Harry Potter. Studious family that we are, we made a bee-line for Hogwarts School of Witchcraft and Wizardry. Unbelievably, however, there were still a few people ahead of us. Despite our very best bat-out-of-hell endeavours, we weren't at the head of the line. Clearly, some kind of skulduggery was afoot. The miscreants up front must have cheated, or sneaked through a side entrance, or had best buddies working for Universal, or, unforgivably, bribed their way into Harry's holy of holies. Whatever the reason, it wasn't acceptable to those of us who got there fair and square. Retribution had to be exacted, if only on behalf of all the innocent customers who'd been injured on the fast 'n' furious footslog to Hogwarts.

Perched atop its concrete crag, Hogwarts was a monument to the plastic arts, polypropylene in particular. Although it looked impressive from the outside, the interior consisted of a huge holding pen, taped off this way and that to channel the seething swarms of Pottermanes. The monotony was broken by themed tableaux taken from the mega-selling novels and movie adaptations—the Mirror of Erised, the Goblet of Fire, the headmaster's office, the Dark Arts classroom, the Gryffindor common room, long corridors with walking, talking portraits, an animatronic Professor Dumbledore who informed us, in Michael Gambon's suspect Irish accent, that the ride was just around the corner, although it was an awfully long corner.

Contrived this may have been, not to say downright cheesy, but it afforded ample opportunities to chastise those who had cheated their way ahead of the Brown hounds. Readers of a nervous disposition are advised to skip the next two paragraphs. But most of you, I'm sure, can appreciate that something had to be done to those who abuse the system and take advantage of law-abiding families who'd flown all the way from Ireland on an overcrowded and understaffed Virgin flight where we were forced to watch a truly ghastly video of Richard Branson telling us how wonderful the Virgin experience was going to be, except that it wasn't. The flight was delayed, the plane was packed, the leg room was minimal, the food was diabolical, the entertainment system was infernal, and a couldn't-care-less flight attendant spilt a cup of complimentary coffee over me—tepid coffee, luckily—and then disdainfully handed me a wad of napkins to dry myself off. Evidently, it was entirely my fault for disrupting her routine. Worse, while sitting there surrounded by discarded tissues, I looked less like a drowned rat than a dirty rat who'd been watching the porn channel all the way to Orlando. It was fifteen minutes max, I swear.

There's only one thing worse than standing in line, and that is standing in line behind shilly-shalliers. The seven-strong party in front, all dressed like lapsed slackers—plaid shirts, low-slung pants, bulging backpacks, Timberland boots from the Bigfoot range—were led by a school-marmish alpha mom who insisted on pausing at every single tableau, oohing and aahing and oh-my-godding, prior to posing for photograph after photograph after photograph. We couldn't get past. Steps had to be taken. Noticing that one of her oversized shoelaces was undone, I knelt down and tied it around a stanchion while she was pontificating about Hufflepuff, Slytherin, the Marauders Map, or some such Hogwartian arcana. When she tried to move on, mayhem ensued. We slipped through in the melee. Better yet, her hysterical reaction unsettled the group directly ahead. Seizing the moment, I ran my fingers up the exposed spine of their leader, casually mentioning that there was a big hairy spider on her back. How was I to know that she was a recovering arachnophobe? People like that shouldn't go into cobwebby places where big hairy spiders are known to foregather. What was she thinking of? I ask you! Frankly, my friends, it's difficult to be sympathetic towards the idiotic amongst us, although there was absolutely no excuse for what happened next. Cynical doesn't begin to describe it. The poor woman was sobbing and screeching and twisting and turning while trying desperately to remove the phantom arachnid. Someone—I know not who—shouted "Fire!!", an exclamation whose impact in a crowded theatre is nothing compared with a theme park holding pen.

It is of course wicked to take advantage of the afflicted. Still, in that frozen moment, before the stampede for the emergency exits commenced, we must have sidled past at least fifty stricken holidaymakers. Hey, we had Express Plus tickets, and, although they didn't actually cover the Forbidden Journey ride, people who pay extra have additional inalienable rights throughout Universal's family-friendly empire. I'm pretty sure they do, anyhow.

Whatever you think of our tactics—and don't pretend you'd do otherwise—we got to the head of the queue, or pretty damn close to it. After being snugly fitted into our "enchanted bench," a four-abreast car with over-the-shoulder restraints, we waited for Harry Potter and the Forbidden Journey to begin, excitement mounting all the while. It was only 9.25 a.m., and by this stage, I was running on my reserve tank of caffeine from the day before—Virgin brand caffeine, which wasn't so much good to the last drop as foul from the first sip.

With a whoosh like a turbo-charged broomstick, our dark ride took off and soared skywards. Thanks to its unique robocoaster technology, prodigious wrap-around projection screens, and the finest audiomatronic soundtrack this side of a Lady Gaga gig, we soon found ourselves flying over the Hogwarts battlements, skimming above the Black Lake, plunging into the Forbidden Forest, and participating in a pick-up quidditch match while being pursued by dragons, tormented by Dementors, thumped by whomping willows, spat at by Aragog's heaving nest of spiders—I was doing that arachnophobe a favour, believe me—and cornered in the Chamber of Secrets by nefarious Lord Voldemort himself. The ride took a grand total of five minutes. Or it would have done if the robocoaster technology hadn't broken down, leaving us hanging at a steep angle while staring into the fang-filled face of an icy-breathed basilisk. Several minutes passed before they managed to restart the thing. However, the magic of the experience had evaporated by then, and they didn't even offer us another go in recompense. Fair enough, we could have re-joined the line and waited our turn once more. But by the time we exited through the gift shop—sorry, Filch's Emporium of Confiscated Goods—the queue was already well past the "one-hour wait" signpost. Many were muttering imprecations as they smouldered in the baking heat. Apparently there'd been some kind of kerfuffle in the hallowed halls of Hogwarts. Whatever next? Where will it end? Some people just don't know how to behave nowadays. They spoil the fun for everyone.

But not for us. We strolled into the nearby village of Hogsmeade, all higgledy-piggledy buildings, faux snow-dusted rooftops and sales opportunities beyond number: Honeydukes sweet shop, Zonko's joke shop, Dervish and Banges magic shop, Ollivanders wand shop, and what have you. They were all present and correct and heaving with people. There was no sign of a Cruciatus coffee shop, sadly. Beverage-wise, it was butterbeer or nothing. In desperation, I bought a bottle of the baleful brew and chugged it down before discretion kicked in. My daughters asked what it was like prior to taking a tentative sip. "I can't believe it's not butterbeer," I quipped, to stony-faced familial indifference. Actually, it tasted more like fermented dragon droppings, IMHO, although I believe the pumpkin juice's even worse. Distilled ogre booger, allegedly.

There was no alternative but to talk our way into The Three Broomsticks, a restaurant-café arrangement smack dab in the middle of downtown Hogsmeade. The uniformed *maître d'* wouldn't let us in without a booking. "We sent it by Owl Post," I wisecracked. He'd heard that one before. He'd also heard the ones about Floo powder, portkeys, and apparating at empty tables for four. He'd heard them on countless occasions, judging by the testiness of his demeanour. "And *Avada Kedavra* to you too, I said cheerily, as we retreated, defeated, to Flight of the Hippogriff, a feeble family roller-coaster that looked like a Coney Island cast-off circa 1950. One drop, two turns, three minutes, four underwhelmed punters later, we were back on the crowded streets of Hogsmeade. "Where to next," I groaned. "Let's shop!" the ladies chorused in unison.

As a marketing evangelist who rejoices in retailing, believes in branding, adores advertising campaigns, worships word-of-mouth, and regards merchandising as little short of miraculous, I suppose I should have exulted in the glory of Rowling's gift-glut. Every character in the HP books had T-shirts and sweatshirts and hoodies to his or her name, in all sorts of sizes and colours and price points. Every tangible object referred to in the seven-volume saga, from invisibility cloaks and sorting hats to sneakoscopes and extendable ears, was on sale in one or more of the emporia. Every line of confectionary imagined by J. K. Rowling—Ton-Tongue Toffee, Bertie Bott's Beans, Pepper Imps, Ice Mice, Chocolate Frogs, Fainting Fancies, and so forth—was flying out the doors of Honeydukes. Every Hogwarts house had a huge array of crest-emblazoned collectibles, knick-knacks, gee-gaws, and bric-a-brac: books and stationary, bedspreads and linens, cosmetics and unguents, coffee mugs and tea towels, and more wizard/witch apparel than you could shake a broomstick at. There were plenty of broomsticks, too.

It was the magic wands that got to me. Ollivander's Wand Shop was not only jam-packed with punters, but a long line of wannabe wand owners stood outside, patiently waiting their turn. The queue, I kid you not, was considerably longer than that for the adjacent Dragon Challenge, an intertwined, twin-track, white-knuckle collide-ride, manifestly retro-fitted from a pre-Potter attraction.[8] Ollivander's, I kid you even less, was charging thirty bucks-plus for a silk-lined box and a little bit of varnished wood. The Potterphiles couldn't get enough of them. It was all I could do to restrain my darling daughters, although I have a sneaking suspicion that they bought a brace when my back was turned. If a wand turns up on my birthday—surprise, daddy!—I'll stick it where. . . .

No I won't. Instead, I'll shed a few sorrowful tears over the depravity of the marketing system, the fact that it defiles everything it touches. When J. K. Rowling sold the licensing rights to Warner Brothers, way back in the early days of Harry Potter fandom, she swore that the merchandising would be tasteful, would be restrained, would be strictly limited, and would be the kind of thing she'd buy for her own children. If that's the case, I can only assume that her kids are big-time tat lovers because the stuff she's buying them nowadays is expensive kitsch at best and extortionate trash at worst. In many ways, of course, it's breath-takingly brilliant. It's nearly as brilliant as the marketing scam in Robert McLaim Wilson's comic novel, *Eureka Street*, where an Irish entrepreneur sells "leprechaun crutches"—bits of twig torn from thorn bushes—to gullible American consumers with a soft spot for differently-abled little people.[9] It's even better than that, come to think of it, because the leprechaun-loving segment of the American market isn't particularly big, a paltry 10 million or so. The market for Ollivander's magical accoutrements, by contrast, is not only inestimable but *actually exists* in the here and now.

Despite J. K. Rowling's very best intentions, it seems to me that Harry Potter has slipped down the slope to marketing perdition, the backsliding chute that carried off Google and Starbucks and Richard Branson's once-iconic brand. Virgin, much as I hate to say it, is a sinner nowadays. How the guy had the gall to record a pre-flight message that's more full of dragon droppings than butterbeer is beyond me. He looked uncomfortable, admittedly, hunched over, leaning into the camera, ostensibly auditioning for the role of Quasimodo, and with those supersized teeth that only an equine fetishist could love. Maybe he has spent so long in pampered upper class, or arranging extra-terrestrial flights to neighbouring planets, that he has forgotten what it's like at the back of the plane. In the old days, they sprayed champagne around; nowadays, they chuck cold coffee on us.

Actually, a cup of cold coffee wouldn't go amiss right now. As you've probably guessed, I'm writing this in Universal Studios' "house of horror," waiting for the cops to arrive. The security people picked me up on the way out of Hogsmeade. They claim to have CCTV footage of my alleged antisocial behaviour in Jurassic Park. They're bluffing. I can tell. It's patently part of the show, a cheap publicity stunt to generate additional word-of-mouth. They're good these dudes, I grant you that. The shackles on the wall of my cell look pretty authentic, as do the branding irons by the brazier. The big sweaty guy in the corner seems to have taken a shine to me, just like they do in the movies. But at my withered age, any expression of amorous intent is welcome, even from someone with man-boobs the size of Mount Rushmore. They'll have to do a lot better than that if they want to scare me. I'll beat their bum rap, brothers and sisters.

It's Richard Branson's fault, you see. The mental stress of that traumatic coffee spill must count for something in my defence. Howard Schultz, Starbuck's CEO, must also share a bit of the blame because that crack-caffeine he sells is the ultimate cause of my downfall. It's J.K. Rowling's responsibility, too, because she wrote those books about a boy wizard to spellbind the more susceptible among us. Muggles like me. Alamo car rental is in on it as well because Beatrice, the enigmatic sat-nav, stopped speaking to me when I needed her most. Who, in any event, would believe CCTV footage produced by Universal Studios? I mean, come on. Get real. This is the organisation that released *Howard the Duck*, don't forget.[10] And the things they can do with CGI nowadays would make your head spin. Literally.

The branding's to blame, your honour. The devil made me do it.

Case dismissed.

NOTES

1. If, on the off chance, an attorney with time on their hands is rooting through this chapter, in search of something actionable, I must make it clear that I'm expressing my legitimate personal opinion. Most of the events recounted in this story actually happened, in one form or another, albeit the narrator is unreliable.
2. See Aherne, A. 2003. "Travels in Retroreality." In *Time, Space and the Market: Retroscapes Rising*, edited by S. Brown and J. F. Sherry, 158–170. Armonk: M. E. Sharpe. Yes, I was that masked marketing man.
3. I still bear the scars, you must appreciate, but if you're looking for a laugh at my expense, check out Brown, S. 2000. "Drove My Chevy to the Levee." In *Imagining Marketing*, edited by S. Brown and A. Patterson, 240–248. London: Routledge.
4. Brown, S. 2001. "Torment Your Customers (They'll Love It)." *Harvard Business Review* 79 (9): 82–88.
5. You might not be familiar with "dandering." The word "dander" is an Irish colloquialism, meaning to walk or stroll in an unhurried manner. It's the Ulster equivalent of *flâneur*.
6. Brown, S. 2005. *Wizard! Harry Potter's Brand Magic*. London: Cyan.
7. Because I don't have space to elaborate, your best bet is to read Ken Auletta's *Googled: The End of the World as we Know It* (London: Virgin Books, 2011). It's a real eye-opener.
8. I know whereof I speak. Many years ago, I worked for a funfair in Atlantic City, where I was responsible for the roller-coaster. I'm not an expert by any means, but I know a little bit about roller-coasters' cultural history.
9. Wilson, R. McL. 1996. *Eureka Street*. London: Secker & Warburg.
10. For those of you with short memories, *Howard the Duck* (1986) is widely regarded as one of the worst movies of all time. It was George Lucas's biggest flop and, arguably, the nearest thing to hell this side of *Phantom Menace*.

8 Locating the Sacred in Consumer Culture
Championing Colin Campbell's Easternization of the West Thesis

Alan Bradshaw

As consumer culture theory studies ranging from the Consumer Odyssey (Belk et al., 1989) to the Burning Man (Kozinets, 2002) inform us, much of consumer culture can be interpreted and analysed from the frame of the sacred. More broadly, general subject concerns with how consumption acts as a site for registering discourses of truth, ethics, meaning, and subjectivity resonate with what metaphysical philosophy calls the "transcendent domain" (Hedley, 2011). Recurrent spiritual and religious terms in consumer culture theory like *sacred*, *divine*, *devotion*, and *transcendent* are all contingent on a spiritual belief system but what sort of spiritual belief system obtains? Now, when religious discourses are typically approached from lenses of postmodernity, anatheism, new atheism, and fundamentalism, it is increasingly difficult to speak of sacred contingencies. However, given the recurrence of the sacred within consumer behaviour, it is crucial to consider the contingencies so that the sacred is more than a tautological labelling device. I reflect on the conditions of the sacred within the literature and seek to champion the recent work of Colin Campbell as offering an important framework. As will be demonstrated, Campbell's *Easternization of the West* thesis offers a significant framework that not just re-orientates and re-orientalizes discourses of the sacred within a contingent system of worldview but also presents a powerful mode for analysing consumption in general.

TAUTOLOGICAL LABELLING OF THE SACRED

Arguably the condition of the sacred within consumer studies marks a convergence in the theoretical co-ordinates of religion and consumer culture; a meeting point between the former's secularization and the latter's sacralization. For instance, a well-thread field of discussion concerns how Christmas is re-cast as a secularized commercial event yet ironically maintains its sacred and transcendent dimension via ritual. Hence, a clear basis exists for arguing a convergence between sacralization of consumer culture with a secularization of religious behaviour. But again the question is posed: If an experience is sacred, it is sacred with reference to what belief system?

The question of contingency is typically by-passed by maintaining an expanded definition of the sacred. For example, the Consumer Odyssey (Belk et al., 1989) tautologically defines the sacred as emanating from "a need to believe in something significantly more powerful and extraordinary than the self—a need to transcend existence as a mere biological being coping with the everyday world" (Belk et al., 1989, p. 2). The tautological approach is mandated by series of references which are themselves tautological and are useful to reproduce beginning with a definition from William James:

> Religion shall mean for us the feelings, acts and experiences of individual men in their solitude, so far as they apprehend themselves to stand in relation to what they may consider to be the divine. . . . We may interpret the term "divine" very broadly, as denoting any object which is godlike, whether it be a concrete deity or not. (cited in Belk et al., 1989, p. 6)

Similarly, Roberts said:

> Religion has to do with a unique and extraordinary experience—an experience that has a sacred dimension and is unlike everyday life . . . the experience of the holy. Such an experience is often called non-rational, for it is neither rational nor irrational. (cited in Belk et al., 1989, p. 6)

And finally a statement from Maus:

> It is not the idea of God, the idea of the sacred person that one finds over again in any religion, it is the idea of the sacred in general. (cited in Belk et al., 1989, p. 6)

Similarly Holbrook (1999) tautologically defines a sacred experience tautologically: "sacred experience . . . involves a receptive form of devotion or worship," while spiritual consumer value is explained as the "faithful, ecstatic, sacred or magical" (p. 23).

Such expanded framings of religiosity are certainly useful for capturing a multitude of activity during an era of fragmented beliefs and also holds the advantage of being an umbrella term across various religious beliefs. Further, such framing locates the sacred in the experientialist domain. However, to transcend "existence as a mere biological being coping with the everyday world" (Belk et al., 1989, p. 2) suggests that there is a higher belief system that can be transcended into, but the article declines to analyse what such a belief system might look like, and tautologically we see words like holy, transcendence, and divinity acting as explanations where in fact they do no such thing. By contrast, in Kozinets' Burning Man (2002) article and analysis of Star Trek's community of consumption (2001), we are provided with analyses of what is being believed and yet the belief systems are so bizarre and far-fetched, in my opinion, that it is left to wonder by what mechanism it is possible to maintain these spaces as sacred. Hence, it would seem to be the case that these papers nod towards a dimension that can be transcended into, but the dimensions of that dimension are barely explored, if at all.

Further, this idea of religion is so expanded that it runs the risk of a framing that is at once incoherent: a frame of analysis paradoxically concerned with everything yet nothing in particular, and this gives rise to a concern that a loose concept of religion emerges divested of any belief and universally applicable. Consequentially, it was possible for the odyssesians to "clinically describe and interpret" all sorts of forms of consumer behaviour as loaded with a "sacred dimension" (p. 2). The expressions of religious-esque behaviours that emerge thereafter range from the sublime to the ridiculous: Barry Manilow as deity (O'Guinn, 1991), the Burning Man festival (Kozinets, 2002), and Star Trek conventions as sacred events (Kozinets, 2001) whilst it is observed that there are uncanny resemblances in representations of Apple founder Steve Jobs with Jesus Christ (Belk & Tambut, 2005). Similarly in his seminal *Theory of Shopping*, Miller (1998) identifies the sacred as being alive and well in a supermarket near you with seemingly pedestrian shopping analysed as, in fact, sites of sacrifice, devotion with sacred subjects and objects.[1] Hence, we see the sphere of consumption as repeatedly framed as sites for the sacred experiences, with no deed or object considered too trivial to be regarded as a site for devotion. As stated, this creates the risk of a tautological and divested idea of the sacred and a concurrent difficulty in conceptually drawing the line between what is sacred and what is profane.[2]

For Hellman (2010), consumption theory is amidst a metaphysical turn as products and brands are less interpreted as performing a role of solving problems in the market—such as consumer loyalty and satisfaction—and increasingly interpreted as solving problems beyond a straightforward conception of the market, such as mediating relationships and identities. Hellman critiques the Consumer Odyssey (Belk et al., 1989) and Holt's (2004) iconic brands framework on the basis that they expropriate or instrumentalise the semantics of sacredness on behalf of consumption and do so without presenting sufficient evidence of any sheer transcendent subjective experience. Hence, Hellman objects that not only does this profanisation of sacredness cut any connection to true religious experience but also is a form of valorisation of brands/consumption that causes a radical devalorisation of the original sphere of reference. On this basis, Hellman raises critical questions: at which point is the experience of transcendence a sign for religiosity? Does it make sense to promote consumption into the field of religion and what are the symptoms to affirm or deny such an analysis?

However, Hellman's (2010) critique seems predicated on the idea that there can still be an original frame of reference for religion. Yet contemporary analyses of religious theory cast doubt on the possibility of any index point of religiosity. For example, Zizek (2001) notes a shift in Western discourse to the extent that religious leaders have strayed from orthodoxy and maintain a concept of goodness not directly grounded in the gospel: "ultimately just a perfidious semblance of itself, its own travesty" (Zizek, 2001, p. 1). This paradox of a post-God God is addressed by Kearney (2009), who considers an opened space between theism and atheism; an 'anatheism' in which we can encounter religious wonder anew and an everyday divinity based on a leap of faith predicated on doubt. In as much as the synthesises described by Zizek and Kearney are paradigmatic, there is fierce reaction from so-called New Atheists such as Dawkins, Dennet, Harris, and Hitchens, who aggressively attack analyses informed by both the sacred and the aetheist, which, as Harris describes it, split "the difference between intellectual integrity and the fantasies of a prior age" (Derbeyshire, 2011, p. 36). Yet any idea of a rational framework contaminated by superstition is purported notwithstanding Adorno and Horkheimer's (1997) observation that enlightenment itself is mythical. Finally, as Toscano (2010) demonstrates, any enthusiastic commitment to the abstract is already regarded as a potentially dangerous excess or fundamentalism to which Christianity has responded by re-creating itself as secular with Islam re-cast as the irrational other. Hence, imbroglio prevails if we attempt to imagine what a contingency for the sacred might be—the conventional basis for Western religion, that is, the external judging God has been displaced by a post-God God in a fundamentalist-fearing secular rationalist order, which itself is predicated on myth and fantasy; a system of religious belief that is atheist to accommodate a rationalism that is mythical. No wonder scholars label consumer behaviour as sacred and leave it at that.

Therefore, the following charges are brought against an expanded framing of sacred experience: that the object for analysis becomes incoherent, divested, and tautological, an axiomatic agenda of secularisation may be pursued, engagement with wider interdisciplinary discussion on the nature of sacred belief is foreclosed, and that the question of the sacred is merely labelled and pointed to with wider ramifications left unexplored. However, an important clarification is needed. The above line of argumentation should not result in a denial of an intensity of experience or devotion to objects and subjects that are such that they may be referred to as a sacred. However, it is to say that it is problematic that the sacred seems to work more as a tautological labelling device than a frame of analysis and that a more sustained framework is required. Such a framework can be found, I submit, in the work of the sociologist Colin Campbell.

CAMPBELL REVISITED

In consumer research, Campbell is mostly associated with the landmark *The Romantic Ethic and the Spirit of Modern Consumerism* (2005). Coinciding with developing interest in consumer hedonism and experientialism (see Holbrook & Hirschman, 1982), The *Romantic Ethic* was a seminal contribution, as marked by the responsive publication of the edited volume *Consumer Research: Postcards from the Edge* (Brown & Turley, 1997). In the *Romantic Ethic*, Campbell adapts the Weberian thesis of *The Protestant Ethic and the Spirit of Capitalism* (see Weber, 2003). In Weber's words, the task is to "ascertain whether and to what extent religious forces have taken part in the qualitative formation and the quantitative expansion of that spirit over the world" (Weber, 2003, p. 91) and also to understand how the impulse to acquisition that lies in the heart of consumer culture and capitalism stems from the Reformation. Campbell (2005) adopted Weberian analysis but re-directed focus away from Calvinistic ascetic dimensions or iron cages of production and instead focused on the rise of sensibility, hedonism, creativity, and the "turn to magic, mystery and exotic religion, manifesting a marked alienation from the culture of rationality" (p. 3) of the Romantic era. In contrast to studies of sacred consumption, Campbell's text allows us to engage with the intensity of emotional investment but does so according to a secular frame—those same "religious emotions" prevail, but during the process of secularization they are transformed in function and meaning:

> For religious doctrines of a Calvinist character to give rise to emotions which might be 'enjoyed' it was clearly necessary that belief should have become considerably attenuated; few individuals could possibly have found much pleasure in the total despair or abject terror which the first Puritans commonly experienced. Once convictions become conventions, however, the possibility of emotional self-indulgence is a real one. At the same time this possibility is extinguished if the beliefs really are abandoned, in form as well as in substance as some of the Enlightenment rationalists desired. In between the two extremes of conviction and dismissal, however, there is a position in which the belief becomes merely a symbol representing an emotional condition or mood, manipulable more or less at will in order to obtain pleasure. (p. 133)

Therefore, it is between the poles of "conviction and dismissal," and hence of the secular and the sacred, that Campbell presents his analysis of the romantic ethic.

Whereas the *Romantic Ethic* is a seminal text within consumer research, Campbell's more recent *Easternization of the West: A Thematic Account of Cultural Change in the Modern Age* (2008) has yet to exert such impact, although, I submit, it holds the potential to be an even more significant work.[3] Campbell returns to the questions in the *Romantic Ethic*, but this time the focus is on the Western imagination of Eastern spirituality and its impact on shifting the Western ethic, a process, Campbell argues, often misinterpreted as a rise in secularization.

For Campbell, a core conceptual basis for his project emanates from his reading of Weber and the idea of 'worldview,' a term that Weber used instead of 'culture,' and relates to a human need to conceive of the world as a meaningful cosmos. Campbell (2007) writes:

> For Weber therefore culture consisted of those ideas and beliefs that serve to meet this universal need, and by so doing help to give meaning to people's experiences of life and the world. It obviously follows, if culture is indeed to fulfil this role of providing a meaningful worldview, that it must approximate to a system rather than a mere aggregation of discrete beliefs and ideas . . . in stressing culture's critical role in providing just such an overarching system of meaning necessarily focuses on culture as a "system", that is, as a comprehensive worldview that humans can employ to try and make sense of the world and all their experiences. (p 11)

Through this Weberian lens, there is a possibility of identifying a contingency for what is regarded as sacred; a 'system' or 'worldview.' Still working on a Weberian foundation, Campbell states that no religious worldview can be entirely satisfactory in meeting the basic human need for meaning, and this produces tension. Further, there is an inherent drive towards a systematizing and rationalizing of these worldviews. Critically, this rationalizing can take one of only two directions, and that these are logically, not empirically, derived hence Campbell acknowledges that what is being theorised are ideal-typical religious orientations. It is also important to note, as Campbell does, that the social and economic circumstances that people find themselves in will affect the kind of meanings that people need.

The first direction that rationalization of worldview can take is that the *ultimate reality* becomes envisaged as a separate form *above* or *beyond* this world, which becomes increasingly profane in distinction: "these alternatives tend to result in the first case in the postulation of a personal god who transcends the world he created and who intends the resolution of all discrepancy by establishing a 'Kingdom of God on Earth' at some future time" (p. 12). This rationalization is identified as being the direction followed by the major Western religions, including Christianity, Judaism, and Islam.[4] The second rationalization typifies religions of the East:

> the postulation of an immanent divine principle, which working itself out over millennia through a moral mechanism involving the transmigration of souls, will also eventually achieve closure once all life has progressed through to the highest level of unity with the "all-soul." (p. 12)

Hence, we are provided with two worldviews that give rise to the meanings and ethics that we find: a Western thought predicated on the idea of an external ultimate reality as distinct from an Eastern thought predicated on the idea of immanent divinity. An important clarification is needed to say that for Campbell the 'East' at stake is actually the West's image of the East, or perhaps a Western alter-ego available for anybody alienated from the Western system, and is not, therefore, an authentic form of cultural importation. Campbell's core argument is that a shift in worldview has taken place and that we are now amidst an era of Easternization: "it concerns fundamental changes in the dominant worldview that prevails in the West, and as such changes that are apparent in all areas of life, including religion certainly but also medicine, the arts, political thought and even science. In that respect the Easternization thesis refers to a fundamental revolution in Western civilisation, one that can be compared in significance to the Renaissance, the Reformation or the Enlightenment" (p. 41). Concurrent with an Easternization of the West is, of course, the de-Westernisation of the West. The import of these claims is huge.

Over the course of Campbell's text, a series of examples of Easternization are provided. An example of the process, at a very basic level, is yoga. At first yoga is imported divested of spiritual content—merely a means to achieve fitness and physiotherapy. However, over time, its spiritual dimension becomes re-inscribed amidst a general popularization of Zen, Taoism, and other Eastern beliefs. Hence. the tendency "to Westernize, that is to secularize it, (is) replaced by an acceptance of its essentially spiritual nature" (p. 35). Of course the process of Easternization probes deeper than an embracement of yoga, and over the course of several hundred pages, Campbell iterates the rise of the New Age as a major cultural transformation of Easternization with enormous consequences. Christianity becomes piece by piece re-packaged as a more Eastern friendly religion; the Devil disappears from theology, as does the idea of God as a "distant, awesome and terrifying judge" (p. 255) as indeed does the idea of the Bible as a text that needs to be read literally—as Campbell states the "form of Christianity that flourishes in the West today . . . bears a considerable resemblance to the New Age movement" (p. 345). Leftist politics are undermined as scepticism of religious dogma and orthodox doctrine spill over, and so projects of social transformation turn away from institutional reform towards existentialism. Concerns with an excess of materialism, free sexual subjectivity, and the notionally emancipated and non-alienated subject become more resonant; a "shift of the focus of radicalism in the West from the political to the cultural and quasi-spiritual realm" (p. 239). In science, the shift is away from "old, classical Newtonian-style scientific worldview" of linear, uni-directional cause and effect towards a more associated holism; a self-organising system that is biological and organic rather than physical and mechanic, a reality that embraces consciousness, mind, and intelligence. Across these various channels, we see the same general Easternization process at work consistent with a reconfiguration of culture according to alternative beliefs. For Campbell, this leads to an undermining of authority of the pillars of the West—politicians, scientists, and religious leaders—who are forced to transform according to the logic of the new ethic. By contrast, Campbell identifies rises in discourses that are consistent with immanent divinity and Easternization; the human potential movement, astrology, animal rights, ecology, and so on.

The question, then, arises, which forms the basis of Campbell's text—how does a major cultural transformation take place? Intriguingly for consumer culture scholars, the cultural change takes place in popular consumption and he identifies England during the 1960s as the critical time that finally brought about, in real terms, a transformation that had been coming for centuries. For Campbell, transformation becomes possible when the existing system is no longer sufficient for a large group of people, and so the case proved to be in the 1960s amongst divergent youth subcultures. To all-too rapidly summarise Campbell's expanded argument, a convergence took place between disaffected youth subcultures in a 1960s counterculture that was predicated on alternative philosophies of radical Eastern spirituality and Romanticism. Campbell argues that such was the explosive impact of this convergence—marked by the radical uprisings of 1968 (generally retrospectively understood as a youth culture war against alienation)—that the process of Easternization became entrenched.

ASSESSING EASTERNIZATION

Campbell seeks to pre-empt critiques of Easternization as simply re-labelling postmodernity by arguing that, to the contrary, postmodernism is a misreading of Easternization. As he argues, "much of the defining features such as ontological dualism, an emphasis on the orderliness and rational comprehensibility of the cosmos together with a distinct historical sense" (p. 361) are distinctive of the West rather than of modernity itself, therefore a more accurate description would be post-Western rather than postmodern. In addition, Easternization, according to Campbell, emphasises the close link between the collapse of faith in modernity with the collapse of faith in traditional Christianity, and finally the Easternization thesis offers more detail into the precise mechanizations of the transformation as opposed to postmodernity, which typically remains locked into philosophical discussion.

Further critique is indirectly provided by Zizek (2001), who seems to pre-empt Campbell by imagining Weber writing a book entitled *The Taoist Ethic and the Spirit of Global Capitalism*—arguably the closest possible thing! For Zizek, such a phenomenon is entirely reconcilable with the postmodern—in fact, it represents the "ultimate postmodern irony" in that at the very moment that the Judeo-Christian legacy is threatened within the

European space by the onslaught of the "New Age Asiatic thought," Taos is establishing itself as the hegemonic ideology of global capitalism; a "perfect ideological supplement" (Zizek, 2001, p. 12). As such this "recourse to Taoism" offers the solution to coping with the acceleration of technological progress and social change, that is, that one should simply reject the momentum as the expression of the modern logic of domination:

> One should instead, "let oneself go", drift along, while retaining an inner distance and indifference towards the mad dance of this accelerated process, a distance based on the insight that all this social and technological upheaval is ultimately just a non-substantial proliferation of semblances which do not really concern the innermost kernel of our being . . . One is almost tempted to resuscitate here the old infamous Marxist cliché of religion as the "opium of the people," as the imaginary supplement of the terrestrial misery: the "Western Buddhist" meditative stance is arguably the most efficient way, for us, to fully participate in the capitalist dynamic while retaining the appearance of mental sanity. (p. 13)

In this way, Western Buddhism or Easternization functions, according to Zizek, as a fetish: it does not resolve any problems raised by Western modernity but displaces the critique. Hence, the West continues in its productive and destructive capacity, but rather than respond to the crises generated, the subject can "fully participate in the frantic pace of the capitalist game while sustaining the perception that you are not really in it, that you are well aware how worthless the spectacle is—what really matters to you is the peace of the inner Self to which you know you can always withdraw" (p. 15). Furthermore, the conviction that religious beliefs, especially once they take the form of a fetish, must be critically engaged with is especially manifest in Adorno's (2002) content analysis of the astrology column in the *LA Times*. For Adorno, the refusal of astrologists to convincingly engage with critiques that there is simply no convincing evidence to suggest that any of the predictions have any transparent interconnection with astronomical observations marks a retreat into narcissism, a dangerous refusal to be critically reflexive, an ideology of dependence, and a smug satisfaction of being one of the few who are "in the know." This unapologetic and committed irrationality contains, for Adorno, the same theoretical co-ordinates as anti-Semitism. Therefore, Adorno saw no progressive element in astrology, only—like Zizek—an operation of potentially dangerous ideology. Of course as Campbell is working within a Weberian mode, the truth of such critiques is beside the point—the task is merely to arrive at a sociological analysis of practice rather than to evaluate their intrinsic goodness; as Weber nicely put it, "whoever wants a sermon should go to a conventicle" (p. 29) .

In any case, for consumer culture theory, in particular, the implications of Campbell's thesis are immense. The text provides a systematic analysis

of the contingencies of the sacred and the devotional—the very theoriza-
tion that I claim is problematically absent from the literature—and it also
locates a fundamental transformation in culture at the very front-line of
issues that are of interest to consumer researchers—hence, the radical
individuality, hedonism and experientialism, the return to nature, ritual,
magic, drug consumption, aesthetics, ethical and green consumption, new
forms of community and tribalism, the recurrence of romantic mythology,
the idea of brands that are iconic, the identification of servicescapes as
utopian, the sacred dimensions, and more besides can be located within a
larger system or worldview; arguably Campbell presents consumer culture
theory with its missing link! In addition, thinking through the label of the
sacred with reference to a wider worldview provides a basis to critically and
reflexively engage to a greater extent with the objects of analysis, and the
critiques offered by Zizek (2001) and Adorno (2002) provide, surely, such
critical frameworks. Overall, however, the import and relevance of Campbell's text locate the spiritual dimension of consumption to be of critical
importance to understanding the world and culture that we inhabit, and
therefore it is worthwhile for the text to receive such engagement alongside
the other chapters in this text.

NOTES

1. At the risk of overstating Miller's position, it is possible to read his work as
   stating that religions themselves are totally contingent on material objects
   for generating the idea of the sacred, thus providing an alternative means of
   considering the problem (see Miller, 2010). However, because Miller is an
   anthropologist, his works stands outside of the domain of consumer culture
   theory and is cited indicatively.
2. This question was explored, if not resolved, during the consumer odyssey.
3. Apparently publishers were keen for the 400-plus-word book to be cut in
   half, and Campbell's perseverance may have condemned the book to a more
   obscure debut. To put the phenomenon into context, a Google Scholar search
   for the *Romantic Ethic* yields 1,645 citations whereas the *Easternization of
   the West* yields only seventeen. Although the former has been around for a
   lot longer, a suspicion prevails that the book is being ignored; hence, there is
   an added need for sympathetic scholars to champion the work, as this chapter seeks to do.
4. Interestingly, Campbell provides an excellent analysis as to why Islamic is
   fundamentally Western.

REFERENCES

Adorno, Theodor 2002. *The Stars Down to Earth* London: Routldege.
Adorno, Theodor, and Horkheimer, Max. 1997. *Dialectic of Enlightenment*. Lon-
    don: Verso.
Belk, Russell, Wallendorf, Melanie, and Sherry, John. 1989. "The Sacred and the
    Profane in Consumer Behavior: Theodicy on the Odyssey." *Journal of Con-
    sumer Research* 16 (June): 1–38.

Belk, Russell, and Tumbat, Guulnur. 2005 "The Cult of Macintosh." *Consumption Markets & Culture* 8 (3), 205–217.

Brown, Stephen, and Turley, Darach, 1997. *Consumer Research: Postcards from the Edge*. London: Routledge.

Campbell, Colin. 2005. *The Romantic Ethic and the Spirit of Modern Consumerism*. London: Blackwell.

Campbell, Colin. 2008. *The Easternization of the West: A Thematic Account of Cultural Change in the West*. London: Paradigm Publishers.

Derbeyshire, Jonathan. 2011. "War on Weak Tea Christians." *New Statesman* (April 11): 36–37.

Hedley, Douglas. 2011. "I'm a Believer" *New Statesman* (April 11): 29.

Hellman, Kai-Uwe. 2010. *Fetische des Konsums : Studien zur Soziologie der Marke*. Wiesbaden: VS Verlag.

Holbrook, Morris. 1999.*Consumer Value: a Framework for Research and Analysis*. London: Routledge.

Holbrook, Morris, and Hirschman, Elizabeth. 1982. "The Experiential Aspects of Consumption: Consumer Fantasies, Feelings and Fun." *Journal of Consumer Research* 9 (September): 132–140.

Holt, Douglas. 2004. *How Brands Become Icons: The Principles of Cultural Branding*. Cambridge, MA: Harvard Business School Press.

Kearney, Richard. 2009.) *Anatheism: Returning to God After God*. New York: Columbia University Press.

Kozinets, Robert V. 2001. "Utopian Enterprise: Articulating the Meanings of Star Trek's Culture of Consumption." *Journal of Consumer Research* 28 (June): 67–89.

Kozinets, Robert. 2002. "Can Consumers Escape the Market? Emancipatory Illuminations from the Burning Man." *Journal of Consumer Research* 29 (June): 20–38.

Miller, Daniel. 1998. *A Theory of Shopping*. London: Polity.

Miller, Daniel. 2010. *Stuff*. London: Polity.

O'Guinn, Thomas. 1991. "Touching Greatness: The Central Midwest Barry Manilow Fanclub." In *Highways and Buyways: Naturalistic Research from the Consumer Behavior Odyssey*, edited by Russell Belk, 102§111. New York: Advances in Consumer Research.

Toscano, Alberto. 2010. *Fanaticism: On the Uses of an Idea*. London: Verso.

Weber, Max. 2003. *The Protestant Ethic and the Spirit of Capitalism*. Mineola: Dover Publications.

Zizek, Slavoj. 2001. *On Belief*. London: Routledge.

Part III

The Commodification of the Spiritual

9   The Veneration of Relics at Glastonbury Abbey in the Middle Ages

Robin Croft

I recently found a forgotten relic in a drawer at home. It is a minute piece of straw, from a mattress belonging to St. Theresa of Lisieux (1873–1897), acquired during a family pilgrimage to Normandy in the late 1950s. It is in a small leather folder, with a short prayer on the cover, and a photograph inside. This item seems to belong in an earlier era of religious pilgrimage, described by historians such as Webb (1999, 2000) and by cultural anthropologists like Turner and Turner (1978). In part, though, the transformation of a piece of straw from mundane to sacred, and its subsequent consumption as a retail artefact, can perhaps be better understood through the work of later anthropological studies on the phenomenon in religion, travel,[1] and shopping (O'Guinn and Belk, 1989).

Relics form an important part of the devotional practices of many religions, including Buddhism, Christianity, Hinduism, and Shamanism. The corporeal remains—the bones or preserved body parts of a holy person—are most commonly revered. But so-called 'secondary relics' or 'contact relics,' including clothing, bedding, and similar items that may have been used by the holy person, are also believed to have taken on their sanctity.

Modern-day veneration of religious relics continues to fascinate social scientists (Coleman & Eade, 2004; Sallnow, 1978) and popular writers alike (Rufus, 1999; Sora, 2005), just as it caught the attention of Chaucer, who wryly described the role of the Pardoner in the Canterbury Tales: this character dealt in primary and secondary artefacts but was created in a period where the cult of relics had passed its peak, and audiences and believers alike were starting to share Chaucer's understated scepticism. How was it that cloths, stones, and "pigges bones" not only were objects of veneration but simultaneously had become commodities to be traded across frontiers?

Whereas contemporary studies have attempted to understand the transformation from profane to sacred based on the testimony of consumers (Belk et al., 1989; O'Guinn and Belk, 1989; Tynan and McKechnie, 2006), the authentic medieval voice is lost to us. The closest we are able to come to an ethnographic understanding of the consumption of religious relics in the Middle Ages are narratives recorded by clerics as part of the process of beatification (where an institution would petition Rome for a holy person to be formally recognised as a saint). These hagiograpical miracle tales (e.g., those in Yarrow, 2006), though, were neither authentic nor reliable, being understandably one-sided in their attempt to influence the authorities, and in many cases they were set down generations after the events took place.

As Carley (1988) noted, modern audiences find the medieval cult of relics "naively superstitious and almost impossible to respect" (p. 120). In this chapter, I adopt Carley's nominalist position, focusing on the tangible evidence presented by the relics and interpreting the uses to which these were put. "Relics depend on faith; they have no extrinsic value and their power derives from the viewer's response to them" (p. 130). I concentrate on the later medieval period, from the 10th to the 15th centuries, in particular studying the role of relics at Glastonbury Abbey in England. Not only was this period the high point of consumption of religious relics in England, but the abbey deserves attention as having amassed probably the largest collection of this type of artefact in the world at the time.[2]

In medieval Europe, relics performed a number of important functions, for both religious and secular groups. On a non-spiritual level, they were collectors' items, signifiers of wealth and prestige. The reliquaries were often themselves works of art, made with precious metals and covered in jewels.[3] As Brown (1981) noted, "Detached fragments of the saints in gold and silver caskets, or in their miniature marble shrines had something of the measureless quality of an *objet trouvé*" (p. 78). The collection of relics was particularly encouraged by what we have come to know as the Crusades (Asbridge, 2010) and papal incentives for pilgrimages to Rome and Jerusalem.

As Geary (1978) noted in his study of the relic trade in medieval Europe, though, it is important to put aside post-Enlightenment considerations of authenticity and evidence and examine instead what can be learned of the people of the period through their use of relics. Although this chapter started by considering the paradox of how the mundane could be transformed into the sacred, to medieval audiences, these items were anything but ordinary, as Geary observed: "There was no class of individuals, be they theologians, kings, or peasants, for whom relics were not of great importance . . . an indispensable part of daily life, accepted as unquestioningly, in fact, as life itself."

This centrality of relics in medieval life helps to explain the extraordinary trade in religious artefacts in the period, a 'commerce,' as Geary's study described, just as often based on outright theft as on buying, selling, and gift-giving. Religious houses competed with one another for the prestige associated with having a significant holy 'person' on the premises, just as merchants and traders saw the value of financing expeditions to acquire important relics, often without the agreement of their rightful owners. Saints were a part of the community, and God worked through their remains: relics provided guarantees of the continuing interest of the glorious individual in his or her host people (Geary, 1986).

Most English centres for pilgrimage were based around a single 'celebrity'[4] saint: Thomas Becket in Canterbury, Swithun in Winchester, John in Beverley, William in York, Thomas in Hereford, Hugh in Lincoln, Edward in Westminster, as well as Saints Alban and Edmund in their eponymous towns. This chapter, however, examines the role of relics at Glastonbury Abbey, where the strategy appeared to centre on acquiring the largest number of saints' relics, rather than merely to promote a single high-profile individual. In this way, Glastonbury sought to position itself as a holy place in its own right, redolent of the sanctity of the multitude of saints who had 'chosen' to make it their resting place.

Glastonbury became constituted as an abbey at some stage in the Dark Ages, having gained renown in Western Christianity by drawing Saint Patrick and other Irish holy men and women to it. During the time of Danish and Norwegian raids on Britain, the site's relative isolation meant it remained relatively protected, a fact that was to feature in many later narratives, including the Arthurian legends. Glastonbury drew support from the Saxons kings both during and after the reconquest of Wessex from the Danes in the so-called Dark Ages. It was rewarded with grants of land and valuables.

However, by the early part of the 10th century, the Glastonbury estate was run down, the community depleted, and the buildings in a poor state of repair. Legend tells how as a boy St. Dunstan was on a family pilgrimage to Glastonbury when he had a vision of the abbey church as the largest and greatest in the British Isles (Wood, 1999). Dunstan set about having Glastonbury identified as a holy place, somewhere equivalent in sanctity to Rome, Santiago de Compostella, or Jerusalem. He and later abbots drew attention to the long line of saintly men and women who visited, stayed, died, and were buried at Glastonbury, most of whom were recorded in contemporary chronicles or who appeared *ex post facto*.

Indeed, such was the popularity of Glastonbury as a final resting place that it was necessary to expand provision. Dunstan had a wall built to the south side of the abbey's cemetery and raised the level of the ground by 2 to 3 metres (Carley, 1988). This effectively opened the cemetery once more for new burials while leaving the holy relics undisturbed below (something confirmed by modern archaeological digs). This strategy appears to have paid off: successive kings and nobles patronized the abbey and endowed it with goods, land, and holy relics.

Glastonbury was to suffer a major setback in the following century when England was conquered by the Normans, much of the abbey's land being confiscated and made over to the country's new military elite. Bishop Henry of Blois shared the abbacy of Glastonbury with an episcopal role at Winchester, and at both places he was instrumental in developing pilgrimage revenues based on holy relics. At Winchester, for example, he promoted the cult of St. Swithun, including constructing a tunnel under the saint's resting place so that pilgrims might get closer to the bones themselves.[5] The bishop realized the importance of a credible narrative, and he commissioned the respected chronicler William of Malmesbury to write the authorized history of Glastonbury Abbey. William's *De Antiquitate* was finished around 1129 and was copied extensively by the monks there and at other Benedictine houses over the next two centuries. William's work was complemented and to an extent supplemented by the later writings of Cardoc of Llancarfan: Caradoc (or Caradog) helpfully addressed the important Celtic audience and started to hint at some of the Arthurian myth that was to feature prominently in the Glastonbury narrative towards the end of the 12th century.

The 'evidence' commissioned by Henry of Blois consisted of historical and hagiographical accounts in an attempt to restore Glastonbury's reputation "as a place of great holiness . . . redolent with divine sanctity" (cited in Scott, 1981, p. 1). As William made clear, the relics, in both the abbey church and the cemetery outside, were central to this:

> [T]there is no part of the church that is without the ashes of the blessed. The stone-paved floor, the sides of the altar, the very altar itself, above and within, are filled with the relics close-packed. Deservedly indeed is the repository of so many saints said to be a heavenly shrine on earth. (Chapter 18 of DA, cited in Scott, 1981, p. 67)

Not only was Glastonbury a special place to visit, but William identified its desirability as a final resting place:

> How fortunate, good Lord, are those inhabitants who have been summoned to an upright life by reverence for that place. I cannot believe that any of those can fail of heaven, for their deaths are accompanied by the recommendation and advocacy of such great patrons. (Chapter 18 of DA, cited in Scott, 1981, p. 67)

Glastonbury's relics covered every important period in Christianity. With royal patronage and a judicious management of the pilgrimage business, the first half of the 12th century saw Glastonbury expand on a massive scale: Henry of Blois built a bell tower, chapter house, cloister, lavatory, refectory, dormitory, infirmary, 'castellum,' outer gate, brewery, and stables (Carley, 1988).

This period of expansion came to an abrupt end in May 1184, when a serious fire took hold of the abbey church and destroyed most of the buildings. The fire consumed almost everything: vestments, ornaments, a priceless library, and almost the entire relic collection. It did not matter that many of the artefacts were widely believed to have been fakes: Glastonbury was now without its principal draw for pilgrims and lacking an infrastructure in which to accommodate them.

Fortunately, Glastonbury's revenue from land holdings was substantial, and rebuilding commenced on a grander scale than had been envisaged before. The relic gap was filled by a number of audacious 'discoveries' and the careful cultivation of new narratives around these. The most significant was the finding of the 'remains' of King Arthur and Queen Guenevere in the churchyard around 1190. There was an obvious draw to being associated with a figure and a literary genre that was very much in fashion in Europe at the time: "Arthur's bones could be seen as Glastonbury relics . . . they attracted pilgrims, enhanced the prestige of the monastery and generated devotion" (Carley, 1988, p. 124).

Perhaps anticipating the public scepticism that would greet this convenient discovery, Glastonbury invited the Welsh scholar Giraldus Cambrensis to describe the Arthurian dig in 1193, his visit being almost contemporaneous (Scott, 1981). Other celebrity relics to appear after the Great Fire include remains of Saints Patrick, Indract, Brigit, David, and Gildas, all appealing to the Celtic elements of the pilgrimage market (Abrams and Carley, 1991).

Glastonbury continued to solicit gifts from powerful benefactors, and as a wealthy abbey, it could afford to buy relics. As the new collection matured, the community commissioned another scholar to develop the narrative: by the middle of the 14th century, John of Glastonbury could proudly boast:

> The stone pavement, the sides of the altar itself are so loaded, above and below, with relics packed together that there is no path through the church, cemetery or cemetery chapel which is free from the ashes of the blessed. (cited in Carley, 1988, p. 128)

Whereas relics served a number of important civic and spiritual roles in the Middle Ages, historians take the view that our understanding of these can only really be advanced by studying how they were used by the actors of the time. At Glastonbury Abbey, it is possible to see three groups 'consuming' the relic collections: pilgrims, benefactors, and the monastic community itself. In fact, of course, these groups are not mutually exclusive, as many benefactors also undertook pilgrimages, just as many of Glastonbury's pilgrims would in time become benefactors. Within the groups, though, we can see a complex interplay of exchange relationships where Glastonbury's relic collection had a crucial mediating role in the production and consumption process.

Conventional ethnographies, as I have suggested, are difficult to apply in historical contexts such as this: indeed, Yarrow (2006) has argued that they can supply misleading readings through the assumption that the texts are capable of being read in a 'static' manner, devoid of historical, cultural, political, and other contexts. However, as Tynan and McKechnie (2006) learned, the cultural insights gained by studies such as Belk et al. (1989) and O'Guinn and Belk (1989) can provide useful templates to hold against data from differing cultures and times (in the case of medieval relics, of course, *ex post facto* interpretations of meanings and events). Initially, however, I will provide a conventional historiographical interpretation before examining this through the interpretive prism provided by consumer anthropologists.

There were many reasons that medieval men and women set out on pilgrimages, the chief of which would invariably have been the spiritual one. There was more to the experience than this, however, and the journey itself was critical:

> Theologians envisaged [pilgrimage] as a form of penance and self-mortification. . . . Through pilgrimage one could transform the linear human progress towards death and disintegration into a circular eternal journey where the heavenly New Jerusalem was the ultimate goal. (Carley, 1988, p. 129)

Relics had an important mediating role in this journey: "Corporeal remains of proven saints were a numinous link with a more heroic age, a higher than human point towards which to yearn in a great chain of being which stretched from the lowest sphere in physical creation to heaven itself" (Carley, 1988, p. 120). Apart from the more general spiritual aspirations, religious practice provided other uses for pilgrimage in the penances exacted on the faithful to atone for their sins. Diana Webb's 1999 study of European pilgrimage showed how the church in many places operated something akin to a tariff system for particular sins, where the penance set for given transgressions was to undertake pilgrimages, whose difficulty reflected the magnitude of the offence.

Healing was another reason for pilgrimage, something that Glastonbury and other institutions worked hard to develop. A sick person cured would bring prestige to an abbey and to its relics, as well as abundant word of mouth publicity. Certain saints were associated with particular ailments, and the relics of Saints Luke, Cosmas, and Damien were sought out as they were known as physicians, Saints Margaret and Pantaleon were invoked in childbirth, while sufferers of syphilis turned to Saints Fiacre and George (Farmer, 1982). Glastonbury's position was that by having the largest relic collection in the British Isles, it would be able to cater for most medical and psychological conditions. As Carley (1988) noted, "an important relic was capable of working miracles: it inspired faith, cured the sick, and gave guidance to the spiritually afflicted. One might even describe relics as the senior consultants of medieval medical practice" (p. 120).

Pilgrimage shrines often not only allowed physical contact with the saints' relics, they encouraged it, providing openings in the sides of reliquaries where pilgrims could reach in and touch the bones. Sickness was associated with sin, and pilgrimage allowed a penitent to escape the grip of physical suffering through spiritual cleansing at the shrine of a saint or in the presence of their remains (Brown, 1981). The physicality was a central part of the popular mindset: as early as the 10th century, the monks at Mont Saint Michel in Normandy realized that pilgrims preferred to venerate saints whose corporeal remains were more tangible (such as St. Aubert) than an ethereal, although arguably more powerful, figure such as Archangel Michael (Smith, 2003). It has to be noted, however, that in the later medieval period at least, saints were able to show their munificence remotely: Webb (2000) offers many examples of miracles attributed to saints where their was no recourse to their physical remains.

For many abbeys, pilgrim offerings were the principal source of revenue and, in the case of major sites such as Canterbury, could represent considerable amounts, sufficient to finance the constant rebuilding of the cathedral. Relying on a single income source, however, was a risky strategy: the cult of individual saints was subject to fashion (Geary, 1986), in the same way as pilgrimage was affected by a range of uncontrollable factors, including the weather, famine, pestilence, and war. All of these national events made travelling for the ordinary pilgrim dangerous (Webb, 1999). Glastonbury's long term planning therefore targeted the wealthy and powerful, building lifetime relationships in order to encourage bequests of property (including relics).

For benefactors the presence of the corporeal remains of so many saints, both those in movable reliquaries in the abbey church as well as those known to be interred in the precincts, was evidence enough of a claim to be the holiest place in the known world outside Jerusalem and Rome. Through the benefaction of estates or other property, a wealthy sponsor could guarantee a burial plot at Glastonbury and so join the queue for a better afterlife in the company of some of the greatest figures of Christianity. Abbey and benefactors would negotiate a programme of *post mortem* exercises for the soul of the deceased: weekly prayers, masses, and other offerings. Providing final resting places to the wealthy and powerful in exchange for land and prestige had been something at which Glastonbury excelled: the early 12th-century William of Malmesbury's authoritative history noted how:

> There is much proof of how venerated the church of Glastonbury was even by the nobles of our country [*primatibus patrie*] and how desirable for burial [*ad sepulturam desiderabilis*], that there especially under the protection of the mother of God they might await the day of resurrection. (cited in Scott, 1981, p. 83)

This targeting of the great and the good entailed some changes in the management of visitors at Glastonbury. Abbots from the 13th century onwards expanded their personal lodgings to create palaces suitable for entertaining high status guests, including the royal family and nobility. In the meantime, new building was undertaken outside the abbey walls to accommodate middle class pilgrim-tourists who now expected a higher standard of

Figure 9.1   The George & Pilgrim Hotel: was this built outside the abbey precincts to house a new class of discerning pilgrim or to separate the profane from the sacred?

lodging than their forebears: the hotel now known as the George & Pilgrim in the town (see Figure 9.1) was built for this purpose by Abbot Selwood (Carley, 1988).

As I have noted, Glastonbury actively solicited, acquired, and 'discovered' relics in order to confirm its claim to be a place of great holiness: this in turn helped build beneficial relationships with the wealthy and powerful as well as supporting the 'Glastonbury brand' that ordinary pilgrims could consume (Croft et al. 2008). As Geary (1978, 1986) reminded us and Brown (1981) confirmed, these were not mere bones, hair, or other body parts: relics were the very presence of the saints themselves in that community. Saints were able to make their wishes and desires known, and they could express their pleasure through miracles such as healing and their displeasure through inclement weather, crop failures, earthquakes,[6] and other events that today might be termed Acts of God.

Relics were also used strategically in the highly competitive tourism market: Glastonbury's burgeoning business was being undermined in the 12th century by competition from Canterbury and Westminster, both of which were physically much closer to the political and cultural centres of gravity in medieval England. King Edward the Confessor (whose tomb was in Westminster Abbey) had been canonised saint in 1160, with the martyred Becket's status at Canterbury being confirmed by Rome in 1161 (Scott, 1981). Both sites were close to the channel ports and could rely on overseas visitors to boost their revenues.

Glastonbury countered the growing influence of Canterbury by claiming to possess the remains of St. Dunstan: although he had died and was buried in Canterbury, the monks of Glastonbury maintained that Dunstan's remains had been taken to Somerset in the 10th century (Carley, 1988). These claims caused predictable outrage in Canterbury, but the Somerset community merely ignored them and continued to develop the cult of St. Dunstan at Glastonbury, building a new chapel to house his supposed remains, right up until the 16th-century dissolution. Relics helped to provide new material to allow the monks to re-write their history "in order to exaggerate the antiquity of their foundations and add to the aura of sanctity that surrounded them in the hope that they would succeed in the competition for pilgrims" (Scott, 1981, p. 27).

Bizarrely, relics were used by Glastonbury in a sophisticated exercise in target marketing. This choice of terminology is not gratuitous and indeed has been employed by some of the pre-eminent historians in the field. As Carley (1988) put it, "Glastonbury had a corner . . . on the Irish market. The relics . . . succeeded on a material as well as a spiritual plane, since they brought Irish pilgrims to Glastonbury throughout the middle ages" (p. 125).

After the Great Fire of 1184, Glastonbury claimed to possess all of the remains of St. Patrick: their 'evidence' was the official chronicler John of Glastonbury, who wrote that the saint had died at the Somerset monastery in 472 and was buried in a position of great honour to the right of the high altar (Carley, 1988). The claim was also made that Patrick's protegé St. Benignus was buried there, too, as was Indract. Secondary relics from

Ireland associated with St. Brigit included her wallet, collar, bell, and weaving implements. Glastonbury enlarged its narrative of St. Patrick with finds of a richly adorned altar said to have been brought by him in the 5th century, as well as what was said to be St. Patrick's charter as abbot (described by Scott [1981] as "fanciful").

Other regions were also targeted in this way. For example, although it was believed that the patron saint of Wales, St. David, had died and was buried in Wales, Glastonbury claimed that his remains had been moved there for safe keeping during the 10th century, as were the bones of others including Gildas (Carley, 1988). In the case of Ireland and Wales, Glastonbury was able to turn its geographical disadvantage in England (far from major centres of population and power) to its advantage: Somerset was well connected to the Celtic world through sea and river connections, a journey that could be sold to pilgrims as re-tracing the steps of Patrick, David, and other culturally significant saints.

Glastonbury also used relics to target pilgrims from the northeast of England, even without this geographical advantage. They claimed that the remains of the great St. Aidan, bishop of Lindisfarne, had to be transferred to Glastonbury for safe keeping during Danish raids of the 8th century. Many others, including the Venerable Bede, St. Hilda (Abbess of Whitby), and St. Paulinus of York, found their way south at the same time.

Finally, on a tactical level, the relics of saints provided Glastonbury and its ecclesiastical competitors with a range of specific events to promote. Saints, for example, would have an official saint's day, usually the anniversary of their birth or death. In addition, many would have their 'translation' celebrated, usually the anniversary of the day when their relics arrived at the abbey or were moved from their original resting place to another. Translations were important events in that they were invariably accompanied by miracles and other signs of the saint's pleasure. Often relics were lost for generations and then found again, the saints showing their pleasure with new miracles or other signs of good favour (Carley, 1988), as happened with Dunstan at Glastonbury. Abbeys learned that translations were also effective ways of reviving tired saintly brands and were talked up with advance publicity (described by Webb, 2000). Better still, translation feasts could be timed to coincide with better travelling conditions: although Thomas Becket's feast day was December 29, for example, his translation on July 7 was much more widely celebrated in Canterbury as roads were in a far better state at this later season. Salisbury's relic feast was moved at least twice during the Middle Ages to make it more attractive to tourists (Webb, 2000).

This chapter opened with the question of how something as mundane as a piece of straw could come to be considered as possessing sacred properties and yet at the same time be commodified as an object of consumption. Glastonbury Abbey's holdings of relics included the bones, body parts, bodily fluids, hair, teeth, clothing, and personal effects of hundreds of Christian saints. I have taken the surviving records about how the relics were used by both provider and consumer and interpreted these in the light of what we know of the political, economic, and cultural contexts of the late Middle Ages.

This approach, of course, rarely gives us the authentic consumer voice: until the end of this period literacy was largely an ecclesiastical preserve, and therefore contemporaneous accounts were invariably re-interpreted by clerical writers. Examining similar phenomena in the 20th century, is it possible that anthropological studies are able to supply *ex post ante* explanations? To an extent this is a curious notion, given that the ethnographies of Star Trek communities (Kozinets, 2001), an evangelical Christian theme park (O'Guinn and Belk, 1989), an anti-consumerist festival (Kozinets, 2002), or the whole experience of secular Christmas gift-giving (Tynan and McKechnie, 2006) rely extensively on earlier religious metaphors. The ethnographic genre itself is largely premised on constructs advanced in the 1989 Belk et al. consumer odyssey. Here a range of explanations of the process of sacralization including ritual and pilgrimage were evidently *a priori* factors in the practice of worship by medieval 'consumers.' We can also see the centrality of gift-giving, particularly in the way in which rulers and church authorities managed relationships with religious institutions such as Glastonbury.[7]

In a similar manner, the language of 20th- and 21st-century studies draws on ideas that are commonplace in wider studies of religious artefacts, including medieval relics (e.g., in 'hierophany' and 'kratophany,' we are reminded that the custodians of relics both respected and feared their collections, whereas the notion of 'contamination' aptly describes the process by which secondary relics came to be venerated). In the same way, the concept of 'sacrifice' applied to early pilgrims whose journeys to relic shrines such as Glastonbury would invariably involve personal discomfort and risk: in the later Middle Ages, critics such as Langland's Piers Plowman were to decry the new class of leisured pilgrim-tourist.

At the same time, I have followed the lead set by historians such as Carley and Webb, who applied the nomenclature of 20th-century business practice to some of the uses to which Glastonbury Abbey put their relic collection. We can see how some decisions being taken in the medieval period were in all but name market segmentation, targeting, and positioning.[8] Glastonbury Abbey emerged from the Dark Ages as a place of quiet contemplation and prayer. By the time of its destruction at the end of the medieval period, it had come to be associated with luxury, wealth, and power. What was arguably the greatest collection of monastic buildings in Europe had been built, to a great extent, on an implicit understanding of consumer behaviour, particularly that of the emerging middle classes in medieval England.

NOTES

1. Lisieux is still a place of pilgrimage, but St. Theresa appears to have acquired celebrity status: her remains have been taken on tour, including Brazil

(1997), Russia and the United States (1999), Canada (2001), Iraq and Australia (2002), New Zealand (2005), Micronesia (2007), Philipines (2008), Britain and Ireland (2009), and South Africa (2010).
2. A 14th-century Relic List survives as the manuscript Cotton Titus D.vii. Folios 2r-13v in the British Library. It has been translated and annotated by James Carley and Martin Howley in chapter 4 of Arthurian Literature, Vol XVI, edited by James Harley and Felicity Riddy (Boydell & Brewer, 1998).
3. Reliquaries formed a major touring exhibition (*Treasures of Heaven*) in Cleveland (2010), Baltimore (2011), and London (2011).
4. This 20th-century term was first used by respected historian Diana Webb (2000). An entire chapter is devoted to the promotional methods used by centres such as Glastonbury.
5. The tunnel still exists, although St. Swithun's shrine was destroyed in the 16th century.
6. An earthquake destroyed St. Michael's Church on Glastonbury Tor on September 11, 1275, and badly damaged the abbey's chapter house (Carley, 1988).
7. An additional concept to consider is that of exchange: Carley (1988) describes how Glastonbury would exchange relics with other Benedictine houses, in much the same way that the collectors of ephemera are described in the 20th-century ethnographic studies of traded artefacts. There is no obvious parallel to the process of systematic and opportunistic theft documented by Geary, though.
8. Watson (2008) showed how the monks of Winchester Abbey had used recognizable PR practices to promote the cult of St. Swithun. I wrote something similar that year which focused on narrative development at Glastonbury (Croft et al 2004)

REFERENCES

Abrams, Lesley. and James P. Carley. 1991. *The Archaeology and History of Glastonbury Abbey: Essays in Honour of the Ninetieth Birthday of C.A. Ralegh Radford*. Woodbridge, Suffolk: Boydell Press.
Asbridge, Thomas. 2010. *The Crusades: The War for the Holy Land*. London: Simon & Schuster.
Belk, Russell W., Melanie Wallendorf, and John F. Sherry, Jr. 1989. "The Sacred and Profane in Consumer Behavior: Theodicy on the Odyssey." *Journal of Consumer Research* 16: 1–38.
Brown, Peter. 1981. *The Cult of the Saints: Its Rise and Function in Latin Christianity*. Chicago: University of Chicago Press.
Carley, James P. 1988. *Glastonbury Abbey: The Holy House at the Head of the Moors Adventurous*. Woodbridge, Suffolk: Boydell Press.
Carley, James P. and Martin Howley (1998), "Relics at Glastonbury in the Fourteenth Century", in *Arthurian Literature XVI,* edited by James P. Carley and Felicity Riddy. Cambridge: D.S.Brewer
Coleman, Simon, and John Eade. 2004. *Reframing Pilgrimage: Cultures in Motion*. London: European Association of Social Anthropologists.
Croft, Robin, Trevor Hartland, and Heather Skinner. 2008. "And Did Those Feet: Getting Medieval England 'on Message.'" *Journal of Communication Management* 12 (4): 294–304.
Farmer, David Hugh. 1982. *The Oxford Dictionary of the Saints*. Oxford: Oxford University Press.

Geary, Patrick. 1978. *Furta Sacra: Thefts of Relics in the Central Middle Ages.* Princeton, NJ: Princeton University Press.

Geary, Patrick. 1986. "Sacred Commodities: The Circulation of Medieval Relics." In *The Social Life of Things*, edited by Arjun Appadurai, 169–191. New York: Cambridge University Press.

Kozinets, Robert V. 2001. "Utopian Enterprise: Articulating the Meanings of *Star Trek*'s Culture of Consumption." *Journal of Consumer Research* 28: 67–88.

O'Guinn, Thomas, and Russell W. Belk. 1989. "Heaven on Earth: Consumption at Heritage Village, USA." *Journal of Consumer Research* 16: 227–238.

Rufus, Anneli. 1999. *Magnificent Corpses.* Cambridge, MA: Marlowe & Co.

Sallnow, Michael. 1978. *Contesting the Sacred: The Anthropology of Pilgrimage.* Champaign, IL: University of Illinois Press.

Scott, John. 1981. *The Early History of Glastonbury, An Edition, Translation and Study of William of Malmesbury's* De Antiquitate Glastonie Ecclesie. Woodbridge, Suffolk: Boydell Press.

Smith, Katherine Allen., 2003. "An Angel's Power in a Bishop's Body: The Making of the Cult of Aubert of Avranches at Mont-Saint-Michel. *Journal of Medieval History* 29: 347–360.

Sora, Stephen. 2005. *Treasures from Heaven.* London: Wiley.

Turner, Victor, and Edith L. B. Turner. 1978. *Image and Pilgrimage in Christian Culture.* New York: Columbia University Press.

Tynan, Caroline, and Sally McKechnie. 2006. "Sacralising the Profane: Creating Meaning with Christmas Consumption in the UK." *European Advances in Consumer Research* 7: 182–188.

Watson, Tom. 2008. "Creating the Cult of a Saint: Communication Strategies in 10th Century England." Public Relations Review 34 (1): 19–24.

Webb, Diana. 1999. *Pilgrims and Pilgrimage in the Medieval West.* London: I. B. Tauris & Co.Webb, Diana. 2000. *Pilgrimage in Medieval England.* London: Hambledon & London.

Wood, Michael. 1999. *In Search of England: Journeys into the English Past.* London: Penguin Books.

Yarrow, Simon. 2006. *Saints and Their Communities: Miracle Stories in Twelfth-Century England.* Oxford: Oxford University Press.

10 Branding Faith and Managing Reputations

Mara Einstein

Implementing marketing strategies in association with religious institutions is on the rise due to a steady fall in traditional religious practice, a trend hypothesized by secularization theory long ago. Practice has decreased whereas belief has not, and thus the marketplace for religion and spirituality remains vibrant. To be competitive within this environment, religious institutions are using promotion to attract parishioners to their congregations. This has been most evident in the United States, where there is a tradition of religious marketing (Finke and Iannaccone, 1993; Moore, 1994), but increasingly this trend is proliferating around the world.

Over the last twenty years, the amount and sophistication of the marketing used by churches, synagogues, mosques, and others have risen to an all-time high (Beaudoin, 2003; Einstein, 2008; Miller, 2004; Schmidt, 1995). In the United States, this is because cultural changes that began in the 1960s led to steeply decreasing church attendance. The most notable change is that large numbers of baby boomers rejected the faith of their family, making one's religious identity acquired rather than ascribed. By the 1990s, being able to choose one's belief system led to a spiritual marketplace (Roof, 1999; Twitchell, 2007), where religious consumers (called seekers) shop for faith. It was not enough, though, to be free to select a faith. Information had to be available about religious alternatives. To that end, new media technologies—digital cable television and satellite providing numerous religious offerings as well as the wide distribution of broadband Internet—allowed for the far-reaching dissemination of religious ideas (Boellstorff, 2008; H. Campbell, 2010; Dawson and Cowan, 2004; Wagner, 2011), including notably Eastern traditions, which were more in evidence after changes in immigration laws in the mid-1960s (Campbell, 2008; Lau, 2000). Thus, with the ability to choose one's faith, the increased diversity of spiritual options and a multitude of methods through which to learn about and even practice one's faith, it is perhaps inevitable that regular church attendance would drop significantly. Although there are conflicting reports as to what the percentage of church attendance is, there is consensus that it is between 20% and 26% of the population, which is down from the 40% annually noted by pollster Gallup (Hadaway and Marler, 1998; Taylor,

2003). Similar trends exist around the world and, in fact, are more pronounced. Attendance in Catholic churches in Latin American countries, for example, has experienced substantial declines because of competition from Pentecostals. Significant decreases are also seen in France, where church attendance has dropped from 27% to 4.5% since 1954, and in Belgium only 11% of the population attends weekly services.[1]

Not attending traditional religious services does not, however, mean there is lack of faith. Rather, there is a panoply of faith practices—association with a church or not (the latter being what Grace Davie [1994] called "believing without belonging"), practicing one religion or combining faiths (syncretism or more pejoratively "cafeteria religion"), or shopping for faith (the seeker phenomenon noted by earlier). An array of options shouldn't surprise us because consumer culture has indoctrinated people to "want what they want when they want it," and this ideology spread to religious institutions. Congregations responded to this market-oriented mentality by creating congregations that appeal to the needs of their religious consumers (Cimino and Lattin, 1998; Twitchell 2004; Warner, 1993). Churches produced shorter and more entertaining services to accommodate congregants' lifestyles. They offered an expanding array of small group options to appeal to the widest number of people. Finally, surveys, focus groups, and demographic mapping are used by churches to plan new congregations and create a religious "product" that will suit the needs of the seeker.

BRANDING FAITH

Brands are made up of a name, an identifying icon, a tagline, and a mythology, which combined help to differentiate one commodity product from another within a category. These images and stories are presented through advertising and marketing as a means to position products in the minds of the consumers.

Importantly, branding is intended to enable consumers to see a logo and immediately access the brand's mythology. The logo appears and the stories connected with that brand come readily to mind. Think of Disney. In truth, it is simply a man's last name. But, if it is written in the company's distinct script and there are a pair of mouse ears in the immediate vicinity, it will come to symbolize dreams coming true, "when you wish upon a star," or it might evoke rage over the reported anti-Semitic leanings of the company's founder. These split-seconds of awareness about a product transmit invaluable information in an overly cluttered media environment (Danesi, 2006; Holt, 2004; Lury, 2004; Williams, 2000).

Brands have become the tools for creating our personal identities, replacing career, family, and, in many cases, religion as signifiers of who we are and what we believe. Brands replaced religious beliefs in part because marketers learned to understand consumers not at a demographic level, but on a psychographic one that taps into the lifestyles, concerns, and beliefs of who we are. Products were no longer marketed based simply on what they do, but what they do for the consumer particularly in terms of their symbolic utility. Thus, even the most basic products are no longer simply necessities; they are stories and badges that tell the world who we are. Think about it: the Body Shop is not just lotions and make up; it is a socially conscious retailer. Nike is not simply a sneaker; it is the best of athleticism and "Just Do It." We buy brands because we connect to the myths they convey—about the product, yes, but ultimately about ourselves. More to the point, people themselves are brands; celebrities and sports figures, of course, but also everyday people—particularly those on the job market—are encouraged to create and maintain their "personal brand" in the world of Web 2.0 (Lair, Sullivan, and Cheney, 2005), and even the most famous advocate against the use of branding—Naomi Klein—has perhaps unwittingly taken on the mantle of a brand (Belk, 2010).

Today, the full spectrum of religious and spiritual practices has turned to branding in order to remain part of the cultural conversation. For many, notably megachurches and their pastors such as Joel Osteen and Rick Warren, marketing and branding are forms of evangelizing (Hoover, 2005; Lee and Sinitiere, 2009; Twitchell 2004). For traditional denominations—which of themselves were a form of branding until they lost their distinct mythologies—branding is a means to re-establish an identity within the spiritual marketplace. As religious marketers have become more sophisticated and more comfortable with branding, it is being used not only to bring people to the faith but also to change perceptions, solidify an identity, and strengthen sagging public reputations. This has become increasingly important since the rise of social media when fully two-thirds of communications about an organization—religious or otherwise—are produced by someone other than the owner of the "brand."

Here, we will examine two recent advertising campaigns—"I'm a Mormon" for the Church of Jesus Christ of Latter-Day Saints and "Inspired by Muhammad" for Islam. These campaigns differ from their faith brand predecessors; although their ultimate objective is to bring people to faith, they also perform the important strategic function of trying to improve sagging public reputations while simultaneously teaching prospects who they are, what they stand for, and why that matters to them.

"AND I'M A MORMON"

Defining ourselves through brands is evident in advertising that uses the phrase "I am." The most ubiquitous version of this was the long-running Apple computer commercials with the copy "I'm a Mac" and "I'm a PC," where a nerdy guy in a gray suit symbolizes the old guard computer and a cool dude in t-shirt and jeans is the ever-hip Mac. This example epitomizes the anthropomorphizing of brands. We don't simply use a product, we are that product. After all, the ads don't say "I *use* a Mac"; they say "I *am* a Mac." Apple is not the only one to employ this languaging. Other examples include "I am Jeep" and "I am Nikon." There's also Microsoft's "I'm a PC and I'm four and a half," said by a young girl who demonstrates the ease of using the more widespread technology, and a T-Mobile phone campaign that flat out mimics the Apple spots comparing their products to the iPhone. The use of "I am," a phrase often associated with Western religions, demonstrates how utterly integrated brands have become to who we are.

Because religious identity is now a choice, it is not surprising to see religious institutions begin to use this copy strategy as well. It is an attempt to again make one's faith a defining aspect of who one is. Two churches—the Latter Day Saints and the Episcopal Church[2]—have opted for this messaging. Here, we will look at the "I'm a Mormon" campaign because it was the first and the most visible.

In the summer of 2010, the Mormon Church launched an advertising campaign that showed everyday people doing (mostly) everyday activities. Each ad ended with the tagline "I am 'Susie Smith' or 'Bob Jones,' and I'm a Mormon." These messages were disseminated via television, radio, and outdoor advertising such as billboards and bus platforms in select mid-sized markets around the United States (J. Campbell, 2010).[3]

Two important components of this campaign are to demonstrate the diversity of church membership—an important message in light of African Americans being excluded from the priesthood until the late 1970s—and to present Mormons as remarkable or special, but not outside the mainstream. According to Scott Swofford, director of media for the church, "We didn't want people that were famous or well-known, but we wanted them to be extraordinary in some way in life" (Schmuhl, 2010). In total there are thirty of these stories.[4] As a group, the Mormons appear accomplished, happy, friendly people from a number of backgrounds, who are decidedly family oriented—an important attribute for Mormons. The following three examples provide a sense of the breadth of the campaign. Note that what I describe here are the long-form videos; each of these has been cut into shorter versions, which are the commercials that aired on TV. In one video, a mother of two children with disabilities and four children in total talks about her life as mom. She speaks directly into the camera and tells us that doctors told her she could not have more than three children. She says she was okay with that because one of her children had cerebral palsy, and she felt like her life was full enough. That said, however, she and her husband adopted a fourth child, this one with Down syndrome. Throughout the video, we see her at home with her family, and we watch the disabled children compete in the Special Olympics. The spot ends with the line, "I'm a redhead, a Texan, a wife, a mom, and a Mormon." In another example, a British singer of Nigerian decent talks of how his mother moved back to her home country when he was only 11 and left him in London to fend for himself, initially through foster care and later falling into homelessness. We then see him in a recording studio; he has grown up to be a successful singer. He tells us that he performs because he wants to help people and not simply to make money—a point he makes explicit when he tells a story about how someone heard one of his songs and decided not to commit suicide. We also see him sitting happily with his white wife and small baby (remember, diversity). The video ends with, "I'm a father, a husband, and a musician. My name is Alex Boye, and I am a Mormon." In a third video, an Asian American woman is teaching math, and we learn she is the winner of the Presidential Award for Excellence in Mathematics & Science Teaching. Throughout the profile, we also see her running, cooking, and sitting at the dinner table with two women who appear to be her roommates. Part of the voiceover says, "I often perceive Mormons as 'you grow up, you turn 20, you get married, you have a family, you become a mom, and that's your life.' That hasn't happened for me. There isn't a cookie-cutter way to be a Mormon." Although the teacher is not married with her own children, the video shows her interacting with her nieces and nephews, thus still presenting the importance of family. It ends with the now familiar descriptive list, "I'm a loyal friend, I'm a middle school math teacher, I'm a huge sports fan. My name is Yvette Yamagata, and I'm a Mormon."[5]

Newspapers and pundits around the country chimed in as to why the church decided to initiate this campaign. Many believed that church leaders were attempting to support Mitt Romney's anticipated second attempt for the presidency; the church denied this (Goodwin, 2010). Others assert that the campaign had much more to do with changing the image of Mormonism in light of negative publicity around Utahan's support for California's Proposition 8 (the anti-gay marriage amendment), the arrest of polygamist and convicted rapist Warren Jeffs,[6] reports of racism in the Mormon church, as well as a number of not-all-flattering depictions of the faith on popular television, notably the HBO drama "Big Love" and the TLC reality series "Sister Wives." Beyond the initial reporting, the expansion of social media amplified these messages many times over, giving further strength to the negative messages.

In all, Mormonism attained a much higher profile than it had in the past, and with this attention came confusion about Mormonism: at a ratio of five to one, Americans are strongly unfavorable towards this faith versus strongly favorable. "Sixty-seven percent are uncertain whether Mormons believe the Bible, 77 percent on whether Mormons are Christians and 75 percent on whether Mormons practice polygamy" (Lloyd, 2010). The statistic that seemed to have most motivated the church to take control of the perception of their institution was that the majority of Americans (51%) have little to no awareness about Mormon practices and beliefs, and an almost equal percentage (47%) look on the faith unfavorably (LDS press release, 2010).

In light of these statistics, the campaign had a two-pronged marketing objective. First, the campaign had to normalize Mormonism, to "brand" Mormons as being "just like you and me." An important aspect of this communication is to let seekers know that Mormons believe in Jesus Christ—another way of saying, "We're just like you" (Machelor, 2010). This is presented prominently on the website. As discussed above, showing a diversity of people is an important factor towards this end. Doing this enables viewers to visualize themselves in the church. Smartly, the site provides visitors with the ability to select the type of Mormon they would like to meet based on age, gender, ethnicity, former religion, and continent, which can be navigated through a series of pull-down menus. In addition, by choosing people who are just a little special but doing everyday things, viewers cannot only visualize themselves but also can come to aspire to be like the people they see in the ads. It's the sense of, "Wow, these people are really interesting, cool, something I would like to be. Maybe it's because of the church." This is problem/solution advertising at its best.

The second goal was to drive current Mormons to the church's website where they can create their own profiles and share their stories much like the people in the commercials.[7] In order to post to the site, someone must have an LDS account, that is, be a church member. Once there, they can write a profile, upload a picture, and submit it for review. According to the church, within the first month of the campaign, thousands of people had created profiles. The church requested this of their members because they believe the best way to dispel myths about the church is to meet a Mormon. As they noted in their press release about the campaign, "Be a virtual neighbor to the thousands who could learn something from you about the Church. Share your story on mormon.org." Thousands of church members responded, and it was reported that they are hoping that number will reach into the millions (Tabor, 2010). These profiles/people become virtual evangelicals for the faith because the website is not static; it is a social network open to anyone. Each person who puts up a profile agrees to act as a representative of the church and voluntarily allows "prospects" to contact them to learn more about what it is to be a Mormon. Mormon.org, however, is just the entryway. From there visitors can move on to converse with Mormons via Facebook, blogs, and Twitter. Through all of this, social media comes to replace going door to door as the new way to meet a Mormon and to bring religion to the seeker.

"INSPIRED BY MOHAMMED"

By and large, Islam is promoted through a hodgepodge of methodologies. Traditional advertising is targeted to attract mainstream religious seekers. Islamic televangelism, while also mainstream, appeals to a younger Muslim cohort.[8] Finally, social networking and viral marketing (particularly rap videos) are used to attract a more violent Jihadi fringe—a minority view, for sure, but one that attracts significant media attention. The branding of Islam broadly is being negotiated in the secular media space via these competing messages. This should, perhaps, not surprise us given there is no centralized Islamic governing body to manage a cohesive communication strategy such as there is for the Mormon church.

However, similar to the "I'm a Mormon" campaign, "Inspired by Muhammad" was implemented in response to negative publicity and a continuingly poor international public image, particularly since the events of September 11th. Created by the Exploring Islam Foundation (EIF), a UK nonprofit, this campaign was launched to help change public perception in light of data which found that "58% of the British population surveyed associated Islam with extremism, 50% associate it with terrorism and 68% feel the religion encourages the repression of women" (Dougall, 2010).

The advertising campaign consists of a series of print ads. One features a Middle Eastern looking male, another shows a Middle Eastern looking female in a veil, and one presents a blonde, white, 30-something female. This last is a well-known MTV Europe personality, Kristiane Backer, who famously converted to Islam. The veiled woman is a barrister, and the man works with a homeless charity. The ads end with a call to action to go to the website ("Find out more at InspiredbyMuhammad.com"). Whereas previous campaigns such as "Islam is Peace" directly addressed the connection between violence and Islam, in this case hostility is not in evidence. Rather the campaign is intended to be optimistic and upbeat, which is emphasized through the use of bright colours, notably in the campaign's logo. The ads appeared in subways, on buses, and on shrink-wrapped taxis.

The campaign uses a pro-social copy strategy, not unlike the "green" marketing and corporate responsibility initiatives used by packaged goods companies. For example, the former MTVer is identified as an "eco-Muslim." Her ad states, "I believe in protecting the environment. So did Muhammad." For the barrister, the ad reads, "I believe in women's rights. So did Muhammad." And the final ad says, "I believe in social justice. So did Muhammad." According to EIF spokesperson Remona Aly, "We wanted to highlight areas that are buzz terms at the moment. . . . The environment is a really hot topic at the moment, and people are not aware Muslims are encouraged to care for the environment by the prophetic teachings and also the Koranic teachings" (Houpt, 2010). Thus, although the visuals of the campaign communicate diversity as much as the Mormon ads do, in terms of messaging, the issue is about dispelling misperceptions about Islamic beliefs through tying the faith to lifestyle issues. Unlike the Mormon ads, the communication is not that I am like you, but that I care about the things you care about and so do the people of my faith. This is a subtle difference but a noteworthy one.

What is fascinating about this strategy is that it is exactly what consumer packaged goods companies are using to improve their image. Cause-related marketing—tying a product to a cause in order to improve the image of the company—is an expanding trend. Think here of pink ribbons and breast cancer or red dresses and heart disease. Companies use these logos to embed shared values into a product's brand (Banet-Weiser and Lapsansky, 2008; Einstein, 2012; King, 2006; Kotler, Kartajaya, and Setiawan, 2010). Remember, we said that brands help make up our identity. Therefore, it becomes incumbent on brands to present our values to the world, much the way wearing a cross might have for earlier generations. If someone was to convert to Islam today, for instance, they would face having to combat the idea that they are a terrorist—the overriding mythology of Islam. What the campaign attempts to do is say, Islam is about social justice and women's rights and environmentalism and you can wear those badges if you are a Muslim.

Fundamentally, the objective of this advertising is to rehabilitate the religion's reputation as well as to "mainstream Islam," the motto of the organization that created this work. As mentioned, like "I'm a Mormon," the advertising points viewers to a website. This site is broken up into three main areas: Inspired Lives, Who was Muhammad, and The Campaign. At the bottom of each page, there are three prominent areas that point visitors to find out more; they are "Who is Muhammad?", "What is Islam?", and "Who are Muslims?" Although there is a Twitter feed running down the left side of the site and there is a YouTube section where visitors can "meet Muslims" (Inspired Lives), this is not a full-fledged social media site like that of the Mormons. There are a handful of videos that show people discussing their social issue—the environment, animal welfare, charity, education, and coexistence, among others—as it relates to Islam. Solidifying the connection to causes, visitors search by the issue, not by who the member is, when wanting to learn more about the faith.

EIF claims that the point of the campaign is to educate people about the progressive values of Islam. "We do not seek to preach or proselytize. We simply wish to provide accurate and accessible information about Islam for a mainstream audience in order to foster better understanding between the diverse communities in Britain" (Houpt, 2010). Although this may be the intention, it is difficult not to interpret these ads as also having an element of evangelization, perhaps in conjunction with image building but certainly there is an aspect of selling the faith via these communications. For example, compare these ads to those of the United Methodist Church (UMC), which has been implementing the "Rethink Church" campaign.[9] In the UMC advertising, they show church members working in daycare centers and helping to build communities in underdeveloped countries. They explain that viewers should "rethink church" as being about helping the wider world and not merely a physical place to attend. InspiredbyMuhammad doesn't do that. By showing people but not specifically presenting how they are changing the world (except in copy, which we know most people don't read), the information conveyed becomes a mixed message of reputation building and proselytizing.

Evidence suggests that InspiredbyMuhammad was created to appeal to a young adult audience. The people in the ads are young. The campaign is based around a website and utilizes some limited amount of social media. It seems EIF could do a lot more to present their case to a younger demographic target. The website, while clean, for example, does not have the depth of information that a seeker—particularly a young, internet-savvy seeker—would be looking for. Without a vibrant backend, the campaign is unlikely to be as effective as the creators might envision.[10]

CONCLUSION

In the midst of a competitive religious marketplace and a dynamic media environment, we can expect to see an increasing number of faiths—traditional and not—turn to marketing and branding strategies. This is so for a number of reasons. First, although secularization theory suggested that industrialized nations would become less religious, that has not turned out to be the case, particularly in the United States (Oswalt, 2003). The vast majority of Americans continue to believe in a higher power, and they have a plethora of options through which to express and participate in their beliefs. Because of this, religious organizations have to continuously prove that their service, their leader, and their community are the best source for fulfilling these needs. Second, because of the shopping mentality surrounding faith, a revolving door exists, with new congregants entering while disenfranchised members leave. Churn requires that congregations market themselves in order to retain membership levels. Finally, in terms of competition, brick and mortar institutions vie for congregants against not only one another but also against do-it-yourself religion, which is often practiced via books, 24-hour religious cable networks, and the internet, notably via virtual churches.

But, as demonstrated in the examples here, branding and marketing are not just about driving people to the pews. It is also about managing reputations and creating a positive image. For Muslims and Mormons, traditional news media were the primary drivers that led to the need for faith branding. However, social media perpetuated these messages. As Facebook, Twitter, and other social media have become widespread, their ubiquity is likely to push more and more faiths toward implementing these strategies—both online and off. Importantly, what we saw here, and what will continue to be true, is that centralized institutions are more successful in these efforts; this is because they have access to more funds, they can better manage the means of message distribution, and this ultimately leads to a more focused—and ultimately a more successful—branding campaign.

NOTES

1. The collapse of the church in France. http://rorate-caeli.blogspot.com/2010/01/collapse-of-church-in-france.html (accessed 9/12/11). For survey data in French, see la-Croix.com http://www.la-croix.com/illustrations/

Multimedia/Actu/2009/12/28/catholicisme-ifop.ppt; Belgium statistics http://www.state.gov/g/drl/rls/irf/2001/5563.htm

2. See http://www.iamepiscopalian.org/

3. The markets were Minneapolis-St. Paul, Minnesota; St. Louis; Baton Rouge, Louisiana; Colorado Springs, Colorado; Rochester, New York; Pittsburgh, Pennsylvania; Oklahoma City; Tucson, Arizona; and Jacksonville, Florida. In June 2011, the campaign also began to run in New York City.

4. They now appear on YouTube on a Jesus Christ of Latter Day Saints channel. The videos run between a minute and a half to over four minutes, and the fifteen-second commercial versions of these spots are cut from the longer pieces.

5. The publicity around this campaign makes much of the fact that these videos were unscripted. Although this may be true, it does not mean they are unedited.

6. He was the prophet of the Fundamentalist Church of Latter Day Saints (FLDS), which is a splinter group not recognized by the church. The FLDS widely practices polygamy, a practice abandoned by Mormons more than a century ago.

7. The strategy the Mormons pursued is similar to that of the Church of Scientology, which faced considerable negative publicity in 2009 in light of a number of high profile defections. While Scientology's commercials were more mystical and elusive, the ultimate goal was to get viewers to visit their newly revised and expanded website (Einstein, 2011).

8. Islamic televangelism has grown exponentially in the last two years because of the expansion of satellite television and the loosening of government restrictions of programming in Muslim countries. Young Islamic preacher present a compassionate alternative to the violence presented in Jihadist online videos and help fill the program schedules of 27 channels dedicated to Islamic religious programming. The most popular of this group is 29-year-old Moez Masoud, who relates religious texts to the everyday lives of his viewers and uses marketing to sell himself and his faith, much like Western televangelists.

9. See rethinkchurch.org

10. Interestingly, the group recently launched a new campaign in January 2011 called "Missing Pages," which promotes unity between Islam and Jews. Focused on the Holocaust Memorial Day, it appears to be targeting an older generation, and we might add one that is unlikely to switch faiths. The website for this campaign is more developed and better designed than the one for the advertising, suggesting that it is not money that is keeping EIF from more fully fleshing out the messaging of the original campaign.

REFERENCES

Banet-Weiser, S., and C. Lapsansky. 2008. RED is the New Black: Brand Culture, Consumer Citizenship and Political Possibility. *International Journal of Communication* 2: 1248–1268.

Beaudoin, T. 2003. *Consuming Faith: Integrating Who We Are with What We Buy.* Chicago, IL: Sheed and Ward.

Belk, R. 2010. "The Naomi Klein Brand." *Women's Studies Quarterly* 38: 293–298.

Boellstorff, Tom. 2008. *Coming of Age in Second Life: An Anthropologist Explores the Virtually Human.* Princeton, NJ: Princeton University Press.

Campbell, C. 2008 *The Easternization of the West: A Thematic Account of Cultural Change in the Modern Era.* Boulder, CO: Paradigm Publishers.

Campbell, H. 2010. *When Religion Meets New Media.* London: Routledge.

Campbell, J. 2010, August 25. Mormon Media Observer: Ad campaign gets mixed reviews. *Deseret News.* Retrieved April 12, 2011. from http://www.mormontimes.com/article/16679/Mormon-Media-Observer-Ad-campaign-gets-mixed-reviews

Cimino, R., and D. Lattin. 1998. *Shopping for Faith: American Religion in the New Millennium.* San Francisco, CA: Jossey-Bass.

Danesi, Marcel. 2006. *Brands.* New York: Routledge.

Davie, Grace. 1994. *Religion in Britain Since 1945: Believing Without Belonging.* Hoboken, NJ: Wiley-Blackwell.

Dawson, L. L., and D. E. Cowan. (2004). *Religion Online: Finding Faith on the Internet.* London: Routledge.

Dougall, J. 2010, June 7). Campaign Launched to Improve Image of Islam. *Sky News.* Available at http://news.sky.com/skynews/Home/UK-News/Inspired-by-Muhammad-Campaign-Launched-To-Improve-Image-Of-Islam/Article/201006115644684

Einstein, M. 2008. *Brands of Faith: Marketing Religion in a Commercial Age.* London: Routledge.

———. 2011, Fall. "The Evolution of Religious Branding." *Social Compass* 58 (3): 1–8.

———. 2012. *Compassion, Inc.: How corporate America blurs the line between what we buy, who we are and those we help.* Berkeley, CA: University of California Press.

Finke, R., & L. R. Iannaccone. 1993. "Supply-Side Explanations for Religious Change." *The Annals of the American Academy, AAPSS 527:* 27–39.

Goodwin, L. (2010, August 11). *In New TV Ads, Mormons Pitch Message to Middle America.* Retrieved April 1, 2011 from http://news.yahoo.com/s/yblog_upshot/in-new-tv-ad-campaign-mormons-pitch-message-to-middle-america

Hadaway, C. K, & P. L. Marler 1998, May 6. "Did You Really Go to Church This Week? Behind the Poll Data." *The Christian Century,* 472–475.

Holt, D. 2004. *How Brands Become Icons: The Principles of Cultural Branding.* Cambridge, MA: Harvard University Press.

Hoover, Stewart M. 2005. "The Cross at Willow Creek: Seeker Religion and the Contemporary Marketplace." In *Religion and Popular Culture in America,* edited by Bruce Ford and Jeffrey Mahan, 145–159. Berkeley, CA: University of California Press.

Houpt, S. 2010, June 11. "Muhammad Gets a Makeover; A British Campaign Peddles the Softer Side of Islam. *The Globe and Mail* (Canada), B8.

King, S. 2006. *Pink Ribbons, Inc.* Minneapolis, MN: University of Minnesota Press.

Kotler, P., H. Kartajaya, & I. Setiawan. 2010. *Marketing 3.0: From Products to Customers to the Human Spirit.* Hoboken, NJ: Wiley.

LDS Press Release. 2010, September 11. *I'm a Mormon.* Retrieved April 2, 2010, from http://www.ldschurchnews.com/articles/59841/Im-a-Mormon.html

Lair, Daniel J., Katie Sullivan, and George Cheney. 2005. "Marketization and the Recasting of the Professional Self." *Management Communication Quarterly* 18 (3): 307–343.

Lau, K. 2000. *New Age Capitalism: Making Money East of Eden.* Philadelphia, PA: University of Pennsylvania Press.

Lee, S., & P. L. Sinitiere. 2009. *Holy Mavericks: Evangelical Innovators and the Spiritual Marketplace.* New York: New York University Press.

Lloyd, R. S. 2010, August 7. "Mormons Need to Work to Increase Favor." *Deseret News*. Available at http://www.deseretnews.com/article/700054363/Mormons-need-to-work-to-increase-favor.html

Lury, C. 2004. *Brands: The Logos of the Global Economy*. London: Routledge.

Machelor, P. 2010, August 21. "Marketing Mormonism: TV Spots Highlight Diverse Backgrounds of Church Members." *McClatchy—Tribune Business News*.

Miller, V. J. 2004. *Consuming Religion: Christian Faith and Practice in a Consumer Culture*. New York: Continuum.

Moore, R. L. 1994. *Selling God: American Religion in the Marketplace of Culture*. New York: Oxford University Press.

Oswalt, C. 2003. *Secular Steeples: Popular Culture and the Religious Imagination*. Harrisburg, PA: Trinity Press International.

Roof, W. C. 1999. *Spiritual Marketplace: Baby Boomers and the Remaking of American Religion*. Princeton, NJ: Princeton University Press.

Schmidt, L. E. 1995. *Consumer Rites: The Buying and Selling of America Holidays*. Princeton, NJ: Princeton University Press.

Schmuhl, Emily. 2010, September 13. *The People in the 'I'm a Mormon' Ad Campaign*. Retrieved April 15, 2010, from http://www.mormontimes.com/article/17068/The-people-in-the-Im-a-Mormon-ad-campaign?s_cid=newsline

Tabor, A. 2010, August 16. *Surfing a Saintly Social Network*. Retrieved April 2, 2011, from http://uscmediareligion.org/theScoop/310/Surfing-Saintly-Social-Network

Taylor, H. 2003, October 15. *While Most Americans Believe in God, Only 36% Attend a Religious Service Once a Month or More Often*. Retrieved April 19, 2011, from http://www.harrisinteractive.com/vault/Harris-Interactive-Poll-Research-While-Most-Americans-Believe-in-God-Only-36-pct-A-2003–10.pdf

Twitchell, J. B. 2004. *Branded Nation: The Marketing of Megachurch, College inc., and Museumworld*. New York: Simon & Schuster.

———. (2007. *Shopping for God: How Christianity Went from in Your Heart to in Your Face*. New York: Simon & Schuster.

Wagner, R. 2011. *Godwired: Religion, Ritual and Virtual Reality*. London: Routledge.

Warner, R. S. 1993. "Work in Progress Toward a New Paradigm for the Sociological Study of Religion in the United States." *American Journal of Sociology* 98 (5): 1044–1093.

Williams, G. 2000. *Branded: Products and Their Personalities*. London: B&A Publications.

11 Economies of Expectation
Men, Marriage, and Miracles in Kenya's Religious Marketplace

Catherine Dolan

> Whether you desire a marriage miracle, a financial miracle or a healing miracle, come believing and the Lord will meet with you at your point of need in Jesus name.—Pastor Chris Ojigbani

In 2010, thousands of women scrambled to reach the gates of Kenya's largest conference center vying to hear charismatic Pastor Chris Ojigbani, the self-confessed Nigerian "apostle of marriage," spread news on "how to get married without delay." For several hours, Nairobi came to a standstill as 10,000 well-dressed women clamored to reach the venue and police struggled to keep the 'expectant' crowds at bay. While the city streets were abuzz with the news of the unfolding pandemonium, inside the convention center, the atmosphere was electric with women singing, raising their hands, crying, dancing, and praying in hopes that the boyish leader of the Covenant Singles and Married Ministries (CSMM) would bless them with an "instant wedding" (Genga, 2010). Like a Christian rock star, Pastor Ojigbani swanned to center stage amid a swirl of lights and gospel music, announcing to an ecstatic audience, "Good men are not all taken. By the end of today, you will get your suitor. . . . The spirit has told me that one of you by morning will have four suitors." With a wry smile, he then asked the exuberant women, "Now, who will you choose?" (Gisesa, 2010). Before the "Set Time of Marriage" (STOM) event had concluded, dozens of women had mounted the stage to testify that they had received marriage proposals via text messages while others left the auditorium buoyed by the prospect of lavish weddings and marital success (Gisesa, 2010). As Sister O testified on the CSMM website,

> After the seminar . . . I met an old friend who has been admiring me since high school. I saw him last three years ago. . . . Within 5 minutes of meeting him he started proposing marriage to me and said he had never stopped admiring me. He said "I want to marry, will you marry me?" He had barely finished talking when I got a call from another man who I broke up with 6 years ago. He asked me where I was from and I told him I was on my way back from a singles programme. And he said, "What single? You are no longer single. I want to marry you.

In fact consider you married." I was amazed! My set time of marriage has indeed come.[1]

Although mega marriage spectacles are relatively new to Kenya, similar charismatic scenes unfold daily in a nation where crusades, radio revivals, and celebrity evangelists pervade all facets of public life, and where the boundaries among religion, commerce, and entertainment are often impossible to discern. The mushrooming of the so-called 'single lady ministries' sits comfortably within this syncretic context and reflects the increased significance of the 'unmarried woman' to Africa's Charismatic ministries as they adapt themselves to an ever-changing religious consumer. Whereas some ministries focus on cultivating women's entrepreneurial dispositions, promising that business acumen will produce an Oprah-style transformation of personal confidence and self-esteem, other ministries cast marriage as the passport to material wealth and worldly success, hitching an imaginary of personal transformation to an industrious, dependable, and prosperous spouse. In both cases, however, the self-interested instrumentalism of the capitalist marketplace is twinned with the prophetic promises of the Bible, forming an interpretive frame through which all aspects of everyday life are navigated and managed.

This chapter uses the CSMM founded by Pastor Ojigbani as a prism through which to explore the interplay of spiritual belief and material well-being among a group of 'born again' women in Kenya. Building on consumer research that highlights the sacred and profane aspects of consumer behavior and anthropological studies that describe the slippage between ostensibly discordant spheres of market and religion, the chapter argues that while Christianity construes marriage as a harbor of sanctity distinct from the impersonal world of market capitalism, Pentecostal-charismatic Christianity (P/c),[2] and Single Women Ministries in particular, diffuse the boundaries among religious, domestic, and market spheres, rendering conjugal relations a site for spiritual and financial transformation. It is through rather than against the rationality of the capitalist market that women attain the "spiritual gift" of P/c: a marriage proposal from a well-to-do provider.

THE CONFLUENCE OF SPHERES

Since Durkheim's seminal "separate sphere" thesis,[3] the relationship between sacred and profane realms of social life has commanded significant attention across the social sciences. Within marketing, consumer culture theorists have empirically demonstrated the significance of material objects and consumption activities to the constitution of consumers' spiritual lives across cultures and commodities (Arnould and Price, 1993, 2004; Arnould et al., 1999; Belk et al., 1989; Curasi et al., 2004; Sherry and Kozinets, 2003; O'Guinn and Belk, 1989; Wallendorf and Arnould, 1991).

This literature approaches the sacred/profane dichotomy from two vantage points: one strand focuses on how consumers sacralize mundane goods and services, turning prosaic commodities and everyday consumption practices (e.g., shopping) into vehicles for transcendent experience (Arnould and Price, 2004; Arnould et al., 1999; Belk et al., 1989; Firat and Venkatesh, 1995; O'Guinn and Belk, 1989), whereas the other strand explores how the realm of the sacred is commoditized, as religion becomes a market commodity that is packaged, marketed, and sold in global consumer culture. Twitchell (2005, 2007) and Einstein (2008), for example, describe how the marketing machine of Christian megachurches lures evermore-discriminating 'customers' through celebrity pastors, fitness facilities, and food courts, while O'Guinn and Belk (1989, p. 227) describe how the shopping mall, auctions, and water park of the Christian theme park, Heritage Village, convert heaven into a site of "luxury, play, celebration . . . and shopping." Indeed, while "spiritless" consumerism is typically deemed as anathema to a relationship with the divine, this body of research points to the often-symbiotic relationship between the worlds of money and morality.

Although marketing the sacred is not a new phenomenon (see Miller, 2004; Parker and Baker, 2007; Turner and Turner, 1978), the intermingling of sacred and secular realms has intensified under late capitalism as individuals seek to manage the instability and uncertainty of globalization through a diversity of 'irrational' spiritual practices, products, and services. Ethnographic research in Asia (Kitiarsa, 2007; Sinha, 2010), for example, documents how the global market economy has intersected with longstanding ethno-religious landscapes to produce new forms of religious commoditizations and economies of charisma. Similarly, scholars of Africa have shown how contemporary symbols and practices of both the occult and Christianity are integral to the experience of modernity as individuals seek to manipulate, navigate, or control the opportunities and tensions engendered by global capitalism (e.g., Bornstein, 2002; Comaroff and Comaroff, 1993, 2000; Geshiere, 1997; Gifford, 2004; Meyer, 2004). These studies, to cite but a few, unsettle Durkheimian binaries and Weberian predictions that modernity (i.e., rationality) would produce a "disenchantment of the world," pointing instead to the fluid, malleable, and persistent imbrication of the sacred and the profane.[4]

Whereas the entanglements between sacralization and secularization are becoming clear, less is known about how the intimate world of marriage and family figure in the interpenetration of these processes. Like religion, contemporary forms of marriage are positioned as antithetical to the detached world of market capitalism, a private sphere of affective ties cordoned off from the instrumentalism of commercial exchange. Described by Zelizer (2005) as the "hostile-worlds view," this perspective views economic activities and intimate relations as distinct domains, with "disorder resulting when the two spheres come into contact with each other" (pp. 20–21). Christianity, for instance, holds marriage to be an institution ordained by

God—a holy sacrament that reflects Jesus' relationship to the Church—whose sanctity is threatened by a "globalized secular culture" and a mercenary consumer society (Armstrong, 2011; Catholic News Agency, 2007). However, there is little discussion of how the private realm of conjugal relations serves as fodder for processes of religious commodification, as an object of consumerism in the same way as Mecca and the megachurch (Gillette, 2000; Twitchell, 2005). As the following discussion illustrates, marriage too is a site that bridges the seemingly antagonistic worlds of religious devotion and economic gain, one that facilitates the accumulation of financial as well as spiritual capital.

THE RISE OF PENTECOSTALISM IN AFRICA

Over the last few decades, P/c[5] has grown into one of the most powerful socio-economic forces on the African landscape, eclipsing the dominance of mission churches—Catholics, Anglicans, Baptists, Lutherans, and Methodists—to become the continent's most vital and rapidly expanding popular religion (Maxwell, 2006).[6] Thousands of churches and ministries of P/c persuasion now flourish across Kenya and other SSA countries, offering miraculous healing, divine illumination, and both spiritual and economic salvation through Christian ministry. Described as a "metacommentary on the ill-doings of capitalism and globalization" (Moore and Sanders, 2001, p. 14), the P/c movement adeptly reconciles the tensions between the local and global, individual and community, and tradition and modernity that mark the topography of contemporary African economies, penetrating seemingly non-religious spheres such as politics, business, mass communication, and entertainment with increasing ubiquity (Maxwell, 2006; Parsitau, 2008; Ukah, 2003). Today Africa's urban centers are suffused with forms of religious production and consumption that extend well beyond the revival gatherings, air-rallies, and healing ministries often associated with born again movements. A midday stroll through Nairobi's city center, for example, reveals a dizzying array of Christian images, symbols, and practices: acquaintances greet each other with the words *"bwana asife"* (praise the Lord), scriptural banners flutter at street intersections, born again graffiti embellishes streetlights and public notice boards, Christian slogans (e.g., "Keep cool, Jesus is in control") are inscribed on *matatus* (local transport) (Parsitau, 2008), and the signs of local businesses—"Blessed Cereals Store" and "Answered Prayer Boutique"—create a roadside iconoscape that transports Jesus from the altar to the capitalist marketplace (Dolan and Johnstone-Louis, 2009). At the same time, representations and discourses of salvation are increasingly diffused through the world of electronic and digital media. Media-savvy "pastorpreneurs" fill television airwaves with religious programming and recorded church services, FM stations run a steady soundscape of audio sermons, phone-in talk shows and gospel

music, and the internet facilitates virtual evangelism through PayPal blessing opportunities and Facebook prayer networks. These 24 hour stream-
ing 'mediascapes' (Appadurai, 1997) pair spiritual sustenance and worldly
well-being, offering Kenyan audiences new affinities with transnational
religious networks.

This "spiritual marketplace" reflects a now common pattern of fetish-
ism, whereby religious symbols are unmoored from their original referents
and repackaged as consumer goods, as capital objectifies evermore aspects
of religious experience from Mecca to Jerusalem (cf. Marx, 1867[1977]).
However, Nairobi's blend of market and morality specifically represents the
forms of cultural production associated with "Faith churches," notably the
"materialist ethos of the Prosperity Gospel" (Coleman, 2004, p. 423).

PROSPERITY GOSPEL

In the Christian context, the "Prosperity" gospel refers to a set of loosely
defined yet globally uniform doctrines and liturgical practices that attribute
illness and poverty to demonic influence and promise believers physical health
and material success on Earth through divine intervention (Dolan and John-
stone, 2010; Robbins, 2004). Also termed the "health and wealth" gospel,
the prosperity teachings originated among independent pastors, churches,
and popularizers in North America and fanned out across Europe, Africa,
and Latin America. Prosperity Gospel teachings are distinct from more traditional interpretations of the Christian faith in that they promise not only
salvation but also financial transformation (Coleman, 2000, 2002; Gifford,
2003; Hunt, 2000). Unlike older, mission-style churches that eschew materialism as unholy, the prosperity doctrine not only condones but promotes
displays of acquired wealth, equating visible consumption with religious
virtue. Pastors are expected to emulate 'modern' entrepreneurs, showcasing
upmarket lifestyles and a transnational cosmopolitanism, whereas followers are encouraged to display their "gifts of the spirit" as testimony to their
"redemptive uplift" (Marshall-Frantani, 1998; Maxwell, 1998). As Elizabeth, a 25 year old unemployed women living in Nairobi, told me, "When
you testify to be a child of God someone should look at you and see you
really are the child of God. . . . You can't just testify to be a child of God yet
you are so poor that everyone can tell. They will wonder which God is this
that you worship that lets you be so poor." Acknowledging the blessing of
God thus requires that material gifts are publicly witnessed, creating a spiritual economy where evangelism and consumption walk hand in hand.

The Prosperity Gospel has found a receptive audience in many African
countries where its tantalizing promise of Western-style success offers the 'disenfranchised' a palliative to a world turned upside down by 'modernity,' globalization, and neoliberal capitalism (see Meyer, 2004, for Ghana; van Dijk,
1995, for Malawi; and Maxwell, 1998; Mate, 2002, for Zimbabwe). The

"instantism" of Faith teaching (Hunt 2000: 334), in particular, is a natural fit in a landscape where cravings for 'fast wealth' have fuelled a diet of pyramid and Ponzi schemes, gambling and speculation, and other forms of what Krige (2009) terms "'Fong Kong' Finance." Indeed, faith ministries unabashedly peddle financial salvation as in the words of Pastor Obigjani, "No matter what you desire, you will have it in Jesus' name," which is typically not eternal life but "cars, houses, and fashionable clothes." For example, at the STOM seminar, it was not only husbands who were secured but also lucrative business contracts as illustrated by Alice. A poised, doe eyed-woman with delicate features, Alice mounted the stage to announce that when she followed Pastor Ojigbani's advice to declare her intentions, she won a contract worth billions of shillings from a European firm, a "testimony" that now travels the world via YouTube. Such performances are often fodder for critics, who equate adherents of the Prosperity teachings to a cargo cult, in which the mere currency of faith and belief buy the material rewards of modernity. However, as I will explore later, whereas consumption is as likely as prayer to signal religious devotion, it would be a mistake to interpret the 'economic miracles' of CSMM as free gifts from the Divine. Rather, good fortune is a return on spiritual investments, investments that begin with conversion and encompass a clear set of practices, behaviors, and rituals. In the remainder of this chapter, I explore how women interpret three aspects of spiritual investment—prayer, tithing, and self-improvement—as avenues to marriage, an institution shaped as much by monetary as moral imperatives in CSMM circles.

The discussion is based on twenty-five in-depth interviews conducted with women who attended Pastor Obijani's "Set Time for Marriage" seminar in Nairobi, Kenya, in September 2010. Women were selected through a purposive sample that reflected varying demographic profiles (age, family size, employment, etc.). All informants are self-identifying born again Christians. The purpose of the interviews was to understand women's motivations and rationale for attending the seminar, and explore how they interpret the relationship among marriage, material wealth, and their Christian beliefs within the expanding capitalist economies of charisma.

MINISTRY AND THE SINGLE WOMAN

Research around the world has repeatedly found that women underlie the rapid expansion of evangelical, mostly P/c, around the world. According to Martin (2001), women constitute three quarters of the world's evangelicals, a figure supported by studies of individual P/c churches (Robbins, 2004). Much has been written about P/c's apparent gender paradox—why it is that countless women flock to a religion that endorses patriarchal norms of female subordination and deference (Brusco, 1995; Gill, 1990; Robbins, 2004), particularly in contexts where discourses of gender equality are often most vehemently promoted by international aid agencies (Martin, 2001). While the motives for women's participation in P/c are multi-faceted, several aspects are relevant to understanding the appeal of Single Ladies ministries. First, in sub-Saharan Africa poverty, illness, and misfortune are frequently interpreted through the idioms of the supernatural (e.g., witchcraft, occult, and sorcery). Pentecostalism offers a vehicle to combat these malevolent forces, one that is particularly attractive to women, who are far more likely than men to be branded as witches (Quarmyne, 2011; Smith, 2001). Second, P/c emphasizes the personal development of individuals, particularly women, and encourages women's engagement in activities and processes that foster confidence and self-esteem (Soothill, 2010). In a context like Kenya, where approximately one third of households are headed by a single woman (World Bank, 2003), the importance that single ladies ministries' place on financial empowerment, and in particular the assistance they provide to unskilled women to start small-scale businesses or obtain employment, fulfills both spiritual and economic ambitions, as laziness and poverty are deemed inimical to God's will (see www.slif.net). In fact while marriage is cast as an avenue for future economic stability, it does not preclude the need to develop a strategy for financial security in the here and now.

Third, although P/c doctrine upholds men's position as "master of the household" (Chestnut, 1997, p. 112), in practice ministries place a high value on conjugal and family development (Brusco, 1995), proscribing the irresponsible exercise of male power and reining in aspects of male behavior that are potentially damaging to women, such as domestic violence, adultery, and drunkenness (Brusco, 1995; Martin, 2001). Through what Smilde (1997, pp. 354–355) calls a "religiously bounded patriarchy," Pentecostalism imparts a religious justification for confronting untoward male authority and offers women some security, albeit within the confines of marriage. Single Ministries like CSMM reinforce this vision by stressing the importance of finding the 'right' and 'correct' spouse, one who will protect women emotionally, physically, and financially. Finally, the P/c movement offers women a valued sense of moral community. Because converts are required to sever ties with the past and specifically with non-believing kin and community, the church becomes the locus of both religious and associational life, providing women with new networks through which to negotiate the country's shifting economic and political landscape (Smith, 2001).

These opportunities for self-renewal and empowerment are circumscribed by a theology that affirms rather than contests dominant concepts of masculinity and femininity and that places marriage as the source of women's fulfillment. According to Catherine, for example, in weekly women's meetings, "women are taught how to keep yourself if you are single, and how to cope with marriage challenges if you are in a marriage," teachings that focus on cooking, cleaning, grooming, and conduct. As Camilla noted, women were created to help men, and "there is no man who wants a wife who will not cook or wash for him." However, the fact remains that the prospects for any marriage can be dim, particularly in urban areas where women delay marriage to pursue education or careers. As Kanini said, "this thing of getting married is becoming a problem to so many people. You know those career women, who decided to work first and after sometime, they realize they are getting old and they don't have a husband. . . . Now they realize the years are passing without notice. Nowadays, you can find women at 40 who are not married." This is why, she said, Single Ministries attract so many women.[7] They need "that spiritual intervention" to find a husband in a lackluster marriage market, an intervention that ministries like CSMM are eager to fulfill. Pastor Ojigbani, founder of CSMM, claims that God commissioned him to liberate marriages through the preaching of the Word, which he does through a range of avenues from stadium-style ministries and televangelism to video prayer sessions and marriage school. His liberation includes removing devices that cause his 'fans' delay in marriage, empowering singles to marry, restoring broken marriages, and making marriages work. As he states on his Facebook page:

> I have decided to consistently teach and impart my fans with the right knowledge that will empower them to marry easily and also empower the married to enjoy their marriages. I will also, on a daily basis, pray for you. The combination of the right knowledge and the right prayer gives rise to testimony. Amazing marriage testimony! I decree that your set time of marriage has come in Jesus name! Talking about testimonies, visit our website, www.singlesandmarried.org to read some amazing testimonies of attendees of our marriage seminar. (https://www.facebook.com/topic.php?uid=143851529492&topic=10606)

An author of several self-help marriage books (e.g., *Spiritual Warfare, Activating the Grace of Marriage*, and *I want to Marry You*) and DVDs (e.g., *The Power of Sex* and *The Trick of Love*), Pastor Ojigbani has become a global commodity in his own right, a site for the production, consumption, and circulation of enchantment from London to Lagos. He is aired on television stations around the world, has a sermon circuit that draws thousands of fans in major European and African capitals, and courts contributions through PayPal (http://www.singlesandmarried.org/PASTORCHRIS/tabid/63/Default.aspx). Indeed, Ojigbani serves as a microcosm for the transnational flows of media, money, moralities, and imagined modernities that define the space of charismatic and Pentecostal Christianity, as its ministries manufacture and spread the promise of health and wealth through the circuits of consumer culture.

"I WANT TO GET MARRIED, LIKE YESTERDAY"

Marriage in Kenya is often derided for its patriarchal character, with culturally sanctioned power differentials in access to resources and opportunities that privilege men. Women's hunger for marriage can thus appear puzzling, particularly as maternal and matrimonial roles are largely decoupled, especially in urban areas. There is, of course, the desire for the emotional and physical intimacy conferred through marriage, an intimacy that is increasingly showcased through mass mediated images of Western-style romance as the model for contemporary gender relations. Yet as Gacheri, a participant at the STOM seminar, argued, "Most women can't get married for love, because they will not eat love." They would, she said, rather "cry in a Mercedes Benz than laugh on a motorbike." Similarly, Lucy claimed that women "are running after old men with money who can buy them houses and cars. Not because they love them [but because] they do not want poor men who cannot support them. Nobody wants someone who will bring *sukuma wiki* [collared greens] every day. It sounds better if you can go out on weekends for *nyamachoma* [roasted meat]." As a participant in Pastor Ojigbani's seminar observed, "In times of economic uncertainty, marriage is a good way to hedge your bets. . . . Marriage is the new sacco [Savings and Credit Co-operative]." These narratives are not uncommon; they circulate widely through commercial media and a public sphere that broad brush Kenyan women as 'gold diggers' who enter transactional relations with sugar daddies for modern material goods. Yet such representations trivialize the "patriarchal risk" (Cain, Khanum, and Nahar, 1979) single women often confront—a threat of economic insecurity, social ostracism, and potentially long-term deprivation. Indeed in a Kenyan context, the link between marriage and financial security can be anything but inconsequential, as marriage is not only a proxy for economic security but also for social identity and belonging.

As a result, the pursuit of a spouse is a consumption choice that demands a careful weighing of a man's potential for economic stability and upward mobility. For example, most of the women interviewed for this study portrayed marriage as a way that they could bankroll their futures. As Kanini, a mother of two, said to me, "You don't want to hustle the whole of your life. You want a guy whom you know when you have kids they will go to a nice school, because you can't rely on the government schools. You also want to live in a nice place. You don't want to stay in a place where there is no security; you want to live in nice comfortable place." In nearly all conversations, the affective sphere of marriage was entangled with the logic of capital, requiring an intervention that would deliver not just any husband but "someone earning big money, with a big bank account." The pairing of commodification and intimacy—the way marriage is fetishized, commercialized, and objectified—emerged clearly in women's descriptions of their anticipated weddings. Anne, a single, 26 year old service worker, told me that she would host a buffet for her 300 to 400 guests at a hotel garden with a live band, flowers, and cakes, and travel to Jomo Kenyatta airport in a limousine, where she would board a plane for a South African honeymoon. When I asked Anne what kind of wedding she would actually have, she looked at me with surprise, telling me that "Nothing will change. God is my father who owns everything on earth. He will grant me what I desire," even if such glamorous scenarios bore little resemblance to her current circumstance. Anne is not alone, however, in ascribing a link between religious convictions and consumerist fantasies. For nearly all informants, the pursuit of marriage was framed through a similar mixture of evangelical morality and economic accumulation, a mixture captured in three themes of the STOM seminar—tithing, praying, and self-development—to which I now turn.

TITHING: THE SPIRIT OF GIVING AND RECEIVING

P/c movements emphasize *charismata pneumatika* or "spiritual gifts" that are available to all believers (Asamoah-Gyadu, 2004). These gifts, however, are neither unconditional nor free of obligation (cf. Mauss, 1925[1967]). Rather, they are nested in an exchange relationship animated through tithing. The obligation to tithe and give offerings is fundamental to Pentecostal culture (Robbins, 2004). While the extent and nature of tithing (seed planting) varies across denominations, it is generally expected that followers will tithe at least 10% of their income to the church in accordance with the scriptures. In Kenya, as in other parts of SSA, the prosperity gospel explicitly tethers the biblical edict to tithe with the prospect of material wealth. Several U.S. megachurch preachers who broadcast regularly on Kenya's Christian airwaves (e.g., Joel Osteen and Joyce Meyer) often parade the 'beneficiaries' of tithing—that is, those who have acquired jobs, houses, cars, etc.—in front of congregations to underscore the relationship between giving and getting. Tithing also assumes a central position in CSMM. For example, during the first offertory collection at the STOM seminar, Pastor Ojigbani showed video clips of various women who 'testified' to the miracle marriage proposals and magnificent weddings they had experienced thanks to CSMM. At the second round of giving, women were told to fill out two forms—prayer requests and financial commitment—thus making explicit the ties that bind piety and prosperity (Muiruri, 2010). However, paying to be freed from marital poverty isn't unproblematic. As Ann M commented, "I was like, if I don't plant a seed I won't get a husband?" Her ambivalence mirrors wider criticisms of tithing, which has come under fire for reproducing the greed, selfishness, and materialism of modern consumer society, transforming Christianity into a casino where the highest bidder prevails. Several women I spoke to claimed that Kenyan pastors are peddling an expectation of abundant wealth while stuffing their coiffeurs with congregants' money. As Lucy described, "In every church in Kenya they are preaching prosperity not heaven any more. . . . After prayers you plant a seed—an offering—so you can get the prosperity they are talking about. But these pastors [are] becoming millionaires while you are still there planting seeds and no harvest." Another young teacher, Melissa, said that her pastor requests that followers send offerings through M-pesa (an electronic money transfer service) so that miracles can be delivered without delay whereas others decried the introduction of minimum payments for *sadaka* (blessing). This "fee for service" exchange (Comaroff and Comaroff, 2000, p. 314) is what Obiora (1998, p. 58) describes as "Holy Deceit"—the irreverence of marketing fortune in God's name.

Yet while some circles discredit tithing as crude commercialism, many women believed that "when you worship God with your wealth, the Lord will bless you more." Far from viewing tithing as separate from their economic well-being, women emphasized the need to give to God in order to achieve prosperity, viewing spiritual investment and financial returns as intrinsically aligned. Citing the gospel of Luke, "Give, and it will be given to you . . . for with the same measure that you use, it will be measured back to you." Prudence told me that she knows that the more she gives, the more business contracts she will be awarded. A giving hand shall receive, she said. Similarly, Faith claimed that in her church, they are told the truth: "There is no prayer to get money. You have to give in order to receive." Yet giving is neither simply anticipatory nor unreciprocated. Gacheri, whose estranged husband returned following her attendance at the STOM seminar, contributed an offering of 1,000 Kenyan shillings (approximately $11) in gratitude. Indeed for many followers of the CSMM, tithing is as much an economic as a spiritual calculation, a strategic deployment erected so that God could bless their home with a husband and thereby gain the fruits of material success that their spouse will bestow.

PRAYER

For many women, the mere act of giving tithes and offerings did not alone guarantee a return gift (cf. Mauss, 1925[1967]). Rather, tithing operated in tandem with the practice of prayer, construed as an unmediated channel to God through which all His blessings pass (Soothill, 2010). As Catherine said, "It is important to pray for a life partner. . . . God has to be involved in the connection of the two. . . . He knows who you are suited for. . . . That is why we really need to pray for a husband." Yet even the relationship between prayer and marital success is more ambiguous than Catherine's words imply. On the one hand, like tithing, the CSMM knits together prayer and prosperity through sermons, testimonies, and trainings that equate purposeful prayer with imminent matrimony (e.g. *"Two Marriage Proposals in 5 minutes!"*). For example, on Pastor Ojigbani's Facebook page, he exhorted Kenyans attending the STOM seminar to "attend with expectations" and "to stand up and declare what u want to happen next week!" The nexus between clarity of prayer and the realization of imagined futures is repeated across the ministry. As Maggie told me, "You have to lay down your vision, tell God I want ABCD. You need to have a plan. . . . Because even when you are doing a prayer to God, you must be specific. It is in the book of Mathew. Specify." Sarah agreed, "You know the Bible says God knows me and He knows my needs and He will grant the desires in my heart . . . [so] I put my prayer for a husband, for a job and for all these other things before God." Importantly, the "shopping list" (O'Guinn and Belk, 1989) not only maps desire, enabling women to envisage a married life dissociated from their current reality, but converts it into a tangible expectation.

For other women, however, material benefits are not understood as the passive rewards of prayer and clear intention, or as blessings extended through the sheer beneficence of God. Rather, inciting God's gifts required more than prayer; prayer had to be twinned with action. As Anne described, "Prayer alone can't work . . . you pray to God to give you an idea that will help you to get money. . . . Then you also have to work hard when you get that idea. You can't expect God to do everything for you. . . . You can't pray for God to give you something when you are doing nothing. You have to work hard and also worship God unconditionally to get what you want." Martial prosperity is thus hinged on initiative, rendering a protestant virtue of industriousness a natural counterpart to the power of prayer. As Catherine commented, "You get busy in the kingdom of God as you wait for the right person to come." This, as I will next discuss, coheres seamlessly with the renewal of self-hood at the heart of P/c doctrine.

SELF-IMPROVEMENT: RIGHT THINKING, RIGHT DRESS

P/c aims to deliver women from the shackles of mind and body, promoting self-affirmation through 'right thinking' and the development of a positive self-image (Soothill, 2010, p. 87). The CSMM, for example, links women's marital aspirations to the wider P/c discourse of self-improvement, claiming that two avenues in particular—Right Thinking and Right Dress—will inspire a process of self-transformation that will unblock women's path to marriage. In the ontology of CSMM, developing right thinking is equated with a battle. As Ojigbani describes,

> No power is strong enough to cause delay, disappointment, or crisis in your marriage. External force does not have power over a person. Only an internal force can affect a man negatively or positively. . . . Spiritual Warfare is a game of the mind . . . when a person's mind is renewed, he or she is empowered to achieve what he or she couldn't achieve previously (Romans 12:2). (https://www.facebook.com/topic.php?uid=1438 51529492&topic=10606)

Renewing the mind occurs through a process of spiritual cleansing and purification, as well as reconstitution (deliverance). To illustrate, one oft-cited cause for women's "delay and disappointment" in marriage is what CSMM terms a generational curse, that is, "events from the past that affect the present in negative ways" (Asamoah-Gyadu, 2004, p. 390). Such curses are believed to underlie a range of afflictions from household poverty and chronic diseases to miscarriages, deaths, and marital woes (Asamoah-Gyadu 2004). They can, however, be lifted through the power of the Holy Spirit, which works through the hands of an anointed person of God such as Pastor Ojigbani. According to participants at the STOM seminar, Pastor Ojigbani liberated women from the errant ways of their progeny through his "ministry" of "breaking curses," a healing process in which the Holy Spirit banished the "power of darkness" and released women to marry without delay. As one participant, Edith, described, "The pastor was breaking barriers . . . he would look at you and tell you that there is a spirit in your family against marriage . . . and that is why you too are having the same problems. He would then pray to break those barriers." Yet as Edith added, it is only "by planting a seed to the man of God" that "those barriers will be broken," insinuating that liberation from the 'curse' of the unmarried requires monetary as well as spiritual intercession.

CCSM's emphasis on right thinking is part of a broader circulation of narratives on positive thinking, affirmation, and self-care within P/c that reflect a shift from "self-denial (epitomized by earlier forms of evangelicalism) to self-affirmation and the promotion of the individual Self" (Soothill, 2010, p. 87). Pastor Ojigbani, for instance, casts negative thinking as "the devil using his tricks," impregnating women's' minds with self-doubt and subverting their opportunity for worldly success. As Maggie, who was visibly moved by her STOM experience, said, the devil infests the mind with toxic thoughts such as, "I will never get married, I am not beautiful, I will not get a good job." It becomes, she said, "like a cage. You will never get out. All you see is evil." Sarah described how Pastor Ojigbani delivered participants from the "bondage they were in" by renewing their minds through the grace of the Holy Spirit, his relentless insistence on the power of positive thinking, and by instilling a certainty that "a man was coming" their way. As Rebecca described, "I thought I was not good enough to be out there. . . . But now I know that I am beautiful, made in the image of God. I was delivered big time." Such deliverance, however, allows for new logics of accumulation as women are encouraged to cultivate their self-esteem and positive outlook by tending to their behavior, image, and appearance. As Sarah said, Pastor Ojigbani informs singles how "you are supposed to carry yourself if you are expecting to get married . . . how you are supposed to relate with other people. . . . The way you are supposed to talk to them and how you answer back in conversation." Women are also coached on the relationship between feminine deportment and marital success as, according to Martha, "being smart, making your hair, [and] being attractive, will definitely get someone to like you," although, she added, accentuating feminine virtue "does not mean short skirts or blouses with a cleavage and showing your body." A born again woman, another respondent argued, "should never provoke men with their dressing" by looking like a "prostitute on Koinange Street" but must walk a fine line between observing P/c gender norms and signaling availability on the marriage market. The performance of femininity is thus keyed to religious conceptions of moral behavior as clothing value codes women as both single and Christian. Yet whereas consumption of beauty and fashion may produce respectability and ward off allegations of disrepute by delineating between proper and improper women, it is also a salvific investment made in the hopes of concrete financial and spiritual returns: the economically stable Christian man.

CONCLUSION

The sacred and the profane are often seen to index incompatible domains of social practice, pitting the public against the private, the rational against the irrational, the mundane against the transcendent, and a moral economy against immoral accumulation. Whereas the relationship between these spheres assumes different forms across time and space, the delineation is nonetheless upheld as axiomatic, a powerful explanatory tool for categories of human experience. Recently, however, this binary has been disinfested of some of its clout as scholars identify the myriad ways that consumers sacralize and desacralize goods and religious organizations leverage the enchanted for calculative and commercial ends. As marketing studies suggest, in a world where Allah appears on bumper stickers (Lukens Bull and Calbeck, 2006) and Jesus is as likely to be visible in a holiday theme park as the altar, the distinction between material and spiritual spheres is becoming ever less clear.

Although the ironies of today's sacred/secular couplings are striking, the intermingling of sacred and secular realms is hardly new in Africa, where the production, circulation, and consumption of goods have always been seen as inextricable from other worldly forces. Yet the commodification of the sacred, and in particular its instrumental appropriation for commercial gain, has intensified in recent decades as the predatory forces of globalization give rise to a proliferation of prosperity cults, pyramid schemes, and "occult economies" across the continent. The case of Pastor Ojigbani and the wider P/c ministry fits squarely within this context, offering many women a spiritual and financial palliative to an uncertain future.

Yet whereas the sacred is increasingly recast in market form, the private sphere of marriage has been relatively untouched by these sorts of spiritual commodifications. The intimate world of conjugal relations, an embodiment of God's covenant with his believers, has only recently emerged as grist for the marketing machinery of P/c. The flourishing of single women's ministries, which tout a personal transformation premised on material gain (whether through market endeavors or marital success), have brought marriage squarely into the frame of P/c's global enterprise as congregations seek to appeal to an ever-changing religious consumer. In Kenya, in particular, single women represent a particularly promising market segment, an opportunity to diversify P/c's product portfolio by bringing the nation's substantial numbers of single women into the fold of the Christian market.

There is little difference, however, between the prosperity doctrine's message of health and wealth and the product peddled through single women's ministries. Like his counterparts, Pastor Ojigbani has hitched P/c's promise of 'instant' salvation to the figure of a financially stable Christian man, using his mega marriage spectacles to market and distribute the lure of a marriage proposal among expectant women. He creates an imaginary—marriage as an avenue of wealth creation—that animates women's spiritual investments in tithing, prayer, and self-improvement, investments that aim to yield a tangible financial return in the guise of a well-to-do provider. Yet as single women's ministries retool and extend this brand of Christianity into ever more domains, it is not only the distinction between the sacred and secular that is called into question but the nature of intimacy and marriage itself.

NOTES

1. http://singlesandmarried.org/READAMAZINGTESTIMONIES/tabid/58/Default.aspx
2. This is derived from Robbins (2004).
3. Durkheim (1953) argued that the dichotomy between the sacred and the profane is the central characteristic of religion.
4. Berger (1999), in fact, argues that modernity has fueled a desecularization of the world.
5. The term "Pentecostalism" is an umbrella term that refers to a form of Christianity that emphasizes the role of the Holy Spirit in Christian life and worship. The term "charismatic" refers to Pentecostal movements operating outside major Pentecostal denominations, although the terms Pentecostal and charismatic are often used interchangeably (Asamoah-Gyadu, 2004).
6. A 2006 Pew Forum on Religion and Public life found that out of a total population of 890 million, an estimated 147 million Africans are "renewalists," with more than a quarter of Nigerians, a third of South Africans, and 56% of Kenyans self-identifying as Pentecostal or charismatic Christians (Phiri and Maxwell, 2007).
7. Many single women's ministries focus on providing women with the skills, advice, and support they need to become economically productive. These aspects are not emphasized by CSMM.

REFERENCES

Appadurai, Arjun. 1997 *Modernity at Large: Cultural Dimensions of Globalization*. Delhi: Oxford University Press.
Armstrong, Kurst. 2011. *Why Love Will Always Be a Poor Investment: Marriage and Consumer Cultures*. Eugene: Wipf & Stock.

Arnould, Eric, and Linda Price 1993. "River Magic: Extraordinary Experience and Extended Service Encounters." *Journal of Consumer Research* 20 (June): 24–45.

Arnould, Eric, and Linda Price. 2004. Rethinking the Sacred and the Profane in Postmodernity: "Abstract for Special Session Summary" Accessed at http://www.acrwebsite.org/volumes/v31/acr_vol31_45.pdf.

Arnould, Eric, Linda Price, and Cele Otnes. 1999. Making (Consumption) Magic: A Study of White Water River Rafting." *Journal of Contemporary Ethnography* 28 (1): 33–68.

Asamoah-Gyadu, J. Kwabena. 2004 Mission to "Set the Captives Free": Healing, Deliverance, and Generational Curses in Ghanaian Pentecostalism." *International Review of Mission* 93 (370–71): 389–406.

Belk, Russell, Melanie Wallendorf, and John Sherry. 1989. "The Sacred and the Profane in Consumer Behavior: Theodicy on the Odyssey" *Journal of Consumer Research* 16 (June): 1–38.

Berger, Peter. 1999. "The Desecularization of the World: A Global Overview." In *The Desecularization of the World: Resurgent Religion and World Politics*, edited by P. Berger, 1–18. Rapids, MI: William B. Eerdmans Publishing Co.

Bornstein, Erica. 2002. "Developing Faith: Theologies of Economic Development in Zimbabwe." *The Journal of Religion in Africa* 32 (1): 4–31.

Brusco, Elizabeth. 1995. *The Reformation of Machismo: Evangelical Conversion and Gender in Colombia*. Austin: University of Texas Press.

Cain, Mead, Khanam, Syeda Rokeya and Shamsun Nahar. 1979. "Class, Patriarchy, and Women's Work in Bangladesh." *Population and Development Review* 5 (3): 408–16.

Catholic News Agency. 2007. "Defend Marriage and Family Life at All Costs, Benedict XVI Tells Africans. *Catholic News*. Accessed at http://www.catholicnewsagency.com/news/defend_marriage_and_family_life_at_all_costs_benedict_xvi_tells_africans/

Chestnut, Andrew. 1997. *Born Again in Brazil: The Pentecostal Boom and the Pathogens of Poverty*. New Brunswick, NJ: Rutgers University Press.

Coleman, Simon. 2000. *The Globalisation of Charismatic Christianity: Spreading the Gospel of Prosperity*. Cambridge: Cambridge University Press.

Coleman, Simon. 2002. "The Faith Movement: A Global Religious Culture?" *Culture and Religion* 3 (1): 3–19.

Comaroff, Jean, and John Comaroff. 1993. "Introduction." In *Modernity and its Malcontents*, edited by J. Comaroff and J. Comaroff, vii–xxxvii. Chicago: University of Chicago Press.

Comaroff, Jean, and John Comaroff. 2000. "Millennial Capitalism: First Thoughts on a Second Coming." *Public Culture* 12 (2): 291–343.

Curasi, Carolyn, Linda Price, and Eric Arnould. 2004. "How Individuals' Cherished Possessions Become Families' Inalienable Wealth." *Journal of Consumer Research* 31 (December): 609–622.

Dolan, Catherine, and Mary Johnstone-Louis. 2009. "Bargaining with God: Religion, Advertising, and Commercial Success in Kenya." *Advertising and Society Review* 10 (4).

Durkeim, Emile. 1953 *Sociology and Philosophy* New York: The Free Press.

Einstein, Mara. 2008. *Brands of Faith: Marketing Religion in a Commercial Age*. New York: Routledge.

Firat, A. Fuat, and Dholakia Venkatesh. 1995. "Liberatory Postmodernism and the Reenchantment of Consumption." *Journal of Consumer Research* 22 (December): 239–267.

Genga, Shirley. 2010. "It's Raining Men." Standard Media, September 10, 2010 http://www.standardmedia.co.ke/InsidePage.php?id=2000018112&cid=300

Geshiere, Peter. 1997. *Modernity of Witchcraft*. Charlottesville, VA: University of Virginia Press.

Gifford, Paul 2003. *Ghana's New Christianity: Pentecostalism in a Globalising African Economy*. London: Hurst.

Gifford, Paul. 2004. "Persistence and Change in Contemporary African Religion." *Social Compass* 51 (2): 169–176.

Gillette, Maris Boyd. 2000. *Between Mecca and Beijing: Modernization and Consumption Among Urban Chinese Muslims*. Stanford, CA: Stanford University Press.

Gill, Lesley. 1990) " 'Like a Veil to Cover Them': Women and the Pentecostal Movement in La Paz." *American Ethnologist* 17 (4): 708–721.

Gisesa, Nyambega. 2010. "Kenya: Women Flock to City Prayers for Husbands." *Daily Nation*, September 2011. http://allafrica.com/stories/201009060484.html

Hunt, Stephen. 2000. " 'Winning Ways': Globalisation and the Impact of the Health and Wealth Gospel." *Journal of Contemporary Religion* 15 (3): 331–347.

Kitiarsa, Pattana, ed. 2007. *Religious Commodifications in Asia: Marketing Gods* London: Routledge.

Krige, Detlev. 2009. " 'Fong Kong' Finance." Research report presented to workshop on Popular Economies and Citizen Expectations, LSE, London, June 17–18.

Lukens-Bull, Ronald, and Alethia Calbeck. 2006. "Youth Culture and the Negotiation of Religious Identity." In Religious Harmony: Problems, Practice and Education, edited by M. Pye, E. Franke, A.T. Wasim, and A. Mas'ud, 303–312. Berlin: de Gruyter.

Marshall-Frantani, Ruth. 1998. "Mediating the Global and Local in Nigerian Pentecostalism." *Journal of Religion in Africa* 28 (3): 278–315.

Martin, Bernice. 2001. "The Pentecostal Gender Paradox: A Cautionary Tale for the Sociology of Religion." In *The Blackwell Companion to Sociology of Religion*, edited by R. K. Fenn, 52–66. Oxford: Blackwell.

Marx, Karl. 1867[1977]. *Capital Vol. 1*. Translated by Ben Fowkes. New York: Vintage Books.

Mate, Rekopantswe. 2002. "Wombs as God's Laboratories: Pentecostal Discourses on Femininity in Zimbabwe." *Africa* 72 (4): 549–568.

Mauss, Marcel. 1925.[1967]. *The Gift*. Translated by I. Cunnison. London: Cohen and West Ltd.; New York: W.W. Norton and Company.

Maxwell, David. 1998. " 'Delivered from the Spirit of Poverty?' Pentecostalism, Prosperity and Modernity in Zimbabwe." *Journal of Religion in Africa* 28 (3): 350–373.

Maxwell, David. 2006. *African Gifts of the Spirit: Pentecostalism & the Rise of a Zimbabwean Transnational Religious Movement*. Oxford: James Currey.

Meyer, Birgit. 2004. "Christianity in Africa: From African Independent to Pentecostal-Charismatic Churches." *Annual Review of Anthropology* 33: 447–474.

Miller, Vincent. 2004. *Consuming Religion: Christian Faith and Practice in a Consumer Culture*. New York: Continuum Publishing.

Moore, Henrietta, and Todd Sanders. 2001. "Magical Interpretations and Material Realities: An Introduction." In *Magical Interpretations, Material Realities: Modernity, Witchcraft and the Occult in Postcolonial Africa,* edited by H. Moore and T. Sanders, 1–27. London: Routledge.

Muiruri, Billy. 2010. "Do We Have a Husband Crisis?" Saturday Magazine, *Kenya Daily Nation*, September 10.

Obiora, Fidelis. 1998. *The Divine Deceit: Business in Religion*. Enugu: Optimal Publishers.

O'Guinn, Thomas, and Russell Belk. 1989. "Heaven on Earth: Consumption at Heritage Village, USA." *Journal of Consumer Research* 6 (16): 227–238.

Parker, Jerry, and Joseph Baker. 2007. "What Would Jesus Buy?" *Journal for the Scientific Study of Religion* 46 (4): 501–517.

Parsitau, Damaris. 2008. *From the Fringes to the Centre: Rethinking the Role of Religion in the Public Sphere in Kenya*. Yaound, Camerousn: CODESRIA.

Phiri, Isaac, and Joe Maxwell. 2007. "Gospel Riches: Africa's Rapid Embrace of Prosperity Pentecostalism Provokes Concern—and Hope." *Christianity Today*. Accessed April 24, 2011. www.christianitytoday. com/ct/2007/july/12.22.html

Quarmyne, Maakor. 2011. "Witchcraft: A Human Rights Conflict Between Customary/Traditional Laws and the Legal Protection of Women in Contemporary Sub-Saharan Africa." *William and Mary Journal of Women & Law* 17 (2): 475–507.

Robbins, Joes. 2004. "The Globalization of Pentecostal and Charismatic Christianity." *Annual Review of Anthropology* 33: 117–143.

Sherry, John, and Robert Kozinets. 2003. "Sacred Iconography in Secular Space: Altars, Alters, and Alterity at the Burning Man Project." In *Contemporary Consumption Rituals: A Research Anthology*, edited by Cele Otnes and Tina Lowrey, 291–311. Hillsdale,NJ: Lawrence Erlbaum Associates.

Sinha, Vineeta. 2010. *Religion and Commodification: "Merchandizing" Diasporic Hinduism*. London: Routledge.

Smilde, David. 1997. "The Fundamental Unity of the Conservative and Revolutionary Tendencies in Venezuelan Evangelicalism: The Case of Conjugal Relations." *Religion* 27: 343–359.

Smith, Daniel. 2001. " 'The Arrow of God': Pentecostalism, Inequality, and the Supernatural in South-Eastern Nigeria." *Africa* 71 (4): 587–613.

Soothill, Jane. 2010. "The Problem with 'Women's Empowerment': Female Religiosity in Ghana's Charismatic Churches." *Studies in World Christianity* 16 (1): 82–99.

Turner, Victor, and Edith Turner. 1978. *Image and Pilgrimage in Christian Culture: Anthropological Perspectives*. Oxford, England: Basil Blackwell.

Twitchell, James. 2005. *Branded Nation: The Marketing of Megachurch, College Inc., and Museumworld*. New York: Simon & Schuster.

Twitchell, James. 2007. *Shopping for God: How Christianity Went from in Your Heart to in Your Face*. New York: Simon & Schuster.

Ukah, Asonzeh. 2003. "Advertising God: Nigerian Christian Video-Films and the Power of Consumer Culture." *Journal of Religion in Africa* 33 (2), 203–231.

van Dijk, Rijk. 1995. "Fundamentalism and ils Moral Geography in Malawi. The Représentation of the Diasporic and the Diabolical." *Critique of Anthropology* 15 (2): 171–191.

Wallendorf, Melanie, and Eric Arnould. 1991. "We Gather Together: Consumption Rituals of Thanksgiving Day." *Journal of Consumer Research* 18 (June): 13–31.

World Bank. 2003. "The Kenyan Strategic Country Gender Assessment." World Bank. Accessed May 14, 2011. http://siteresources.worldbank.org/EXTA-FRREGTOPGENDER/Resources/KenyaSCGA.pdf

Zelizer, Viviana. 2005. *The Purchase of Intimacy*. Princeton, NJ: Princeton University Press.

Part IV

The Consumption of Spiritual Goods

12 Framing Sacred Places and Possessions
Pilgrims at St. Brigid's Holy Well

Darach Turley

Over the past two decades there has been a growing realization of the sacred and ritual underpinnings of many aspects of consumer behavior (Arnould et al., 1999; Belk et al., 1989; Muniz and Schau, 2005). Apart from illuminating the presence of the sacred beyond the confines of formal religions, these studies have also shown how the sacred can be experienced in places as well as in objects and artefacts (Forbes and Mahan, 2005).

Studies of consumption at sacred places have arguably paid insufficient attention to theoretical divergences in how the sacredness of such locations is understood. Chidester and Linenthal (1995) have identified two broad definitional approaches: substantial and situational. Substantial theorists claim that the divine 'irrupts' as a hierophany, a superhuman appearance, manifesting itself in such a way that space is subsequently rendered heterogeneous; a radical disjuncture between sacred and profane space is inaugurated, giving rise to experiences of awe, power, and ultimate significance on the part of the believer or 'insider' (Eliade, 1959). Ritual at such sites serves as a ceremonial reprise of the initial superhuman consecration, "a repetition of the work of the gods" (Shiner, 1972, p. 426). The second, situational approach, with Durkheim as one of its more notable protagonists, insists that no place is inherently sacred. The symbolic polarity between a sacred and profane space is a function of historical cultural consecration. In this sense, the concept of a sacred space is an indeterminate one, "an empty signifier" (Chidester and Linenthal, 1995, p. 6); however, once instituted, it instates a radical divide between sacred and profane spaces. Thereafter, the profane does not impinge on the sacred (Durkheim, 1976[1915]).

Chidester and Linenthal (1995) question the radical disjuncture between sacred and profane space central to both of these essentialist formulations insisting that both spatial categories can coexist and comingle with each other. They also take issue with the substantial view that the sacred is 'given' because this "erases all the hard work that goes into choosing, setting aside, consecrating, venerating, protecting, defending, and redefining sacred places" (p. 17). They proffer three characteristics or pointers that inform how specific sites are produced precisely as sacred. First, the site is consecrated through the enactment of ritual practices. Second, a sacred place is construed as a meaningful place, in that devotees anchor a worldview there. Third, a sacred space, precisely because it is being formed as a meaningful place, will involve contested negotiation over symbolic ownership.

PILGRIMAGE

If places are sacred, then journeys to such sites—pilgrimages—can also be considered sacred (Belk et al., 1989; O'Guinn and Belk, 1989). The motivational substratum for pilgrimage is far from monochromatic, and the task of decoupling religious, superstitious, touristic, curiosity, and voyeuristic underpinnings is a formidable one (Reader, 1993). Indeed, there is growing evidence of consumers adopting a 'supermarket approach' (Digance and Cusack, 2001) to pilgrimage, where, on foot of globalized technology, they can avail of a less regulated and multicultural symbolic inventory coupled with a more dispersed and eclectic choice of destinations to tailor and combine different genres of pilgrimage.

Discussion on the nature of pilgrimage has been dominated by a structure versus anti-structure debate. For Durkheim (1976[1915]), the pilgrimage, like all religious ritual, serves to bond and unify the body social. In this sense, its function was an organic, reparative one directed at maintaining existing social structure. At the other end of the spectrum, anti-structure proponents (Turner and Turner, 1978) see pilgrimage as quintessentially liminal. The pilgrim is an initiate, a 'liminoid' who has withdrawn voluntarily from quotidian routine and social structuration, "entering into a new, deeper level of existence than he has known in his accustomed milieu" (p. 8). Pilgrims find themselves divested of social roles and obligations, in a world where normal social and kinship hierarchies have been suspended, an anti-structure where an egalitarian ethos of fellow-feeling—*communitas*—prevails.

Pilgrimages can mean travel to 'modern secular' (Alderman, 2002; Davie, 1993; Glass, 1995; Jindra, 2005; King, 1993), prehistoric/pagan (Bowman, 1993; Digance, 2003; Digance and Cusack, 2001), as well as traditional religious destinations (Reader and Walter, 1993). In all cases the pilgrimage consists of more than the physical journey to and from the site; it also includes what Turner and Turner (1978) term the "pilgrimage system." "Some will doubt the propriety of extending the notion of a pilgrimage system to embrace the entire complex of behavior focused on the sacred shrine. But we insist . . . that we must regard the pilgrimage system . . . as comprising all the interactions and transactions, formal or informal, institutionalized or improvised, sacred or profane, orthodox or eccentric, which owe their existence to the pilgrimage itself" (p. 22). This chapter reports on a study of the pilgrimage system centered on a Holy Well in rural Ireland dedicated to Saint Brigid. The choice of this site was prompted by two main considerations. First, practices and rituals at the Well speak to debates on the nature of both sacred place and pilgrimage. Second, pilgrims' personal possessions and artefacts appear to play pivotal roles in both processes.

ST. BRIGID

St. Brigid, a sixth century Irish abbess, holds pre-eminent and emblematic status among Irish Catholics. There is increasing evidence that the Christian St. Brigid is in fact the outcome of euhemeric enterprise, where the attributes and powers of a pre-Christian goddess were "baptised" into a historical Christian personage (O'Cathasaigh, 1982). In this sense, the cult of St. Brigid is a syncretic one (Brenneman and Brenneman, 1995). For instance, the pre-Christian Brigit was a goddess of fertility and growth and the guardian of livestock; miracles attributed to St. Brigid are characterized by lavish abundance, multiplication of foodstuffs, and fecundity. Grounding the cult of St. Brigid firmly in the Irish landscape—in this case, a well—further served this syncretic agenda. Celtic spirituality has consistently privileged place over object, image, or relic as the point of contact with the sacred (Carroll, 1999). Pilgrimages to Holy Wells in Ireland serve the same function as pilgrimages to more distant locations for those lacking the requisite health and resources (Harbison, 1991).

Figure 12.1   St. Brigid's Well exterior.

St. Brigid's Well is situated near the Cliffs of Moher, one of Ireland's most visited tourist attractions. The Well itself is located to the front of a small wooded graveyard that slopes up to the Cliffs. Behind a grotto statue (see figure 12.1) is a man-made tunnel about 20 metres long, at the end of which, in a rectangular stone opening, sits the well. The only formal celebrations at the Well take place on February 1st, St. Brigid's feast-day, and the eve of August 15th, a Marian feast-day that coincides with a former pre-Christian harvest festival. On these occasions, a local priest celebrates mass outside the Well. Apart from these two occasions, pilgrims come and go with little or no ecclesiastical scrutiny, mediation, or control. Most visits involve "taking the waters" either by way of drinking water directly from the well or administering it to some part of the body. As with many other Irish pilgrimage sites, there is a "rounding ritual" or "pattern" associated with the Well (Nolan, 1983; O'Duinn, 2005), a pre-liminal ritual consisting of sun-wise circumambulations of the area outside the Well with prayers being recited at particular landmarks.

On entering the Well passage (see figure 12.2), the pilgrim encounters shelves on each side adorned with an array of devotional and not so devotional bric-a-brac, a potpourri of personal belongings and artefacts. First impressions are of dizzying chaos, clutter, and disorder. The moss that

Figure 12.2   Inner passage to St. Brigid's Well.

grows around the Well creeps down the passage, leaving objects with a greenish pallor, adding to both the sense and smell of decay and decomposition that pervade the shrine. The atmosphere is dark and dank year round, giving a penumbral, liminal feel as though the passage serves as a spatial separator of the profane world outside and the sacred within.

Items on the shelves seem to fall into two broad categories. The first are those objects possessing some devotional or religious pedigree: statuary, rosary beads, medals, religious pictures, and petitionary notes penned to St. Brigid, usually concerning an illness or pregnancy-related matter. This assortment of religious goods is redolent of "Catholic kitsch" (Primiano, 1999), artefacts that appear anachronistic, clichéd, derivative, mass-produced, populist, and in poor taste. At pilgrimage shrines, this designation is sometimes given to objects purchased at the site and brought home as souvenirs or mementoes. At St. Brigid's Well, they are brought *to* the shrine. In fact, no financial transaction of any form occurs here, and, as Belk et al. (1989) note, the absence of commercial activity can heighten the perceived sacredness of such places.

The second, and more numerous, category of items features objects that are small, secular, portable, and quite personal. These objects include gimcracks, bows, baseball caps, babies' toys and pacifiers, belts, scarves, neckties, handbags, pins, keys, reading glasses, and walking sticks. Collectively, they exude an aura that is singular, personally intimate, and yet anonymous. All are second-hand, most are worthless, and many are broken, something that need not however detract from an object's sacredness (McDannell, 1995). Indeed, O'Duinn (2005) suggests that they may have been broken deliberately by those who placed them there to signal that their use in the world outside the Well was now at an end, that they were now consecrated.

Six visits were made at varying times of the calendar and liturgical years to observe how pilgrims behaved and to study the Well's interior. Interviews were conducted with both pilgrims and local residents (four males and six females). As interviews progressed, it became clear that the majority of those depositing items at the Well were in fact members of the Irish Traveller community, that their visits were irregular and at "off peak" hours, and that their settled counterparts' feelings towards their behaviour were both complex and ambivalent.

Although ethnically distinct, Irish Travellers have often been compared with their nomadic gypsy counterparts on mainland Europe. On foot of a valorisation of sedentarism, the settled majority have tended to marginalise and stigmatise their nomadic fellow countrymen (Griffin, 2002). Begging and hawking are their most common modes of interaction with the settled community, practices that are often peppered with religious invocations and prayers promised. Contact was made with a group of travellers at a halting site about forty miles from the Well. The only travellers willing to be interviewed were female, seven in total.

SACRED PLACE

Sites of pilgrimage and ritual are deemed sacred places (O'Guinn and Belk, 1989), and pilgrims from both groups were in no doubt that St. Brigid's Well was such a sacred pilgrimage site. However, its sacredness was articulated in a variety of registers and modalities.

> My father used to work for a builder from Galway and his brother back in the forties and their sister had TB. And some local told them they should come up to St. Brigid's Well and do the rounds. And they both did that and she got better. Like she only died there about seven or eight years ago. (Peter, settled)

This account was one of numerous stories confirming the shrine's thaumaturgic repute, a repute that extended to a broad range of human and bovine ailments. Crutches and walking sticks deposited in the passage were testament to the curative powers that made the Well a sacred place.

This same sacredness was also underscored by the air of mystique and otherness surrounding the purpose and provenance of the objects in the passage. Comments from settled pilgrims about these objects were often prefaced with terms such as, "as far as I know," "we think it's the Travellers," and "I don't really know what's the idea behind it." Although the items are visible to settled pilgrims, their meanings are not; "only themselves and St. Brigid knows." Several travellers recounted a legend that gave further texture to the perceived sacredness of the shrine:

> And a long time ago I heard that the Well was down the field. And a woman got up one morning and she washed potatoes in the well. And when she got up next morning the well was gone completely from there back up where it is now. It was shifted because it was a Blessed Well. They shouldn't have used it for washing anything. (Anna, traveller)

Some Holy Wells have dried up in the past (Logan, 1980), so this legend could be seen by those with a scientific bent as making a mythological virtue out of a geological necessity, of "embroidering the new location with mythic explanation" (Nolan, 1983, p. 431). However, for these pilgrims, it illustrated how Brigid's Well, precisely because it was a sacred place, removed itself and its powers from those who failed to accord it due reverence and respect. This, in turn, may explain an observation on the part of local devotees that the stereotypical penchant of travellers for opportunistic pilfering was put on hold while at the shrine: "The travellers would never touch anything in a sacred place. There was never a flower taken from it, not even a pot" (Joan, settled).

Turner and Turner (1978) noted how liminal sacred spaces represent a normative and an egalitarian counterpoint to everyday life and structuration.

There were intimations of such an experience in the accounts of some traveller pilgrims who had deposited items at the Well. For example, one participant indicated how being a sacred space entailed it being essentially a shared space:

> Then again we don't mind. Because no one has their own particular place up there. If I've a place there, you can put something up there, that's no harm. Anyone else who goes up there, they'd never take them down and say 'Look that's ours'. You can hang anything up there. (Bridie, traveller)

If sacred space is seen as shared space, it is also seen as a safe space. Traveller families are usually large families who live in relatively small cramped caravans or homes. In such an environment, possessions can intentionally or unintentionally get broken or go missing. Depositing items at the Well consecrates them and, in the process, guarantees them a safe and secure future.

> You know if we had something belonging to someone who had died back at the caravan, maybe the grandchilder would be saying 'What's this?' and maybe taking it or putting it round their neck or round their hand. But God forbid, the way I look at it is, if anything was to happen to me tomorrow morning, maybe it'd get thrown out, I wouldn't know what they'd do. So I said 'Look, if it's left in St. Bridget's Well they won't touch it because it'll be safe.' (Joyce, traveller)

Overall, for both groups of pilgrims, the sacredness at the Well appeared to derive more from the spiritual magnetism of the place than from any devotion to the person of a historical St. Brigid. Indeed, only one of the participants made any reference to the historical St. Brigid: "She was around 500 plus AD, or was it BC?"

SACRED OBJECTS

The vast majority of the items deposited in the Well passage were, on their own admission, left there by travellers. This was suspected by many pilgrims from the settled community, although none had actually witnessed this happening. The motivational tapestry underpinning the travellers' behaviour was both intricate and wide-ranging. Leaving goods at sacred sites is a practice found in many religious traditions (Carroll, 1999; McDannell, 1995). In Latin Catholic countries, this behaviour has a clear *ex voto* purpose. Goods are left as votive offerings in thanksgiving for some favour received (O'Duinn, 2005). At Brigid's Well, however, the performative role of goods is not a votive, contractual one. Instead, they serve as material embodiments of the disease or illness for which a cure is sought. "If a child was sick, parents would bring a shoe or teddy bear . . . little things like that. Something that was associated with the child." None of the travellers reported leaving objects in thanksgiving for favours or cures. Small intimate belongings, such as buttons and belts, as well as pieces of clothing can have a cathectic relationship with parts of the body and can thus "serve as metaphorical representations of the process of detachment from physical and spiritual ailment that was the primary purpose of visiting the well" (Carroll, 1999, p. 34). In this sense, objects "foreshadow what could be" (Csikszentmihalyi and Rochberg-Halton, 1981, p. 27), a theme echoed in the views of settled pilgrims in their views on these same objects.

> They tend to leave a lot of those things there. Babies' bibs, or children's shoes or socks. I think what they're supposed to mean like they've something to do with fertility. So it's mostly I think travellers who would hang that stuff there. . . . People who want to get pregnant and that. That's what I heard anyway. (Nora, settled)

Apart from its tone of mild disapproval and its concluding disclaimer, this verbatim is an illuminating example of how goods at the Well are seen as having an agentic, performative role, of being complicit in bringing the desired outcome—pregnancy—about.

Items deposited at the Well by travellers appear to play a further sacral role in the service of deceased travellers. At St. Brigid's Well, there was evidence of deliberate and ongoing divestment of their material possessions.

> There's personal things belonging to the dead in the St. Brigid's Well; it's great. Mass cards, photographs, everything belonging to them, rosary beads, jewelry, we've great faith in it. Years and years we go up. We leave something up there each time. I've my mother's scarf for 28 years at home and I'm going to leave it up there. It'll be safe up there. (Teresa, traveller)

Nomadism is part of travellers' DNA; their homes are usually mobile ones. With such a lifestyle, establishing a "home" for the departed family member can be a significant concern. There was repeated reference to the way in which belongings left at the Well served as an anchor, a material foothold for the deceased, and in doing so facilitated communion between the living and the dead that would not otherwise have been possible.

> There's a child's bottle up there. The young fellow got killed there in Dublin. He was a toddler boy. His uncle reversed back on top of him. He was three years of age, one of the O'Connors. So they got his little bottle and people brought it back to St. Brigid's Well. Dead or alive, if they leave something there, it's very special. So, dead or alive, you leave something there—and everyone gets together, the dead and the alive gets together. (Eileen, traveller)

The multiplicity of functions served by these sacred objects at the Well clearly invests them with symbolic weight. Their sheer volume necessitates that, on occasions, members of the local settled community have to remove some of them, a task they view with mixed feelings. Those charged with this duty reported a reluctance to tamper with these objects even though they did not share the same views as traveller pilgrims on their sacredness.

> It needs a big clean out but you can't just come along and take everything away like. It's kind of sacred like, people have their own reasons for leaving things there. (Phyllis, settled)

Apart from drawing travellers' ire, disturbing these objects clearly gives rise to an element of kratophany (Belk et al., 1989), a sense of apprehension that lack of due deference to the sacred, albeit "sacred" on traveller terms, could result in some negative supernatural retribution.

All pilgrims from the settled community agreed that traveller pilgrims were the main depositors. However, they also reported that there was one class of artefact that had been left there by non-traveller visitors—framed religious prints of Jesus, the Virgin Mary, and a variety of Catholic saints. It emerged that the principal motive for leaving these items at the Well was one of expediency, although there was a sacred substrate. Lastovicka and Fernandez (2005) showed how some dispositions can involve an attempt to relinquish negatively valenced former selves. These pictures, most of which have been inherited from an older generation, are very much the "stuff" of a traditional Catholic image that young people may wish to distance themselves from. Several settled pilgrims had witnessed dispositions of these pictures:

> God forgive me for saying it, but it isn't from a devotional point of view that a lot of them are left there. When a young woman comes into a new house she'll say, 'Oh, that's getting on my nerves, bring that over to St. Brigid's Well.' It's for the sake of getting rid of it. It isn't in gratitude at all. (Rita, settled)

Although the ostensible reason behind such dispositions was profane, the mode of disposition was not, and intentionally so. These pictures could have been thrown in dustbins; however, in order to assuage any lingering misgivings or guilt, a sacred repository had been identified as a suitable home for unwanted artefacts that their parents at least viewed as sacred—just in case.

> They might think that there might be a bit of bad luck attached to dumping these holy pictures whereas if they bring them to a holy place, that they're kind of doing the right thing. (John, settled)

A local priest has essayed to reinstate and revalorise devotion to the historical St. Brigid, incorporating ritual objects traditionally associated with her into both of the annual Catholic ceremonies at the shrine. These have included butter and "St. Brigid's crosses," lozenge-shaped crosses made out of reeds and a commonplace in both homesteads and barns in rural Ireland up until recently. This echoes a wider phenomenon in Ireland of "tidying up" rituals at early Christian pilgrimage sites in the interests of recovering neglected elements of Celtic spirituality and local identity (Brenneman and Brenneman, 1995; Ó Giolláin, 2005). However, there was no evidence of the travellers themselves or their material assemblage playing any part in these revived liturgical proceedings at the Well. Similarly, none of them had ever performed "the rounds," a core element of pilgrimage in the Celtic tradition. For most settled devotees, traveller pilgrims were spiritual outliers, dancing to a different devotional and interpretative drumbeat, and subscribing to a narrative that has more to do with superstition and post-mortem communication than with penitential orthodoxy and practice.

> They can come at any time and they leave all those little bits and pieces, those childish things. They're very ugly like and I feel like cutting them down but I don't want to get myself in trouble. (Nora, settled)

CONCLUSIONS

At one level, the cult of St. Brigid at this Holy Well can be seen as an idiosyncratic and relatively obscure admixture of Celtic Christian and pre-Christian religious beliefs and practices. However, it can also be viewed as a site where significant themes relating to pilgrimage and the nature of sacred space and possessions are being played out. Many of its rituals are extra ecclesiastical, demotic, and redolent of what Williams (1980) terms "Little Religion" (p. 10). Traveller pilgrims in particular seemed to straddle the border between orthopraxis and superstition, sacred and profane with consummate ease.

The profusion of material objects at the shrine, most of them deposited by travellers, seems overpowering at first. For settled pilgrims, this was definitely "matter out of place" (Douglas, 1966, p. 35), akin to litter, and seemed to chime with the widespread, if exaggerated, stereotype of travellers' halting sites after they have moved on. However, for the researcher, the symbolic possibilities are so alluring and tantalising that the temptation to leave the concrete materiality of these objects behind and cut to the interpretive chase is difficult to resist. Daniel Miller (2010, p. 155) notes how "Stuff has a quite remarkable capacity for fading from view, [it] achieves its mastery of us precisely because we constantly fail to notice what it does." At St. Brigid's Well, the accumulation of deposited artefacts and objects on both sides of the narrow passage, apart from confronting and discommoding pilgrims making their way up to the Well, both confirms and contributes to friction between settled and traveller pilgrims. They were irksome to settled pilgrims not just because they were symbolically jarring.

Both Durkheimian and Turnerian approaches to pilgrimage were outlined earlier and framed as structure versus anti-structure. Neither perspective sits well with pilgrimage as instanced at St. Brigid's Well. In particular, the Turners' contention that social structuration and divisions do not impinge on relations between pilgrims at shrines is very much at odds with what emerged from this study. There were limited elements of *communitas* in evidence, but these were primarily among travellers in their toleration of each other's space and artefacts in the passage. It should however be conceded that pilgrimage to this site does not typically involve prolonged Chaucerian journeys, "once in a lifetime" visits, and lengthy stays, all of which might give rise to greater communal interaction among pilgrims.

The overriding impression of pilgrimage to St. Brigid's Well was one of multiple discourses about what makes the site itself and the artefacts deposited there sacred. Many of these discourses are contested, and, in this sense, findings approximate more closely to the views of Eade and Sallnow (1991) for whom pilgrimage is constituted precisely by the confluence of competing discourses. Any deterministic, essentialist model of pilgrimage that is divorced from everyday conflicts and socio-cultural conditioning will inevitably be limited. The sacral power of a pilgrimage site resides in its ability to serve "as a religious void, a ritual space capable of accommodating diverse meanings and practices" (p. 15). Chidester and Linenthal (1995) emphasize the contrast at sacred places between limited physical space, on the one hand, and unlimited possibilities of signification, on the other. The defining contestation at sacred spaces is one "over symbolic surpluses that are abundantly available for appropriation" (p. 18). In a tautological sense, it is the receptivity to multiple meanings and the capacity to absorb differing interpretations of the sacred that constitute a site as sacred.

Coleman (2002) cautions against too literal a view of contestation in this context and wonders whether a more nuanced form is called for at certain sites. Contestation between agonistic constituencies may sometimes subsist more in the musings of academic observers than at the shrine itself. This seems eminently sensible in the case of St. Brigid's Well. Here, differences between both pilgrim groups do not result in overt contestation. Travellers have won the spatial battle in the Well passage; settled pilgrims do not want to place anything there anyway. Added to this, interaction between both groups is minimal. Traveller pilgrims are more often suspected than seen. The travellers who were interviewed displayed no reflexive awareness of adverse reactions to their activities on the part of their settled counterparts. In turn, settled pilgrims appeared to lack both the resolve and opportunity to voice their disapproval of traveller devotion and deposits at the shrine openly. Contestation at the Well may be *sotto voce* and asymmetrical, but it is no less significant for that. Differences between traveller and settled beliefs, between Celtic Christian and Pre-Christian spiritualities, between sacramental and secular artefacts, between living and dead and between superstition and orthopraxis all find a home in a cult, famed from the outset for its lavish abundance.

REFERENCES

Alderman, Derek H. 2002. "Writing on the Graceland Wall: On the Importance of Authorship in Pilgrimage Landscapes." *Tourism Recreation Research* 27 (2): 27–33.

Arnould, Eric, Linda L. Price, and Cele Otnes. 1999. "Making (Consumption) Magic: A Study of White Water River Rafting." *Journal of Contemporary Ethnography* 28 (1) (February): 33–68.

Belk, Russell W., Melanie Wallendorf, and John F. Sherry, Jr. 1989. "The Sacred and the Profane in Consumer Behavior: Theodicy on the Odyssey." *Journal of Consumer Research* 16 (June): 1–38.

Bowman, Marion. 1993. "Drawn to Glastonbury." In *Pilgrimage in Popular Culture*, edited by Ian Reader and Tony Walters, 29–62. Basingstoke: Macmillan.

Brenneman, Walter L., Jr., and Mary G. Brenneman. 1995. *Crossing the Circle at the Holy Wells of Ireland*. Charlottesville, VA: University of Virginia Press.

Carroll, Michael P. 1999. *Irish Pilgrimage: Holy Wells and Popular Catholic Devotion*. Baltimore, MD: Johns Hopkins University Press.

Chidester, David, and Edward Linenthal. 1995. "Introduction." In *American Sacred Space*, edited by David Chidester and Edward Linenthal, 1–42. Bloomington: Indiana University Press.

Coleman, Simon. 2002. "Do You Believe in Pilgrimage?" *Anthropological Theory* 2 (3): 355–368.

Csikszentmihalyi, Mihaly, and Eugene Rochberg-Halton. 1981. *The Meaning of Things: Domestic Symbols and the Self*. New York: Cambridge University Press.

Davie, Grace. 1993. "'You'll Never Walk Alone': The Anfield Pilgrimage." In *Pilgrimage in Popular Culture*, edited by Ian Reader and Tony Walters, 201–219. Basingstoke: Macmillan.

Digance, Justine. 2003. "Pilgrimage at Contested Sites." *Annals of Tourism Research* 30 (1): 143–159.

Digance, Justine, and Carole M. Cusack. 2001. "Secular Pilgrimage Events: Druid Gorsedd and Stargate Alignments." In *The End of Religions?: Religion in an Age of Globalisation*, edited by Carole M. Cusack and Peter Olmeadow, 216–228. Sydney: University of Sydney Press.

Douglas, Mary. 1966. *Purity and Danger: An Analysis of the Concepts of Pollution and Taboo*. London: Ark Paperbacks.

Durkheim, Emile. 1976 [1915]. *The Elementary Forms of Religious Life*. Translated by Joseph Ward Swain. London: Allen & Unwin.

Eade, John, and Michael J. Sallnow. 1991. "Introduction." In *Contesting the Sacred: The Anthropology of Christian Pilgrimage*, edited by John Eade and Michael J. Sallnow, 1–27. London: Routledge.

Eliade, Mircea. 1959. *The Sacred and the Profane: The Nature of Religion*. Translated by William R. Trask. New York: Harcourt, Brace Jovanovich.

Forbes, Bruce David, and Jeffrey H. Mahan, eds. 2005. *Religion and Popular Culture in America*. Berkeley, CA: University of California Press.

Glass, Matthew. 1995. " 'Alexanders All': Symbols of Conquest and Resistance at Mount Rushmore." In *American Sacred Space*, edited by David Chidester and Edward Linenthal, 152–186. Bloomington: Indiana University Press.

Griffin, C. C. C. M. 2002. "The Religion and Social Organization of Irish Travellers on a London Caravan Site (Part 1)." *Nomadic Peoples* 6 (1): 45–68.

Harbison, Peter. 1991. *Pilgrimage in Ireland: The Monuments and the People.* London: Barrie and Jenkins.

Jindra, Michael. 2005. "It's About Faith in our Future: Star Trek Fandom as Cultural Religion." In *Religion and Popular Culture in America*, edited by Bruce David Forbes and Jeffrey H. Mahan, 159–173. Berkeley, CA: University of California Press.

King, Christine. 1993. "His Truth Goes Marching on: Elvis Presley and the Pilgrimage to Graceland." In *Pilgrimage in Popular Culture*, edited by Ian Reader and Tony Walters, 92–104. Basingstoke: Macmillan.

Lastovicka, John L., and Karen V. Fernandez. 2005. "Three Paths to Disposition: The Movement of Meaningful Possessions to Strangers." *Journal of Consumer Research* 31 (4): 813–823.

Logan, Patrick. 1980. *The Holy Wells of Ireland.* Buckinghamshire: Colin Smythe.

McDannell, Colleen. 1995. *Material Christianity: Religion and Popular Culture in America.* New Haven, CT: Yale University Press.

Miller, Daniel. 2010. *Stuff.* Cambridge: Polity.

Muniz, Albert M., Jr., and Hope Jensen Schau. 2005. "Religiosity in the Abandoned Apple Newton Brand Community." *Journal of Consumer Research* 31 (4): 737–747.

Nolan, Mary Lee. 1983. "Irish Pilgrimage: The Different Tradition." *Annals of the Association of American Geographers* 73 (3): 421–438.

O'Cathasaigh, Donal. 1982. "The Cult of Brigid: A Study of Pagan-Christian Syncretism in Ireland." In *Mother Worship: Theme and Variations*, edited by James J. Preston, 75–94. Chapel Hill: The University of North Carolina Press.

O'Duinn, Sean. 2005. *The Rites of Brigid, Goddess and Saint.* Dublin: The Columba Press.

Ó Giolláin, Diarmuid. 2005. "Revisiting the Holy Well." *Éire-Ireland* 40 (1/2): 11–41.

O'Guinn, Thomas C., and Russell W. Belk. 1989. "Heaven on Earth: Consumption at Heritage Village, USA." *Journal of Consumer Research* 16 (September): 227–238.

Primiano, Leonard N. 1999. "Postmodern Sites of Catholic Sacred Materiality." In *Perspectives on American Religion and Culture*, edited by Peter W. Williams, 187–202. Malden, MA: Blackwell Publishers.

Reader, Ian. 1993. "Conclusions." In *Pilgrimage in Popular Culture*, edited by Ian Reader and Tony Walters, 220–246. Basingstoke: Macmillan.

Reader, Ian, and Tony Walter. 1993. *Pilgrimage in Popular Culture.* Basingstoke: The Macmillan Press.

Shiner, Larry E. 1972. "Sacred Space, Profane Space, Human Space." *Journal of the American Academy of Religion* 40 (4): 425–436.

Turner, Victor, and Edith Turner. 1978. *Image and Pilgrimage in Christian Culture: Anthropological Perspectives.* Oxford: Basil Blackwell.

Williams, Peter W. 1980. *Popular Religions in America: Symbolic Change and the Modernization Process in Historical Perspective.* Englewood Cliffs, NJ: Prentice-Hall.

13 Materializing the Spiritual
Investigating the Role of Marketplace in Creating Opportunities for the Consumption of Spiritual Experiences

Richard Kedzior

Sir Charles Lyell is said to have coined the phrase "mind over matter" in 1863. Perhaps influenced by the work of Darwin, Lyell was referring to the dominance acquired by beings with developed intelligence (humans) over other species and physical objects. However, Western religious traditions have long privileged the immaterial (or spiritual), transcendent sphere of existence over the mundane aspects of human lives reflected in matter. This metaphysical division is said to be rooted in the Judeo-Christian tradition, in which God is represented by a disembodied voice that interacts with embodied human beings (McDanell, 1995). Durkheim's (1915) classic work on the sacred and profane is a well-known example of this tendency to separate the material from immaterial and view them as dichotomous realms—spirit vs. matter; piety vs. commerce—thus marginalizing the material in the study of religious and spiritual practice.

Interestingly, despite religious rhetoric encouraging the transcendence of the material world, the spiritual is often reified in the material. Through ritual engagement, objects have the ability to render tangible what is immaterial and make visible what is normally invisible. Singularized and sacralized, objects bring people closer to the divine realm via contagion (Frazer, 1922). As Moore (1994) argues, although Judeo-Christian dogma discourages the presence of sacralized objects in market exchange, Western societies have a long history of commercializing religion, and even revered sacred objects are frequently sold by marketplace actors (Geary, 1986). Indeed, infusion of the sacred properties to an otherwise mundane good or service can act as a source of differentiation and positioning strategy. As the marketplace acquires an increasingly venerated position in contemporary Western life, commodification blurs the sharp distinction between the sacred and the profane and allows movement between the two realms. Consumers not only have the capacity to sacralize secular objects (Belk, Wallendorf, and Sherry, 1989) but secular consumption can be sacralized in the context of religious practice (O'Guinn and Belk, 1989).

Within the context of religious and spiritual movements, blurred boundaries between the sacred and profane are perhaps most apparent in the New Age movement, where elements of the sacred are mixed with the market economy (Zaidman, 2007). The New Age is frequently labeled a 'spiritual market place,' where the spiritual is commodified and can be traded based on free-market principles (York, 2001). In addition, unlike in many religions with established orthodoxy and ordained clergy, the opportunity to launch new spiritual products is open to all (Zaidman, 2003).

To date, researchers' interest has been largely channeled into understanding the commercialization of tangible spiritual artifacts (e.g., Geary, 1986), with little attention devoted to the role of the marketplace in enabling access to the sacred that dwells in experiences rather than in any one material object. Such experiences are especially prominent in the context of pilgrimages: journeys undertaken by consumers hoping to experience divine energies present at a sacred site.

This chapter addresses this gap by investigating the role of the marketplace in enabling the consumption of spiritual experiences. It does so by delving into the experiences of visitors to Sedona, Arizona, who decide to explore the phenomenon of vortex energy. The findings discussed in this chapter are impressionistic in nature (Van Maanen, 1988) and based on ethnographic data collected during five, three day-long immersions in Sedona over the course of two years: 2008–2009. Data set encompasses author's fieldnotes, interviews with consumers, commercial material obtained from various vendors, free local press, and websites created by businesses that target vortex seeking visitors. In keeping with the impressionistic style of representation, the auto-ethnographic nature of the collected data stems from the author's active participation in the events being described (cf. Hayano, 1979; Kozinets and Kedzior, 2009; Wall, 2006).

I argue that in case of consumption related to spiritual pilgrimage sites such as Sedona, where the lack of physical or historic markers renders the sacred particularly intangible, undefined, and ephemeral, the marketplace fosters and exploits the volatility of consumers' expectations. It does so by creating tensions that are resolved through the consumption of marketplace offerings. Thus, consumption becomes a materializing force through which access to the sacred and spiritual is achieved.

This chapter is structured as follows: first the context of the study is presented, followed by a brief discussion of its significance as a pilgrimage site. Then, the importance of pilgrimage for the New Age movement is presented. Finally, the presentation of findings consists of revealing four major consumer tensions as fostered and exploited by marketplace dynamics. Consumer tensions refer to situations in which the lack of prior experience with the marketplace offering creates ambiguity of consumers' expectations and decrease their certainty related to the outcomes of consuming a particular product or service. The chapter concludes with a short discussion of the role that marketplace plays in enabling the consumption of spiritual experiences.

SEDONA: A TOURIST ATTRACTION OR A PILGRIMAGE SITE?

Located in the Sonoran Desert of northern Arizona, the city of Sedona is known worldwide for the natural beauty of its sandstone formations called the Red Rocks. Whether rising or setting, Sedona's intense sun brings out the vibrant orange and red colors of the fantastically shaped sandstone—a sight so scenic that it decorates many book covers and photo albums. With a population of slightly more than ten thousand people and an average inhabitant age of fifty, this nineteen-square-mile area would seem like a quiet, peaceful town if it were not for the fact that more than four million people visit Sedona annually (City of Sedona, www.sedonaaz.gov).

Given its unique beauty and proximity to other scenic places such as the Grand Canyon and Flagstaff's skiing resorts, it is no wonder that outdoor recreation enthusiasts flock here to take advantage of countless hiking and camping opportunities. However, it is probably spiritual discovery-oriented tourists who are most visible and prominent in the city's social and commercial landscape. The number of those who travel here for spiritual reasons is imprecise, with estimates ranging from a few to more than 40% of all visitors (Coats, 2009). Nevertheless, Sedona's international fame stems from the fact that the local New Age (otherwise also known as metaphysical) community is one of the largest and most geographically concentrated world-wide. Accordingly, Sedona has earned epithets such as "The Vatican City of the New Age" (Ivakhiv, 1997), "New Age Mecca," and "The New Age Lourdes" (Timothy and Conover, 2006).

The New Age movement, often considered an "alternative spirituality" or "secular religion," comprises an eclectic set of beliefs and practices oriented toward personal spiritual quest. Followers of the movement stress each person's subjective truth and the divine nature of the self, which, through the vicissitudes of everyday life, bad karma from previous lives, or life energy deficiency, becomes incomplete and in need of integration (York, 2001). Moreover, energy is a necessary component of healing and integrating of the self, and its constant pursuit is an important motivation for New Age pilgrimage.

Among New Agers, Sedona is known not only as a community center but also as a home to power spots known as 'energy vortexes.' The significance of these power spots is well reflected in Sedona's vernacular, where preference is given to the plural form 'vortexes' instead of the more common 'vortices' when referring to these phenomena. Believers in the existence of vortexes claim to have experienced the strong effects of vortex energy on improving their health and well-being in general. It is no surprise then that many tourists fascinated with the New Age movement visit Sedona with a spiritual agenda in mind.

NEW AGE PILGRIMAGE

According to Timothy and Conover (2006), the New Age movement began to flourish in the United States during the 1970s as a result of the counter-cultural mysticism of the 1960s. New Age spirituality incorporates elements of both Eastern and Western spiritual and metaphysical traditions and blends them with influences from a myriad of other sources, including motivational psychology, holistic health, parapsychology, consciousness research, and quantum physics (Drury, 2004), and it is therefore often referred to as a "secular religion." Followers of the movement stress each person's subjective truth and the divine nature of the self and share a belief that everything is universally connected and part of the same energy.

Pilgrimages occupy a particularly important place in New Age practice because one way to restore the spiritual energy sapped by daily living is to set out on a personal quest that can bring about the necessary integration and unity of energy (York, 2001). The end point of the healing spiritual journey, then, is finding one's connected self, true self, whole self, or integrated self (Tucker, 2002). The movement, also greatly inspired by neo-paganism and other forms of nature worship, is marked by abundant discourses related to Earth Mother (Gaia), her healing vibrations, and the balancing power of contact with nature's pure energies (Ivakhiv, 2001). The tendency of the New Age movement to borrow freely from other traditions has also resulted in the incorporation of rituals and symbols of Taoism, Buddhism, and Native American spiritualism (Hanegraaff, 1998), including meditation, chanting, channeling spirits, engaging in divination (e.g., tarot card or palm readings), past-life regression, and shamanism.

Traditionally, pilgrimage has been defined as a physical journey in search of truth, pursuit of what is sacred or holly (Vukonic, 1996). More recently, however, researchers have argued that the distinction between pilgrimage and other forms of travel is increasingly fuzzy, as the separation of the spiritual from the religious in contemporary Western societies leaves individuals with choices of what they want to consider sacred (cf. Olsen and Timothy, 2006). Because the New Age movement is not a religion in the conventional sense— for example, it lacks a single authority figure who could act as a guardian of orthodoxy as well as a distinct place with a status of a worship center— some scholars suggest that for New Agers, journeys to sites of unique natural beauty containing the vestiges of ancient civilizations have the elevated status of pilgrimage (Ivakhiv, 2003; Timothy and Conover, 2006).

ENERGY VORTEXES

Among destinations frequented by New Agers are places that assert the presence of special energy in the form of power vortexes. Some sources imply the existence of energy vortexes in places such as Stonehenge, Avebury, Pendle Hill, the Great Pyramids in Egypt, or Machu Picchu (Ivakhiv, 2003; Timothy and Conover, 2006). As Ivakhiv (2003) points out:

Such places are believed by many to harbor 'earth energies' of some sort—energies that are thought to be beneficial and health-promoting

in their effects and catalytic to spiritual growth. In the growing body
of popular literature on such power spots, these landscapes are seen as
places of personal transformation, and pilgrimages to them are considered a tool of such transformation. (p. 97)

Experiences with vortex energy are often linked to healing (e.g., Lamb and
Barclay, 1987), mystical journeys, profound states of serenity (e.g., Butler, 2002; Shapiro, 1991), and contact with extraterrestrial forms of life
(Dongo, 1988, 1990; Dongo and Bradshaw, 1995). Frequently, the distinction drawn among vortexes relies on the kind of energy that creates them.
They are often described as 'masculine' or 'feminine,' 'electric' and 'magnetic,' or 'yin' and 'yang' (Ivakhiv, 1997).

Despite numerous attempts to provide scientific evidence for the existence
of vortex energies (cf. Sanders, 1992), no conventional proof of such phenomenon exists (Feder, 2010). Even among members of the New Age movement,
little consensus exists as to the specific number of vortexes or their locations.
Despite this ambiguity, thousands of people each year set out to visit locations around the globe that are heralded for the alleged presence of energy
vortexes, and the destination that tops this list is Sedona, Arizona.

Sedona's preoccupation with vortexes can be traced back to 1950s, when
a local metaphysical community emerged out of the activities carried out by
a group of spiritualists, who believe that spirit is an inseparable element of
reality and that the communication between the dead and the living is possible (Ivakhiv, 1997). However, it was not until the 1970s when a psychic
and self-help guru named Dick Sutphen credited Sedona's 'power spots' with
the ability to heal the body and transform the mind. Concurrently, Page
Bryant, another local psychic and medium, revealed her visions about the
presence of several power vortexes around Sedona (Coats, 2009; Ivakhiv,
2001). As a result, by the early 1980s, local tour guides were already offering vortex tours. With the publication of Sutphen's book *Sedona: Psychic
Energy Vortexes* in 1986, interest in the extraordinary power of vortexes
grew exponentially (Ivakhiv, 1997), and during the 1990s, further percola-
tion of the New Age spirituality into the mainstream media fortified Sedona's position as the New Age Mecca. Among New Agers, the uniqueness
and attractiveness of present-day Sedona lies predominantly in its reputation for having the highest concentration of power vortexes worldwide.
This single fact attracts a sizeable segment of the tourist market.

Despite their potentially positive effects, Sedona's energy vortexes can
also be seen as problematic because there is no unified understanding of
what constitutes energy vortexes, no proof of their existence according
to conventional science, and no clarity as to the impact the vortexes and
their energy have on people. Thus, visitors to Sedona seeking to explore or
experience the phenomenon of vortex energy face a number of challenges,
including determining what and where the vortexes are, how to access and
appropriate their energy, and what effects should be anticipated. These

challenges are termed 'consumer tensions' and serve as analytic backdrop to demonstrate ways in which the marketplace takes a central stage in enabling consumption and facilitates materialization of the spiritual experiences with vortex energy.

What Are the Vortexes?

Upon arrival in Sedona, even those who were not previously familiar with the site's reputation are quickly made aware of the vortexes' existence and their importance. My fieldnotes record the word *vortex* as being prominently featured on countless storefront banners, sandwich boards dotting the side of the streets, copious tourist information flyers (generously distributed), and even from the bodies of local tour jeeps driving through the city. This visual omnipresence of vortex signage activates tourists' interest and motivates inquiries about the phenomenon. According to service providers and retailers with whom I spoke, novice visitors' first question is usually an inquiry concerning the definition of a vortex.

As previously stated, multiple definitions of the phenomenon circulate in the marketplace. Many of them have an institutionalized character by virtue of appearing in promotional materials published by locally-recognized and acknowledged institutions. For instance, one of the biggest New Age stores in Sedona, the Center for the New Age, which has the rank of a local community center, defines a vortex as:

> the funnel shape created by the motion of spiraling energy. The vortexes in Sedona are swirling centers of subtle energy coming out from the surface of the earth. They characterize Sedona as a spiritual power center (. . .) The energy is not exactly electricity or magnetism, although it does leave a slight measurable residual magnetism in the places where it is strongest. (Center for the New Age, www.sedonanewagecenter.com).

Even seemingly secular institutions, such as the Sedona Chamber of Commerce, in its 2009 Official Guide for tourists promotes the idea of a vortex as,

> a hot spot of natural energy that draws thousands of visitors each year. The vortexes are believed to create positive, negative and neutral releases of the Earth's energy and evoke balance, a heightened sense of awareness, an awakening of the spirit and even divine intervention. (*Experience Sedona: 2009 Official Guide*, p. 38)

It is also not uncommon to hear waiters in restaurants and sellers involved in businesses not even directly linked to the New Age movement explain in their own words what vortexes are when prompted by questions from patrons. Regardless of the source of definitions, their central element remains the same: a notion that the abundant energy which creates vortex might be appropriated by people with positive results for their well-being.

Vortex Roulette": Where Are the Vortexes?

Once visitors begin to make sense of what a vortex is, another question presents itself: how to locate vortexes. The areas considered vortexes are generally located in big rock formations or flat mountain tops (e.g., Airport Mesa), both abundant geological forms in Sedona, so finding the exact vortex spot seems almost impossible. Rather than leave a befuddled visitor in an information vacuum, the marketplace comes to the rescue with a cornucopia of options: vortex-themed books (e.g., Anderson, 2007; Sanders, 1992) provide advice, orienting maps are available for purchase, and a wide variety of tours are offered by individual guides or 'jeep tour' operators. For example, the widely available *2009 Official Guide to Sedona* offers a map where vortexes are marked among other Sedona points of interest, including hiking routes, scenic overlooks, medical centers and a public library. Inclusion in a tourist guide among other conventional resources normalizes the hunt for the vortexes and positions them as an indispensable part of the Sedona experience.

Rather than discourage consumers, the lack of clarity about the number of vortexes and their locations encourages engagement with the marketplace as a means of resolving ambiguity. For example, in his guidebook, one of the most popular Sedona's tour guides, the self-titled "Mr. Sedona" recommends:

> If your primary interest is our famous vortex energy, then avoid playing Vortex Roulette. Tourists with too little time race among Boynton Canyon, Cathedral Rock, Bell Rock and Airport Mesa. Yes, there's energy here for sure, but you won't find an "X" that marks the spot. (Andres, 2009, p. 41)

Thus, even when armed with a map, tourists who set out to find vortexes face ambiguity and uncertainty. The lack of a definite mark on the map opens up possibilities for providing visitors with services of an experienced tour guide.

Some vortex enthusiasts attempt a more "objective" way to find the right spot. It is not uncommon to see people walking around the vortexes with specialized tools such as dowsing rods and pendulums trying to gauge where the influence of the energy is the strongest. In one of the fieldnotes from a visit to Bell Rock, I noted:

> The group consisted of a guide and four participants. The guide walked up to a place on the side of the rock and took out a pendulum. I could hear him explain to the group that by observing the direction and force with which the pendulum swings, he can determine the location and

the kind of energy needed for performing a healing ritual. He also said that the exact spot depends on an individual, as different people would need different energy vibration. To the question, "can anyone can use a pendulum?" the guide nodded 'yes' but added that the extensive practice is needed to communicate with the pendulum. And if anyone is interested, pendulums and guidebooks are available for purchase from the new age stores in Sedona but the best way is attending a workshop organized by a specialist" (fieldnote; emphasis added here)

As positioned by this canny service provider, it is not enough to know where the vortex is because individuals have different needs corresponding to different vibrations of the energy. And even if one decides to buy the necessary equipment to find it out, it takes training to learn how to use it. In the language of strategic marketing, the cost of entry is high.

Marketplace mechanisms are equally in evidence to distinguish among offerings. The abundance of available way-finding options motivates providers of vortex tours to differentiate and position their services. For instance, the Sedona Metaphysical Spiritual Association, which "connect[s] spiritual seekers in Sedona to the metaphysical spiritual practitioners and businesses who can best assist them in their journey" (www.sedonaspiritual.com; About Us section), compares vortex tours offered by its members with tours offered by 'jeep tour' companies in the following way:

> As a general statement we dare to say that most jeep tour companies provide services to those who want to enjoy and see Sedona and the vortex sites as a tourist. Taking a vortex tour with each one of our members will offer you a profound personal experience, more focused on the metaphysical spiritual side of life. (Sedona Metaphysical and Spiritual Association, www.sedonaspiritual.com)

Thus, people who are interested in experiencing Sedona spiritually, beyond purely admiring Red Rocks' beauty as tourists, need to choose the "right" guide.

Apart from the four areas mentioned in Mr. Sedona's statement above, some other local guides claim the existence of secondary vortexes in other locations such as Coffee Pot Rock, Schnebly Hills, Courthouse Butte, and the Chapel of the Holy Cross. However, interestingly enough, the influence of the vortex energy often surpasses even the geographic limits of the areas considered "lesser" vortexes. As Anderson (2007, p. 32) states in his guide, "Just being in Sedona is being in a vortex, because the whole place is a vortex." Thus, whether you are climbing the rocks, shopping for art in galleries, or eating dinner at a local restaurant, you still benefit from the presence of the energy. This discursive extension of vortex influence is clearly visible as the raison d'etre of some local businesses. For instance, one of local spa resorts claims:

At Angel Valley an unusually high number of energy lines cross the land. Consequently there are many vortexes and special energy sites. Some are directly aligned with our chakras and meridians, some correspond to various levels of our consciousness, and others connect to the Christ Consciousness, Angels, and Beings of Light. (Angel Valley Sedona, www.angelvalley.org).

Owing to this extension, even businesses that do not find themselves in proximity of a recognized vortex manage to secure their affinity with the energy to attract customers.

How to Appropriate Vortex Energy?

Gaining an understanding of what constitutes a vortex and designates its location usually leads to still another tension: how can one benefit from vortex energy? Practices involved in the appropriation of vortex energy are diverse, but their nature is best understood by looking at them through the notion of energy. As one of my informants whom I met meditating at a vortex explained,

> The whole idea of being here is to use this <vortex> energy, draw it in and balance your chakras. Yesterday, one healer who sees the aura told me that my solar plexus <chakra> isn't working correctly. He was dead-on; I have problems with digestion, too much stress at work and no time to meditate. He gave me this affirmation to meditate with and a piece of amber to charge at the vortex and take home. I am supposed to place it on my body before falling asleep and it should help align my chakras. (vortex visitor; John, 42)

Based on the Hindu beliefs, chakras are the energy centers of the physical body and are located in its different parts. Chakras' vibrations are said to carry the information about an individual's physical, emotional, and spiritual well-being. Often my informants referred to the energy of these vibrations as the aura of their bodies. If their bodies were aching, vortex energy could alleviate the pain. But chakra benefits are not confined to physical body; apart from healing, the energy can be motivating and uplifting. It is interesting that energy is typically described as ubiquitous and everything in the world is seen holistically as an interplay of multiple different energies, some beneficial and others harmful. Also, as the discussion of vortex types shows, energy is often anthropomorphized: it can be good or bad, masculine of feminine, strong or weak.

John's statement above also reveals an interesting property of inanimate objects in relationship to vortex energy (i.e., they can become its reservoirs). This highlights a common practice performed at the vortex sites: charging objects with vortex energy. Objects used for this purpose usually involve crystals, gemstones, and jewelry. As one of my tour guides instructed us,

> often before the crystal can be charged it needs to be cleansed from the psychic residue which they accrue before charging. (tour guide; Scott, 55)

According to Scott, objects are best charged when in direct contact with the vortex. In order to charge them, people place these objects on the ground at the site and leave them lying around throughout their stay at the vortex. Once the crystal is charged, it is recommended that the consumer stores it in a pouch made out of natural fabric or leather. Charged crystals function like a small vortex emanating energy, which later on, at home, can be used during meditation or healing. This way each visitor can have a keepsake of his or her tour, as well as a magical battery-like object that stores vortex energy and has the ability to extend the connection with vortexes beyond time and geography.

Certainly, very few visitors travel to Sedona with their gemstones and crystals. Therefore, not surprisingly, the local New Age shops carry a vast inventory of stones, minerals, and crystals (see Figure 13.1). For those visitors who did not have a crystal while at a vortex or could not make it to the site

Figure 13.1   Variety of stones and gems for purchase at a local New Age shop.

(e.g., due to disability), local shops have a solution—pre-charged pieces of quartz neatly packed in small Ziploc bags with a card that contains information about a vortex where this particular piece of crystal was charged.

Another big group of vortex practices are related to energy healing. It encompasses different set of practices often referred to as "modalities" (e.g., reiki, quantum touch, craniosacral massage, reflexology, or sound therapy). Usually these practices are highly ritualized and can engage a number of objects. For instance, practitioners of reiki believe that the hands of a reiki master have the ability to channel the universal energy ("ki") onto another person and heal ailments of a physical and mental nature. Even though the practice of reiki is not vortex-specific, what makes it unique in this context is the claim that the presence of vortex energy facilitates healing much faster and strengthens the efforts of alternative healers. Ephemeral as the healing energy is, it is often materialized through the incorporation of objects such as stones, musical instruments (harps, tambura, ting-shas) or even piano tuning forks, and singing crystal bowls to produce the right healing vibration, amass, and channel the energy. Because vortexes are also believed to elevate concentration, it is very common to observe guided meditation sessions carried out simultaneously with healing practices.

As previously mentioned, vortex tours are often offered by guides who claim to join the knowledge of vortex locations with ability to appropriate and channel vortex energy for healing purposes. Thus, apart from the multiplicity of healers and healing centers located in the city of Sedona, it is also possible to schedule a healing session that will take place directly at the vortex site. The added value of such a session is of course the fortifying role of vortex energy. Similarly, local psychics and mediums also claim that vortex energy influences the vividness and clarity of their readings. The use of tarot cards or runes mediates and objectifies the contact with the spiritual and concretizes communing with vortex energy.

Setting out to find vortexes under the guidance of a psychic or an alternative healer resembles a product bundling strategy, which resolves two consumer tensions at the same time: how to find a vortex and how to benefit from its energy.

Related to the energy healing practices are collective rituals based on Native American spirituality, which involve drumming circles, medicine wheels, and sweat lodges performed under the guidance of a shaman. They allow participants to "be guided into their own personal journey of releasing, healing and prayer" (Lookinghawk, 2009, p. 5). However, for environmental reasons such as land conservation, these rituals are usually carried out around the areas considered vortexes.

Drumming is a form of prayer during which a shaman uses the steady beat of the drum to induce a trance-like state and help participants access their unconscious mind. Similar in its intended effect is a ritual involving a medicine wheel—an arrangement of stones and rocks in circular shape, which, as Sams and Carson (1999, p. 21) point out:

is a symbol for the wheel of life, which is forever evolving and bringing new lessons and truths to the walking of the path. The medicine wheel is used to gather together the energies.

Finally, a sweat lodge resembles a tent constructed of willow branches covered with blankets and canvas tarps to retain the heat of hot stones, which are placed in a pit located centrally in the ground. As Lookinghawk (2009, p. 5) explains, "This dome shape represents the Mother's womb, which the visitors crawl into, to be reborn."

All of these rituals promise spiritual benefits related to finding one's true self, the meaning of the earthly journey, re-gaining the clarity of existence, etc. The significance of vortex energy for these rituals lies in its amplifying nature. As one of our guides explained,

> the vibration of the drums is strengthened by the presence of vortex. All energy which surrounds us is a form of vibration. Drums are like a microphone, they just intensify the experience. (fieldnote)

It is also not uncommon to see ceremonies which integrate, for instance, building medicine wheel and drumming in one orchestrated ritual. These rituals often take a form of scheduled ceremonies featured in the event listings sections of the local free press available at Sedona's New Age stores and other outlets frequented by tourists. It is also possible to hire a vortex tour guide who specialized in shamanic ceremonies performed on sites. Although shamanism is a domain of Native Americans, many local healers and guides claim familiarity with shamanic knowledge inscribing themselves in the ongoing controversy about commercialization and exploitation of Native American spirituality by non-native "plastic" shamans (Aldred, 2000).

What to Expect?

Given the ephemeral nature of vortex energy and multiplicity of practices involved in appropriating it, it is important to take notice of the way in which the marketplace facilitates managing visitors' expectations concerning the impact of the energy. As recounted earlier, people report various feelings and sensations that they attribute to vortex energy. Copiousness of these reports can be partially credited to an open stance taken by many guides, psychics, and healers. When questioned about the impact of vortex energy, one of the guides during my vortex tour explained,

> I can't tell you what to expect because I would limit your perception, close you to things outside of the box. We all have individual needs and sensitivities. We can feel different things but in order to feel anything you have to be open to anything. (psychic guide; Ann Marie)

This view resonates also with the position taken by the Sedona Metaphysical and Spiritual Association. When acknowledging the uniqueness and the focus on the spiritual aspect of taking a vortex tour with any of its members, the association also emphasizes that, "This experience may differ depending on the personality and the style of each facilitator" (www. sedonaspiritual.com).

A fluid and ambiguous character of the consumer expectations gives marketplace an opportunity to maintain a wider variety of products and services associated with vortexes. As favorable as this position may seem for consumers, it is important to note that many vortex visitors expressed being overwhelmed with a number of available options. Especially, with the increase in the multiplicity of vortex-related products and services, the competition between providers also intensified. As a result, marketplace actors' differentiation efforts nuanced meanings attached to vortexes even more and, by doing so, destabilized consumer expectations, adding to already existing tensions.

Frequently, the effects of vortex energy also can be construed as removed in time (e.g., only from a perspective of time are you able to see that your vortex visit was a starting point for your journey of self-discovery). This discursive tactic wards off the potential for consumer disappointment and dissatisfaction. However, there are also more "objective" attempts to quantify the impact of vortex energy on visitors. For instance, in their advertising flyer, the Center for the New Age offers aura pictures taken before and after a vortex tour. Implicit, of course, is the understanding that, similar to TV makeover shows, the change caused by vortex energy can be unearthed by comparing the pictures, which show colors of a visitor's aura before and after the tour. Even if such change occurs, it still remains debatable what it actually means for the person's well-being because there is no scientifically corroborated interpretation of aura colors.

Conclusions

In this chapter, I attempted to demonstrate that even though the spiritual and commercial belong to two seemingly different orders of our daily lives (i.e., sacred and profane), in consumer society, the marketplace creates opportunities for spiritual consumption and facilitates materialization of the spiritual in order to enable marketplace exchanges. I also posit that the marketplace plays an active role in destabilizing consumer expectations through fostering the presence of various and often contradicting discourses regarding the marketed offering (i.e., vortex energy). This ambiguity exacerbates consumer tensions, which for their resolution require a consumption of specialized products and services (see Figure 13.2).

The dynamics revealed here also indicates that the resolution of consumer tensions is never permanent as the continuously growing number of products and services vying for consumer attention increases competition

Figure 13.2   Spiritual marketplace dynamics.

among marketplace actors who try to differentiate their offering from this of their competitors. This usually takes place through nuancing meanings and discourses related to the main offering (i.e., vortex energy), which only increases consumer uncertainty related to a product that is already intangible and ephemeral in its nature.

Marketing of spiritual experiences can be seen as a process similar to selling credence goods, the quality of which is hard to evaluate even after their purchase and consumption. However, unlike credence goods, where the role of marketer comes down to managing customer expectations, spiritual experiences seem to benefit from strategies that individualize and destabilize consumer expectations in order to allow for an open-ended evaluation. By co-opting consumers' responsibility for the consumption outcomes (e.g., "You need to be open to the energy in order for it to have effect on you"), claiming the longitudinal nature of the results (e.g., "It might be the starting point of a great change in your life but you will know this only from the perspective of time"), and insignificance of geographic distances (e.g., "Effects can be felt after you returned home"), marketers attempt to delay post-purchase evaluation and minimize the effects of buyer's remorse.

Destabilizing multiplicity of discourses related to vortex energy can also have another benefit for marketplace actors. It allows a wider market penetration and access to diverse groups of consumers with different religious affiliations. Existing variety of narratives about power vortex origins, practices necessary for energy appropriation, and its influence on human beings can be easily incorporated into many different religious systems, be it Christian, Buddhist, or neo-pagan.

Finally, destabilization initiated and perpetuated by competing market-place discourses allows even mundane forms of consumption (e.g., dining or shopping in the areas located away from core vortex spots) to become part of a spiritual experience. Typically sacred sites are sharply distinguished from the profane world around it (Shackley, 2001). In Sedona, however, this distinction is being actively blurred by marketplace actors. The indeterminate nature of vortex energy allows its influence to be stretched beyond the physical limits of the Red Rock formations where vortexes are said to reside.

This particular conceptualization of spiritual marketplace dynamics opens new avenues for inquiry into the strategies employed by marketplace actors to materialize and sell experiential offerings. As non-material goods play an ever greater role in the economy and consumption in general (Slater, 1997), marketers encounter a number of problems related to competing on intangible and experiential aspects of their products and services. Hence, thorough theorizations of materializing processes could be of help here. The market dynamics depicted in this chapter can also be of relevance to transformative consumer research. Potential research agenda could tackle issues related to consumer well-being in a lucrative and fast-growing market of self-help education and spiritual services, which remains highly unregulated and frequently lacks appropriate consumer protection.

REFERENCES

Aldred, Lisa. 2000. "Plastic Shamans and Astroturf Sun Dances: New Age Commercialization of Native American Spirituality." *The American Indian Quarterly* 24 (3): 329–352.

Anderson, Richard J. 2007. *The Heart of the Vortex*. Sedona, AZ: Sedona Wind Publishing.

Andres, Dennis. 2009. *Sedona: The Essential Guidebook*. Sedona, AZ: Meta Adventures Publishing.

Belk, R. W., M. Wallendorf, and J. F. Sherry. 1989. "The Sacred and the Profane in Consumer Behavior: Theodicy on the Odyssey." *The Journal of Consumer Research* 16 (1): 1–38.

Butler, Jamie. 2002. *Sedona's Best Vortex Guidebook*. Sedona, AZ: In Print Publishing.

Coats, Curtis. 2009. "Sedona, Arizona: New Age Pilgrim-Tourist Destination." *CrossCurrents* 59 (3): 383–389.

Dongo, Tom. 1990. *The Alien Tide*. Sedona, AZ: Light Technology Publications.

———. 1998. *The Mysteries of Sedona*. Sedona, AZ: Light Technology Communication Services.

———, and Linda Bradshaw. 1995. *Merging Dimensions: The Opening Portals of Sedona*. Sedona, AZ: Light Technology Publications.

Drury, Nevill. 2004. *The New Age: Searching for the Spiritual Self*. New York: Thames & Hudson, Inc.

Durkheim, Emile. 1915. *The Elementary Forms of Religious Life*. London: Allen and Unwin.

Experience Sedona: 2009 Official Guide. 2009. Edited by Sedona Chamber of Commerce Tourism Bureau. Sedona, AZ: Gannett Pacific Publications.

Feder, Kenneth L. 2010. *Encyclopedia of Dubious Archaeology: From Atlantis to the Walam Olum*. Santa Barbara, CA: Greenwood.

Frazer, James George. 1922. *The Golden Bough: A Study in Magic and Religion*. New York: Macmillan.

Geary, Patrick. 1986. "Sacred Commodities: The Circulation of Medieval Relics." In *The Social Life of Things*, edited by Arjun Appadurai, 169–191. New York: Cambridge University Press.

Hanegraaff, W. J. 1998. "Reflections on New Age and the Secularization of Nature." In *Nature Religion Today: The Pagan Alternative in the Modern World*, edited by J. Pearson, R. Roberts, and G. Samuel, 22–32. Edinburgh: Edinburgh University Press.

Hayano, D. 1979. "Auto-Ethnography: Paradigms, Problems and Prospects." *Human Organization* 38: 99–104.

Ivakhiv, Adrian. 1997. "Red Rocks, 'Vortexes' and the Selling of Sedona: Environmental Politics in the New Age." *Social Compass* 44 (3): 367–384.

———. 2001. *Claiming Sacred Ground: Pilgrims and Politics at Glastonbury and Sedona*. Indianapolis: Indiana University Press.

———. 2003. "Nature and Self in New Age Pilgrimage." *Culture and Religion* 4 (1): 93–118.

Kozinets, Robert V., and Richard Kedzior. 2009. "I, Avatar: Auto-Netnographic Research in Virtual Worlds." In *Virtual Social Identity and Consumer Behavior*, edited by Natalie T. Wood and Michael R. Solomon, 3–19. Armonk, NY: Society for Consumer Psychology.

Lamb, Gaia, and Shinan Naom Barclay. 1987. *The Sedona Vortex Experience*. Sedona, AZ: Light Technology Publications.

Lookinghawk, Artie. 2009. "Unearthing Ancient Health Secrets: The Sweat Lodge." *The Red Rock Review* 14 (7): 2–6.

McDannell, Colleen. 1995. *Material Christianity: Religion and Popular Culture in America*. New Haven, CT: Yale University Press.

Moore, R. Laurence. 1994. *Selling God: American Religion in the Marketplace of Culture*. New York: Oxford University Press.

O'Guinn, T. C., and R. W. Belk. 1989. "Heaven on Earth: Consumption at Heritage Village, USA." *Journal of Consumer Research* 16 (2): 227–238.

Olsen, Daniel H., and Dallen J. Timothy. 2006. "Tourism and Religious Journeys." In *Tourism, Religion and Spiritual Journeys*, edited by Dallen J. Timothy and Daniel H. Olsen, 1–22. London and New York: Routledge.

Sams, Jamie, and David Carson. 1999. *Medicine Cards: Revised, Expanded Edition*. New York: St. Martin's Press.

Sanders, Pete A., Jr. 1992. *Scientific Vortex Information: How to Easily Understand, Find, and Tap Vortex Energy in Sedona and Wherever You Travel!* Sedona, AZ: Free Soul Publishing, 1992.

Shackley, M. 2001. *Managing Sacred Sites: Service Provision and Visitor Experience*. London: Continuum.

Shapiro, Robert, ed. 1991. *The Sedona Vortex Guide Book*. Sedona, AZ: Light Technology Publications.

Slater, Don. 1997. *Consumer Culture and Modernity*. Cambridge: Polity Press.

Sutphen, Dick. 1986. *SEDONA: Psychic Energy Vortexes*. Malibu, CA: Valley of the Sun Publishing.

Timothy, Dallen J., and Paul J. Conover. 2006. "Nature Religion, Self-Spirituality and New Age Tourism." In *Tourism, Religion and Spiritual Journeys*, edited by Dallen J. Timothy and Daniel H. Olsen, 139–155. London and New York: Routledge.

Tucker, J. 2002. "New Age Religion and the Cult of the Self." *Society* 39 (2): 46–51.

Van Maanen, John. 1988. *Tales of the Field: On Writing Ethnography.* Chicago Guides to Writing, Editing, and Publishing. Chicago: University of Chicago Press.

Vukonic, Boris. 1996. *Tourism and Religion.* Oxford: Pergamon Press.

Wall, Sarah. 2006. "An Autoethnography on Learning About Autoethnography." *International Journal of Qualitative Methods* 5 (June): 1–12.

York, M. 2001. "New Age Commodification and Appropriation of Spirituality." *Journal of Contemporary Religion* 16 (3): 361–371.

Zaidman, N. 2003. "Commercialization of Religious Objects: A Comparison between Traditional and New Age Religions." *Social Compass* 50 (3): 345.

———. 2007. "The New Age Shop—Church or Marketplace?" *Journal of Contemporary Religion* 22 (3): 361–374.

14 Consuming the Mists and Myths of Avalon

A Case Study of Pilgrimage in Glastonbury

Linda Scott and Pauline Maclaran

A consistent characteristic of religion is the sacred place that draws adherents, often on a periodic basis, as pilgrims. Pilgrimage now constitutes a significant component of world travel. Lourdes, Mecca, and Varanasi, as well as many smaller shrines throughout the world, draw visitors seeking spiritual experience who need accommodation and meals, as well as goods and services that may be required to enact the requisite ritual, achieve the moment of insight, or perform the purification. Providing pilgrimage experience thereby becomes the basis for a local economy whose market trades in spiritual consumption.

We describe a pilgrimage experience in Glastonbury, a place that has held sacred status in England through several religious periods over thousands of years and continues to draw spiritual seekers in these most secular of times. Our intention is to show local vendors producing pilgrimage experience, acting independently of any single religious institution, yet using history and landscape, along with an eclectic selection of stories and practices from established faiths, to produce a distinctly 21st-century spiritual experience for a new generation of independent pilgrims.

OTHE LITERATURE

In consumer research, there are no studies on pilgrimage as such. Heritage Village, a Christian theme park studied by O'Guinn and Belk (1989), drew millions of consumers who may be very loosely characterized as pilgrims. However, Heritage Village was a purpose-built space sponsored by a single religious institution, equal parts theme park, conference center, and church space. Further, O'Guinn and Belk's analysis focused on the political and technological underpinnings of Heritage Village, rather than the quest for spiritual experience that typifies pilgrimage.

Kozinets (2002) studied the Burning Man festival at Black Rock, Nevada, whose attendees might view their journey as a pilgrimage. However, the site was chosen opportunistically when the festival grew too large for its original site at Baker Beach in San Francisco, and the rituals do not seem intended to result in spiritual experiences strictly speaking, although much of the experience is ritualistic and communal. A primary objective of Burning Man is for consumers to distance themselves from exchange, although Kozinets calls attention to ironies in the exchange behaviors. Our case study will identify similar ironies.

Other work investigates the interface among the power of place, market, and consumption in a secular domain. One group studies market-directed places such as flagship brand stores (Kozinets et al., 2004), brand museums (Sherry, 1998; Peñaloza, 1999), and shopping malls (Maclaran and Brown, 2005). The ubiquitous presence of 'strategic place marketing' (Kotler, Hinder, and Rein, 2002) makes it easy to forget that places can create markets rather than vice versa.

In many ways, the purpose-built sites of Burning Man and Heritage Village are more similar to flagship stores and brand museums than to sacred sites like Lourdes and Varanasi. We argue that 'place-directed markets'— sites of exchange created by the crowds drawn to a sacred place—are at least as numerous and certainly as important as those created by marketers or even anti-market promoters. Consider, for example, that Our Lady of Guadalupe in Mexico, stemming from a sighting made in 1531 by a local peasant, now draws more than fifteen million tourists per year, thus producing a flourishing marketplace of spiritual services and goods. Yet, none in consumer research have looked at the many places around the world with histories of sacred status or at the overtly commercial behaviors that are required to support them. Thus, we seek to conceptualize how the spirits of place drive marketization. We will draw specifically on a recent stream of research on pilgrimage in anthropology.

THEORY: THE PILGRIMAGE

Anthropological work on pilgrimage was limited until the 1990s primarily because the cultural boundary crossing that is often a pre-condition of pilgrimage worked against the intensely local focus of ethnographic work (Coleman and Eade, 2004). Most work before that built on Victor and Edith Turner's (1978) work, which actually focused on rites of passage (see Coleman and Eade, 2004). However, scholars have begun studying pilgrimage intensely in the past twenty years, proceeding by building up case studies of individual pilgrimage sites (Coleman and Elsner, 1995; Morinis, 1992). Whereas the analysis sometimes addresses the overlap with globalization or tourism, the focus understandably is not on the commercial basis for the site and so virtually never looks at the local market.

Pilgrimage makes an appearance in most religions, so the particulars vary a great deal. We begin, therefore, by distilling from this broad literature characteristics that seem broadly typical, but we make no claim that these are universal traits or are always present in a pilgrimage experience.

There is usually a geographic journey, although there are now claims for "virtual pilgrimage," and some feel drug-induced or deep meditative states can be classified as pilgrimage. Usually, though, a trip through space is a condition of pilgrimage, and sometimes the manner and method of travel is an important aspect. Often, indeed, the journey is as much a part of the pilgrimage as is the destination, sometimes presenting obstacles, trials, and hardships that act as a prelude to or preparation for spiritual experience. Importantly, the journey itself, especially if long or challenging, creates the sense of separation from the mundane world that many feel is necessary.

The company of other, like-minded pilgrims is also often a condition. Although it is possible to make pilgrimage alone or to designate a site of special meaning to oneself, the general phenomenon of pilgrimage usually involves the collective movement of a community of believers, sometimes all at once, as in the Hajj, but sometimes continuously, as with visitors to Lourdes. People who accompany a pilgrim can be formative of the experience, as in *The Canterbury Tales*.

Indeed, a challenging condition for the study of pilgrimage is its simultaneous occurrence on communal and individual planes. There is normally an anticipated spiritual outcome—purification, enlightenment, ecstasy, visions, healing, pacification of gods, forgiveness of sins, and so on—that may or may not be finally achieved, but it is usually an individual experience or achievement, even when it occurs in the company of others. The personal experience often results from a ritual for which preparation is normally needed. This ready-making may involve fasting, meditation, walking counterclockwise, or any number of things. Often the preparation includes obtaining certain objects—a pitcher, a robe, a candle, and so forth.

The spiritual outcome is supposed to result from following the correct steps, sometimes in prescribed order, from embarkation to epiphany. Therefore, pilgrimages are often rule-governed. Specialists may be engaged to assist and advise. These people may be clergy or merely self-appointed guides. Interestingly, tension between pilgrims and guides has also been observed to be typical.

Pilgrimage does not always have the desired result. If the outcome is not achieved, the trip is still a pilgrimage, but the intention to reach the outcome must be there or the trip is not a pilgrimage. In our case, for instance, the experience has many features of pilgrimage, but we ourselves were not on a pilgrimage because our intention was to conduct research. Tourists come to Glastonbury without expectation of spiritual experience; they are not pilgrims. Random visions are not pilgrimages; Saul was not a pilgrim on the road to Damascus, although he was radically changed along the way. How the pilgrim interprets failure may determine whether they attempt the journey at a future date and may result in enough disillusion to make the supplicant leave the faith. As intense spiritual turning points, pilgrimages can have life-changing effects.

METHOD

We draw on a three-year-long ethnographic study of Glastonbury, a small English town whose main economic basis has been pilgrimage for centuries, despite radical changes in the religious climate. We have studied Glastonbury through immersion, going to conferences, retreats, and fairs, but also by observation of ceremonies and processions, and by interviewing merchants and visitors. One strategy has been to attend events held on celebratory days, including pagan feast days such as Samhain, Beltane, and Imbolc, but also Christian days such as mark the Anglican and Catholic churches in Glastonbury, and the main secular event, the annual Guy Fawkes Day Parade.

Here we report a trip made for Imbolc, the deep winter pagan day, for a ritual drumming workshop. Although the three-day weekend was termed a "workshop," it was advertised as a series of rituals that would be performed by participants and did not include lessons in drumming. The workshop convened in the seminar room at Glastonbury's famous Chalice Well Gardens and then proceeded to three group outings to nearby holy sites, at which ritual drumming and chanting were performed. Themes and props drew on multiple traditions and attracted an equally mixed bag of participants.

The mapped journey for the ritual made use of a cartographic conceit popular in Glastonbury, the Michael and Mary lines, also known as "the dragon lines." The Michael line, also called "St. Michael's ley," is an imagined straight line that runs through English churches and monasteries dedicated to St. Michael, who, like St. George, is a dragon slayer and associated with legends of England. The Mary line is an imagined energy line that curls, like an electric current, around the Michael line. These two lines echo a common motif in Glastonbury lore, the interdependent balance between female and male energies. By walking, chanting, and beating a drum from point to point where the Michael and Mary lines are thought to cross, the workshop participants were given a pilgrimage experience the organizer called "Drumming the Dragonlines."

In order for readers to make sense of the peculiar combination of places, imagery, and practices involved, we first overview Glastonbury's history, showing how the interaction among geography and history give the place its 'genus loci' (Sherry, 1998). We draw on an extensive collection of history and archaeology of Glastonbury assembled during this project, but also on English folklore and popular belief. Because Glastonbury is an important site in Britain, there is much besides fairy tales written about it, and we will merely be summarizing here (see, for instance, Ashe, 2002; Howard-Gordon, 2010; Mann, 2004; Mitchell, 1997).

LAND AND LEGEND

Archaeologists speculate that Glastonbury has been a spiritual site from the time of the first humans in England. The most outstanding topographical feature is a tower of land with a flat top, which can be seen from miles on approach because there is no other rise of land to compete. From the top of the "Tor," as it is called, a prehistoric viewer would have had a complete, 360-degree view of the night sky as it revolved through the year. In those times, the surrounding area was a dense swamp, which not only made access to the Tor difficult, but surrounded it with thick mists, adding to its mystical appearance. Internally, the Tor is a catacomb of caverns, a space suited for secrets, rituals, and tales of underground colonies. From this network of mineral spaces flow two springs, a red and a white. The red is iron and the white is calcium; the two colors from a single source have supported dualistic metaphors—especially of male and female powers— over millennia of human speculation.

Yet the Tor is unfriendly to human habitation. The soil is stony and the sides steep; the land is covered by a thin veneer of grass, and a handful of weak trees cling to the angled grade. Although archaeological evidence reveals attempts to cultivate the land, this imposing mass has been uninhabited through most of history. Instead, humans have used the Tor as a sacred site, regardless of the religion dominant at the time.

From the Tor, you can see three opposing landmarks: the Chalice Well Garden, Wearyall Hill, and Glastonbury Abbey. The Chalice Well Garden nestles into the side of the Tor, a high array of hilly spaces, waterfalls, pools, and wells, all red with iron, including one dramatic grotto called the Chalice Well. The topography of the Chalice Well Gardens, with its rounded shapes, flowering plants, and red waters, is a clearly female contrast to the imposing, sparse, but unmistakably phallic Tor next to it.

The Tor and the Chalice Well have figured often in British folklore. The king of the Fairies, the Welsh figure Gwynn Ap Nudd, is said to live there. The mystical Avalon, where King Arthur's half-fairy half-sister, Morgan Le Fay, lived, is said be in and around the Tor. The goddess worshipped by Morgan's priestess cult was called, "The Lady of Avalon." Arthur's Camelot is said to have been Cadbury Castle, twelve miles away. The Chalice myth is much entangled with the Arthurian legend of the Holy Grail.

From the Tor and the Chalice Well Garden, you look across Glastonbury to Wearyall Hill. According to a surprisingly widely held belief, Joseph of Arimathea, the uncle of Jesus, came to Britain after the Crucifixion, accompanied by eleven apostles. They stopped, all of them weary, on this hilltop, now known as Wearyall Hill. Joseph stabbed the earth with his staff and it immediately flowered, becoming the tree that is now called "the Holy Thorn." Taking this as a sign, Joseph declared that the Christian Church in Britain would be founded there. He also allegedly took the Cup from the Last Supper, carried from the Middle East, and put it in the Chalice Well.

The first church was actually built in the valley below, visible from the Tor, Wearyall Hill, and the Chalice Well Gardens. The Abbey and the Holy Thorn tree on Wearyall Hill both became Christian pilgrimage sites. After an excavation in 1185 unearthed the alleged remains of Arthur and

Guinevere, the bones were buried below the altar of the Abbey's "Mary Chapel," sometimes called the "Lady Chapel."

A monastery dedicated to St. Michael was built on the Tor in the 13th century, but it was destroyed by earthquake, all except a tower at the top. This tower is a node on the Michael line; the Mary line crosses just below the summit and again at the Chalice Well, as well as near the place where Arthur and Guinevere are buried in the Lady Chapel.

The discovery of Arthur and Guinevere's bodies points to clues about Glastonbury's economy. Some historians insist that the discovery was a hoax designed to pump up Glastonbury's tourism, which was in decline at the time (Croft et al., 2008). Records also indicate that there was tension between the Abbey, which sought to bring market activity closer—now the site of the High Street—rather than nearer the Tor, which still drew the pilgrims. Considerable elaboration on mythical visits by popular saints, such as Brigid and Patrick, skillfully blended history, Celtic legend, and official doctrine—and established the site as one with multiple special spots and associated rituals.

By the 16th century, the Catholic Church in England was rich, especially the abbey at Glastonbury, and the town was known as "the English Jerusalem." However, the only industry there was the church and its associated influx of travellers. When Henry VIII dissolved the monasteries, closing Glastonbury Abbey in 1539, his men killed the last of the Catholic Abbots, Richard Whiting—at the time the most powerful cleric in England—by drawing and quartering him atop the Tor, then fixing his head on a pike. Glastonbury went into a deep slump, emotionally and economically, from which it never really recovered. During the long period of religious strife that followed, many church observance days were outlawed by Protestant England, including Halloween (which was replaced with Guy Fawkes Day in honor of a failed Catholic plot against the crown), the Holy Thorn was cut down by Oliver Cromwell, and the Abbey fell into ruin.

In the centuries since Glastonbury Abbey was closed, authorities have made various attempts at rescuing the town from persistent economic decline. Because a network of swamps made access from the outside difficult, there was no real basis for Glastonbury to be a "market town," in the traditional sense used by agricultural economies. Flemish artisans were brought in during the 16th century to stimulate a weaving industry. In the 1750s, Glastonbury enjoyed a short period of prosperity when the waters of the white spring were thought to be curative. A smallpox outbreak put an end to that. In the 18th century, a canal was built in an attempt to stimulate trade, but it had to be closed because it could not be maintained. In the 19th century, some success was finally achieved in building an industry around tanning and producing leather goods, notably by Clark's shoes. Overall, however, the town has never had a solid economic foundation other than as a pilgrimage site.

As England became one of the most secular-minded nations in the world, then, we might have expected that Glastonbury would decline and disappear. Instead, beginning in the late 1920s, it reawakened as a mystical site for a variety of spiritual practices, while still drawing in pilgrims for two annual Christian processions, one Catholic and one Protestant, as well as the secular parade for Guy Fawkes Day. In the 1920s, it drew a splinter group of the Hermetic Order of the Golden Dawn, a collection of spiritual seekers, many of them well-known (W. B. Yeats and Maud Gonne among the members), who dabbled in astrology, tarot, and other occult practices. The Chalice Well Trust was formed in 1959 by Wellesley Tudor Poole, a seer but also a soldier and businessman, who had worked on behalf of various persecuted faiths, especially during the world wars. A member of the B'hai faith, which attempts to unify the visions of world prophets like Jesus, Buddha, and Mohammad, Pole dedicated the Chalice Well Gardens as a sanctuary for all faiths in the name of world peace. Then, in the late 1960s, Glastonbury drew a "hippy" community, which brought further interest in alternative spiritualities, including goddess worship. During the 1970s, the Glastonbury music festival began—it is held some distance from town and has little effect on the local economy, but furthered the association between Glastonbury and counterculture. The interest in the divine feminine begun in the late 1960s grew over the next twenty years, in Glastonbury, as elsewhere in the industrialized nations. A Goddess Temple was built in central Glastonbury, just off the High Street, in 2002, and the town's largest annual gathering is now the Goddess Conference in July.

Today, the first thing striking a traveler to the town is the visual impact of Glastonbury's high street with its array of small shops, proffering creative displays of mystical merchandise. These brightly colored storefronts have wonderfully evocative names (e.g., Speaking Tree Bookshop, The Celtic Thread, The Goddess and the Green Man, The Psychic Piglet, Yin Yang, Gothic Image). Together they present a spiritual bricolage of shopping that reflects the mosaic of myth and legend surrounding the region and enables a "pic n' mix" approach to a personalised spirituality. Sandwich boards on the sidewalk also offer tarot and aura readings, reiki healing, and chakra adjustments. The local paper, called "the Oracle," is packed with adverts announcing lectures on Christian theology, art shows of goddesses around the world, African drumming demonstrations, and astral travel workshops. So, a range of spiritual services also contribute to Glastonbury's economy. The spiritual diversity is vast, encompassing Wiccans, druids, and goddess worshippers, as well as welcoming Christianity, Buddhism, Hinduism, and Islam. The town is as keenly attuned to the pagan calendar as to the Christian, and the shops and services adapt their offerings to tie in with its ancient seasonal festivals.

More established institutions also have a stake in the town. Glastonbury Abbey is owned and maintained by the Church of England, and the Tor is now owned by the National Trust. From a retail perspective, these two landmarks can be likened to anchor stores. Both the Anglican and Catholic annual processions begin near the Tor and proceed down the High Street to the Abbey; the Goddess March, however, begins near the Abbey and proceeds up the High Street to the Chalice Well and the Tor (see Bowman, 2006). What this means, however, is that the bright landscape of the shops along the High Street are ritual space as well as ritual suppliers.

DRUMMING THE DRAGONLINES

At this stage in our research, we were targeting the major pagan holidays. It was winter, so the next trip to Glastonbury was to be for Imbolc. An observance that heralds the end of winter, Imbolc normally falls at the full moon nearest the midpoint between the winter solstice and the spring equinox. It is normally on either February 1 or 2 and coincides with the Gaelic Brigid's Day. It is a festival associated with weather-watching and finding the earliest signs of spring.

No public ritual was planned in Glastonbury, as normally would happen for bigger festivals, such as Beltane. So, we chose to attend a drumming workshop being advertised online because we were interested in the function of drumming at rituals we had attended and because the proposed schedule included rituals to be performed at both pagan and Christian sites, as well as liturgical elements from each tradition.

We came separately to Glastonbury, one by train and one by car. It had snowed heavily during the week. The train does not actually come to Glastonbury, so the one arriving by public transport on Thursday night took a taxi through a snow storm from Bristol Temple Mead to Glastonbury. By midnight, the snow was heavy, and there was concern that the one coming by car would not be able to get through the following morning.

By Friday noon, however, we were both in town and ready for the workshop. One of us had purchased drums on a recent trip to Africa explicitly for the event. We were proud to be prepared with what we felt were authentic drums for this purpose. However, when we walked into the seminar room at the Chalice Well Garden, we were greeted by a shrill voice admonishing us for bringing the wrong kind of drum.

Freda, the convener of the workshop, informed us in an imperious tone that we had to use a ritual drum. Her meaning was not immediately clear, as we had observed many kinds of drums being used in Glastonbury rituals—and the African drums were as much "ritual drums" as one could want. Freda showed us a set of what she insisted were Native American drums. Only these flat leather drums, about 24 inches in diameter, were permitted. We could buy or rent one from her. Purchase prices began at £150, and the weekend rental was £20. The drums for purchase were simply beautiful, with elaborate patterned skins, and the rentals were made of a simple white covering, possibly paper or plastic. We were offended at the obvious commercial manipulation and took the rentals.

The workshop began much later than scheduled because many of the participants were delayed by weather. We sat in a circle, exchanging stories of our travel troubles with our new classmates, interrupted from time to time by a cell phone call from someone stranded in the snow. England, in truth, does not experience serious snowfall very often and is ill-prepared for it. A snowstorm of this magnitude is remembered for years.

Our fellow travellers were a mixed lot. One was an ordained Methodist minister, on a grant from her church to learn how neo-pagans were attracting so many followers. Another was a medium from Germany who claimed to channel a variety of spiritual characters. Freda herself was a long-time resident of Glastonbury, a local poet and drummer, who wrote and recorded chants for local ceremonies (CDs were available for sale). Ten of us were gathered around a small table set with a lace tablecloth and various ritual objects, such as crystals, candles, religious statues, and fresh spices. We were invited to bring our own special objects for this "altar." On the floor was an oriental rug; the main wall had a huge representation of St. Michael. The room had many windows and a skylight, so when the snow stopped, a bright glow diffused through the room.

That afternoon we prepared for three "walking meditations," during which we would drum and chant at the Chalice Well, the Tor, and the Abbey where the Michael and Mary lines crossed. Freda drew expansively, and probably also inaccurately, from several traditions for our preparations. We learned the colors and parts of the body associated with the chakras—a common conceit in Glastonbury—but also learned to sing the sounds of each chakra (something we thought might be Freda's invention). We recited a version of the Lord's Prayer translated directed into contemporary English from the Ancient Greek. We learned Native American chants and pounded our drums with mallets wrapped in soft animal skins. We were served herbal teas and a vegetarian meal. Periodically, Freda stood to take our photograph for her website, and we obediently smiled.

The night of the first day was clear but cold. We did not really think Freda would stick to the planned outing, given the weather, but she insisted that we take our drums out into the Chalice Well Gardens and follow a prescribed path among the pools, falls, and wells. The snow was white and undisturbed. We walked silently, shivering, into the gardens. Frieda began to drum and chant. We obediently followed her lead, drumming and chanting as instructed, through the shrubbery, stopping at points to meditate. In some places, the foliage was thick and the dark impenetrable. We had no flashlight, so some steps were treacherous. But at the top of the gardens, you could see the full moon over the Tor, and the sky was bright with stars and the reflected snow. We sang and then just stopped, silent, watching. It was a beautiful moment.

Such a joyous evening created great expectations for the main event the following morning: a drumming walk up the Tor. We warmed our hands and our drums during tea in the seminar room and then walked out into the early sunshine. We stopped first at the White Spring Chapel, a newly-opened shrine converted from a 19th-century waterworks building just outside the Gardens. There was no electric light, so we plunged, drumming with bravado, into total darkness. Freda's assistant, a bald man in a Day-Glo vest, lit candles. We could then see the flow of the spring through a room that had clearly been abandoned for decades and was never intended as a shrine. Yet, as Freda's assistant set about placing the candles along the stream of water, the place began to take on the appropriate aura, and, in the growing light, we could see a mural of Brigid just above the place where the water pooled. We drummed and sang for what seemed like a long time, enjoying a sense of dank mystery that contrasted nicely with the crisp experience of the previous night.

We then headed for the far side of the Tor because the Oaks of Avalon provide the traditional Druidic entry point and are a crossing for the dragon lines. The sun was high, and the snow had melted from the mostly treeless Tor. The grade of the Tor on the back side was very steep, the ground was soft, and all the plant life superficially rooted. As we tried to climb, mud slid beneath our feet, and any plant we grabbed gave way. Several members in our group were seniors and several very unfit. Yet we were trying to climb a glass mountain. Freda stood aside, drumming and chanting as we crouched close to the grass and struggled up the Tor. When we reached a ledge about three feet deep, we all stood against it, relieved for a moment, and Freda shouted at her assistant to take our picture for the website. We smiled and held up our drums, but some were getting angry.

At long last, we reached the St. Michael Tower. We sat, exhausted, on the stone benches inside the small open room at the base. Freda began to drum and sing, motioning us to join her. The German medium, smiling rather inappropriately, began to sing as well. Most of us mumbled along. One or two remained stubbornly silent. The assistant took more photographs. Finally, the pilgrims were allowed to walk down the public path, a gentler descent. The research duo headed straight for the pub, furious.

The next morning, a rainy Sunday, we gathered again at the Chalice Well room. Freda showed us the photographs from the previous day. We looked manically happy on the ledge at the far side of the Tor, obediently displaying the beautiful ritual drums (no doubt to be sold on the website). We then appeared to be stunned with fatigue under the Michael tower. Freda, however, was focused not on her customers, but on some white globes that appeared in the photographs at the summit, calling them "orbs" and implying that they were some kind of spirit matter. It appeared obvious a sprinkle of water had hit the camera lens, but such prosaic interpretations are not the stuff of pilgrimage.

The pilgrims now trudged in the rain toward Glastonbury Abbey, stopping at the gate to pay the entrance fee. We went first to the Abbot's kitchen, a great space with a high ceiling that magnified our drumming and Freda's admittedly marvelous singing voice. Once more, there was a glimmer of spiritual excitement as our collective sounds filled the room.

Then we were back out in the mist, to drum in the Mary chapel, at a crossing point for the lines, but also over the spot where Arthur and Guinevere had allegedly been entered. There is no roof on the Lady Chapel, but the space does have an appealing mystique. Freda arranged us for several photographs.

Amidst a fresh shower, we went into the yard where Freda ordered us to hold hands and pray. She marched several meters away to stand by her assistant while he photographed us. We were beginning to feel rebellious—the time had come for the end of the workshop, and we were losing patience. But we stood in the pouring rain with our fellow pilgrims: the photos later showed a group of nine, bundled up with shoulders hunched and heads bowed. It is difficult to discern whether the visible attitude is prayerful, frustrated, or merely suffering.

After this prayer, the pilgrims said goodbye to each other and to Freda. We strode toward the parking lot, keen to return to the secular world.

ANALYSIS

The intention of the "Drumming the Dragonlines" workshop was to make money by providing a pilgrimage experience, a line of work within the long tradition of Glastonbury. Although this group was small, one could see that our travel to the town provided a bit of income to many vendors: buying or renting drums, buying CDs, paying entry fees, the room rental for the seminar, the meals we were provided, as well as the fee for the workshop, the rental for our lodging, and the much-needed trip to the pub. The organizer was observably intent on building an income stream by photographing our experience at key points along the way—by the time of this writing, there are several subsequent pilgrimages in and around Glastonbury promoted through pictures on Freda's website.

The design of our pilgrimage intentionally used the landscape and legends of Glastonbury as a scaffolding, but it also integrated practices from other traditions and New Age beliefs. Thus, it was designed to appeal to the do-it-yourself spirituality of a contemporary seeker and reflected the pluralistic ethos that now characterizes Glastonbury. This eclecticism was sometimes suspect, as with the chakra sounds, but was generally conducive to creating a collective sense of spirituality among a group of people who might arrive from various faith backgrounds and were unlikely, any of them, to be particularly dogmatic about purity of practice.

Reflecting on the negative aspects of the experience actually led to some particular insights about the nature of pilgrimage. The journey itself, with the treacherous snow-covered roads, did provide a kind of imaginary portal through which, once passed, we travellers felt a certain isolation from everyday life, a common aspect of pilgrimage. The relative discomfort did produce a modicum of suffering for spirituality, also typical of pilgrimage rites. Even the climb up the Tor had potential to bind the group together and to lend a narrative edge for story-telling later that the trip would otherwise not have had. We were reminded that part of the power of Glastonbury is its dark side, the last abbot's death being the primary (but not the only) example, and that locals often talk of the place as a spiritual challenge, rather than an easy escape.

And we admit that the moment at the top of the Chalice Well Gardens, as well as, to a lesser extent, the candlelit chant in the darkness of the White Spring, did have the uplifting quality of spiritual experience. Finally, the tension caused by Freda's rigid insistence on staying with the prescribed order for the weekend, regardless of snow or mud, was probably also typical of pilgrimage experience, as the proscriptions of guides apparently often clashes with the individualistic nature of the desire behind pilgrimage.

What was jarring and ultimately defeating was the overt commercial intent behind every move made by the organizer and her assistant.

CONCLUSION

Remember, however, that pilgrimage has been the backbone of the Glastonbury economy for a very long time, and that, worldwide, tourism and pilgrimage are closely identified. We suspect that the dissonant tone of commerce infects many pilgrimage experiences—and that this fact is no modern anomaly but has been true since at least the times of Chaucer. When traveling, it is easy to see that the cathedrals of Europe are crawling with guides for hire and their plazas cluttered with souvenir stalls. In Asia, we have seen that sacred sites are often overtly commercialized by myriad "spiritual entrepreneurs." Therefore, while we would tend to agree with others that there is a distinction to be made between pilgrimage and tourism generally, we suspect that the widespread expectation that tourism is commercial in nature while pilgrimage is not reflects only nostalgia.

REFERENCES

Ashe, Geoffrey. 2002. *The Traveller's Guide to Arthurian Britain*. 3rd edition. Glastonbury, UK: Gothic Image.

Bowman, Marion. 2006 "The Holy Thorn Ceremony: Revival, Rivalry and Civil Religion in Glastonbury." *Folklore* 117: 123–140.

Coleman, Simon, and John Eade. 2004. *Reframing Pilgrimage: Cultures in Motion*. London: Routledge.

Coleman, Simon, and John Elsner. 1995. *Pilgrimage Past and Present: Sacred Travel and Sacred Space in the World Religions*. London: British Museum Press.

Croft, Robin, Trevor Hartland, and Heather Skinner. 2008. "And *Did* Those Feet in Ancient Times: Getting Medieval Glastonbury on Message." *Journal of Communication Management* 12 (4): 294–304.

Howard-Gordon, Frances. 2010. *Glastonbury Maker of Myths*. Glastonbury, Somerset: Gothic Image Publications.

Kotler, Phil, Donald Hinder, and Irving Rein. 2002. *Marketing Places*. New York: Free Press.

Kozinets, Robert V. 2002. "Can Consumers Escape the Market?: Emancipatory Illuminations from Burning Man." *Journal of Consumer Research* 29 (1): 20–38.

Kozinets, Robert V., John F. Sherry, Jr., Diana Storm, Adam Duhacheck, Krittinee Nuttavuthisit, and Benet DeBerry-Spence. 2004. "Ludic Agency and Retail Spectacle." *Journal of Consumer Research* 31 (3): 658–672.

Maclaran, Pauline, and Stephen Brown. 2005. "The Center Cannot Hold: Consuming the Utopian Marketplace." *Journal of Consumer Research* 32 (2): 311–323.

Mann, Nicholas R. 2004. *Energy Secrets of Glastonbury Tor*. Sutton Mallet, Somerset: Green Magic.

Mitchell, John. 1997. *New Light on the Ancient Mystery of Glastonbury*. Glastonbury, Somerset: Gothic Image Publications.

Morinis, Alan, ed. 1992. *Sacred Journeys: The Anthropology of Pilgrimage*. London: Greenwood Press.

O'Guinn, Thomas C., and Russell W. Belk. 1989. "Heaven on Earth: Consumption at Heritage Village." *Journal of Consumer Research* 16 (2): 227–238.

Peñaloza, Lisa. 1999. "Just Doing It." *Consumption, Markets and Culture* 2 (4): 337–400.

Sherry, John F., Jr. 1998. *Servicescapes: The Concept of Place in Contemporary Markets*. Chicago, IL: NTC Business Books.

Turner, Victor, and Edith Turner. 1978. *Image and Pilgrimage in Christian Culture: Anthropological Perspectives*. Oxford: Blackwell.

Part V

Issues of Method and Representation

15 Reflections of a Scape Artist
Discerning Scapus in Contemporary Worlds

John F. Sherry, Jr.

[T]he universe is a communion of subjects, not a collection of objects.
—Thomas Berry

After scrapping several false starts on this chapter, I've decided to craft it as a personal essay, rather than as a social scientific inquiry or a managerial treatise. While I hope to engage both social scientists and marketing managers in the process, I've adopted a more humanistic approach in conveying the way in which I attempt to apprehend—that is, both understand and represent in reciprocal fashion—a sense of place.

I've spent three decades trying to make some scholarly sense of this phenomenon and twice as long unpacking it as a stranger in strange lands. I usually describe the enterprise in terms of resonance, and I use the metaphors of tuning fork and dowsing stick (or maybe, better suited to the volume's theme, divining rod) to make my point with friends, family, colleagues, and students. As an ethnographer and part-time poet, I believe the researcher *is* the instrument, just as dancer and dance are one. Unlike some fellow travelers, I believe that I study contexts, not merely study *in* contexts. As I roam the earth in more and less circumscribed orbits, I expect to vibrate, as space and place attempt to seize my attention and make themselves known to me.

It might happen on a mist-shrouded wilderness lake, the teeming midway of a periodic market, on a dusty artery clogged with pilgrims and art cars in Black Rock City, in the collision of vernacular genres on an upper story of a flagship brand store, or at home in my man cave or office eyrie. It has happened as I've peered up at the oculus of the Pantheon or down into a deep cenote. It happens routinely here on my own university campus (which has been described just half-jokingly as "Catholic Disneyland"), whose precincts are dotted with shrines both formal and informal, invested with the aura of sacred and profane (the two occasionally fused), as in the multistory mural on the library that sports fans have christened "Touchdown Jesus," which I can contemplate from my hallway window. It has happened at Zen Central in Bangkok and at my local grocery store. Ball parks often seem to do the trick. Whether the place has been predictably spectacular or profoundly ordinary, its capacity to induce resonance in me has been a perpetual source of wonder.

A confluence of life experiences has likely heightened my sensitivity to place. Being born in Chicago and raised there and in its nearest suburbs, as the conurbation converted cornfields into housing tracts, strip malls, and industrial parks while sparing vast expanses of riverine forest, afforded me the opportunity to shuttle between worlds, as did proximity to bucolic Wisconsin and pure Michigan. Being reared in an Irish-Catholic cultural tradition attuned to the numinous in everyday life, being immersed in classical and comparative mythology and folklore as a result of a liberal arts education, and being trained as an anthropologist with a peripatetic disposition and plenty of opportunity to wander the globe all provoked in me a receptivity to the vitality of space and place. As a consumer researcher, I've gravitated to marketplaces not merely because they comprise a convenient locus of stakeholder subjects, but also because markets thrum with a vibe that shapes thought, emotion, and behavior. I've written across genres in celebration of this elusive thrum, trying to capture it and its reverberations in me.

In those attempts, I have sought to describe the commingling of the material and the mystical that presents itself to me as the spirit of the place. In this chapter, my goal is to review some of the intellectual traditions that have helped calibrate my awareness of the *genius loci* and to sketch some of the ways I go about apprehending spirit. The fields of marketing and consumer research are just being touched by the "spatial turn" that has ramified throughout the social sciences in recent years (Soja, 2010). Like the interpretive turn before it, the spatial turn promises to reshape our discipline profoundly. Consumers' lived experiences of place frequently lend themselves to the kind of geomantic exploration I have in mind.

THE ARGUMENT

I take "How is this place happening?" to be the central question animating my chapter. Drawing on the social scientific and humanistic intuitions of such traditions as indigeneity, actor network theory, and phenomenological ecology, I outline an approach to the field study of the spirit of place that shapes and reflects consumption. I am especially interested in exploring the role of non-human agents and non-human personhood as elements of *genius loci.* I use just a handful of references in this chapter to situate my premise, and I rely extensively on just one—May (1993)—to motivate interested readers to summon emplaced spirits. For purposes of brevity, I've bracketed the experimental literature on servicescapes (Kearney, Kennedy, and Coughlan 2007) and stayed within the CCT fold, but I acknowledge the promise of the work of our positivist brethren for informing the study of genius loci.

I also give the enterprise of spatial spiritual sounding a name (or brand, as it were) to stake it out as an ongoing project in marketing and consumer research. In this chapter, I am concerned with the *scapus* and with states and conditions *scapular.* I recall the former term from its virtual retirement and redeploy it to capture the quintessential, singular aura of a place. I refurbish the latter term by yoking it to the spatial turn and invoking the ethereal qualities it suggests.

Scapus conjures shaft or stem, staff or scepter, and connotes a foundational, majestic, local axis mundi that ensouls a place. Scapular evokes a literal and figurative cloaking proclaiming membership and is redolent of the totem and fetish. Scapular connotes a shouldering in service to load bearing and to divination that connects to the geomantic. The scapular envelopes and contains a place, imparting sensuous boundaries and rendering it distinctly recognizable to its apprehenders.

I introduce these terms to relieve the servicescape construct of a burden it can no longer bear, as our inquiries into place push persistently past the realm of the merely commercial. I also intend to exploit the synergies of the terms with those of poet Gerard Manley Hopkins—inscape and instress— that I have explored elsewhere (Sherry, 2008, p. 87):

> Inscape is the essence of an entity sensually apprehended and rendered in description (Everett n.d.); it is the unique, differentiated quality of that entity. Instress is the ineffable experience of the beholder occasioned by the inscape that flouts description (Peters 1948); it is the resonance we feel in contemplation of inscape.

Scapus I take to be a specific instantiation of these terms. The ethnographic enterprise seeks to apprehend inscape as meticulously as possible and to represent instress as genuinely as our genres permit.

SPIRITUAL RESOURCE MANAGEMENT

I offer an unconscionably brief and temporally disjointed variation of salvage archaeology in the following paragraphs. The thesis is uncomplicated. Other eras and peoples have been more attuned to genius loci than are postmodern marketers and consumers. As we have inexorably erased nature and embraced the built environment, and as commerce and the state have relentlessly appropriated the cultural commons, there are ever fewer active wild sources of inspiration and imagination available to guide our premodern sensibilities with respect to the emplaced numinous (Latour, 1993; Sherry, 2005). This apperceptual occlusion produces insensitivity in our ability to design for and appreciate the spirit of place, and it induces a hunger for sense of place that feels abidingly right. We crave environments that are edifying and nurturing, no matter their secular cast.

For most of us, the default destination for discussions of spirit of place is likely the classic era of great world civilizations. In the Greco-Roman world, every locality embodied a genius that articulated the gestalt of the site, rendering the foundational character of the locality recoverable by humans. Over time, this genius evolved from an incomprehensible daimon through a guardian or protector of environs to a prosecutor or an advocate of place, and from thence to an internal transcendental human condition, until it was eventually regarded as a creature intermediate between gods and humans (Hamilton, 1969; Murray, 2010; Onions, 1966). As the governing spirit of a place, the genius represented the entire store of meaning (denotative and connotative) animating the site. The tutelary function of the genius ensured the site's integrity. Meanwhile, in the Chinese world, the philosophy of feng shui arose to account for and manipulate the systemic spiritual forces that resided in the landscape and affected bodies and built environments of all kinds. This geomantic orientation—divination via meanings recovered from the locality—is common across cultures and time.

I've long lobbied for a millenarian marketing focused on sustainable consumption rooted, inevitably, in place, which would encourage a mythopoeic stance in our comprehension and behavior, and acknowledge ecopoetics as the necessary driver of ecopragmatics. A properly turned mythology, and its enactment in ritual, will compel sustainability just as assuredly as it has heretofore impeded it. I've even maundered a heretical call for a non-teleological ecotheism that would champion a hylozoic form of animism capable of re-emplacing our mystical relationship with goods back into nature, from whence it originally arose (Sherry, 2000a, 2001). That is, we would redirect our premodern animistic impulses, which modernism has deflected from the natural world and into the world of goods, back toward the natural world, broadly construed, and inexorably to place. My chiliastic consumerism was grounded in an encounter with deep ecologists and radical economists, and lodged in a tradition of anthropological advocacy. A decade of subsequent reading has helped refine my musing, and three sources in particular bear on the present attempt to comprehend the spirit of place: TEK, ANT, and PE/EP.

Traditional Ecological Knowledge (TEK). In evolutionary perspective, the most successful and enduring resource management practices have involved religious and ritual representation. (Hence, my belief in mythopoeic motivation.) Our aboriginal ancestors and indigenous hunter gatherers of ethnographic record inhabited a broad ethical context that did not separate culture from nature (Berkes, 2008). Theirs was a "sentient ecology" whose entire world was "saturated with powers of agency and intentionality" (Ingold, 2000, pp. 25). All things were ensouled (Abrams, 2010; Harvey, 2006). Indigenous groups embraced a humans-in-nature rather than a dominion-over-nature worldview, and they experienced a synaesthetic engagement with the land that can be characterized as "interagentivity" (Abrams, 1996; Berkes, 2008; Ingold, 2000).

These hunter gatherers recognized a wide range of nonhuman personhood and attributed life and spirit to everything in the environment ((Berkes, 2008). Or, rather, in their "animic ontology," life was a "generation of being in an incipient world" (Ingold, 2000, p. 113), immanent in the relations between the world's constituents (Abrams, 2010). Spirit of place was an "expressive presence," and landscape was an "active participant" in human life (Abrams, 1996, 2010).

Indigenous ecology is a challenge to our positivist, materialist cosmology (Skowlimowski, 1981) and a source of corrective insight in our quest for sustainable consumption, whether we embrace either the Gaia (Lovelock, 1995) or the Medea (Ward, 2009) hypothesis. The TEK worldview resonates with the themes of stakeholder orientation and co-creation afoot in our disciplines. Ingold describes TEK as a "poetics of dwelling," and this posture has much to contribute to the recovery, discovery, and creation of spirit of place.

Actor-Network Theory (ANT). A revised ontology for sociological analysis has gradually diffused from Science, Technology, and Society studies into consumer research and marketing over the past decade, as we have struggled to unpack such key constructs as materiality and the extended self (Latour, 1986; Prior, 2008; Schau et al., 2009; Shove and Pantzar, 2005; Swidler, 2001; Warde, 2005). I draw my understanding of this revision from Bruno Latour (2005, pp. 54–55), who has described ANT as being "half Garfinkel and half Greimas," a hybrid of ethnomethodology and semiotics that taps the "inner reflexivity" of actors and texts. ANT attempts a thorough exploration of "who and what participates in the action," on the way to creating a "science of the social" (Latour, 2005, p. 72). Latour (2005, p. 116) asserts that there are "simply more agencies in the *pluriverse*, to use William James' expression, than philosophers and scientists thought possible." A good ANT account is one that traces a "string of actions where each participant is treated as a full-blown mediator" (Latour, 2005, p. 128). This involves recognizing the agency of nonhuman actors in the world-making activities of our informants and not exalting the human over the nonhuman as a unit of analysis. Latour's (2004, p. 74) premodern project is to "get rid of the tiresome polemics of objects and subjects." Entities are cybernetic assemblages of human and nonhuman components, and artifactuality embodies animation. These assemblages exist in a dynamic of relational materiality, are performed into being, and are sustained in a variety of practices (Law, 1999).

ANT properties and propensities are inherent in many of my own accounts of servicescapes, and in current work I am striving for precise articulation. Alone (Sherry, 1998) and with colleagues (e.g., Sherry and Kozinets, 2007; Borghini et al., 2010), I have explored the ways in which consumers, products, architectural affordances, advertising and merchandising strategies, channels of embodied engagement, and cultural categories have conspired to produce retail theatre and therapy, festal community and chorography, and ritual giving and getting. I've plumbed brand for essence, from construction to deconstruction and back again. Place has been central to these undertakings. Scapus emerges as it is enacted by stakeholders manipulating mutually influential, interagentic properties and ideologies on the site, and it can be conjured with any aspect of the ecosystem by contemplation of any aspect of the network.

Phenomenological Ecology & Environmental phenomenology (PE/EP). A confluence of disciplines in the social sciences and humanities is giving rise to a field that has been described variously as phenomenological ecology and environmental phenomenology. This emergence has been fueled by the "spatial turn" sweeping across domains of inquiry, which has most recently touched our fields of marketing and consumer research. This emerging field—which I will (by collapsing terms) call ecophenomenology—is focused on the practice of "dwelling," broadly construed. Ecophenomenology attempts to provide an account of the lived experience of dwelling. In this account, concern for the spirit of place usually arises at the intersection of the poetics and ethics of dwelling.

Rather than revisit positions I have reviewed elsewhere (Sherry, 1998, 2000b), I recognize just a few of the fundamental pillars of ecophenomenology. The principal preoccupation of this field is "immersion-in-the-world," and this "in-worldness" contrasts with the dualisms inherent in positivist projects (Hay, 2002, p. 145). Goethean science (Seamon and Zajonc, 1998) tries to reconcile these positions. Focus on the visceral experience of being-in-place characterizes the work of ecophenomenologists; "seeing" places from the "inside out" is the goal of inquiry (Hay, 2002, p. 156). A Heideggerian emphasis on authentic being and authentic dwelling is elevated above a functional and utilitarian view of place as mere real estate. To dwell authentically would entail recognition and cultivation of the being that place authentically is: the scapus.

In the social sciences, cultural geographers (Harding, 2006; Tuan, 1977), sociologists (Gibson, 2009; Lefebvre, 2008a, 2008b, 2008c), and anthropologists (Messer and Lambek, 2001) have been in the vanguard of ecophenomenological research. In the humanities, philosophers (Bachelard, 1994/1958; Deleuze and Guattari, 1987), theologians (Berry, 2006; Fox, 1988; Kearns and Keller, 2007), historians (Berman, 2000; Roszak et al., 1995), architectural scholars (Seamon, 1993), and poets (Snyder, 1995) have led the charge.

Consumer research has been receptive to this tradition. Inquiry into retroscapes (Brown and Sherry, 2003) has built on this perspective. Much of my own current work on place, undertaken with a host of colleagues (Anderson, Borghini, Bradford, Diamond, Joy, McGrath, Visconti), in venues stretching from the mundane to the extraordinary, assumes an ecophenomenological shape. Perhaps our account of street art (Visconti et al., 2010) is the most succinct illustration of a jointly negotiated narrative of place, where urban residents conspire to reclaim and recreate a commons capable of sustaining authentic dwelling. Recent intriguing work by Linnet (2009) on the homologies of place extends this tradition into productive new arenas.

A VIEW FROM ARCHITECTURE

For almost two decades, I have used an elemental template developed by May (1993) as an improvisational platform for sounding the scapus. I discovered the template in the pages of *Environmental and Architectural Phenomenology*, a newsletter of original and reprinted contributions edited by David Seamon out of Kansas State University, which celebrates qualitative inquiry into the lived experience of dwelling. May (1993) reports the details of a workshop he conducted, mostly with other architects, designed to promote a Goethean (Seamon and Zajonc, 1998) approach to observation of the built environment and to enhance "conscious awareness" of participants' "responses and feeling" to their "physical surroundings."

The exercise began with a meticulous examination of the material environment, continued with a consideration of sensuous changes experienced as participants moved across a course ranging from natural to built environments, culminated with an examination of participants' personal responses to the environments, and concluded with a bracketing of that experience in an attempt to determine what might "speak through" to reveal "a particular wholeness and sense of place" (May, 1993, p. 3). The unpacking in discussion of their sensual immersion allowed participants to gauge the degree to which their reliance on their predominant sensory modality impoverished perception and diminished capacity for enriched dwelling (and, by extension, designing). Discussion also facilitated the translation of sensory experience to meaning, helping each participant become a "self-conscious and integral part of a more fully understood environment" (May, 1993, p. 3).

May (1993, p. 2) has developed a set of "observational themes" that can guide inquiry into the scapus. He uses a quasi-geomantic classificatory system based on the four essential elements—earth/physical, water/etheric, air/astral, and fire/ego—to characterize these themes. The earth theme seeks an answer to the question "What is here?" and elicits formal, material, sensual, and geographic inputs. It results in a physical description of a bounded area. The water theme seeks an answer to the question "What is happening here?" and elicits inputs on facilitators and inhibitors of movement (into, out of, and within an area), atmosphere (sound, light quality), sheltering and exposure, social usage and rhythms. It results in a description of incentives and impediments to wayfaring and wayfinding. The air theme seeks an answer to the question "What do I feel here?" and elicits introspective inputs on emotion, sensation, motivation, compatibility, archetypicality, evocation, and resonance. It results in a comprehensive visceral description of being-in-the-place. The fire theme seeks an answer to the question "What is the personality of this place?" and elicits imagistic inputs such as character, strength, complexity, function, and honesty. It is intended to result in a holistic description of the essence of the place.

Despite the obvious utility of May's battery of probes and their ability to illuminate stability and fluidity, inspiration and authenticity, I have long felt that the fire theme and its focus on personality fell short of capturing the genius loci. It seems to me that a fifth essence is required to fix the quintessential experience of the scapus and would pose the question "How is this place happening?" Or, if not an essence (and because May has co-opted other usual suspects), something more like a chakra, and in particular the crown chakra, *sahasrara*, might do. This would encompass the synthesis of the dialectic of immanence and transcendence that results in our transfiguration as inscape and instress are reconciled. I imagine an integrative, epiphanic energy reflecting the connection and identity of beings and reminiscent of Bateson's (1972) ecology of mind.

May's framework helps me discern scapus in several ways. First, the elemental themes establish minimal parameters for discovery, and the scope of each theme is broad enough to permit me to both generate many micro inventories of dimensions and customize inventories to suit the site. Second, the themes can be plumbed as a developmental sequence, allowing me to move systematically and organically from the material to the numinous (or, retrospectively, from resonance to sources). Third, the themes can be pursued in a less linear fashion by readjusting my focus from transitions to

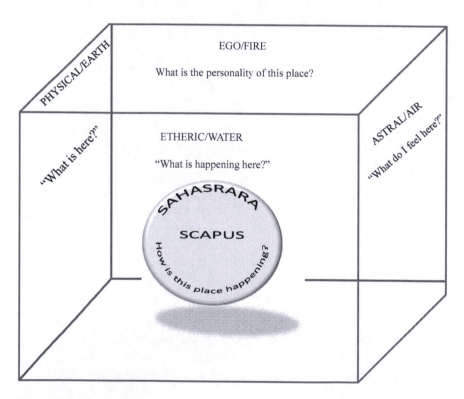

Figure 15.1 Scapus.

overlaps and shifting my conception of progression from scalar or vector to mobius strip. Fourth, I've played with graphical representations of the themes, and the configuration I find to be the greatest impetus to insight is the open-ended cube of Figure 15.1. I imagine the quintessence, the scapus, to manifest in the interior, as I move, metaphorically, through the cube as a participant observer, in various degrees of merger.

DIVINING SPIRIT OF PLACE: A BRIEF EXCURSUS

Whether it manifests in places public or private, hermetic or hestial, or profane or sacred, the scapus will inevitably be revealed as a creature of both the singular and the commercial. The Mad River canoe that conveys me to the glorious floating carpet of pitcher plants, the Rockport shoes that hasten my ascent of the five hundred stairs to the top of St. Peter's basilica, and the Dell computer that delivers the first digital image of my newborn granddaughter in her birthing room each demonstrates the interpenetration of the technological and the experiential, the natural and the cultural, the material and the spiritual. The scapus may be sought outdoors or indoors, in geography or architecture. In a simple illustration, I situate my own practice in the built environment.

What follows is a brief exploration of my ground floor Department Chair's office (my "official" office, as opposed to my regular faculty office on the third floor) at the University of Notre Dame. This exercise—a lineal relative of Russ Belk's "Unpacking My Library" (2002) and a collateral relative of his "A Cultural Biography of My Groucho Glasses" (2000) and Dennis Rook's "I Was Observed (*In Absentia*) and Autodriven by the Consumer Behavior Odyssey" (1991)—serves as a quick-and-dirty autoethnographic approximation of my approach to divining spirit of place. I have chosen it simply to facilitate readers' introspection (as most will have offices) and acknowledge the limitations my familiarity imposes on my acuity. The account is neither exhaustive nor extensively corroborated, but simply illustrative. As with Freud and his clutch of fetishes, my room is a projective echo chamber. Because I am a co-creator of and dweller in the place, my experience reflects both managerial and consumer perspectives.

THROUGHWAYS

Outside Looking in. My office is in the corner of an interior suite, whose outer precinct is an expansive, brightly lit open bullpen occupied by departmental assistants and student workers, a bustling venue full of movement, voices, ringing phones, and humming office equipment. Immediately outside my door is an alcove that houses a water cooler, a coffee machine, and a microwave oven, ensuring that snatches of conversation and aromatic clouds of caffeine and cuisine waft into my office when my door is open, which invariably it is. My nameplate is posted on the wall beside the door-frame, along with a photocopied logo of the Burning Nerds. Just below, there may be Post-It noted instructions for current students and frequently an empty Amazon box awaiting recycling. On the other side of the door-frame, a table and chairs are arranged for visitors

Inside Looking out. Inside my office, on the wall opposite the door, is a large ground floor window, which, because of its western placement, allows little natural light into the room until the end of the day. It does afford a clear view of a large evergreen tree directly outside my office, the squirrels, rabbits, ducks, and occasional dog attracted to the tree and its companion bench, and glimpses of activity on the neighboring quad. I am able to open the window to allow fresh air, whether warm, cold, or damp, to circulate through the room, carrying seasonal sounds and odors along with it. I always know summer is over when I look out the window and see battalions of young girls twirling their batons on the quad, their training camp about to end.

Lines of Sight, Sound, and Smell. Spatially, then, the interior space of my office is bracketed by an expansive, kinetic clerical antechamber and a serene, bucolic landscape, the contrast apparent to anyone poised on the threshold or seated within the room. Visitors always perch about midway between these worlds and are aware of their own suspension, especially given the contrast with the room itself. Entrance and exit are one.

WALL SPACE

Interior-Exterior Boundaries. The wall facing the bullpen is seen last by visitors, who typically face away from it until departure. A rack on the door holds an assortment of sport coats to be deployed in unforeseen emergencies (to mask when needed my habitual campus casual style) and regalia worn for commencement ceremonies. A credenza stands against the wall and holds an overflowing inbox, stacks of file folders and documents casually sorted by project, and a table lamp. Above the credenza, two wall hangings are mounted, one a reproduction of a page from the book of Kells and the other a photograph of Stonehenge. Their frames are usually askew, thanks to vibrations and wind current generated by the swinging door. The thermostat is set into this wall. I keep a set of Allen wrenches in my desk to defeat the governor and to try to keep the temperature of the room in the high sixties (Fahrenheit), as my metabolism runs high and a warmer setting makes me sluggish. The light switch panel is located here as well and goes untouched by me. I use table lamps with incandescent bulbs to light the room, which produces gentler, more intimate, and less penetrative illumination than the harsh fluorescent tubes overhead.

The wall facing the outdoors is seen first (or a close second) by visitors and is dominated by the window, the Levolor blinds adjusted as required by natural light. On one side of the window, monastic busts of two of the seven deadlies—greed and envy—are mounted near the ceiling. Just below, the nameplate from my deceased mentor's office door is hung, intentionally askew to mimic its original haphazard placement. If not precisely a meditation corner, these objects of contemplation remind me of the personal and professional challenges inherent in my chosen career. On the other side of the window, the wall holds a cluster of plaques awarded by various scholarly organizations, commemorating career achievements. I regard this corner as the requisite "brag wall" of administrative authority, a reassurance to my visitors that I probably know what I'm doing and a chastisement (and perhaps comfort) to myself to acknowledge the toll that administrivia exacts on scholarship.

Adjacent-Lateral Boundaries. The two long walls that separate my office from the rooms of neighboring administrators are the artifactually busiest dimensions of the built environment. The south wall faces my desk. Mounted close to the ceiling are a series of five wall hangings: a photo of Ken Kesey riding his bus "Further," a Gary Larson cartoon depicting natives hiding technology from anthropologists, a large reproduction of the bow of the Queen Mary II, a reprint of Durer's "Knight, Devil, and Death," and a Richard Shorty print of "Raven Stealing Sun." Each of these wall hangings has a deep, evocative connection with my life as a scholar.

Figure 15.2 Office south wall.

Just beneath them, a set of five mahogany book cases runs the length of the wall. Their shelves house three sorts of artifacts. First, the shelves are crammed with books and journals, standing upright and wedged in sideways on top of other books and stacked in piles on top of some of the cases. Second, the shelves contain stacks of photocopied articles, file folders full of research materials, and piles of trade press clippings destined for lecture notes. Third, the shelves are studded with a wide range of photographs, memorabilia, tchotchkes, product samples, gifts, and the bric a brac of a research life focused on experiential consumption. This stuff is not curated in any conscious sense so much as distributed across the shelves. Because this assemblage has proven endlessly fascinating to visitors, and because it is the occasion of an endless number of my own mental mini-vacations from tasks at hand, I spend a long paragraph cataloging some of its contents. Figure 15.2 captures a section of this area.

The top shelf holds such gifts from friends as a Chinese doll dress wine bottle cover, a Burmese prayer fan, an 18-inch Santa effigy in the guise of Jerry Garcia, a red brick from the demolished Belfast home of Seamus Heaney, and a St. Paddy's day pimp hat. Chocablock with these gifts are such products as Italian baby food containing prosciutto, design-centric orange juice packages embodying the genius and hubris of Peter Arnell, a jar of Notre Dame salsa, and an eco-aesthetic vodka bottle. Interspersed are photographs of such subjects as Ali taunting Liston, the Jordan statue at the United Center decked out in Blackhawks regalia, street art from around the world, Northwest coast aboriginal art, and Celtic manuscript illustrations. Baseball caps, a takraw ball, a pith helmet an electric fan, our MBA Code of Ethics, and a stack of books also rest on the top of the cases. The first row of shelves is bestrewn with personal photographs (family members, friends, classroom moments), gadgets (puzzles, gimmick mugs), and a host of miniature objects (a globe in a shopping cart, a tiki idol, a Oaxaca pot, a boxing glove, a runic amulet). The second row of shelves contains more photos (including one of Kurt Vonnegut), product samples (such as an aluminum Coke bottle and a Heinz ketchup bottle), various Adbusters post cards, bibelot exotica (jawbone of an ass, glass pumpkin), gifts (an anthropomorphic Alessi wine opener, from which I have suspended a sign that reads "When the student is ready, the master appears"), a moai tissue dispenser, a statue of St. Clare (patron saint of television), mini Azteca fantasy figures, a number of image-shifting holographic placards, a reproduction of a Palaeolithic cave painting, a shadowy (how Jungian) figurine of a pondering Freud seated in an armchair, and a personal shrine (containing Burning Man sacra, a figurine of a polar bear, a wire sculpture of a leafless tree, and a resin cast of the skull of Peking Man). More objects (magic 8-ball, fabric softener ball, AMA paperweights), personal photographs, signs, and dangling doodads (the sole of a running shoe, a mini canoe paddle) grace the third row of shelves. And, as Clifford Geertz might quip (and as Figure 15.3 suggests), there are similar knickknacks all the way down.

The north wall, behind my desk, is much less crowded. Hung on the wall are stark images of the Irish countryside, a pencil drawing of a curving Belgian streetscape, an etching of a riverine forest, an Adbusters image of Santa sitting zazen, and a reproduction of Rembrandt's painting "Philosopher in His Study." Like their counterparts across the room, these pictures embody aspects of my professional identity. In the center of these images, I have framed the championship boxing glove trophy patch won in my wayward youth, as a student at the very institution that now employs me as a professor. Part *memento mori*, part *memento vivivere*, it helps account for my lecture style and acts as leverage in negotiations with students and colleagues. At the far end of the wall, above the wardrobe, I have hung an old Coca Cola advertisement that has a certain retro appeal. The wardrobe itself is pasted over with Post-It notes, calendars, photo rosters, poems about consumer behavior and winter, and a number of memorable fortunes from Chinese cookies. Atop the wardrobe is a shrine comprising many family photographs (and a few of revered colleagues), gifts (a remnant of a shattered statue of the Virgen de Guadeloupe, mugs), bibelots (a statue of a Mexican monk, a fragment of the Berlin Wall), and several boxes of hard-to-part-with floppy disks. Waste baskets stand on the floor beside the wardrobe, along with some old presentation posters from a long ago class.

Grounding Boundaries. My floor is covered with a dark grey short-napped industrial carpet, which seems to be effective in muffling sound and masking stains. The suspension ceiling is covered in white sound-absorbent tiles, and embedded in it are a bank of lights, a heating and cooling duct, and a return vent. The colors of each of these surfaces complement the institutional off-white color of the walls.

FURNITURE

Two principal fixtures remain to be described. The first is a simple round table, accompanied by two chairs and a floor lamp, which sits just about in the center of the room. This is the principal site of my visits with the outside world, where others come to consult, confer, and converse. It also sometimes doubles as a lunch table and repository for the overflow of stacks and piles. Books not yet read often accumulate on the floor between this table and the shelves. The surface of the table hosts two mugs full of pens and pencils, a paperclip holder, a few stacks of Post-It notes, and a tape dispenser.

The second fixture is my work surround, comprising a desk, wrap around computer table, and file cabinets, all of dark mahogany, arranged into an open U configuration, allowing me to swivel my Aeron chair 360 degrees to accommodate personal paperwork and facework with visitors. The desk fronts the bookcase, the computer fronts the window, and the file cabinets lie along the north wall. There is no barrier between me and visitors to the office. Access is unimpeded.

Figure 15.3 South wall close up.

My desk is lined along its perimeter with books, active files, current administrative paperwork and research manuscripts, photographs of family and colleagues, business cards, the now familiar assemblage of knick-knacks (gifts, gags, puzzles, statuary, memorabilia), mugs and holders full of pens, pencils, paperclips and Exacto blades, drinking bottles, thumb drives, a calculator, and an assortment of to-do lists. It holds a table lamp (itself supporting a calendar), behind which sits an altar populated with artifacts created by my youngest son when he was a child. At the far end, closest to the window, I have arranged two realistic artificial plants, a concession to the poor sunlight that has prevented me from sustaining green life. Near the plants I have propped several inspirational note cards. The very circumscribed center of the desk's surface is where I do all my writing. Beneath the desk, I've stuffed old file boxes, numerous video cameras, and several pairs of shoes deployed on wintry days when I've worn snow boots to work.

My computer table affords space for a telephone, a monitor, a photo reader, and a cantilevered keyboard; the tower and subwoofer are stored beneath the table. Photographs of field sites and canoe trips, an artificial rose, some snippets of poetry, a Chinese yo-yo, and a mug full of pens and pencils grace the table top. Residing there as well is a heavy lithic tool I use to hold open my Day Timer. I park a shillelagh between my keyboard and the table; I swing the club absentmindedly while thinking, speaking on the phone or working the typing kinks out of my neck. My printer sits on the far corner of the table top and also houses photos and posted notes.

The top of my file cabinets holds a flatbed scanner, a small stereo (from which issues only classical music or songs in a language I can't speak, so as not to interfere with work, as well as the occasional NPR broadcast), stacks of working files, a large collection of CDs, DVDs, and videos, family photographs, a Zen admonition to "Don't Just Do Something, Sit There," a box of business cards, stacks of yet-to-be laterally cycled Altoids tins, several retro-style post cards, and a table lamp. I also use this surface as a place to park drinks, snacks, and other food items that I don't want messing my desk.

INTERPRETIVE SUMMARY

Having suffered through this self-indulgent itinerary (with so many curios thankfully still unpacked), the reader has earned a divination of scapus that might then be compared with his or her own. This public space has been reworked into a personalized place where the affairs of administration—from clinical spreadsheet (mis)calculation to intimate, sometimes loud or tearful interpersonal interaction—can be conducted in comfortable seclusion. Simply described, the room is dimly lit and relatively cool; it smells occasionally of brewing coffee, cooked food, and fresh air; it contains an abundance of books on many topics and a Victorian profusion of artifacts; and it is encircled by photographs and piles of documents. Once seated within, a visitor is viscerally poised between a garish bureaucratic servic-escape and a manicured Midwestern landscape, embraced by an enclosure that is not quite cave, not quite grotto, but sanctuary nonetheless. The scapus is the academic equivalent of McCracken's (1989) "homeyness." I have sought to temper the hermetic with the hestial.

As I sit by myself in the office, I am embraced by family, friends, colleagues, and academic ancestors. I am encircled by gifts, reminding me of my enmeshment in an intimate and intricate circuit of relationships. I am embedded in the trappings of knowledge, established and emergent; I'm wrapped (and rapt) in reminders of my vocation. The tonal prompts from Outlook Calendar, the endless processing of actual and virtual paperwork that sets strategy in motion (or derails it), the anticipation of the next visitor, and the sanctuary-seeking after offsite meetings shield my administrative perspective from distraction. My office is a sanctum, its scapus, as I intuit it, one of generativity, creativity, and centeredness.

The place is intended to be inviting and challenging, comfortable and diverting. Its aura is intended to be collegial, conversational, and predominantly informal, seeded with reassuring clues to the proprietor's persona so that a visitor might feel less like an intruder and more like a guest. The artifacts and their arrangement evoke curiosity (visual, tactile, aural, and olfactory) and often elicit a call for narrative. Stuff is assumed to be storied, and visitors often share spontaneously what they find evocative as a spring-board for inquiry into an object's cultural biography, and hence to a discussion of our mutual interests. The artifacts are alive, animated by dialectics of meaning emplacement and displacement, investment and recovery, and projection and introjection.

Visitors have described my office as "comfortable," "homey," and "cool." It is a "cozy" place into which some feel able to "nestle." Sometimes I hear, "It's just what I imagined a scholar's office might be." I get variations of "It's like a house, or a home" or "It's normal" (as contrasted with the artificial sterility of cubicle land). I've been told it's "a place you'd like to be on a cold rainy day." The room has been described as an "armchair journey around the world." Some have found it a "smorgasbord for the imagination," which "arouses curiosity." Others have called it "nostalgic." Most are too kind to criticize it as the museum of precipitous piles and mismatched mementos it must appear to the organized mind. Part port in a storm, part tempest in a teapot, the scapus reveals itself to visitors pretty much as it does to me, with both lesser and greater nuance.

CONCLUSION

If indigineity—the sustainable tie between an aboriginal people and its agentic, sentient landscape (Johnson, 2010)—were a hallmark of our pre-modern forebears, then *indigenteity* might be said to characterize our post-modern condition. *Indigenteity* would be the unsustainable disconnection felt by an increasingly mobile, transient, urbanized people from its com-modified (even if branded) landscape. Under indigeneity, place making is an everyday practice, wayfinding is an act of storytelling, story is emplaced on a landscape, and place is a mnemonic for narrative recall: places represent the "embodiment of cultural process realized through travel and storytell-ing" (Johnson, 2010, p. 14). Under *indigenteity*, we delegate much of our public storytelling to marketers and architects, and we recover many of our narrative lessons from branding, design, themeparking, flagshipping, tour-ism, and a host of other immersive commercial practices and affordances as we transit through locales.

Consumers hunger for the authenticity—as cultural a construct as it may be—they imagine their premodern ancestors to have enjoyed, and they learn to read it into (or lament its absence from) the environments others have built for them. The particular hierophany that marketers intend may or may not result from their [in]attention to design, but the shining through of spirit will occur only if consumers are inspired to summon it. As CCT research has shown over and again, consumers also engage in creative and resistant readings, smuggling their own singularized authenticity into the environ-ments they build for themselves from the wherewithal the culture industries provide. Bricolage and curation, appropriation and subversion, and accommodation and acquiescence are each a part of this place making.

In this chapter, I have asserted that spirit resides in and emerges from place, that spirit is emplaced and displaced through the practices of stakeholders, and that spirit is a pliable entity summoned by a primordial mode of perception (Harding, 2006) repurposed for a postmodern medium. I have further asserted that marketing and consumer researchers (but less our managerial cousins) have been neglectful of spirit of place largely because of our impoverished toolkits and our reluctance to treat non-materialist topics. I have attempted to provide some insights from the orientations and methods of other disciplines that might make our investigation of the spirit of place more attuned to the interplay of the material and the numinous. Finally, I have encouraged inquirers into servicescapes to cast a broader net, to ply their trade in contexts beyond the overtly commercial, to explore the scapus.

Our pursuit of the scapular—its enlightened discernment or design—may be guided by the work of "geologians" (Harding, 2006, p. 21) whose patient and persistent probing and engaged dwelling reveal the ways in which place is ensouled. When we ask "How is this place happening?", the intimations of the scapular become detectable. But our consultation ought not to be confined to the clerisy, whether academic or managerial. The scapular arises in the everyday practices of dwelling, which is to say in the intimate details of consumer behavior. Consumers-as-dwellers disclose through their placeways just how scapus may be conjured. So also do affordances both architectural and natural, artifacts both fashioned and found, and assemblages both ideological and behavioral. Holistic appraisal affords the surest sounding and the best bet for nudging spirit from stuff back into nature. Our discipline has helped and hindered reverence for place. Perhaps closer attention to the poetics of dwelling will earn us a better seat at the table of ecological revitalization.

REFERENCES

Abrams, David. 1996. *The Spell of the Sensuous*. New York: Vintage.
Abrams, David. 2010. *Becoming Animal: An Earthly Cosmology*. New York: Pantheon.
Bachelard, Gaston. 1994/1958. *The Poetics of Space*. Boston, MA: Beacon Press.
Bateson, Gregory. 1972. *Steps to an Ecology of Mind*. Chicago: University of Chicago Press.
Belk, Russell. 2000. "A Cultural Biography of My Groucho Glasses." In *Imagining Marketing:Art, Aesthetics, and the Avant-Garde*, edited by Stephen Brown and Anthony Peterson, 249–259. London: Routledge.
Belk, Russell. 2002. "Unpacking My Library: The Marketing Professor in an Age of Electronic Reproduction." *Journal of Marketing* 66 (January): 120–125.
Berkes, Fikret. 2008. *Sacred Ecology*. New York: Routledge.
Berman, M. 2000. *Wandering God: A Study in Nomadic Spirituality*. Albany, NY: State University of New York Press.

Berry, Thomas. 2006. *Evening Thoughts: Reflecting on Earth as a Sacred Community*. San Francisco: Sierra Club Books

Borghini, Stefania, Nina Diamond, Robert Kozinets, Mary Ann McGrath, Albert Muniz, andJohn F. Sherry, Jr. 2010. "Why Are Themed Brand Stores So Powerful? Retail Brand Ideology at American Girl Place." *Journal of Retailing* 85 (3): 363–375.

Brown, Stephen, and John F. Sherry, Jr. 2003. *Time, Space, and the Market. Retroscapes Rising*. New York: M. E. Sharpe, Inc.

Deleuze, Gilles, and Felix Guattari. 1987. *A Thousand Plateaus: Capitalism and Schizophrenia*. Minneapolis: University of Minnesota Press.

Everett, Glenn. n.d. "Hopkins on 'Inscape' and 'Instress.' " In *The Victorian Web: Literature, History & Culture in the Age of Victoria*, edited by George Landow Available at http://www.victorianweb.org/authors/hopkins/hopkins1.html

Fox, Matthew. 1988. *The Coming of the Cosmic Christ*. San Francisco: Harper and Row.

Gibson, James. 2009. *A Reenchanted World: The Quest for a New Kinship with Nature*. New York:Holt.

Hamilton, Edith. 1969 *Mythology: Timeless Tales of Gods and Heroes*. New York: Warner.

Harding, Stephan. 2006. *Animate Earth: Science, Intuition, and Gaia*. Wild River Junction, VT:Chelsea Green.

Harvey, Graham. 2006. *Animism: Respecting the Living World*. New York: Columbia University Press.

Hay, Peter. 2002. *Main Currents in Western Environmental Thought*. Bloomington, IN: Indiana University Press.

Ingold, Tim. 2000. *The Perception of the Environment: Essays in Livelihood, Dwelling and Skill*. New York: Routledge.

Johnson, Leslie. 2010. *Trail of Story: Reflections on Ethnoecology and Landscape*. Edmonton, AB: AU Press.

Kearney, Treasa, Aileen Kennedy, and Joseph Coughlan. 2007. "Servicescapes: A Review of Contemporary Empirical Research." School of Marketing Conference Papers, Dublin School of Technology, Dublin, Ireland.

Kearns, Laurel, and Catherine Keller, eds. 2007, *Ecospirit: Religions and Philosophies of the Earth*. New York: Fordham University Press.

Latour, Bruno. 1986. "The Power of Associations." In *Power, Action, and Belief: A New Sociology of Knowledge*, edited by John Law. London: Routledge, Pp.264–280

Latour, Bruno. 1993. *We Have Never Been Modern*. C. Porter Trans. Cambridge: Harvard University Press

Latour, Bruno. 2004. *Politics of Nature: How to Bring the Sciences into Democracy*. Cambridge, MA: Harvard University Press.

Latour, Bruno. 2005. *Reassembling the Social: An Introduction to Actor-Network-Theory*. New York: Oxford University Press.

Law, John. 1999. "Complexity, Naming and Technology." In *Actor Network and After*, edited by John Law and John Hassard, 1–14. Oxford: Sociological Review and Blackwell.

Lefebvre, Henri. 2008a. *Critique of Everyday Life, Volume 1*. NewYork: Verso.

Lefebvre, Henri. 2008b. *Critique of Everyday Life, Volume 2: Foundations for a Sociology of the Everyday*. New York: Verso.

Lefebvre, Henri. 2008c. *Critique of Everyday Life, Volume 3: Form Modernity to Modernism*. New York: Verso.

Linnet, Jeppe. 2009. "Money Can't Buy Me *Hygge*: Danish Middle Class consumption, Egalitarianism and the Sanctity of Inner Space." Unpublished manuscript University of South Denmark, Odense.

Lovelock, James. 1995. *The Ages of Gaia: A Biography of Our Living Earth.* New York: W. W. Norton.

May, J. Bruce. 1993. "Experiencing Place in Nature and in Architecture." *Environmental and Architectural Phenomenology* 4 (1): 2–3.

McCracken, Grant. 1989. "Homeyness: A Cultural Account of One Constellation of Consumer Goods and Meaning." In *Interpretive Consumer Research*, edited by Elizabeth Hirschman, 168–183. Provo, UT: Association for Consumer Research.

Messer, Ellen, and Michael Lambek, eds. 2001. *Ecology and the Sacred: Engaging the Anthropology of Roy A. Rappaport.* Ann Arbor, MI: University of Michigan Press.

Murray, Penelope. 2010. "Genius." In *The Classical Tradition*, edited by Anthony Grafton, Glenn Most, and Salvatore Settis, 387–388. Cambridge, MA: Belknap Press. Onions, C. T., ed. 1966. *The Oxford Dictionary of Classical Etymology.* Oxford: Oxford University Press.

Peters, W. 1948. *Gerard Manley Hopkins: A Critical Essay Towards the Understanding of His Poetry.* Oxford: Basil Blackwell.

Prior, Nick. 2008. "Putting a Glitch in the Field: Bourdieu, Actor Network Theory and Contemporary Music." *Cultural Sociology* 2 (3) (November 1): 301–319.

Rook, Dennis. 1991. "I Was Observed (*In Absentia*) and Autodriven by the Consumer Behavior Odyssey." In *Highways and Buyways: Naturalistic Research from the Consumer Behavior Odyssey*, edited by Russell Belk, 48–58. Provo, UT: Association for Consumer Research.

Roszak, Theodore, Mary Gomes, and Allen Kanner, eds. 1995. *Ecopsychology: Restoring the Earth, Healing the Mind.* San Francisco: Sierra Club Books.

Schau, Hope Jensen, Albert M. Muñiz, Jr., and Eric J. Arnould. 2009. "How Brand Community Practices Create Value." *Journal of Marketing* 73 (September): 1–35.

Seamon, David, ed. 1993. *Dwelling, Seeing and Designing: Toward a Phenomenological Ecology.* Albany. NY State University of New York Press

Seamon, David, and Arthur Zajonc. 1998. *Goethe's Way of Seeing: A Phenomenology of Nature.* Albany, NY: State University of New York Press.

Sherry, John F., Jr. 1998. *Servicescapes: The Concept of Place in Contemporary Markets.* Chicago IL: NTC Business Books.

Sherry, John F., Jr. 2000a. "Distraction, Destruction, Deliverance: The Presence of Mindscape in Marketing's New Millennium." *Marketing Intelligence and Planning* 18 (6/7): 328–336.

Sherry, John F., Jr. 2000b. "Place, Technology and Representation." *Journal of Consumer Research* 27 (September): 273–278.

Sherry, John F., Jr. 2001. "Sometimes Leaven with Levin: A Tribute to Sidney J. Levy on the Occasion of His Receiving the Converse Award." In *The Fifteenth Paul D. Converse Symposium*, edited by Abbie Griffin and James Ness, 54–63. Chicago: American Marketing Association.

Sherry, John F., Jr. 2005. "Brand Meaning." In *Kellogg on Branding*, edited by T. Calkins and Tybout, 40–60. New York: John Wiley.

Sherry, John F., Jr. 2008. "The Ethnographer's Apprentice: Trying Consumer Culture from The Outside In." *Journal of Business Ethics* 80: 85–95.

Sherry, John F., Jr., and Robert Kozinets. 2007. "Comedy of the Commons: Nomadic Spirituality at Burning Man." In *Consumer Culture Theory*, Vol. 11 of *Research In Consumer Behavior*, 119–147. Oxford: Elsevier.

Shove, E., and Pantzar, M. 2005. "Consumers, Producers, Practices: Understanding the Invention and Reinvention of Nordic Walking." *Journal of Consumer Culture* 5 (1): 43–64.

Skowlimowski, H. 1981. *Eco-Philosophy.* London: Boyars.

Snyder, Gary. 1995. *A Place in Space: Ethics, Aesthetics and Watersheds*. Washington, DC: Counterpoint.

Soja, Edward. 2010. *Seeking Spatial Justice. Minneapolis*, MN: University of Minnesota Press.

Swidler, Ann. 2001. "What Anchors Cultural Practices" In *The Practice Turn in Contemporary Theory*, edited by Theodore Schatzki, 74–92. London: Routledge.Tuan, Yi-Fu. 1977. *Space and Place: The Perspective of Experience*. London: University of Minnesota Press.

Visconti, Luca, John F. Sherry, Jr., Stefania Borghini, and Laurel Anderson. 2010. "Street Art, Sweet Art: The Reclamation of Public Place." *Journal of Consumer Research* 37 (3): 511–529.

Ward, Peter. 2009. *The Medea Hypothesis: Is Life on Earth Ultimately Self-Destructive?* Princeton, NJ: Princeton University Press.

Warde, Alan. 2005. "Consumption and Theories of Practice." *Journal of Consumer Culture* 5 (2): 131–153.

16 Spirituality as Introspection and Introspection as Spirituality in Consumer Research

Stephen Gould

There are probably as many definitions of spirituality (and its alleged doppelganger or opposite, religion) as there are people defining it. This is, after all, a poststructural age in which meaning is greatly dispersed and decentered (but see James [1929] on the *Varieties of Religious Experience*, which quite pre-dates poststructuralism). For me here, spirituality is totally embodied in the very life I lead, and introspecting about it is part of my spiritual journey. I can characterize that spirituality in many ways, such as connectedness, the transpersonal, a set of 'spiritual' practices and discourses, fully inhabiting the time-space matrix, and links to specific culturally-defined forms of spirituality, such as Buddhism or chi-gong. How I think about it and more importantly experience it may paradoxically have a certain coherence in being something "I" experience but also a certain incoherence in that my experience is never quite repeated the same way. I definitely do want to say that it is not merely intellectual or even intellectual at all, but rather it is the fullness of being involving something I can only call the mind-body-energy-spirit continuum with duality showing up more in language than in experience.

Famously as is said in various spiritual disciplines, what we think and say intellectually is at best like a finger pointing to something else. From that starting point, then, I will introspect on my own spirituality knowing full well that it may not apply to or resonate with everyone. That gives me a certain freedom that in many ways reflects my own personal experience. Still, and on the other hand, this is neither a completely solipsistic effort nor one for which I do not expect others to resonate with. Otherwise, why write this chapter? Indeed, I think there will be insights that I can share with others and even theory to be applied in future research endeavors. In this regard, I seek to problematize or deconstruct duality and in particular dualities between the spiritual-sacred/profane, material/non-material, phenomenal/epiphenomenal, introspection/extrospection, and consciousness/non-consciousness. One tool that I have applied to make my introspective deconstructions more relevant is to provide introspective thought and feeling exercises, which I have derived from my own introspections and in which I invite you the reader to actively participate.

THE HERMENEUTIC OF SPIRITUALITY AND INTROSPECTION

There are several ways that I can employ introspection in relation to spirituality. Similar to how I have defined two types of introspection, narrative and metacognitive introspection, I view recounting my spirituality through introspecting about it as narrating the story of my spiritual journey. However, I also view introspection as a metacognitive exploration of my being, both conscious and unconscious (to the degree I can become aware of it) and that through both my outer and inner encounters constitutes for me spirituality. Based on meditation, of which there are many types and forms and which is often if not always associated with spirituality, I view such introspection as encompassing these and therefore as constituting spirituality. While using both of these approaches, I have developed and applied introspective exercises through which I can explore the various aspects of my consciousness and also share them as research applications, deconstructions, and narratives with others.

Telling my story and developing my perspective here to this particular audience at least as I perceive in this writing has driven me to think about these issues in a different way than I may have before. If nothing else, I'm inscribing my research perspective into my spiritual practice in some new ways beyond what I had done before. Thus, not only is a major part of it informed by my spiritual experiences, but is actually inscribed in them. This is not a 'singularity' however because all my work on Asian perspectives, introspection, self, culture, and vital energy involved one step after another in my personal spiritual evolution. As many people might describe it, this is part of the "spiritual path" through which I engage myself and any others involved. I should also state that my work owes so much to many teachers and teachings, both in oral and written form, of which I can cite but a few, among many, many from a vast array of cultures and perspectives. Here I will cite the work of three Tibetan Lamas, Chogyam Trungpa (1973), Namkhai Norbu (1999), and Tarthang Tulku (1977), whose perspectives inform so much of what I am sharing here.

One key approach is to consider embodiment. In this regard, although some may regard spirituality as a transcendent non-material experience, others including myself view it in terms of immanence and embodied physical manifestations that is something you can observe, feel, or otherwise sense, simultaneously transcendent and immanent. For example, in meditative states one can observe through various signs that one is in a certain state or other. In other contexts, I have called this vital energy, which is something one can experience, feel, and observe. This psychophysiological materiality is not separate from spirituality; indeed it is the very manifestation of it.

However, how one interprets this materiality is very much at issue. In one article (Gould, 1991a), I drew on the Tibetan Wheel of Life mythology to illustrate how there are different levels of perceived materiality. For example, one may see oneself as being in the hells or in some sublime utopian and god-like realms. In these non-material realms one feels (or literally is in the mythology) non-material in terms of human perception, but one is still attached to something or some realm—one is grasping. Thinking, judging, constructing, and desiring are all forms of this grasping. Thus, in many respects materialism or beliefs in materiality are as much an attitude, a construction, or a perception as they are reflective of something 'objectively' solid (Gould, 1992). This perspective seems to differ from traditional consumer research perspectives on materialism, which emphasize attachment to goods (e.g., Belk, 1985). Although that perspective continues to be useful, it seems necessary to excavate the assumptions behind it. Thus, to consider these levels or perspectives in consumption terms, I view them as part of my spiritual development in which I apply these as metaphors for what is going on with or around me.

Hell is a familiar metaphor in many cultures (I make no claims here one way or another about the literalness of hell or hells or for that matter any other regions beyond everyday human perception; there is enough for us to consider in our human realm). We all may feel at times that we are in hellish states. There actually are many forms of hell, such that we experience deprivations or pains of various sorts. In some hellish states the suffering may be that consumption does not move us at all. For example, there may be times when we feel so stunned by events that we do not want to even eat or drink, much less enjoy any pleasures. Other times we may drown our sorrows in these same things. Thus, hellish manifestations are many and diverse.

The god realms, of which there also can be many and may be likened to heaven in some cultures, are centered on unlimited pleasure of various sorts ranging from unlimited fulfillment of sexual or consumption desires to states of meditative bliss beyond all thought. This is perhaps the best metaphor for the marketing and consumer universe, utopia especially for those who have means. However, all of these have one downfall, which is that they end and that end is death.

Beyond these realms that are rooted in a material view of the world, one may embody something beyond these realms, at once rooted in materiality but embarked on a path of spiritual realization. Even within this path, there is any number of path variants. As Eliade, 1954/1973, p. 263) has famously said, "By the same acts that cause some men to burn in hell for thousands of years, the yogin gains his eternal salvation." One way to view these paths involves three main levels, although there are also sublevels beyond our scope here. The first level, which we may recognize in many religions and spiritual paths, involves renunciation that is some sort of withdrawal or abstinence with respect to the material world. For example, for moral reasons, one may decide not to drink alcoholic beverages or abstain from/ restrict sexuality. This is a well-worn and known path in many religions.

Less known is a path of transformation. In this path, one challenges the usual restrictions of certain practices frowned on in some spiritual-religious circles by engaging in them. For example, certain Tantric practices in Buddhism might have one utilize alcohol or sex so that one transforms the energy of such acts into spiritual energy. The final path involves the liberation of everything by being present in phenomenal experience without any cognitive effort or interpretation, including even transformation. Thus, one encounters phenomena in all manner of ways, but one's perspective of being present-aware does not change.

In my own life, I reflect all these levels at various times. For example, I may feel that I need to restrict my behavior because it seems out of control. Then I may engage in renunciation. Alcohol is one product that I may say to myself that I need to restrict because I may lose control in ways I would not want to. However, I may recognize alcohol as a realizational tool through which I can experience different states of consciousness and interact not only with the environment but myself. I engage in self-transformation/self-fashioning, but in the end it is to lead to a place where alcohol does not become a fixation or I cling to drinking. In the end (and this is somehow the final stage, although it is always there if I let it be) is a presence in which all experience self-liberates—it just disappears even as it manifests. In marketing, services may be characterized as being produced and consumed at the same time. But in fact, everything may be viewed as arising (produced) and disappearing (consumed). In this and all, if I grasp at alcohol or transformational experiences with it or even renouncing it, I would be engaging in spiritual materialism in which one collects spiritual objects, practices, and experiences in much the same fashion as profane goods (Trungpa, 1973), at least so far as I had some sort of conceptual grasping of this alcohol ideology that I have constructed. I have to know how to use the tool without becoming attached to it.

This view of spiritual materialism problematizes the sacred-profane as laid out in consumer research in the seminal article on relating spirituality and consumption by Belk, Wallendorf, and Sherry (1989). Their article contributes to our thought especially in discussing the sacralization of the secular, often through consumption. In the context I have applied here, it fits well with many of the levels or realms of existence as I developed above. For instance, in the human realm, people clearly make distinctions between the sacred and profane: "This is my sacred-special place, time, object," etc. The very existence of different realms implies to a certain degree that certain existences might seem to be more holy or sacred than others (e.g., the god realms versus the animal realms).

However, the sacred-profane might be problematized in two different ways. Following Derrida (1991), who deconstructed-problematized all dualities, there is no distinct sacred or profane. In terms of the idea of being present in whatever happens, they are not different nor the same; they are mere conceptualizations that might tie up our minds and prevent us from being present in the full experience of whatever is there. Labeling something as sacred or profane may really obscure the holiness that is present in all encounters with space-time phenomena and our own minds. Now that said, I may not always be that present. And certainly I have likes and dislikes, pains and pleasures, which operating in this perspective drive my own sacralizations (i.e., if I like something I may sacralize it as part of my own experience). I also recognize and honor the formal holiness that resides in various religions, spiritual practices, and secular forms as well. But still if I am aware and self-observant, I'm also cognizant not to get too attached to my conceptualizing and emotionalizing of these forms. This is one of the most tricky and paradoxical aspects of my spirituality, that is, in dealing with thought about experience as something always arising but not to be grasped at as representing anything especially sacred or important.

PHENOMENAL AND EPIPHENOMENAL

I've always had to deal with experience, especially spiritual experience, as something that poses phenomenal versus epiphenomenal aspects. When people describe their own spiritual experiences to others, especially 'mystical' ones, they are often involved with phenomena that those others may not experience and therefore doubt. It seems also there may be individual differences in sensitivities and sensibilities regarding spiritual experience. There may even be 'unique' experiences. However, because in this volume we are dealing with 'consumer research,' we recognize that such a perspective is not easily pursued or rewarded. Averages are usually pursued in such research. Yet, can we conclude anything but that individuals are unique? Moreover, is not their experience, even the most ordinary, not something unique?

But then can we describe anything akin to shared experience? My exercise approach, which I developed in the face of the controversies over introspection, constitutes my way of seeing what unique experiences can be understood in shared ways. I have borrowed from Thompson (1990) in the past (Gould, 1991b) and do so here again to suggest that people may grasp experiences conceptually even if they do not share them phenomenologically whereas others may more directly share in those experiences. The exercises constitute a further advance in that direction either at a minimum by making things more clear conceptually or by posing the possibility of describing an experience and having others find similar things in their consciousness/experience (cf. Gould, 1995a, 1995b, 2006, 2008). This method is not reductionist because it does not assume others will have the same experiences or even frame them the same way. It also seems poststructural to me in that each person is a particular, different site of meaning. I may describe a certain meditation state as spiritual whereas others assuming they experience something comparable may see it as something else altogether. Even our very writing as academics may be seen to constitute an exercise in which we pose what we write as something for others to consider. We may or may not think of our writing this way, but consider it. One could argue that the very idea of exercises makes certain assumptions about spirituality and related foundational ideas, but I will leave that for others to ponder. You may try what I'm suggesting and see if it makes sense to you at all. I will provide basic exercises that I have derived from introspective mediation and which I find crucial in developing the relationship between materiality-consumption and spirituality.

Basic Thought Exercise

Watch your thoughts. Just let them go without any particular 'thinking' about them.

Notice how they keep coming. You can contextualize them by watching what they are about and even pursuing them by thinking about what you are thinking about. Then alternately you can decontextualize them by not looking at what the thoughts mean but just observe them as they arise. We all probably have had the experience of trying to stop thinking. Try it now. What happens? One thing is that thoughts arise on their own, such as thinking about trying to not think. When thoughts arise on their own consider the relationship of conscious deliberation and non-conscious automaticity.

Try a similar exercise with feelings, alternately feeling with meaning and then without thinking about or giving meaning to them. How different, for example, does the material world look when you actively think about it versus when you don't? What is consumer desire in this context?

The paradox of this basic exercise is that thinking may not be intentionally (consciously) thought into being. A recent article mentioned that of all our brain activity, about 2% is conscious (*New York Times*, 2010). However, that takes nothing away from the sublimity of that 2% or that it exists at all. Moreover, the ability to enhance that 2% by amount or quality may exist by reaching into other realms of the brain, hence the idea that meditation reaches those aspects and changes the whole dynamic of my(our) experience (cf. Hözel et al., 2011). For example, when I extend my consciousness into dreaming (lucid dreaming), this is one such dynamic. Or I observe where different sounds or music hit me in the body, a kind of body-environment resonance, one of many forms of 'oneness.' This may correspond to synesthesia in which one's senses are mixed, as here in 'hearing' sounds in one's body-feelings. However, although the reactions are involuntary, they become conscious in a way that extends my consciousness and links me even more tightly through it to the external world.

Another related element of thinking and consciousness concerns the experience of fragmentation versus wholeness as a key aspect of my spiritual experience. This idea may be familiar to you because in postmodernity, fragmentation is all pervasive. We are multiple selves torn in many directions. Does this ever cohere in any way as a single self (cf. Gould, 2010)? I find that such does happen in non-conceptual meditative space.

All thought is fragmentation in this sense, and its lack renders us whole. Where thinking and directing any activity with intention is tricky is in the sense of remaining whole or not. I see something I like in a store and develop desire for it. Can I have this object in a whole way? This is the paradox of fragmentation and wholeness in every moment. But this paradox only exists if I think about it. Also if I make the division between sacred and profane, the profane would be conceptuality and the sacred, non-conceptuality. But that too is riven with paradox because all may be seen as sacred; however, even that is a concept, and there is really no such division, is there?

INTROSPECTION VERSUS EXTROSPECTION

Another category to problematize is the introspective-extrospective dimension (Gould, 1993a). It would seem that in everyday culture outward-viewing extrospection seems to dominate whereas introspective-inner viewing may seem self-absorbed or withdrawn. Here, I would suggest that these two categories are not really so separate, if they are even separate at all. After all what is it we observe when we look out on the world? It is our own mind! Yes, depending on the philosophical or other understanding you might have, there is something out there in the world. But what is it you observe?

Introspective-Extrospective Exercise

View the outer world as reflections of your own mind. As you look upon the world around you or focus on any object what do you observe? (When I say look you may include all senses by themselves or altogether. For example, hearing may be applied as easily as seeing in this context.) Observe for a while as long as you may feel. Note if and how things may blend together so you do not distinguish outer and inner unless you make an effort to do so. When this occurs, what happens to your sense of self? Who or what are you?

Opposite: view your own mind and thought as external. Repeat elements of the outer as inner but do not be restricted by them. Observe your own mind as something that may not be 'you.' Try having a watcher self which watches your mind. Of course this watcher self may have a recursive loop in that one can construct many watcher selves in a kind of infinite regress. But while that can be of interest in observing what the self is, the central element here is how you relate the inner to the outer.

This leads to viewing consumption as an inner versus external matter. I've been exposed to the idea that in Chinese medicine, when one cannot heal oneself internally through energy practices (Chi Gung), one must then seek out external means such as medicines, medical herbs, acupuncture, etc. For me this has become a model for all consumption. When I can function more within, I will seek out less externally and vice versa.

CONSUMPTION AND SPIRITUAL DECONSTRUCTION

I have considered Jacques Derrida as a kind of Zen master, certainly not in his complicating of things conceptual, but in his deconstructive approach, which operates to bring out the self-effacing aspect of all conceptualizations. However, as I have also considered in the past (Gould, 1994), his efforts stop short of going beyond concept. In other words, erasing all concepts is itself conceptual, so then where are you? While Derrida operates in a realm similar to Buddhist and probably other spiritual philosophies, many of those philosophies point beyond themselves to the non-conceptual. Consumption in this realm of conception and non-conception is not inherently bad or good. Over-attachment to the material world and the goods it entails can certainly be a limitation to spiritual realization. But from the perspective of spiritual materialism, so can over-attachment to spirituality, which abhors the pleasures of the material world and the flesh. There is no escaping embodiment, which, interestingly enough, a stream of current consumer research is dealing with, although not spiritually. We can just as easily say we are emminded (Gould, 1993b), which means we live in our minds. Or probably most appropriately, we live in our mind-body continuums, in which mind and body are not dualistic entities even if we often operate as if they are.

Consumption and Spiritual Deconstruction Exercise

Try abstaining from something you regularly consume, if not everything. How does that make you feel? For instance, does this make you feel purified, especially if it is something you desire but feel is not otherwise in your best interest?

Now try indulging in something perhaps the same thing. How does that make you feel? For instance does it make you feel guilty as though out of control? Or does it make you feel somehow liberated and in touch with something deep and rich in your world that you can do this?

Then alternate over time with different goods and experiences. What does this exercise make you feel and how do you interpret those feelings? Are these 'spiritual' or they just artifacts of experience which bear no such label? Does thinking they are spiritual make them so?

Finally, apply different readings to this exercise and ultimately to this chapter and even book. For instance, you might read them from spiritual, introspective and consumer research-materialism viewpoints, one at a time. Do they synergize, converge, diverge, hybridize or otherwise problematize/inform your perspectives. Integrating the levels of perceived materialism discussed above may further help develop this exercise.

CONCLUSION

Because I see spirituality in terms of spiritual practice, it is also worthy of note that I am seeking to engage in self-fashioning, much as applied by Gould and Stinerock (1992). In this sense, spirituality is a set of practices, a practice, and a conscious attempt to shape my life in terms of things or a path(s) I think of as spiritual. Even as I do so, I am aware of the many things that may arise beyond my intentional practice or expectations. This is a paradoxical result. Related to my self-fashioning is self-experimentation (Gould, 1991a, 1995a; Roberts, 2004), in which I try out spiritual practices and see what happens. Sometimes I have a hypothesis or *a priori* concept whereas at other times I take a grounded-theory approach in trying something and interpreting the data of my experience. Really both of these often occur together in a dynamic hermeneutic and emergent relationship in which I go back and forth between the experience, my own prior experience and thought, literature, and discussions with others to characterize the experience. The continual practice of self-fashioning and self-experimentation comprises my spiritual path, a constant dynamic of attempting to grasp what is largely ungraspable. We want to comment, to interpret, to provide meaning. In particular, we want to embody in material terms that meaning. Indeed, through meditative-introspective practices, we mentally transform our very materiality! In many ways, that may seem to be what spirituality is. But if the non-conceptual is 'the spiritual,' we are left with a bind when we want to apply conceptual mind to it.

Consumption is an aspect of embodiment of/in the realm where spirituality takes place. In relation to spirituality, it is in one sense like fire (cooks or burns things)—it can create the environment for spiritual realization or it can be the thing that blocks it. Although in some respects much of what I am saying involves what is ostensibly sacralization of the mundane, it all depends on if one constructs a sacred-profane duality. In this regard, it also depends on the level at which one is viewing materiality. Thus, it can be said that paradoxically there is one spirituality and many. Also although I am informed in this view by my own spiritual practice, which is largely Asian-based, I feel that it relates to virtually any form of spirituality as a way of locating it. However, this is not necessarily to construct an overarching metanarrative or subsume or problematize others' spirituality. But it does provide a perspective that researchers and others might find useful.

REFERENCES

Belk, Russell W. 1985. "Materialism: Trait Aspects of Living in the Material World." *Journal of Consumer Research* 12 (December): 265–280.
Belk, Russell W., Melanie Wallendorf, and John Sherry, Jr. 1989. "The Sacred and the Profane in Consumer Behavior: Theodicy on the Odyssey." *Journal of Consumer Research* 16 (June): 1–38.

Derrida, J. 1991. *A Derrida Reader: Between the Blinds.* Edited by P. Kamuf. New York: Columbia University Press.

Elidade. 1954/1973. *Yoga, Immortality and Freedom.* Princeton: Princeton University Press.

Gould, S. J. 1991a. "An Asian Approach to the Understanding of Consumer Energy, Drives and States." In *Research in Consumer Behavior*, Volume 5, edited by E. C. Hirschman, 33–59. Greenwich, CT: JAI.

Gould, S. J. 1991b. "The Self-Manipulation of My Pervasive, Perceived Vital Energy through Product Use: An Introspective-Praxis Perspective." *Journal of Consumer Research* 18 (September): 194–207.

Gould, S. J. 1992. "Consumer Materialism as a Multilevel and Individual Difference Phenomenon: An Asian-Based Perspective." In *Meaning, Measure, and Morality of Materialism*, edited by F. Rudmin and M. Richins, 57–62. Provo, UT: Association for Consumer Research.

Gould, S. J. 1993a. "Introspective Versus Extrospective Perspectives in Consumer Research: A Matter of Focus." In *Marketing Theory and Applications*, Volume 4, edited by Rajan Varadarjan and Bernard Jaworski, 199–200. Chicago: American Marketing Association.

Gould, S. J. 1993b. "The Circle of Projection and Introjection: An Introspective Investigation of a Proposed Paradigm Involving the Mind as 'Consuming Organ.'" *Research in Consumer Behavior*, Volume 6, edited by J. A. Costa and R. W. Belk, 185–230. Greenwich, CT: JAI.

Gould, S. J. 1994. "An Asian-Based Perspective on Postmodern Consumer Culture and Consciousness: The Nature of Mind." In *Asia Pacific Advances in Consumer Research*, Volume 1, edited by Joseph A. Cote and Siew Meng Leong, 306–310. Provo, UT: Association for Consumer Research.

Gould, S. J. 1995a. "Researcher Introspection as a Method in Consumer Research: Applications, Issues and Implications." *Journal of Consumer Research* 21 (March): 719–722.

Gould, S. J. 1995b. "The Buddhist Perspective on Business Ethics: Experiential Exercises for Exploration and Practice. *Journal of Business Ethics* 14 (January): 63–70.

Gould, S. J. 2006. "Unpacking the Many Faces of Introspective Consciousness: A Metacognitive-Poststructuralist Exercise." In *Handbook of Qualitative Research Methods in Marketing*, edited by Russell W. Belk, 186–197. Northampton, MA : Edward Elgar.

Gould, S. J. 2008. "Introspection as Critical Marketing Thought, Critical Marketing Thought as Introspection." In *Critical Marketing: Issues in Contemporary Marketing*, edited by Mark Tadajewski and Douglas Brownlie, 311–328. Chichester, West Sussex UK: John Wiley & Sons.

Gould, S. J. (2010), " "To Thine Own Self(ves) Be True": Reflexive Insights for Etic Self Theory from Consumers' Emic Constructions of the Self," *Consumption, Markets & Culture*, 13 (June), 181–219.

Gould, S. J., and R. N. Stinerock. 1992. "Self-Fashioning Oneself Cross-Culturally: Consumption as the Determined and the Determining." In *Advances in Consumer Research*, Volume 19, edited by J. Sherry and B. Sternthal, 857–860. Provo, UT: Association for Consumer Research.

Hözel, Britta K., James Carmody, Mark Vangel, Christina Congleton, Sita M. Yerramsetti, Tim Gard, and Sara W. Lazar. 2011. "Mindfulness Practice Leads to Increases in Regional Brain Gray Matter Density." *Psychiatry Research: Neuroimaging* 191: 36–43.

James, William. 1929. *The Varieties of Religious Experience: A Study in Human Nature.* New York: Modern Library.

Norbu, Namkhai.(1999. *The Crystal and the Way of Light: Sutra, Tantra and Dzogchen*. Ithaca, NY: Snow Lion Publications.

New York Times. 2010. http://www.nytimes.com/2010/11/14/business/14stream.h tml?scp=1&sq=nueromarketing&st=cse.

Roberts, Seth. 2004. "Self-Experimentation as a Source of New Ideas: Examples About Sleep, Mood, Health, and Weight." *Behavioral and Brain Sciences* 27: 227–262.

Thompson, Craig J. 1990. "Eureka! and Other Tests of Significance: A New Look at Evaluating Interpretive Research." In Advances *in* Consumer Research, edited by Marvin E. Goldberg, Gerald Gorn, and Richard W. Pollay, 25–30. Provo, UT: Association for Consumer Research.

Trungpa, Chogyam. 1973. *Cutting Through Spiritual Materialism* Boston, MA: Shambhala Publications.

Tulku, Tarthang. 1977. *Time, Space and Knowledge: A New Vision of Reality*. Berkeley, CA: Dharma Publishing.

17 The Autothemataludicization Challenge

Spiritualizing Consumer Culture Through Playful Communal Co-Creation

Robert V. Kozinets and John F. Sherry, Jr.

In the past quarter century of consumer research, a recurrent theme has been the persistent interrelation of religious culture and contemporary American consumer culture. Religious practices, rituals, and meanings—and those looser beliefs termed "spiritual," "magical," and "sacred"—have been located in fan communities (Kozinets, 2001; O'Guinn, 1991), in historical re-enactments (Belk and Costa, 1998), among touristic gatherings (Arnould, Price, and Otnes, 1999; Hetherington, 2000), in technology groups (Belk and Tumbat, 2002; Muñiz and Schau, 2005), in online and offline groups devoted to food (Kozinets, 2002a; Thompson and Troester, 2002), in consumer activism (Kozinets and Handelman, 2004), at raves and doofs (St. John, 2001), at shopping malls and themed retail locations (Kozinets et al., 2004; Ritzer, 1999), as well as in collections, at swap meets, and in American society generally (Belk, Wallendorf, and Sherry, 1989; Sherry, 1990).

Although the presence of sacred forms of consumption is oft-noted by scholars in mainstream consumer practice, explicitly sacred forms of consumption are rarely theorized beyond this point. We know that contemporary consumption has blurred the boundaries between sacred and profane (Belk, Wallendorf, and Sherry, 1989), and that some contemporary variants of traditional religious belief have been deeply transformed by their situation within acquisitive, materialist, and consumer-centered society (O'Guinn and Belk, 1989). However, as studies in the social sciences attest, alternative forms of religion and spirituality have flourished (e.g., Mazur and McCarthy, 2001; Pike, 2004; York, 1995), yet their mutual imbrication with consumer culture has yet to be fully examined. In this chapter, we seek to contribute to this growing and important stream of thinking, one to which this volume makes an important contribution. We focus our efforts on a particular phenomenon of interest in this "self-help" and "consumer-generated" age of consumerized spirituality. We seek to offer up a meaningful initial theory that examines the experience, the substance, and the ideologies of so-called alternate religious and spiritual practices and relate them to studies of consumer culture by looking at the do-it-yourself elements of a popular contemporary spiritual festival. Through that enterprise, we try to develop novel insights into the nature of the consumption of contemporary spirituality and the spirituality of contemporary consumers. We begin by describing contemporary alternative spiritual movements and practices and then relating them to consumer culture. We then detail some of the spiritual consumption practices occurring in our field site, the Burning Man project. In our concluding section, we speculate freely about this new area of spirituality and consumption and its investigation and representation in contemporary consumption and cultural studies.

CONSUMPTION AND SPIRITUALITY

Consumer Society and Transcendence

Many scholars, including many in this very volume, have noted that the consumption of religion, especially in contemporary North American contexts, can be categorized as a "spiritual marketplace," a veritable smorgasbord of alternate beliefs that can be mixed and matched like courses at a broad buffet (e.g., Csordas, 1997). Many have also found that religious sentiments and meanings have moved from more formal, organized locations such as churches and temples to events and gatherings such as festival, concerns, workshops, and fairs (Taylor, 2002; York, 1995). Chief among the new or disestablishment religious forms we wish to explore are genres broadly labeled "New Age," which includes a vast variety of religious forms, including those influenced by Native American and Eastern religions; some reforming Wiccan, shamanic, and Pagan beliefs and rites; and others focusing on extraterrestrial intelligences, channeling, mysticism, and UFOs (Ferguson, 1980; Pike, 2004; York, 1995). New Age is, in short, an eclectic mélange of syncretic expressions that converge on the goals of personal experience and insight, and for whom ritual is the touchstone of identity and community (Pike, 2004; York, 1995).

It would, however, be a mistake to conflate the fluidity and heterodoxy of New Age spirituality with postmodernity and to consign institutional or organized religions—with their tendency towards rote and dogma—to affiliations of modernity. Better perhaps would be to think of the institutions of religion as premodern or traditional and to note the pervasiveness of modern impulses in religious and spiritual forms. It has been widely argued in sociology and anthropology that consumer culture is bound up with the whole of modernity (e.g., Campbell, 1989; Miller, 1987; Ritzer, 1999; Slater, 1997). This view contrasts concepts of modern and premodern society, or traditional and post-traditional society, defining consumption in relation to the major themes and features of modernity.

But in order to elaborate the influence of modern consumer culture on spiritual experience, and without claiming to be exhaustive or authoritative on the matter, we cleave these guiding modernistic themes into three supporting cultural themes or pillars, which we then locate in contemporary American spirituality. The first pillar of modern consumer culture is the premise and promise of *freedom of choice*: a conflation of democracy, autonomy, ostensibly rational self-interest, and individualism. The second pillar is that of the *mutable self*: a conflation of constant desire blended with identity creation and re-creation, competition, and uncertainty. The third pillar is *popular spectacle*: the deep interrelation of the meanings and values of daily life with the mass mediated (and increasingly global) creations of news, sports, entertainment, and other identity brands. Each of these elements is implicated in consumers' religiosity or quest for transcendence, yet these important links have thus far remained, for the most part, indistinct. In total, they constitute the three fundamental underlying principles of a type of religious practice called *autothemataludicization*, which we define, theorize, and develop later in this chapter. As preliminary theoretical groundwork for that exposition, we explain each of them in turn here before proceeding to theorize their more intimate linkage.

Freedom of Choice. Over the course of modernity, a vision of market society arose that focused on liberalism and neo-liberalism, emphasizing choice, autonomy, and individualism and valorizing the consumer as a hero of modern freedom and progress. Supplanting old notions of fealty, responsibility, and communal obligation, the individual has but to freely choose based on selfish desire, and the morality of the innate marketplace will raise his or her action to a level of valor (Campbell, 1989).

Yet central social tensions have arisen in relation to this portrayal, namely, how individuals relate with one another and with the wider world of meaning in the atomistic, hedonistic, individualist, and self-serving consumer society (see, e.g., Cushman, 1995). We see this tension among individuals, society, and the communal search for transcendence meaning in consumer society as a central and commanding theme present in a number of past investigations (e.g., Belk, Wallendorf, and Sherry, 1989; Kozinets, 2001, 2002a, 2002b; Kozinets et al., 2002; Muñiz and O'Guinn, 2001). The present study recasts the dichotomies and uneasy mergers between brands and communities, between markets and communities, and between profane and sacred in modern consumer culture as arising from these central social issues about authoritarian narratives governing collective social logics. Our study suggests how autothemataludicization allows a rapid and communal construction and communication of varieties of religious experience that can be and are used to rapidly transcend, and in some sense transform, systems of consumer culture.

Mutable Self and the Quest for Transcendence. The second pillar of contemporary consumer culture is the *mutable self*: a conflation of constant desire blended with identity creation, a romantic ethos, and a quest for the transcendence of the old through embracing the new. A founding pillar of modernism was the idea that the person could learn, grow, and transcend their past or their inherited condition. After millennia of serf-doms, thralldoms, caste cultures, and bluebloods, individual selves were finally viewed as capable, through their own acts of will, of pulling them-selves up and bettering their conditions. By the modern era, this capability had turned into an imperative.

According to Cushman (1995), Americans suffer from an uncertain, reflexive, and doubting self due not only to the loss of religious certainty and community, but because of the destabilizing influence of markets and pop-ular consumer culture, which demand constant newness, constant change (Brand, 1999), and a constant reach towards the future (Brooks, 2004). Just as Christianity first nurtured the sense of human sin and depravity, offering consolation through confession and the church's acceptance, so capitalism flourished on the broken terrain of the isolated and empty self facing a frighteningly uncertain tomorrow, which it promised to make whole in the future, through the transformative power of fantasy (Cushman, 1995; Firat and Venkatesh, 1995; Martin, 2004).

As other contemporary anthropologists have done (see, e.g., Hether-ington, 2000; York, 1995), our study relates the constantly striving and searching self of contemporary consumer culture to the quest for religious experience and the spiritual seeking of contemporary New Age movements. Like Pine and Gilmore (1999), we see an important and noteworthy ten-dency in the shift from the search for things to the seeking of meaningful experiences, but we cast the quest for new experience as spiritually charged. Through the notion of autothemataludicization, we redeploy notions of the empty, fragmented, and mutable self to answer questions about how con-temporary consumers can slake their thirst for authenticity, take control of the role of time in their experience, and make spiritual shifts fit into the busy schedules of a well-adjusted consumer operating in a therapeutic consumer society.

Popular Spectacle and the Quest for Transcendence. The third pillar of consumer culture is the deployment of public popular images in per-sonal ways. Postmodern, cultural studies, subcultural, and media studies literature fields have long debated whether consumer culture manipulates and inoculates consumers with its values, or whether it provides them with resources for creativity and resistance. Research indicates that it does pro-vide them with images powerful enough to act as spiritual and religious analogs (see, e.g., Belk, Wallendorf, and Sherry, 1989; Brown, Kozinets, and Sherry, 2003; Porter and Maclaren, 1999; Schouten and McAlexan-der, 1995). This appropriation and repurposing of popular culture images creates tensions between control and autonomy, self-expression and self-control, and it requires individuals and communities to form expressive rituals around meanings that belong to them in spirit, but that are actually owned and controlled by others. Autothemataludicization and its projects allow them to collectively meet these sometimes conflicting challenges in elegant and meaningful ways.

Sites of Spiritual Consumption Investigation

Our investigation explores these central themes of choice, self, and spectacle in the context of sites designated as spiritual social spaces. We ethnographically and netnographically engaged a variety of alternative religious events—including several psychic fairs, strip mall channelers and roadside Tarot readers, and an alternative church—in search of spiritual consumption enlightenment. The investigations of these sites informed our central inquiry but will be analyzed and reported in detail elsewhere. Due to the richness of the data it provided, we elected to put our study's primary focuses on Burning Man, an event that is a hotbed of spiritual experimentation and individualization.

For one week each year, a vast tract of the lifeless Black Rock desert near Gerlach, Nevada, is transformed into Black Rock City, the fourth largest city in the state of Nevada, site of Burning Man. In the 2011 event, which ended just as we were finalizing this chapter, the event attracted 50,000 participants and was limited to this number by legal constraints. Many of the event participants describe themselves as spiritual seekers and their Burning Man experience as containing the most profound and sacred moments of their lives. The event has been chronicled in many other places (e.g., Brill and Lady Bee, 2003; Doherty, 2004; Kozinets and Sherry, 2004; Kreuter, 2002; http://burningman.com/; Sherry and Kozinets, 2004, 2007).

This chapter is based within a larger ethnographic and netnographic project of inquiry into Burning Man, conducted with participants and organizers drawn from all quarters of the event. We attended Burning Man in 1999, 2000, 2001, 2003, and 2005. We also attended the event virtually in a myriad of different ways in all of the other years since the inception of our research in 1999. Hundreds of hours of physical and virtual immersion in the sites were capped with participant-observation in Black Rock City in the desert near Gerlach, Nevada, and in-person, on-site interviews of hundreds of Burning Man participants. We recorded data manually in fieldnotes, electronically in photographs and in both audio- and videotape formats. We also drafted research participants (some of whom were fellow academics and other professors) to assist us in member checks. Because this work is part of a long-term and ongoing project, we also have many other related findings reported in a variety of other outlets (see, in particular, Kozinets and Sherry, 2004; Sherry and Kozinets, 2004, 2007, which deal with some related spiritual consumption themes). In keeping with the enacted, embodied, ritual nature of the event and the New Age movement as a whole (Pike, 2004; York, 1995), we opt in this chapter to provide a richly observational account that privileges longer fieldnote excepts over longer interview verbatims (although both are included).

AUTOTHEMATALUDICIZATION

Considering Consumption, Shopping, and Spirituality

Resisting Imposed Meaning and Individualized Choice. Because the ritual of the burning of Burning Man is both physically and metaphysically central to the event, located in the center of the semicircle that forms Black Rock's city, we begin with an exploration of the event as reconstructed through our combined fieldnotes.

> The burning of the Man occurred last night, Saturday night. The effigy had been assembled on Monday, trimmed with neon lighting and installed on its stage. It acted as a devotional shrine for the pilgrims who traverse its structure often in the balance of the week. As the week wore on, participants' talk turned inevitably to the coming burn. The Burn itself turns out to be a major spectacle of the grandest, and most Hollywood and Disneyesque proportions. Yet it's a creation and eternal return of an ancient (or it somehow *feels* like it is ancient) ritual that brims with authenticity, although it is deliberately staged. Tonight, in the gathering darkness, pilgrims stream down the dusty avenues, across the Esplanade where they promenade. They fan out over the playa, staking out their places around the neon-lighted Man. Dressed in full regalia, armed with glow sticks and el-wire, bearing musical instruments and cameras, they banter with each other and the rehearsing performers. The surrounding throng is boisterous and rowdy as the momentum of the previous week achieves its peak. The "Ranger" police force urges the crowd to sit, to ensure maximum visibility for the greatest number. Several hundred fire dancers on foot, on stilts, in costumes, and in wheelchairs parade around the Man, inciting the crowd with the promise of imminent conflagration.

An extremely powerful and engaging ritual, the Burning of the Man is also remarkable because of its lack of imposed meaning. The Burn has no meaning, or, more accurately, it has only the meanings imposed on by the individual participants. Perfectly, almost hermetically in keeping with the New Age, Situationist, and artistic ethos that the ritual or act has no meaning beyond itself, the organizers of Burning Man are extremely careful to leave the significance of the burn polysemic, ambiguous, open, and flexible. As participant-author Black (1998) relates it:

> Burning Man is a veritable tar-baby of interpretation. The organizers and many of the participants refuse to assign or acknowledge any specific meaning to what happens at this festival. The event's founder and chief spokesperson Larry Harvey once told a journalist: 'Representing nothing, the Man becomes tabula rasa: any meaning may be projected

onto him.' This viewpoint is one of the few doctrines that Burning Man attendees can agree on. And so it becomes the sum of everyone's individual experience. Tar baby or teflon? Does a phoenix of understanding rise from the ashes, or is that a black hole bending the light, denying certitude and insight into what, if anything, it all means?

This resistance to imposed meaning runs directly counter to traditional organized religion whose denominational foundations are formed on the collectively shared interpretation of the meaning of particular symbol systems. In this sense, Burning Man defies definition as a culture, subculture, or belief, but a congerie of questers who are rooted strongly to no particular belief but openness to many beliefs. The openness invites personalization, which invites relevance. As Mazur and McCarthy (2001, p. 4) put it when explaining the religious significance of popular culture, "Church is church, but rock concerts, for instance, seem to be nearly whatever their followers want them to be, often including experiences of intense spiritual transformation."

"Trying to explain what Burning Man is to someone who has never been to the event is a bit like trying to explain what a particular color looks like to someone who is blind," states the Burning Man website, by way of an introduction and explanation of the event (http://www.burningman.com/whatisburningman/). Another posting by a participant states, "At the end, though your journey to and from Burning Man are finished, you embark on a different journey—forever." As with the spiritualized participants in post-raves (Tramacchi, 2000), in neo-pagan rituals (Pike, 2001), at New Age fairs like Confest (St. John, 2001), and in gatherings like the annual Rainbow Family gatherings (Niman, 1997), the ritual events themselves have a profound significance that many people find ineffable and mysterious.

Shopping for Experiences in the Spiritual Marketplace. On the morning after the Burning of the Man, we witnessed pilgrims rubbing themselves with the ashes of the burnt Man, a ritual reminiscent of both Hinduism and crematory funerary rites (see Figure 17.1). To us, it suggested that participants seek ever deeper, more physical, more profound, and more personal contact with the ritual moment that so moved them the evening before. In keeping with the flavor of the entire event, this sacred polysemy manifests itself through a marketplace phenomenon that we also encountered in psychic and New Age fairs, and that St. John (2001) describes in detail at the Australian ConFest festival (see also Niman, 1997; Pike, 2001, 2004).

This is the sacred theming, the encampment on particular ground and the making it specifically sacred that Burning Na's guiding organization has institutionalized in its provision of "theme camps." Participants at Burning Man both create and simultaneously choose from a vast variety of constructed experiences, many or most of which have the express purpose of providing spiritual insights or transcendent experiences. Black Rock City can be conceptualized as a New Age/neo-pagan mirror image of the spiritual supermarket its residents have encountered in the world. The New

Figure 17.1 Gleaners the morning after the burn.

Age emphasis on Eastern mysticism revealed itself in widespread yoga and meditation sessions offered in Burning Man theme camps. Typically New Age, various forms of massage are also widely offered for free throughout the encampment. Many of the massage camps drew on the human potential movement of the 1960s and 1970s to encourage safe exploration of one's own and others' bodies.

New types of beliefs were also represented. The Burning Man encampment of the Church of Mez became a place to pragmatically discuss not only the benefits of living intentionally, and of following belief systems that are frivolous and playful, but the pragmatics of life extension. As the Church of Mez's website states, "The Church of Mez is a Transhumanist religion. Transhumanism is the belief that through technology it is possible for us to fundamentally change the so-called human condition, and in so doing to transcend the limitations that we take for granted, and transform ourselves into whatever beings we wish to become. . . . Unlike some religions, we believe that life is to be enjoyed. That enjoyment comes from play, from pleasure, and from sharing that play and pleasure with others" (http://www.mezziah.org/church).

Massages, yoga, and meditation are almost always offered in a playful, pleasurable, yet serious (i.e., non-parodic) fashion. However, a variety of interestingly skewed variations on familiar occult and Christian rites such as exorcism, confession, and baptisms are regularly offered. For example, the "Sacred Temple of the Enigmata" offered its own dogma and confession booth, and it featured a new Christian religious text that expounded a story of Jesus stepping in canine excrement. At Burning Man 2002, one theme camp presented a book that detailed, in words and vivid paintings, child abuse at the hands of Catholic clergy from a first-person perspective. As they are at other spiritual gatherings like psychic fairs and New Age festival, Tarot readers, fortunetellers, and other personality readers and prognosticators are abundant. At Burning Man 2003, we interviewed the founders of the "Temple of Boobfoot," who had developed a method of interpreting personality traits from readings of female (and male) breasts. A cursory check of the theme camp manifest suggests no metaphysical ailment or curiosity need go untreated during the pilgrim's sojourn through Burning Man.

Markets and Spiritual Marketplaces. Both Pike (2001) and St. John (2001) describe spiritual marketplaces that were positioned largely in the commercial realm and were contested. For Pike (2001, pp. 74–75), vendors were located in "Merchant's Row" assigned to special places in the neo-pagan camp and were "approached more ambivalently by festival goers." At ConFest, St. John (2001, p. 53) describes how commercial offerings created tensions between festival participants, as some chose to contest "the apolitical frivolity of on-site consumerism."

Burning Man is noteworthy because of the individualization of participation. With very little central organization, participations themselves create a vast spiritual marketplace of offerings and then share these offerings with one another at their own cost (similar to the Rainbow Family gatherings; see Niman, 1997). Like ConFest, neo-pagan and Rainbow Family gatherings, this is not an event of pure harmony, but one where profound differences breed fundamental schisms, where harmony may be one goal among many. Burning Man is a good example of an "alternative cultural heterotopia," as St. John (2001, p. 48) described ConFest, "a matrix of performance zones occupied by variously complementary and competing neo-tribes and identity discourses," a realm of competing discourses that somehow cohere together around a single event.

The reason for this unanticipated coherence, we propound here, is that they are enmeshed in, and to some extent formed by, a consumer culture that celebrates choice as diversity, and that fosters the growth of heterotopic society as a byproduct of a segmentation-driven marketing culture. The resulting events exemplify economies of experience and customization that provide participants with an access to and variety of choices that they use, as our next section details, to experiment with the transformation of self.

Transforming Self and Others

New Therapies, Confessions, Wedding, and Funeral Rituals. Transformative experiences form the core of many of the syncopated rituals that in total create Burning Man alternative cultural heterotopia. At Burning Man, the pursuit of the sacred self is cast in parodic terms as often as it is cast in a therapeutic form that blends healing and play with spirituality. Indeed, we would argue that much of the therapeutic quality of the Burning Man experience lies in its combination of openness and playfulness.

We witnessed several weddings that took place during Burning Man. For some, the bride and groom were nude for the ceremony. At others, they were dressed in wildly expressive garb that riffs on traditional wedding wear. Each of the weddings was marked by a high degree of individual expression and expressive outpourings of emotion. In an interesting turn of events, funerary and memorial rituals have become institutionalized as part of the Burning Man experience through David Best's series of great Temples that he has built since 2000. But those Temples, including 2011's Temple of Transition, always act as an alternative memorial ritual, a way of remembering the dead in a way that is deeply personal, and yet co-constructed by the community. It is both auto (or personalized) and collective, and therein lies much of its semiotic strength. The structure of the building invites deep inscription and evokes empathic, cathartic, therapeutic response in its dwellers. As they contemplate the meaning of others' deaths, many participants find themselves ruminating about the meaning of their own lives. There is a frequently heard saying that "no one returns from Burning Man unchanged." The experiential event is valued and renowned for its transformative abilities, which celebrate and accelerate modern consumer culture's mutability of the self.

The Liminoid Body. The mutability of the self is also manifest in participants' costumes. This garbing is often reinterpreted as an intentionality of being, an expropriation of self-creation away from the institutions of fashion and industry (cf. Thompson and Haytko, 1997), and an expression of larger truths. We asked "Mustard Sally," a long-term attendee, festooned in twisting metal spirals, crepe, and yellow body paint, to tell us about her costume.

Mustard Sally: I like the idea of it not being a thing, that it actually is what reality is.
Interviewer: It being the costume?
Mustard Sally: Yeah. The way I am is the way everything should be and is. And people that are dressed like you should feel really odd and out of place.
Interviewer: Okay [laughs].

"This is who I really am" is a commonly asserted affirmation of the playa self that a pilgrim comes to discover in a week of aesthetically mediated leveling and bonding rituals that draw him or her into intimate association (or in this case, demarcated insider-outsider boundaries) with her fellow travelers. The adoption of pseudonymous but self-revelatory "playa names," similarly, are seen as a chance to reform the self, to choose one's own self and self-representation, at least for a few days per year. The costumes worn by nomads as gifts to one another are effective masks, allowing multiple personae to emerge from the multiphrenic self, harnessing play in the service of self-discovery and self-disclosure, and expressing it in carnal form.

The burning of things, including money, is also highly symbolic of transformation and the revelation of essence. This burning is a literal form of consumption, a wastefulness and lack of environmental sensitivity not unlike the waste for which consumer society is frequently criticized. "Nevada Joe," the creator of a theme camp that burned a lot of diesel fuel argued as follows: "Look, companies dump a ton of stuff, they pollute the Earth all the time, right, but they do it for greed, for money. Yeah, I'm creating my own little environmental disaster right here. I know it. But I'm doing it for a much more important cause, right? I'm doing it for fun" (Burning Man 1999 interview). Nevada Bob is here arguing that his unenvironmental campaign is transformative. It is important because it defies and discharges the rational logic of the marketplace. Like potlatch, it is wasteful consumption that changes self and world by enchanting them both. As with many holidays, the festive behavior at Burning Man is "built in large part on wastrel prodigality, on surplus and abundance, on conspicuous consumption" (Schmidt, 1995, p. 8). It may be "the new American holiday" (Sterling, 1996), but it is a DiY holiday, a holiday not created by Hallmark or Macy's. It is a new holiday that consumers call their own.

Offering further symbols of the liminality of transformative potentiality were the ubiquitous and often inverted clowns, demons, angels (see Figure 17.2), butterflies, and shamans (see Figure 17.3) who appeared often in the guise of witch doctors, magicians, soothsayers, ecstatic drummers, clerics, and the like. Cross-dressing, which St. John (2001) asserts indicates the body's potential as "a site of resistance," is extremely common.

Figure 17.2 Participants costumed as angelic figures.

Figure 17.3 A modern primitive in shamanic garb.

The chance to regress to childhood is another important tool used by participants to emphasize the added malleability of self-present at Burning Man. In this regression equation, playgrounds of diminutive and gigantic scale are scattered throughout Black Rock City. Trampolines, swing sets, life-sized interactive board games, toy boxes, and sports equipment are offered by nomads to one another in theme interactive camps. Doll Camp, a theme camp, makes huge inventories of dolls and actions figures available to participants, who sit, pose, caress, model, and play with dolls—alone and in groups. One of the founders of Doll Camp told us of the way his doll camp had evolved to take on elements that blended humor and spirituality with Burning Man's participatory culture:

'Action Man':   Porn stars are one kind of ultimate action figure, but so is a guru, a cult leader, right? A spiritual action figure. So we decided to start out own cult. And we have a guru we just made up and we have people contribute dogma to our cult. And once we get enough dogma we can start manipulating the world. 'Pigneesh' is our guru, over there (smiling widely, points to an image on an altar).

Interviewer: Is this non-serious or does it have a serious side to it?

'Action Man':   Everything always has a serious side to it. (Interview, Burning Man 2003)

Although it might seem strange at first, Action Man's notion that sexuality, play, and spirituality are interrelated is common at Burning Man, and in a range of other popular New Age belief systems, such as the human potential movement (including Werner Erhard's est) and Tantric Yoga (for an example closer to home, see also Gould, 1991). At Burning Man, sacred play includes human sexuality. "Sacred sexuality" is preached and practiced in many of the theme camps. Consider, for example, the 2004 theme camp called "TempleWhore," whose description reads: "TempleWhores are historically recognized and defiled hellions who bliss ya out and open the doors to the vault of heaven. TempleWhore camp is an outgrowth of our Seattle gang, and we will provide massage, Reiki, herbal teas, and hotsauce, all served or bartered with a Kali-smile" (from burningman.com website). Another camp, "Camp Cunt," was founded on a mission to reclaim the ancient and sacred meaning of the currently defiled word "Cunt."

Similarly, consider the description of the long-standing theme cam, the Temple of Atonement: "Black Rock city's premier BDSM [bondage, domination, sadism and masochism] camp. Take part in our sanctuary of decadence as we pursue transformation, education and personal development amidst our dark fantasies. . . . TOA is a complete 2500 square foot sanctuary and dungeon with wall-to-wall carpet, lots of SM equipment & a chill space. It is a place where we make our (& your) dark fantasies a reality." Sexuality and gender are publicly problematized and communally celebrated. Nudity is common. Public displays of hetero- and homosexual affection abound, and, as this fieldnote excerpt demonstrates, alternative forms of sexual expression are almost unavoidable.

> After a wandering night that started with shots of Kahlua, we were walking back to our campsite with X and Y. We were turning the intersection before our campsite at Daguerrodrome when suddenly, from out of the darkness, came a she-male of awesome proportions (who we later discovered was named "She-Ra"). S/he was at least 6'1", impressively muscle-bound with huge thick, chiseled arms, clad in black leather chaps, with large fully exposed round breasts and an equally impressive man-thing dangling down between his/her thick, well-defined legs. Immediately commanding our full attention, s/he rapidly approached us, scanning us, raising her whip. John and I cowered and instinctually held back, and poor X (a Burning Man first timer) was her target. S/he commanded him to bend over and good-naturedly, he did. S/he began by stroking his behind with the whip, then slapped him with it, calling him "Slut!" She called him a few other choice names, increasing the power and venom of each stroke, and by the time she reached "Bitch!" the whipping sound of leather hitting X's pants almost made my eyes tear. With those huge biceps, s/he packed quite a whallop. As s/he angrily calling X a "Cunt!" you could see the real pain on X's good-humoring face. (Fieldnotes, Burning Man 2003)

Burning Man is a liminal zone on almost any level that invites self-reassignment, as the story of our close encounter with "She-Ra," a transsexual pilgrim in a stage of gender reassignment, exemplified (She-Ra is also an entrepreneur who has an extremely successful Internet web-page). Our encounter shows how the sexuality, experimentation, and liminality of the place are almost unavoidable. As the experiential immediacy of choice was emphasized in the last section, the carnality of embodiment is the focus of the mutable self, a self whose boundaries can dissolve quickly in the crucible of Burning Man's liminoid zone.

Defining Autothemataludicization

Although the term is a tad unwieldy, we believe that, somewhat like the infamous Mary Poppins tongue-twister supercalifragilisticexpialidocious, whose constituent parts signify (somewhat like German words) a particular thought, namely, "atoning for educability through delicate beauty," the word signifies an important phenomenon or process that no other social scientific term yet does. Autothemataludicization describes a process in which meaningful experiences are self-created (auto as in "autobiography" or "auto-erotic") not only by individuals but also by collectives. The term "themata" relates historically to the administrative divisions established in the mid-seventh century after the Muslim conquests of Byzantine territory. These initial themes were military in nature and represented a form of governance of an area of land by the military units that had conquered them. In our conception, themata resonates with the idea of a particular area of land (we also include online spaces as well as intellectual real estate in our definitional domain) being encamped on and taken over. It also relates to themes as broad, general ideas, messages, or morals, as in the notion of theme parks or themed flagship brandstores (see, e.g., Gottdeiner, 1997; Kozinets et al., 2002). Although the past of themata dealt with warfare, the next and final term, "ludic," indicates that the process we are considering deals with fantasy, play, and the boundless human imagination.

Thus, our term autothemataludicization refers to *a contemporary process in which consumers collectively create of their own initiative, customized, meaningful, and playful spiritual experiences in a particular location, following some particular, and likely proscribed theme.* These ideas demonstrate how an overarching event like Burning Man can suggest and manage a coordinated set of individual themed camps, each of which individualizes and shares a playful spiritual expression.

Participation in Playful Spiritualized Spectacle

Clowns originate as sacred characters. Bast, the Egyptian cat-headed goddess, was a patron of play and playfulness. Games of changes have sacred oracular origins. The spirit of play consumes us still; the playfully spiritual is all around us. In a society where religion becomes popular culture (O'Guinn and Belk, 1989), it should come as little surprise that popular culture becomes religion (Kozinets, 2001; Mazur and McCarthy, 2001; Porter and Maclaren, 1999). For, as Mazur and McCarthy (2001, p. 12) explain, for many Americans " 'religion' is identified with institutional religion, and it is precisely their resistance to those institutions that makes such things as music, food, sports, and film attractive alternative sites for meaning making."

This meaning-making tendency takes on enormous fecundity in the barren spaces of the Black Rock desert, as a fantastic array of parareligious forms with popular culture roots branch out and intertwine. Elmo is crucified. Spock Mountain Research Labs forms their endlessly logical religion on a Star Trek character. McDonald's becomes McSatan's Beastro. Photoshopped Absolut Ads parody every aspect of the event. The ancient Wheel of Fortune becomes the basis of a lewd gameshow. Religion itself is parodied as a type of random, chance, set of spiritual beliefs (see Figures 17.4 and 17.5). Canadian hockeymen battle it out in a full-scale rink in the middle of the Nevada desert. Nude Twister is a popular game. The Thunderdome, based on the Mad Max movie series, enacts simulated bloodsport to the thrill of onlookers. Every aspect of culture and popular culture is contained and parodied. Burning Man as it is known could not exist if it

Figure 17.4   A theme camp's religious parody.

Figure 17.5   An anonymous parody of religious prayer displayed in center camp.

did not partake of and invert ordinary, mainstream society. Like all New Age religions, it exists and gains meaning in opposition to the dominant belief systems and spiritual systems of its day, but it uses them in a manner that is perhaps most overt of all. As surely as it takes over the space of public land, the imaginary communities of popular culture are co-opted.

Figure 17.6   The Temple of Honor, 2003.

Jesters and Jokers. Devils, angels, and interesting hybrids also populate the event. Sacred clowns of many sorts pervade the festival, and, relatedly, there are manifold expressions of political parody and calls to action as well. In 2003, a complex piece of sound and light art combined a projected visual image of President George W. Bush's gigantic head (like an Orwellian Big Brother image) onto he billowing cloth of a dome tent. The head was accompanied by clips from Bush's speeches that were altered, according to the artist, "to take the lies that were said and splice them together to make them say the truth" (Interview, 2003). Some of the many sayings it offered, in George Bush's own voice, include: "God will help the American economy," "Your enemy is running your country," and "Innocent Iraqi women and children will be killed." Another artwork vividly displayed George W. Bush as the Antichrist 666. In 2004, a major installation depicted President Bush and his cabinet as the Mad Hatter and his cohorts from Alice in Wonderland, all spinning in a mad teacup party. Another installation piece, glowing green in the middle of the desert, was the Statue of Liberty locked in a cage. In the Temple of Honor in 2003, there were many memorials dedicated to innocent Iraqis killed in the invasion (see Figure 17.6). Like good art, these examples use the image of culture to critique it. United by the context of the spiritual meanings of the event, they appear as mobilizing forces in a religiously charged movement.

Undermining the status quo by using its core images, the spectacle serves an authentically self-expressive function that many have propounded is missing from traditional religion and spirituality, which emphasizes rationalized, conformist values like obedience, discipline, and self-denial over creativity, innovation, experimentation, self-expression, and authenticity. The theme of the festival in 2003 year was "Beyond Belief," and many installations created an Alice in Wonderland effect that encouraged people to playfully question their beliefs. That year, Zachary Coffin's "The Temple of Gravity" was an engineering and logistical marvel. It presented a pair of crossed metal pieces from which hung several slabs of granite ranging from 15,500 to 18,000 pounds each, dangling from chains (see Figure 17.3). These megaton slabs swayed as pilgrims climbed and then danced on them to the theme's rap and rave music. Writer Brain Doherty (2004, p. 180) reflects meaningfully on the significance of the artwork: "As its name suggested, it made you contemplate the core forces in this universe, weight and solidity and their undeniable reality—and the equally undeniable reality that we are clever enough to defeat these forces, to keep the tons of stone suspended for out contemplation and play. It all added up to a mighty victory for the spirit of mankind."

As with the Temple of Gravity, this artwork often incorporates ingenious technology, such that stationary sculptures of swimmers stroke to life under the influence of stroboscopes, or musical tones emanate from invisible lyre strings as pilgrims move their hands through empty space or laser beams trace out the shape of the Man overhead, for the amusement of any watchers from

Figure 17.7   The Temple of Gravity.

the sky. Humble works are present as well, from elegant postings of poetry, through terra cotta warrior-type battalions of statuettes, to the occasional nonfunctional phone booth or drinking fountain. One phone booth offered a direct line to God (usually busy). These many examples demonstrate not only how the serious and playful intersect, but also how they are co-created in the intersection between managed production and communally co-created encampment. The next section of our chapter draws some conclusions about how these ideas fit together into our conception of autothemataludicization and how they can further advance our thinking about the nature of spirituality in contemporary consumer culture.

Re-enchanting a Disenchanted Consumer Consciousness

In a society where much religion is seen as divisive, distant, and ossified, Burning Man provides a way to recharge self and belief. The state of flux and encampment that typifies the process of autothemataludicization translates well into both Bey's (1991) terminology of "temporary autonomous zones" of resistance to authority and Jenkin's (1992) notions of involved consumers as "poachers" on corporately copyrighted textual territories. As with McKay's (1998, p. 2) conjecturing of do-it-yourself (DiY) culture as "a kind of 1990s counterculture" in which youthful expressions of resistance combine "party and protest," Burning Man combines parody with art, performance with resistance, and inversion with expression. The "party/protest pleasure/politics fusion" (St. John, 2001, p. 51) combines political activism and personal growth into a single experiential and experimental endeavor. In the service of re-enchanting the world, individual and tribal identities are exalted, and spirituality is decommodified.

One of the key processes enabling and establishing these sacred fusions is autothemataludicization, the contemporary process of collective consumer co-creation that involves customized, meaningful, and playful spiritual experiences manifesting in a particular location, following some particular and likely proscribed theme. Through autothemataludicization, we may understand better how identity, ritual, and self-transformation— themes often visited by consumer researchers interested in consumer culture and community (e.g., Kozinets, 2001; Schouten and McAlexander, 1995; Thompson and Haytko, 1997)—can be theorized as responses to consumer culture. The essence of autothemataludicization seems to be a suspension of the routines and guiding social logics of everyday life into a mythical realm where higher-order questions of meaning, self, and existence can be pondered and, at least momentarily, suspended. We can see the hallmarks of its creative communal customization across many consumption experiences. For example, Harley riders experience "a spirituality derived in part from a sense of riding as a transcendental departure" (Schouten and McAlexander, 1995, p. 50); Star Trek fans see the show as "a myth, a sacred text, a type of holy relic" (Kozinets, 2001, p. 81); Newton user groups are filled with "supernatural, religious, and magical motifs" (Muñiz and Schau, 2005, p. 745); and social media and technology users tend to have a history of utopian, religious, and spiritual communal formation (Davis, 1998; Kozinets, 2008).

Many scholars and thinkers from a vast variety of disciplines have argued that consumer culture withers the human soul (see, e.g., Cushman, 1995; Debord, 1995[1967]; McKibben, 1990). Revealed by our own powerful spiritual experiences, and the revelation of self-transformation by informant after informant, Burning Man offers and delivers a mystical moment ingredient of the first order that is largely, but certainly not entirely, absent from both wider, secular consumer society (e.g., Ritzer, 1999) and most people's experiences of organized religion. Although choice, the mutable self, and popular culture are distinct consumer culture themes contained, and even embraced, by the Burning Man event, the event transcends them, flips them on their heads, and reveals the paradox within them. It does this by linking deep play and consumer co-creation with a dialectics of reenchantment: this is the essence of autothematizaton, its driver.

However, autothematization is also wider than this. It also is fueled by the importance of marginality, liminality, stigma, sacrifice, and struggle. Positioned at the margin, Burning Man gives consumers not only what they want but also much of what they do not want. The structure of the themata is constraining, as are the boundaries of communal sacrifice and display. Often the initially undesired is present in the unbounded physical, natural being, which is positioned as the literal ground of what is real, true, and authentic, and it can signal and actually contain considerable danger (cf. Arnould and Price, 1993), as do the many modes of freed, expressive, individualistic social and human beings (cf. Brown et al., 2003; Schouten and McAlexander, 1995; St. John, 2001).

Burning Man's "unconsumers" assert that the event shocks them out of their normal daily consciousness, which we term here a *consumer consciousness*. The notion, originating from Weber's work on rationalization, that modern consumer consciousness is, to some large extent, rationalized and "McDonalidized" has been an underlying theme of much sociological, critical, and consumer research critique which asserts that the end result is consumer emptiness and disenchantment, a form of soullessness (e.g., Cushman, 1995; Firat and Dholakia, 1998; Firat and Venkatesh, 1995; Ritzer, 1999). To ameliorate this state, consumers turn to extraordinary experiences like energizing natural retreats (Arnould, Price, and Otnes, 1999), deep play (Kozinets et al., 2004), or communally constructing mysteries and enchantment from commercial texts (Brown, Kozinets, and Sherry 2003; Kozinets 2001; Muñiz and Schau 2005) to re-enchant their worlds. Lately, these consumer culture theorists have noted that commercial offerings have been rejected, or their aura of commercialism bracketed through subculture and ritual, in the service of re-enchanting the world, adding back the transformative possibility of authenticity and mystery, portending a shift in consumer consciousness.

We have portrayed the Burning Man experience in terms of a pilgrimage-like search of the sacred. We imagine Burning Man to represent a flight from dullardism, through a re-engagement with the sacred, to a reconnection with paradoxical consciousness. Like a memetic virus disguised as part of the cultural immune system, this paradoxical consciousness works from within consumer culture. Autothemataludicization plays an important focusing and decentering (from the center of consumer consciousness) role in this transformation. As related in the findings sections above, the process of autothemataludicization takes the model of consumer choice and applies it to the notion of belief—joining a variety of sacred temples, partaking in the rituals of varieties of New Age and neo-pagan experience—but it limits consumer choice itself. The theme dictates. The community dictates. The proscriptions are a form of scripture and of stricture, and they must be followed. And, although one can choose to be or become almost anything at Burning Man, one cannot choose to become a typical consumer. The event's edicts and social norms demand participation and expression. Autothemataludiciation demands not only compliance, but that one takes the events into one's own mattering, that one invest one's self into it, breathe personal and communal life into its meaning, and, perhaps most remarkably of all, *have fun doing it*.

Similarly, the costumes, playa names, new identities, and rituals of transformation treat self as a highly mutable construct, as it is in consumer culture. But these changes are cast at Burning Man as a type of unfolding of an actual or true underlying self, a paradox not lost on participants. When all fashion and ritual are socially constructed as social constructions, revealing the hidden corporate puppeteers of the systems of consumer culture control, the quest for a truer self becomes self-involving rather than merely self-absorbing, a site of endless experimentation with true self rather than never-ending simulation of self.

Accelerated far past its normally supersonic speed, the pace of self-creation rapidly reaches a critical mass that reveals an underlying profundity, a calm center of enchantment within the consumer's normally rationalized hurricane of doing and being. The engagement of popular culture images, ideas, and icons in the context of the autothemataludicized experience involves inversion, reversion, critique, and parody. Like Macbeth's witches, participants at Burning Man combine in a seething cultural cauldron an ear of Spock with an altered logo and a clipped Bush phrase to create an alternate mirror-world, a funhouse version of mainstream popular culture that permits a diving beneath its bubbling superficial surface, a conscious deep drink from the intoxicating mythical brew it has become.

Choose from a million beliefs, but you cannot choose to be a consumer; change yourself a million times in a week while finding your true self; celebrate the million milieu of the mainstream as a mythic cultural realities, but worship them with inversion and parody. Step out and step aside, step up, then step inside. Make your own world: that is the imperative, the injunction of the autothemataludicization challenge. Play with your reality. Make your reality. With guiding themes and the cushioning of communal involvement, create something radical and expressive and new. Finally, the moral of the theme grows simpler and even more powerful: make reality. At this level, Burning Man's autothemataludicization is simultaneously a sacred playground and a serious lesson. At this point, in our final analysis, it looks a lot like life itself.

REFERENCES

Arnould, Eric J., and Linda L. Price. 1993. "River Magic: Extraordinary Experience and the Extended Service Encounter." *Journal of Consumer Research* 20 (June): 24–45.

Arnould, Eric J., Linda L. Price, and Cele Otnes. 1999. "Making Consumption Magic: A Study of White-Water River Rafting." *Journal of Contemporary Ethnography* 28 (February): 33–67.

Belk, Russell, and Janeen Costa. 1998. "The Mountain Man Myth: A Contemporary Consumer Fantasy." *Journal of Consumer Research* 25 (3): 218–240.

Belk, Russell, and Gulnur Tumbat. 2002. *The Cult of Mac.* Videography presented at the 2002 ACR Film Festival.

Belk, Russell, Melanie Wallendorf, and John F. Sherry, Jr. 1989. "The Sacred and Profane in Consumer Behavior: Theory on the Odyssey." *Journal of Consumer Research* 16 (1): 1–38.

Bey, Hakim. 1991. *T. A. Z.* Brooklyn, NY: Autonomedia.

Black, D. S. 1998. "Burning Man as Ephemeropolis and the Refusal of Meaning." Paper presented at the North American Interdisciplinary Conference on

Environment and Community, University of Nevada, Reno, February 20, 1998. Available at http:// www.spiralgirl.com/ARCHIVE/dsBlackEssay.html.

Brand, Stewart. 1999. *The Clock of the Long Now*. London: Phoenix.

Brill, Louis, and Lady Bee. 2003. "The Art of Burning Man." *Leonardo* 36 (5): 339–370.

Brooks, David. 2004., *On Paradise Drive*. New York: Simon and Schuster.

Brown, Stephen, Robert Kozinets, and John F. Sherry, Jr. 2003. "Teaching Old Brands New Tricks: Retro Branding and the Revival of Brand Meaning." *Journal of Marketing* 67 (3): 19–33.

Campbell, Colin. 1989. *The Romantic Ethic and the Spirit of Modern Consumerism*. Oxford: Basil Blackwell.

Csordas, Thomas J. 1997., *The Sacred Self: A Cultural Phenomenology of Charismatic Healing*. Berkley, CA: University of California Press.

Cushman, Philip. 1995. *Constructing the Self, Constructing America*. Boston, MA: Addison-Wesley.

Davis, Erik. 1998. *Techgnosis: Myth, Magic and Mysticism in the Age of Information*. New York: Three Rivers Press.

Debord, Guy (1995 [1967]). *The Society of the Spectacle*. Trans. Donald Nicholson-Smith. New York: Zone Books.

Doherty, Brian. 2004. *This Is Burning Man*. New York: Little, Brown and Co.

Ferguson, Marilyn. 1980. *The Aquarian Conspiracy*. Los Angeles, CA: J. P. Tarcher.

Firat, A. Fuat and Nikolesh Dholakia. 1998. *Consuming People: From Political Economy to Theaters of Consumption*. London: Routledge.

Firat, A. Fuat, and Alladi Venkatesh. 1995. "Liberatory Postmodernism and the Reenchantment of Consumption." *Journal of Consumer Research* 22 (December): 239–267.

Gottdeiner, Mark. 1997. *The Theming of America*. Boulder, CO: Westview.

Gould, Stephen J. 1991. "The Self-Manipulation of My Pervasive, Perceived Vital Energy Through Product Use: An Introspective-Praxis Perspective." *Journal of Consumer Research* 18 (September): 194–207.

Hetherington, Kevin. 2000. *New Age Travellers*. London: Cassell.

Jenkins, Henry. 1992. *Textual Poachers*. New York: Routledge, Chapman and Hall.

Kozinets, Robert V. 2001. "Utopian Enterprise: Articulating the Meanings of *Star Trek*'s Culture of Consumption." *Journal of Consumer Research* 28 (June): 67–88.

Kozinets, Robert V. 2002a. "The Field Behind the Screen: Using Netnography for Marketing Research in Online Communities." *Journal of Marketing Research* 39 (February): 61–72.

Kozinets, Robert V. 2002b. "Can Consumers Escape the Market? Emancipatory Illuminations from Burning Man." *Journal of Consumer Research* 28 (June): 67–88.

Kozinets, Robert V. 2008. "Technology/Ideology: How Ideological Fields Influence Consumers' Technology Narratives." *Journal of Consumer Research* 34 (April): 864–881.

Kozinets, Robert V., and Jay M. Handelman. 2004. "Adversaries of Consumption: Consumer Movements, Activism, and Ideology." *Journal of Consumer Research* 31 (December): 691–704.

Kozinets, Robert V., and John F. Sherry, Jr. 2004. "Dancing on Common Ground: Exploring the Sacred at Burning Man." In *Rave Culture and Religion*, edited by Graham St. John, 287–303. London: Routledge.

Kozinets, Robert V., John F. Sherry, Jr., Diana Storm, Adam Duhachek, Krittinee Nuttavuthisit, and Benét DeBerry-Spence. 2004. "Ludic Agency and Retail Spectacle." *Journal of Consumer Research* 31 (December): 658–672.

Kozinets, Robert V., John F. Sherry, Jr., Diana Storm, Adam Duhachek, Krittinee Nuttavuthisit, and Benét DeBerry-Spence. 2002. "Themed Flagship Brand Stores in the New Millennium: Theory, Practice, Prospects." *Journal of Retailing* 78 (Spring): 17–29.

Kreuter, Holly. 2002. *Drama in the Desert*. Berkeley, CA: Raised Barn Press.

Martin, Brett A. S. 2004. "Using the Imagination: Consumer Evoking and Thematizing of the Fantastic Imaginary." *Journal of Consumer Research* 31 (June): 136–149.

Mazur, Eric Michael, and Kate McCarthy. 2001. "Introduction: Finding Religion in American Popular Culture." In *God in the Details*, edited by Eric Michael Mazur and Kate McCarthy. New York: Routledge, 1–16.

McKay, George. 1998. "DiY Culture: Notes Toward an Intro." In *DiY Culture: Party and Protest in Nineties Britain*, edited by George McKay, 1–53. London: Verso.

McKibben, Bill. 1990. *The End of Nature*. New York: Anchor Books.

Miller, Daniel. 1987. *Material Culture and Mass Consumption*. Oxford: Basil Blackwell.

Muñiz, Albert M. and Thomas C. O'Guinn. 2001. "Brand Community." *Journal of Consumer Research* 27 (March): 412–432.

Muñiz, Albert M., Jr., and Hope Jensen Schau. 2005. "Religiosity in the Abandoned Apple Newton Brand Community." *Journal of Consumer Research* 31 (March): 737–747.

Niman, Michael I. 1997. *People of the Rainbow: A Nomadic Utopia*. Knoxville, TN: University of Tennessee Press.

O'Guinn, Thomas C. 1991. "Touching Greatness: The Central Midwest Barry Manilow Fan Club." In *Highways and Buyways*, edited by Russell W. Belk, 102–111. Provo, UT: Association for Consumer Research.

O'Guinn, Thomas, and Russell Belk. 1989. "Heaven on Earth: Consumption at Heritage Village USA." *Journal of Consumer Research* 16 (2): 227–238.

Pike, Sarah. 2001. *Earthly Bodies, Magical Selves: Contemporary Pagans and the Search for Community*. Berkeley, CA: University of California Press.

Pike, Sarah. 2004. *New Age and Neopagan Religions in America*. New York: Columbia University Press.

Pine, B. Joseph, and Kames H. Gilmore. 1999. *The Experience Economy*. Boston, MA: HBS Press.

Porter, Jennifer E., and Darcee L. Maclaren, eds. 1999. *Star Trek and Sacred Ground*. Albany, NY: SUNY Press.

Ritzer, George. 1999. *Enchanting a Disenchanted World: Revolutionizing the Means of Consumption*. Thousand Oaks, CA: Pine Oaks/Sage.

Schmidt, Leigh Eric. 1995. *Consumer Rites*. Princeton, NJ: Princeton University Press.

Schouten, John W., and James H. McAlexander. 1995. "Subcultures of Consumption: An Ethnography of the New Bikers." *Journal of Consumer Research* 22 (June): 43–61.

Sherry, John F., Jr. 1990. "A Sociocultural Analysis of a Midwestern American Flea Market." *Journal of Consumer Research* 17 (June): 13–30.

Sherry, John F., Jr., and Robert V. Kozinets. 2004. "Sacred Iconography in Secular Space: Altars, Alters and Alterity at the Burning Man Project." In *Contemporary Consumption Rituals: A Research Anthology*, edited by Cele Otnes and Tina Lowry, 291–311. Mahwah, NJ: Lawrence Erlbaum.

Sherry, John F., Jr., and Robert V. Kozinets. 2007. "Comedy of the Commons: Nomadic Spirituality at Burning Man." In *Consumer Culture Theory, Vol. 11, of Research in Consumer Behavior*, edited by Russell Belk and John F. Sherry, Jr., 119–147. Oxford: Elsevier.

Slater, Donald R. 1997. *Consumer Culture and Modernity*. Cambridge: Polity Press.

St. John, Graham. 2001. "Alternative Cultural Heterotopia and the Liminoid Body: Beyond Turner at ConFest." *Australian Journal of Anthropology* 12 (April): 47–66.

Sterling, Bruce. 1996. "Greetings from Burning Man." *Wired* 4 (November): 196–207.

Taylor, Charles. 2002. *Varieties of Religion Today*. Cambridge, MA: Harvard University Press.

Thompson, Craig J., and Diana L. Haytko. 1997. "Speaking of Fashion: Consumers' Uses of Fashion Discourses and the Appropriation of Countervailing Cultural Meanings." *Journal of Consumer Research* 24 (June): 15–42.

Thompson, Craig J., and Maura Troester. 2002. "Consumer Value Systems in the Age of Postmodern Fragmentation: The Case of the Natural Health Microculture." *Journal of Consumer Research* 28 (March): 550–571.

Tramacchi, Des. 2000. "Field Tripping: Psychedelic *Communitas* and Ritual in the Australian Bush." *Journal of Contemporary Religion* 15 (May): 201–213.

York, Michael. 1995. *The Emerging Network*. Lanham, MD: Rowman and Littlefield.

Contributors

Gary Bamossy has a Ph.D. from the University of Utah and is a professor at Georgetown University. Prior to joining Georgetown, he was a professor of marketing at the University of Utah and the Vrije Universiteit, Amsterdam. He has published widely in the field of globalization and consumer culture and is coeditor with Janeen Costa of *Marketing in a Multicultural World: Ethnicity, Nationalism and Cultural Identity*. He has coauthored many bestselling marketing textbooks that have been translated around the globe and has published articles in the *Academy of Management Journal, Journal of Consumer Psychology, Journal of Business Research*, and others.

Russell V. Belk is the Kraft Foods Canada Chair of Marketing at the Schulich School of Business at York University. He is past president of the Association for Consumer Research and the International Association of Marketing and Development and is a fellow in the Association for Consumer Research. He has received the Paul D. Converse Award, the Sheth Foundation/*Journal of Consumer Research* Award for Long Term Contribution to Consumer Research, two Fulbright Fellowships, and honorary professorships on four continents. He is the co-founder of the Association for Consumer Research Film Festival, the Consumer Behavior Odyssey, and the Consumer Culture Theory Conference. He had published more than 500 books, articles, chapters, papers, and videos. His research involves the meanings of possessions, collecting, gift-giving, and materialism and is often cultural, visual, qualitative, and interpretive.

Stefania Borghini is an associate professor of marketing at Università Bocconi, Milan. Her research interests are related to consumers' behaviour in the marketplace and their connections with brands and retail spaces in particular. Her current projects are focusing in particular on children's and women's behaviour. In her studies she adopts a consumer culture perspective and privileges ethnographic methods. She has published her works in books and academic journals such as *Journal of Consumer Research, Journal of Marketing, Journal of Retailing, Journal of*

Advertising, Journal of Business Research, Industrial Marketing Management, Journal of Business & Industrial Marketing, and *Journal of Knowledge Management.*

Alan Bradshaw teaches and learns at Royal Holloway, University of London.

Stephen Brown is a professor of marketing research at the Ulster Business School, Northern Ireland. Best known for *Postmodern Marketing* (Routledge, 1995), he has written numerous books including *Free Gift Inside* (Capstone, 2003), *The Marketing Code* (Marshall Cavendish, 2006), and *Wizard: Harry Potter's Brand Magic* (Cyan, 2005).

Margo Buchanan-Oliver is a professor of marketing and a director of the Centre of Digital Enterprise (CODE) at The University of Auckland. Her current research focuses on socio-cultural perceptions of digital technologies, the politics of the body, and the semiotics of representation. She has published in leading marketing journals and is a frequent peer reviewer.

Robin Croft is a reader in marketing at the University of Bedfordshire in England. He has written extensively around a range of topics, mostly involving interpersonal communication: in politics, the arts, and in general discourse. More recently he has been exploring how powerful elites in medieval and early modern Britain used popular narratives to achieve commercial, spiritual, and political objectives. At the same time he has been studying how 21st-century tools of person-to-person communication, particularly social media, are forcing brands and consumers back into earlier narrative-based structures.

Catherine Dolan is a Fellow of Green Templeton College and a University Lecturer in the Marketing, Culture, and Society Program at the University of Oxford. She is an anthropologist specializing in the cultural and political economy of markets, particularly in sub-Saharan Africa. She has written extensively on the intersections between markets and contemporary moralities, focusing on practices of corporate social responsibility, alternative trade, and ethical consumption. She is currently engaged in a research program examining the relationship between market-based approaches to development and women's economic empowerment.

Mara Einstein is the author *Brands of Faith: Marketing Religion in a Commercial Age* (Routledge, 2007), a critique of promoting religion in today's consumer-oriented culture. This title was named a CHOICE Outstanding Academic Text in 2008. Dr. Einstein has been working in or writing about the media industry for the past twenty years. She has enjoyed stints as an executive at NBC, MTV Networks, and major advertising agencies, working on such accounts as Miller Lite, Uncle Ben's, and Dole Foods. Her first book, *Media Diversity: Economics, Ownership and the FCC* (Lawrence Erlbaum Associates, 2004), was the cause for much debate when research from this work was used by the FCC to redefine the media ownership rules. In addition, Dr. Einstein has written for *Newsday* and *Broadcasting & Cable* as well as having her work appear in academic journals and edited texts. Her new book, *Compassion, Inc.: How Corporate America Blurs the Line Between What We Buy, Who We Are and Those We Help*, is being published by the University of California Press and will be released in April 2012. This work examines the growing trend of promoting and selling consumer products as a means to fund social causes and effective social change. Dr. Einstein is an Associate Professor at Queens College and an independent marketing consultant.

Stephen Gould is a professor of marketing in the Zicklin School of Business, Baruch College, The City University of New York. He has published numerous articles in such outlets as the *Journal of Consumer Research, Psychological Review, Journal of Business Ethics, Journal of International Business Studies, Marketing Theory, Consumption, Markets and Culture, Journal of Business Research,* and *American Journal of Preventive Medicine*, among others. In particular, his work is informed by his lifelong spiritual quest in its personal, sociocultural, and transpersonal dimensions. He is especially grateful to each and every person who has shared anything at all with him in this pursuit.

Mary Johnstone-Louis is a doctoral candidate based in the Marketing, Culture and Society Program of Saïd Business School, University of Oxford. Her research interests include advertising and consumption in emerging economies and the interplay between religion and the market. She is a Green Templeton College Management Scholar and an Economic and Social Research Council Scholar for the United Kingdom.

Elif Izberk-Bilgin is an assistant professor of marketing and holds a B.A. in Sociology from Boğaziçi University in Istanbul, Turkey, an M.B.A. in Marketing and International Business, and a Ph.D. from University of Illinois-Chicago. Her research focuses on consumer activism, Islamic marketing, and sociological aspects of consumerism in emerging countries. Dr. Izberk-Bilgin's research has been published in *Journal of Academy of Marketing Science, Consumption, Markets and Culture, Advances in Consumer Research, Developments in Marketing Science,* and *Frontiers of Entrepreneurship Research*. She also has book chapters in *McDonaldization: The Reader, Oxford Handbook of Happiness,* and *Beyond Hofstede: Culture Frameworks for Global Marketing and Management.*

Richard Kedzior is a doctoral candidate at the Hanken School of Economics in Helsinki, Finland. As a visiting scholar at the University of Arizona in Tucson and the Schulich School of Business in Toronto, Canada, Richard developed a keen interest in consumer culture theory and pursed a research program that is focusing on the materiality of consumption. In his netnographic dissertation, he investigates the nature of digital materiality as experienced by digital denizens of a virtual world.

Robert V. Kozinets is a globally recognized expert on social media marketing. He is an award-winning professor who has won top teaching honors at both the Kellogg School of Management in Chicago and the Schulich School of Business in Toronto. He has authored more than 80 research publications, including many in the world's top marketing journals, a textbook, and two books. He is frequently cited in the international press and has been quoted or featured in the *New York Times*, *Chicago Tribune*, *Newsweek*, Germany's *Handelsblatt*, Brazil's *Bites Magazine*, Canada's *National Post*, New Zealand's *The Independent*, Australia's *Boss Magazine*, and on the *Discovery Channel* and the *CBS National News*. He is also an accomplished change agent supporting global organizations such as Amex, Merck, eBay, HSBC, Campbell's Soup, Valio, Nissan, and Sony. An anthropologist by training, he is a professor of marketing at York University's Schulich School of Business, where he is also chair of the marketing department. He is also an affiliate faculty member at MIT. His feed is available as kozinets on Twitter. Brandthroposophy, his popular blog on marketing and social media, is available at www.kozinets.net.

Pauline Maclaran is a professor of marketing and consumer research at Royal Holloway, University of London. Pauline's research interests focus on cultural aspects of contemporary consumption. She has co-edited various books, including *Marketing and Feminism: Current Issues and Research*, *Critical Marketing: Defining the Field*, and the *Handbook of Marketing Theory*. She is also co-editor in Chief of *Marketing Theory*, a journal that promotes alternative and critical perspectives in marketing and consumer behaviour.

Diego Rinallo is Associate Professor of Marketing and Consumer Culture at Euromed Management, Marseille. Previously, he was Assistant Professor of Marketing at Bocconi University, Milan, which also granted his Ph.D. in Business Administration and Management, and Visiting Scholar at the Schulich School of Business, Toronto, and the University of Wisconsin-Madison. His research interests include consumer culture, fashion, masculinities, magic and spirituality; critical perspectives on advertising; and trade shows, fashion shows and other marketing events. His work has been published in *Journal of Marketing*, *Journal* *of Business Ethics, Journal of Business Research, Industrial Marketing Management* and other international academic outlets. He is also the author of a textbook on marketing events and a forthcoming volume for Oxford University Press on the role played by trade shows in the globalising knowledge economy.

Hope Jensen Schau is an associate professor of marketing and holds the Gary M. Munsinger Chair in Entrepreneurship and Innovation at the Eller College of Management, University of Arizona. She earned her Ph.D. from the University of California, Irvine. Her research focuses on the impact of technology on marketplace relationships, branding, identity-salient consumption practices, and collaborative consumption. Professor Schau has published in *Journal of Consumer Research, Journal of Marketing, Journal of Retailing, Journal of Advertising, Journal of Macromarketing,* and *Business Horizons*.

Linda Scott is a professor of marketing at Saïd Business School, University of Oxford. She has written extensively on cultural issues related to advertising and consumption. She is on the board of the Advertising Educational Foundation in New York and is the editor of *Advertising & Society Review*. Her current research interests focus on women's empowerment in emerging markets and changing symbol systems in the globalizing consumer culture.

John F. Sherry, Jr., Raymond W. & Kenneth G. Herrick Professor of Marketing and Department Chair, joined the Notre Dame faculty in 2005, after two decades at Northwestern University. He is an anthropologist who studies brand strategy, experiential consumption, and aesthetics. He is a Fellow of the American Anthropological Association as well as the Society for Applied Anthropology. Sherry's work appears in numerous journal articles and book chapters; he has edited six books. He has won awards for his scholarly work and poetry. He is an avid flatwater paddler and is still trying to perfect his seventeen foot jump shot.

Darach Turley is adjunct professor of marketing at Dublin City University. His research interests focus primarily on the relationship between consumer behaviour and human mortality with particular emphasis on how goods are used to negotiate grief and bereavement. In 2007 he was made a Fulbright scholar.

Index

An environmentally friendly book printed and bound in England by www.printondemand-worldwide.com

PEFC Certified

This product is
from sustainably
managed forests
and controlled
sources

www.pefc.org

PEFC/16-33-415

This book is made entirely of sustainable materials; FSC paper for the cover and PEFC paper for the text pages.

#0030 - 170413 - C0 - 229/152/16 [18] - CB